EMOTIONS MATTER:
A RELATIONAL APPROACH TO EMOTIONS

Edited by Dale Spencer, Kevin Walby, and Alan Hunt

The sociology of emotions has recently undergone a renaissance, raising new questions for the social sciences: How should we define and study emotions? How are emotions related to perennial sociological debates about structure, power, and agency? *Emotions Matter* brings together leading international scholars to build on and extend sociological understandings of emotions.

Moving beyond reductionist approaches that frame emotions as idiosyncratic states of mind, the contributors to this collection conceptualize emotions within the experience of social relations. Empirical and theoretical chapters demonstrate how emotions relate to sociological theories of interaction, the body, gender, and communication. Pushing the boundaries of sociology and stimulating debate for related fields, *Emotions Matter* offers diverse relational approaches that illustrate the crucial importance of emotions to the sociological imagination.

DALE SPENCER is a Banting Postdoctoral Fellow in the Department of Sociology at the University of Alberta.

KEVIN WALBY is Assistant Professor in the Department of Sociology at the University of Victoria.

ALAN HUNT is Chancellor's Professor in the Department of Sociology and Anthropology at Carleton University.

EDITED BY DALE SPENCER, KEVIN WALBY, AND ALAN HUNT

Emotions Matter

A Relational Approach to Emotions

UNIVERSITY OF TORONTO PRESS
Toronto   Buffalo   London

© University of Toronto Press 2012
Toronto Buffalo London
www.utppublishing.com
Printed in Canada

ISBN 978-1-4426-4413-7 (cloth)
ISBN 978-1-4426-1253-2 (paper)

Printed on acid-free, 100% post-consumer recycled paper with vegetable-based inks.

Library and Archives Canada Cataloguing in Publication

Emotions matter : a relational approach to emotions / edited by
Dale Spencer, Kevin Walby, and Alan Hunt.

Includes bibliographical references and index.
ISBN 978-1-4426-4413-7 (bound),   ISBN 978-1-4426-1253-2 (pbk.)

1. Emotions – Sociological aspects.   2. Emotions – Social aspects.
I. Spencer, Dale, 1979–   II. Walby, Kevin, 1981–   III. Hunt, Alan

HM1033.E46 2012   302   C2011-906610-6

University of Toronto Press acknowledges the financial assistance to its
publishing program of the Canada Council for the Arts and the Ontario Arts
Council.

University of Toronto Press acknowledges the financial support for its
publishing activities of the Government of Canada through the Canada
Book Fund.

Contents

Acknowledgments

We thank the Social Science and Humanities Research Council of Canada for their funding of the Emotions Matter workshop from which this volume stems. At Carleton University, we thank the Faculty of Arts and Social Sciences, the Faculty of Graduate Studies and Research, the Office of the Vice-President (Research), and numerous departments for their financial support. At the University of Victoria, we thank the Faculty of Social Sciences. Without such support, we would not have been able to bring this project together.

Our thanks go to the reviewers at the University of Toronto Press. Thanks also to Virgil Duff and Doug Hildebrand for helping us navigate the brave new world of academic book publishing.

Our gratitude is to the authors, not only for their chapters, but also for their energy at the workshop. Thanks to Aimee Campeau for helping organize the workshop. We thank Sean P. Hier and Chris Hurl for their comments on the introduction and the section summaries.

Contributors

Sara Ahmed is professor of race and cultural studies at Goldsmiths, University of London. Her publications include *Differences that Matter: Feminist Theory and Postmodernism* (1998); *Strange Encounters: Embodied Others in Post-Coloniality* (2000); *The Cultural Politics of Emotion* (2004); *Queer Phenomenology: Orientations, Objects, Others* (2006); *The Promise of Happiness* (2010); and *On Being Included: Racism and Diversity in Institutional Life* (forthcoming).

Sonia Bookman is an associate professor in the Department of Sociology, University of Manitoba. She obtained her doctoral degree in sociology at the University of Manchester. Her research interests include branding, consumer culture, and urban life. She is currently working on a research project that explores the branding of the Exchange District in the city of Winnipeg.

Ailsa Craig is a sociologist interested in questions of art, gender, and sexuality. She is a Fulbright almunus and assistant professor of sociology at Memorial University of Newfoundland. Her publications include a contribution to *Practicing Culture* (2007), *The Journal of Material Culture*, and *Poetics*.

Joyce Davidson is associate professor of geography at Queen's University, Kingston, ON. Since *Phobic Geographies* (Ashgate 2003), she has developed a research program focused around health, embodiment, and different or 'disordered' emotions. Organizer of the First and Second Interdisciplinary Conference on Emotional Geographies (Lancaster 2002, Queen's 2006), she is founding editor of the Elsevier journal,

Emotion, Space and Society, and has co-edited *Emotional Geographies* (Ashgate 2005), and *Emotion, Place and Culture* (Ashgate 2009).

Jillian Deri is a PhD candidate in sociology at Simon Fraser University, Vancouver, BC, with degrees in women's studies, social ecology, and geography. She has co-published work on transgendered athletes and queer culture, as well as research on pain within aerial dance.

Andrea Doucet is professor of sociology and women's studies at Brock University. She is the author of *Do Men Mother?* (University of Toronto Press 2006), and co-author of *Gender Relations: Intersectionality and Beyond* (with Janet Siltanen, Oxford 2008). She and Natasha Mauthner have co-written on themes of reflexivity, feminist approaches to methodologies, subjectivity, and the Listening Guide approach to narrative analysis.

Alan Hunt is chancellor's professor at Carleton University. He is the author of *Governing Morals* (Cambridge University Press 1999) and *Governance of the Consuming Passions* (Macmillan 1996). Previous books include *Foucault and Law* (with Gary Wickham, 1994), *Explorations in Law and Society* (1993), and *The Sociological Movement in Law* (1978). He is currently writing a book on governing through anxiety.

Jack Katz is professor of sociology at UCLA. Currently he is writing an ethnography of the Hollywood area of Los Angeles covering transformations in the area's 150-year social history; how meanings of contemporary neighborhoods are shaped by how residents make money, develop household relations, and establish routines in their local area; and how politics, retail culture, and sociological theories represent, and misrepresent, the lived realities of urban life.

J. Scott Kenney is an associate professor of sociology at Memorial University. His interests include deviance, victimology, social psychology, and emotions. His prior research includes studies of coping among families of homicide victims and analysis of the interactional dynamics of restorative justice sessions. He is currently involved in studies of 'illegitimate pain,' as well as conducting research on the construction of meaning among Freemasons.

Alexandre Lefebvre is lecturer in the School of Philosophical and Historical Inquiry, and the School of Social and Political Sciences at the University of Sydney. He is author of *The Image of Law: Deleuze, Bergson, Spinoza* (Stanford University Press 2008), and co-editor of *Bergson, Politics, and Religion* (Duke University Press 2012).

Natasha Mauthner is a reader at the University of Aberdeen. She has published in the areas of health and well-being; gender, work, and family; knowledge production in the academy; and methodological and epistemological issues in qualitative research.

Mick Smith is associate professor of philosophy and environmental studies at Queen's University. He is author of *An Ethics of Place: Radical Ecology, Postmodernity, and Social Theory* (SUNY 2001) and *Against Ecological Sovereigny: Ethics, Biopolitics, and Saving the Natural World* (University of Minnesota Press 2011).

Dale Spencer is a Banting postdoctoral fellow in the Department of Sociology, University of Alberta. His interests include embodiment, emotions, violence, and victimization. He is author of *Ultimate Fighting and Embodiment: Violence, Gender and Mixed Martial Arts* (Routledge 2011) and co-author (with Karen Foster) of *Reimagining Intervention in Young Lives* (University of British Columbia Press 2012).

Laura Suski is a University-College Professor in the Department of Sociology at Vancouver Island University. She also teaches in the Liberal Studies Department and the Global Studies Program. She holds a PhD in social and political thought from York University. Her current research interests include the analyses of political emotions, humanitarianism as an Enlightenment project, notions of the family and childhood in global ethics, and new theories of consumption and taste.

Catherine Theodosius is a lecturer in health in the School of Science, Technology and Health at University Campus, Suffolk, UK. Her main area of interest is in the sociology of emotion and emotional labour. Her recent book *Emotional Labour in Healthcare* (Routledge 2008) was awarded an Honourable Mention for Distinguished Contribution at the 2010 ASA convention in Atlanta. She is currently editing a textbook on health and well-being, and co-authoring a book on safeguarding vulnerable adults.

Peggy A. Thoits is the Virginia L. Roberts professor of sociology at Indiana University in Bloomington. Her interests are in mental illness, stress and social support processes, and emotion. Her research focuses on the psychological determinants and consequences of holding multiple role-identies, the social distributions of emotional deviance, and the conditions under which individuals label themselves as mentally ill or resist such labelling.

Kevin Walby is assistant professor of sociology, University of Victoria. He is author of *Touching Encounters: Sex, Work, and Male-for-Male Internet Escorting* (University of Chicago Press, forthcoming), and editor (with M. Larsen) of *Brokering Access: Power, Politics, and Freedom of Information Process in Canada* (University of British Columbia Press, forthcoming). He has recently published in *International Sociology* (with S. Hier), *British Journal of Criminology* (with J. Piche), *Punishment and Society* (with J. Piche), *Policing and Society* (with J. Monaghan), and *Social Movement Studies* (with J. Monaghan). He is the Prisoners' Struggles editor for the *Journal of Prisoners on Prisons*.

Melanie White is senior lecturer in the School of Social Sciences and International Studies at the University of New South Wales. She is co-editor of *Bergson, Politics, and Religion* (Duke University Press, 2012).

EMOTIONS MATTER:
A RELATIONAL APPROACH TO EMOTIONS

Introduction

KEVIN WALBY, DALE SPENCER, AND ALAN HUNT

The chapters comprising this edited volume originate from a workshop organized at Carleton University in May of 2009. Funded by the Social Science and Humanities Research Council of Canada and Carleton University, the workshop was an opportunity for scholars connected to the sociology of emotions to have a dialogue. The resulting volume fosters a diversity of relational approaches to emotions, many of which represent the discipline of sociology, whereas others are more indebted to geography, critical criminology, and cultural studies.

While waiting at the airport for incoming flights of workshop participants, we held a sign upon which was written 'EMOTIONS MATTER.' We received jeers (primarily from men) and puzzled looks. At one point, an elderly woman came up to Kevin and said, quietly in his ear, 'You know, they really do.' We recall this moment to suggest that it is not only in lay settings where a mention of emotions draws mixed responses. Academics seem to be suspicious of emotions. Responses to the question of how emotions matter range from conjectures by colleagues that 'emotions are not important to sociology,' to doubtful queries such as 'emotions . . . don't psychologists study them?' How emotions matter is not always self-evident to social scientists. This volume highlights varied sociological approaches to emotions, but also aims to stimulate debate across the disciplines.

The sociology of emotions is a growing sub-discipline influenced by interactionist sociology, which is often dubbed 'micro-sociology,' although more and more sociologists have theorized emotions in connection to social structure (see Clay-Warner and Robinson 2008; Barbalet 1998). The sociology of emotions also draws from newer subfields, such as cultural studies. Despite a diversity of approaches, there has been little dialogue between emotions scholars, especially between scholars at work in different countries, one consequence being that definitions of emotions in sociology can sometimes lack conceptual clarity. In addition, there is considerable disagreement amongst theorists of emotion. Emotions scholars either fail to communicate with each other, or hotly contest each new contribution to the literature.

Despite these disputes, or because of them, the social study of emotions is a highly productive area of research. While the popularity of the sociology of emotions has waxed and waned, emotions remain salient to understanding social life. The point that Shilling (2002) raises, which we reiterate, is that 'classical sociologists were concerned with the effects of emotions on the moral content of social orders and the ability of individuals to act morally. To lose this concern would be to lose an essential part of the discipline' (28). More broadly, emotions matter to sociological understandings of action, culture, and the self. This volume features chapters that build on existing sociological conceptualizations of emotions and develops new ones as well. We bring various approaches to emotions into dialogue, not only to stimulate debate but also to further develop theories and methodologies.

Why and How Emotions Matter

The sociology of emotions has recently undergone something of a renaissance. Despite being vital to the rise of the discipline, emotions and sociology did not get along during the middle of the twentieth century. It was only in 1975, when, with Arlie Hochschild's introduction of the idea of 'emotional labour' as well as Thomas Scheff organizing the first American Sociological Association session on emotions, that this area of study regained legitimate status (Wouters 1992). The American Sociological Association Section on Emotions has worked hard to legitimize this as an area of study.

A common thread that runs through the chapters of this volume is a conceptualization of emotions as the experience *of social relations,* rather than an idiosyncratic condition. Relations cannot be reduced to an individual state, but relations are not fully determined by social structure either. The reason why the relational cannot be subsidiary to the structural is that action would be eschewed and social structure would be reified. Much of what constitutes contemporary discussions of emotions within the sociological literature is purely analytical (e.g., Turner and Stets 2005), and is not overly concerned with emotions in action. This volume fosters theories and methodologies that take into account the relational genesis of the experience of emotion as physical, phenomenal, and structurally located (see Barbalet 1998). Some of the chapters engage in studies of emotions in situ, using a variety of methodological techniques.

A relational approach to emotions: (1) cannot reduce emotions either to the self or social structure but must analyse the interface between these two levels of analysis; (2) is more concerned with overlapping emotions in a milieu than with singular states; (3) is more concerned with what emotions do than what they are; (4) must borrow from sociological or related theory in order to guide the analysis; and (5) ought to borrow from methodological traditions in sociology and anthropology to investigate emotions in situ as they occur during sequences of interaction.

Our main purpose here is to forward an argument for a relational approach to emotions in sociology and related disciplines. To avoid reducing emotion, affect, and feeling to one another, and to keep our focus on the interface between the self and structural shaping, we must turn to sociological literature and other relational approaches to emotions. In addition, this volume addresses the question of emotions in relation to power. Though Barbalet's (2002) edited volume did emphasize the importance of thinking about emotions as relational, it did not include a consideration of post-structural theorization of power and its influence on the sociology of emotions. There is a small literature concerning emotions and power. For instance, Kemper and Collins (1990) argue that more 'micro' emotional processes are the basis of social differentiation and stratification. Clark (1990) contends that emotions are gendered and mark inequality in the workplace. Furedi (2004) has argued that a therapeutic culture, which encourages people to think of themselves as emotionally 'at risk,' has created new platforms for governance of the self and of others. The volume by Clay-Warner and Robinson (2008) pulls the emotions literature away from social psychology towards structural analysis. Yet there are more ways for the sociology of emotions to focus on how the governance of human conduct is attempted by agencies that hone in on emotions as pathological. The following chapters try to extend this argument about the link between power and the politics of emotions.

Breakdown of the Volume

Emotions Matter is organized in two parts. Part I engages with conceptual issues. These chapters offer conceptual clarification as it concerns emotions in everyday life, especially at the group level. In chapter 2 Jack Katz enriches the pragmatist tradition by examining how emotions arise, moment by moment, out of co-present interaction. He argues there is a corporeal and immanent emotional sense that emerges through everyday collaborative forms of sociality. Extending the phenomenological work of Schutz and Merleau-Ponty, Katz writes of a crucible of emotions, referring to the work people do in aligning actions with the habits, routines, and movements of others.

Sara Ahmed develops an argument concerning happiness as a form of sociality in chapter 3. She argues that if emotions are sociable, then sociability may be approached in terms of the limitation as well as the enjoyment of company. Happiness requires suppression of conflict, which has significant consequences for people who are marginalized as a result. Ahmed cites the 'feminist kill-joy' and the 'angry black woman' as examples of those whose sociability is an affront to the happiness of some (which, ironically, always requires the unhappiness of others). Situating the neurophysiological work of Damasio (2000) on emotion in a bio-psycho-social perspective, Catherine Theodosius challenges and offers insights into current social scientific understandings of the nature of embodied emotions in chapter 4. Adding to the literature on emotion management, Theodosius critically engages with the work of Hochschild regarding surface and deep acting, as well as Archer's (2000) concept of the inner dialogue.

Other chapters draw from scholars outside of sociology in an effort to exorcise conceptual problems that haunt the definition of emotions. In chapter 5 Scott Kenney and Ailsa Craig develop the concept of 'illegitimate pain' to describe situations when pain is hidden for fear of shame and stigma. Drawing from developments in queer theory, Kenney and Craig utilize and develop the concept of illegitimate pain to discuss the pain experienced by lesbian and gay men. In chapter 6 Alexandre Lefebvre and Melanie White revisit the work of Kant and Bergson to reveal the contributions of these philosophers to the sociology of emotions. Lefebvre and White argue that both Kant and Bergson not only critique and avoid the opposition of emotion and reason, but also, through their respective discussions of religion, assess the nature, function, and source of emotion. In chapter 7 Laura Suski offers an examination of the historical development of emotions, placing emphasis on moral emotions as they concern humanitarian projects. Suski focuses on debates concerning sympathy and suffering.

There has been a call in the emotions literature to consider the histories of particular emotions (see Dixon 2003), and this volume includes chapters that draw attention to the socio-historical basis of emotions. Drawing on the texts of Williams (1977) and Elias (1978), in chapter 8 Alan Hunt considers the tendency in the history of emotions for specific epochs to be associated with specific emotions. As with other key thinkers in the historical sociology of emotions (see Stearns 2000), Hunt is not interested in periodizing emotions. Instead, he offers an analysis of the contemporary emotional climate of advanced capitalist societies, which he characterizes as exhibiting a tension between two distinct processes: one that manifests an intensification of emotionality, and another which yields an emotional climate that is distinctively hollowed out.

Part II of *Emotions Matter* is called Emotions and Empirical Investigations. The discussion of emotions, reflexivity, and research methods, contributed by Andrea Doucet and Natasha Mauthner in chapter 9, marks the transition in the volume from the discussion of conceptual issues to research on emotions in action. Drawing from feminist debates concerning the epistemological issues that arise in friendships and relations with research participants, Doucet and Mauthner call for social scientists to focus on how emotions matter to issues such as fieldwork, data analysis, and writing. Some chapters in this volume examine particular settings of interaction that tend to be overlooked in mainstream approaches to emotions. Based on a case study of an earth sciences department, in chapter 10 Kevin Walby and Dale Spencer argue that consideration of emotions as the experience of relations with humans and objects supplements understandings of how work is organized. Drawing on narratives of earth scientists regarding their relationship to a mass spectrometer named 'Shiri,' Walby and Spencer's analysis of emotions and organizations illuminates how humans experience relations together but also the experience of emotions in object-centred sociality. In chapter 11 Peggy Thoits further develops her concept of 'emotional deviance' to examine a subset of mental disorders that are viewed as deviations from emotional norms. Thoits argues that emotion norms are shaped by ideology, and, leading from this assertion, shows that disagreements among clinicians about the presence of disorder may be traceable to ideological differences among them.

While concepts are necessary to understand the relational genesis of emotions, this volume includes chapters that reflect on individual emotions and their specific effects. For instance, in chapter 12 Jillian Deri explores jealousy in polyamorous relationships, an emotion scarcely analysed in the sociology of emotions literature. Deri shows that existing approaches to jealousy are based on heteronormative and gendered knowledges not attuned to the intricacies of polyamorous lifestyles. Deri focuses on the contextual nature of jealousy and the types of relations involved in the experience of jealousy. In chapter 13 Sonia Bookman examines the relationship between branding, consumption, and cultural configurations of cosmopolitanism in everyday urban life. Based on ethnographic research of Starbucks and Second Cup, she posits that people interact in an embodied process of consumption; through this 'affective cosmopolitanism' forms a 'structure of feeling' that is drawn on to orientate selves in the city. Drawing from 45 autobiographical accounts, the final chapter by Joyce Davidson and Mick Smith highlights the emotional relations to 'natural' things and places experienced by people diagnosed with autistic spectrum disorder (ASD). Relying on hermeneutic phenomenology, Davidson and Smith reverse assumptions concerning people with ASD (i.e., that they are asocial and 'unemotional'), showing that their personal geographies are characterized by emotional and meaningful relationships with the wider more-than-human world.

PART I

Conceptual Issues in the Sociology of Emotions

This section maps out major theoretical trends in the sociology of emotions and also situates our contributors in relation to these trends. Just as the contributions to *Emotions Matter* follow a relational approach to emotions whilst drawing from different conceptual resources, the origins of this field of study are diverse.

It is possible to claim that emotions have been salient to sociology since the beginning. In the fourteenth century, Ibn Khaldun, the reputed father of sociology, placed great importance on group cohesion and affection. Khaldun (1989) argued that group cohesion was a result of desire to avoid shame.[1] His attention to emotions was only a small part of his broad focus on social organization, which rejected natural and theological explanations of human development.

Sentiments and emotions were also imperative for Scottish moral philosophers. Adam Smith's ([1759] 2006) *Theory of Moral Sentiments* is an enduring account of self and subjectivity. Smith argues that sentiments such as sympathy play a principal role in maintaining social order. He contends that there exists a moral duty to guard against what he calls the 'selfish passions,' which undermine the propriety of individuals and the laws of nations. Given what he writes about emotions and good governance, it becomes clear that Smith's *Theory of Moral Sentiments* was the groundwork for his widely read *Wealth of Nations*. Though Karl Marx's writings on alienation are not an explicit explanation of emotions, Marx's inversion of Smith's comments on propriety and wealth does account for how the capitalist mode of production creates particular subject positions. The chapters by Hunt and Suski follow this line of argument concerning the historical context of moral emotions.

Emotions also had great importance in sociology's foundational statements (see Shilling 1997), such as writings on order by Comte and Durkheim as well as writings on the individual by Simmel and Weber. In early French social theory, the focus on 'society' as an entity over and above the individual is prominent. Comte argued that the impulse to act comes from emotions and not intelligence. Durkheim picks up on this claim, arguing that emotion spreads almost contagiously through symbolic and collective forms. For Durkheim, collective effervescence, the partaking in shared emotion, is the basis of religious ideas and group solidarity. Whereas Comte and Durkheim start from the social whole, Simmel and Weber begin with the creative and imaginative potentials of individuals. Influenced by Nietzsche's vitalism, they focus on the nature-transcending and self-determining individual. Simmel theorizes emotions and social capacities. Weber argued that a rationalized social system eroded emotions as a motivator for action through disenchantment, but he also argued that rational actions harness emotions. This divergence of French and German thinkers concerns the location of emotions (Shilling 1997). In Comte and Durkheim, emotions are stimulated from outside the individual, binding people in a moral community. In Simmel and Weber, emotions emanate from individuals and are stripped out of them by modern social formations.

At the turn of the twentieth century, there is also a move towards emotions from thinkers on the fringes of sociology. Henri Bergson considered emotion to be part of the open or creative tendency of life, whereas habit and obligation are associated with the closed tendency. For Bergson, emotions allow humans to move beyond simple repetition of habit, towards newness in social forms and life itself. As Bergson ([1935] 1956:45) puts it, 'creation signifies, above all, emotion . . .' The chapter by Lefebvre and White in this volume follows Bergson's argument. Another scholar related to the pragmatist tradition and marginally related to sociology, William James, positioned emotion as continuous with rationality, arguing that choice is determined by emotion. For James, emotions are an embodied experience that is generative of all action, both in terms of goal orientation but also energizing capacities. Cooley and Mead developed their thoughts concerning emotions through a dialogue with pragmatism. The chapter by Jack Katz in this volume extends the pragmatist heritage and puts it in contact with phenomenology. The sociology of emotions, early on, benefited from a dialogue with scholars who did not necessarily identify with sociology but placed a considerable emphasis on emotions as relational phenomena.

In existential philosophy, both Nietzsche and Heidegger highlight the significance of emotions. Nietzsche (2007) discussed *ressentiment* and located it as part of the Judeo-Christian religious doctrines. Nietzsche understands the Judeo-Christian religious doctrines as being based on charity, which undermines the quest for self-assertion. Ressentiment, defined as vengeful desire not readily consummated, is more related to structural forces, as opposed to resentment, which refers to a short-term reaction to affronts to the self. The concept of 'ressentiment' is useful for theorizing the historical relations involved in power struggles and governance processes.[2] For Heidegger ([1926]1962), emotions frame an object as mattering in a particular way – as fearful, boring, cheerful, or hateful. In Heidegger's *Being and Time*, emotions are relational; individual emotion not only affects but is affected by our relations with others (see also Heidegger 2001). Heidegger's work has spawned a phenomenological stream that continues to shape the sociology of emotions (see Ahmed, as well as Davidson and Smith, this volume).

Though the sociology of emotions today is fragmented, marked by divergent methodological strategies (see the introduction to Part II), the various theoretical traditions live on. The connection between the interactionist tradition and the contemporary sociology of emotions in America is especially strong. Two prominent figures in American sociology, both drawing from Goffman's Durkheimian writing on dramaturgy and ritual, are Arlie Hochschild and Randall Collins. Arlie Hochschild can be credited with renewing interest in emotions in sociology. In *The Managed Heart*, Hochschild (1983) argued that societies maintain an emotion culture consisting of emotion ideologies that delineate apposite attitudes, feelings, and emotional responses in basic spheres of activity (see also Hochschild 1979). It is through socialization that people acquire the feeling rules. Feeling rules prescribe how an individual should feel, and display rules specify when and how the overt expression of emotions is to occur. The chapters in this volume by Theodosius, Kenney, and Craig, Walby and Spencer, as well as Thoits, engage with the idea of emotion management. Emotion management becomes emotional labour when conducted as paid work. Hochschild initiated an important feminist stream in the sociology of emotions, but also extended Marx's structuralist concern with alienation and the capitalist mode of production. Continued debates concerning 'emotional labour' (see Brook 2009; Bolton 2009) confirm how pivotal Hochschild's contributions have been to sociological understandings of emotion, gender, and work.

Collins's (1975, 1981, 2004) theory of interaction ritual chains argues that co-presence, mutual awareness, common focus, rhythmic synchronization, and symbolization of the group arouse emotions. Interaction rituals are created when individuals become engaged in common actions or involved in the same event. Collins is concerned with the build-up of emotional energy that compels them to engage in interaction rituals (or not). As emotional energy is built up, rituals take on greater value. For Collins (2004), emotional energy gives the participants 'confidence, elation, strength, enthusiasm and initiative in taking action' (48–9). Emotional entrainment results in the intensification of mutual focus and shared mood.

The work of Hochschild and Collins speaks to the pervasive influence of Durkheim (filtered through Goffman) on the sociology of emotions today, insofar as interaction rituals and effervescence remain the starting point. Yet Hochschild and Collins move beyond classical works. Specifically, the writings of Collins link micro-level experiences of emotions with macro-processes, insofar as interaction ritual chains serve as the basis of organizations. Drawing from Marx, Hochschild accounts more for alienation than a Durkheimian perspective allows.

Hochschild and Collins represent American sociology. A great deal of scholarly interest in the sociology of emotions emanates from the United Kingdom as well. The sociology of emotions in the UK is more influenced by continental sociological theory as well as the phenomenological tradition. For instance, both Barbalet (1998) and Ahmed (2004) offer relational approaches to emotions, the former situating his work in classical sociological theory and the latter positioning her work as phenomenological. Barbalet (1998) stresses the emotional basis of action. Emotions are not experienced as idiosyncratic feelings, but are part of a social transaction. Barbalet's key contribution is his notion of collective emotion. An 'emotional climate' does not require all to experience the same emotion, and emotions differ in a group depending on the social positions of those people. His work displaces the contagion model of emotions (found in Durkheim and Collins) while arguing that group emotions are experienced in varying intensities.

Borrowing from the phenomenological tradition, Ahmed (2004) presents a less structuralist model of emotion. She suggests that emotions move between bodies, aligning subjects with some and against others.

The more emotions circulate, the more affective they become. Through the circulation of emotions, bodies and worlds materialize and take shape. Emotions are crucial to the way bodies become problematized in relation to other bodies, producing the effect of collectivities (39). The contribution that Ahmed makes is moving beyond outside-in and inside-out ontologies of emotions (a problem which is prevalent in existing sociological and psychological theories of emotion). Emotions circulate in an affective economy and it is through emotions that boundaries between the 'I,' the 'we,' and the 'other' are shaped (also see Ahmed as well as Kenney and Craig, this volume).

There are numerous conceptual models in the sociology of emotions, past and present. One commonality in the history of the sociology of emotions is an emphasis on emotions as part of social relations, and *Emotions Matter* continues in this direction. We are not implying that the scholars mentioned above constitute the only noteworthy contributors to this field. Numerous other sociologists have made eminent contributions that are oft cited in the following chapters (e.g., Wouters 2001; Scheff 2000; Katz 1999; Clark 1990; Kemper 1978). We also do not mean to suggest that sociology as a discipline has a stronghold over the study of emotions, or that disciplinary boundaries are always useful. For instance, numerous important contributions to understanding emotions have also been made in organizational studies (see Fineman 2004, 1993; Fineman and Sturdy 1999), criminology (see O'Malley and Mugford 1994; the 2002 special issue of *Theoretical Criminology*), and geography (see Bondi 2005; Thien 2004; as well as the new journal *Emotion, Space and Society*). Many of our contributors do not locate themselves in sociology. Davidson and Smith are geographers, while Bookman and Deri are aligned closely with cultural studies. These different bodies of thought feed into one another, further developing a relational understanding of emotions.

NOTES

1 For more on Khaldun, see Spickard (2001), as well as Dhaouadi (1990).
2 For more on the concept of ressentiment, see Meltzer and Musolf (2002).

2 Emotion's Crucible

JACK KATZ[1]

Introduction

Late in his academic career, Ralph Turner, an eminent social psychologist in UCLA's sociology department, still had a vivid awareness of his first teaching experience some 50 years earlier. Turner had meticulously worked up lecture notes for several of the class sessions. His initial lecture ran without hitch or tangential indulgence. Pleased with the flow of the session, at the end he consulted his notes. He had gone through all the preparations he had made for the course.

On hearing Turner's story, Ted Sarbin, an eminent social psychologist whose career as an academic psychologist stretched over about the same span at UC Berkeley and then at UC Santa Cruz, recalled his first teaching experience. He had put lecture notes into a stack of three-by-five cards, which he turned as the hour progressed. Coming to the end of the deck he checked on the time: about 15 minutes of the 50-minute hour had elapsed. What to do? Trying to comfort himself with the psychologists' understanding that repetition improves memory, he flipped the deck. Fifteen minutes later he flipped the deck again.

Lecturers' tactics for fitting preparation to the teaching hour will differ, and when they realize their preparation was inadequate, so will their emotions. However it is handled, the challenge is emotionally provocative, which is to say that professional horror stories from the biographies of perhaps the two most famous 'role theorists' are useful for focusing on an existential vulnerability in social life. With experience, novice teachers usually develop resources for minimizing the risks of fitting their anticipated performances of self to the immaterial yet

obdurate frames of scheduled class times, but life cannot be completely insured by preparations, no matter how fully rehearsals
maybe dressed. From the insurance that the teacher can seek in advance, there is always a deductible demanded in the historically
unique, socially situated durations of real time. However imaginative
in origin, symbolic in interaction, and ephemeral, the performed self
always congeals in something palpable that is always more and less
than anticipated.

The teacher may seek assurance by reading the lecture. Scripted details may include timed pauses, delimited segments for questioning
and answering, even joking asides. Still there are risks, including losing one's place and train of thought when looking up to indicate to
the audience that those present in the immediate situation are being
given respect.

Lecturing implies being pre-organized. In the context of the strati-
fied power relations in a class, pauses, which in a conversation would
be provocations for a correspondent to take a turn in speaking quickly,
stand out as awkward. But if lecturing implies a degree of preparation
that is inconsistent with the tenor of spontaneous monologue or conversation, it also implies being alive to the instant situation. If he or she
never looks up from notes, the lecturer runs the risk of a prosody that
suggests that nothing more than reading is occurring. For lecturing to
hold onto its raison d'être, something more responsive to the moment
is usually required.[2] If the lecturer is not doing something to fit preparation to the immediate situation, why incur the trouble of assembling
students in a common, designated place? Why not distribute the text
'for free' in digital form, transferring the costs of lighting, heating, security, roof maintenance, and fire insurance to the dispersed, individual
accounts that someone else already is paying?

Putting aside personality and strategy differences, the sources of
emotional provocation as experienced by lecturers are continuous
with emotional provocations that arise generally out of the narrative
structuring of social life. If we examine how, in the most general sense,
social life is constituted by narrative structuring, we can see how personal style acknowledges and with practice eclipses emotions. Over
time, lecturers commonly develop an occupational aesthetic with
which they tame the insistent explosive potential of their defining
work situation.

Feelings are distinctively three-dimensional experiences. In order
to find the sources of emotions in social life, we are advised to look

for matters of texture, or how the practice of behaviour becomes sensible to the practitioner. Our feelings are ways that our corporeality comes into our awareness in two directions, as an awareness of internal depths and recesses and as a sensibility guiding and attending our reach into the world. The foundational question, then, is how does behaviour, what we do in projecting ourselves into the world, become self-sensible?[3]

The three dimensionality of the subject's experience of social life is founded in the very processes through which action is made social. At a first level, action becomes social by becoming socially situated. This occurs in the narrative sequencing that makes behaviour meaningful as a recognizable kind of doing. Structuring experience into a familiar form of conduct does not require that any other person be present. To appreciate how action in becoming social becomes sensible, we need to drop temporarily the focus on lecturing, which implies a co-present interactive relationship with others, and turn to an example that does not. A simple example such as putting on one's own shoes will do.

When a person acts in the responsive co-presence of another, his/her action becomes social in a compounded way. The narrative that the person uses to structure action must itself be narrated. To see the emergence of this second way in which action becomes palpable to the actor, we can look at how one person puts on another's shoes.

For a full appreciation of how behaviour takes on corporeal resonance as it becomes social, a third inquiry is required. At a first level, which is observable when acting alone, the person feels the rhythms, flow, and hitches in the narrative structure through which he/she makes action socially meaningful. When acting with another, a second level comes into play: each feels the push and pull by which two versions of a project become the collaborative production of a single executed narrative. But something more is also always involved. The person knows that his/her life transcends any situation he or she maybe in. Masking various transcendent meanings is also a required part of acting collaboratively with another. Emotions arise to register situation-transcending meanings that must not be displayed to the other.

These three processes create an ontogenetic dialectic in which action becomes socially meaningful through private practices, then becomes social in a publicly shared way, then again becomes privately meaningful in ways others cannot appreciate.[4] Somewhere along the range of this three dimensional composition of social life, all feelings and emotions take shape. Emotions and feelings are ways of grasping, appreciating, and corporeally reflecting on the very structuring of life into social forms. Lecturers' emotions emerge as they realize aspects of the in-class situated structuring of their behaviour that the audience cannot know. And over time, lecturers' transform the sensate substrata of their professional lives – we might say, depending on the subject's mood and the analyst's political perspective, that lecturers control, tame, discipline, manage, or civilize their emotions – by developing aesthetics for structuring their working behaviour at each of these three levels.

Putting on Shoes: Evocative Aspects of the Social Situation

With few exceptions, from the time an adult in the contemporary West awakens until the time for bedding down to sleep, he or she is in an unbroken continuum of situations. The situation, a subjectively understood, narratively framed sequencing of physically mobilized action, is the basic unit, the most universal, ubiquitous, and simplest whole unit of social life. Situations are sometimes encountered, as occurs when a student enters a class in progress, or they may be constructed in solitary phases of living, as when a lecturer prepares class notes. Whether collaboratively or individually shaped, situated action makes up the stuff of social life.

Each situation is a strip of sequential actions, coherent moment-to-moment as what the actor understands to be narratively interrelated behaviours. Action is narratively meaningful when in its execution it references former and subsequent behaviour as occurring within a course of terminable conduct, which it may do at any given moment by heralding, initiating, continuing, or advancing; pausing in, departing from, or abandoning; restarting, reviewing, or finishing some kind of colloquially recognizable 'doing.'

As a rough test of the claim that in our wide-awake life we are almost always in one or another situation, we may ask about any moment of our daily life: 'What am I doing?' There is usually a gerund-like answer that will fit the moment. Each moment's doing is shaped with reference to an overarching course that is substantively known. Each 'ing' is at least a mini narrative. The narrative structuring usually goes on without announcement, but should anyone ask, it will seem natural to answer with phrases such as 'putting on my shoes.'[5]

One reason for working with the example of putting on shoes is that for most readers, putting on shoes will come early in the day's situations. What comes before is a transition from repose to motility and then often a trip to the bathroom for eliminations and ablutions, the latter being routines that are culturally recognized, elaborately commented upon strips of activity that are often learned through emotionally charged, close supervision. That urination, defecation, bathing, or 'washing up' are so obviously socially structured for the individual makes them too robust as examples for focusing on the prior question of how, by shaping behaviour according to situated narratives, the individual structures social character into his or her life. Putting on shoes is a more innocent, stripped down, usefully unimportant example. And unlike 'getting up' from a sleeping position and bodily eliminations, putting on shoes is a social construction, not a physical imperative.

We can briefly note several ways that sequential narrative meaning is used by the person to constitute the situation of putting on shoes. There is the matter of recipe and the effect of dramatic result. Putting on shoes requires the ordering of constituent actions. For example, in most cases the shoe should be put on the foot before laces are tied. Multiple, sequenced actions are required to get to the end of the process, at which point an effect is achieved, a qualitative change on the order of an ontological transformation. With shoes on, a new being emerges, a life form with a bundle of capacities for simultaneously probing and getting energy from the world. If not quite winged sandals, shoes gird the wearer with a new competency to carry on the journey ahead, altering traction, often enhancing endurance. Of course not always: shoes may make balance exceptionally precarious and rapid travel dangerous, in which case their use incidentally demonstrates a certain talent. In either case shoes affect the physics of the body's movements through space, changing the muscles engaged in transportation and creating a new posture, in the process revealing self in the form of capacities to self, even as the world is revealed in different angles and rates of passing landscape.

We are looking for the grounding of feeling in behaviour. The routine of putting on shoes is marked by corporeal changes at its onset and at its terminal boundaries, and also in the shaping of its constituent stages as they are produced within the social logic of accomplishing the project. Thought or self-reflection in an abstracted sense is not necessarily involved. Feelings arise in the physical practicalities of structuring personal life into social form.

This is not to say that all situations have recipes leading to transformations that change one's practical competency for being in the world. Making the bed, for example, is a ritualization of the ending of sleep, a sentimental resource for starting the day but not a preparation that in some other, practical sense will facilitate later actions. Indeed, making the bed routinely will require additional work, the work of unmaking the bed, before the bed is again treated as practically useful for sleep. This practice, a making that requires an unmaking, is doubly ritualistic. It guides people to move on to the next situations, whether in the world of wide-awake practical action or into a drowsier routine, in the way that prayers do; it allies one with patterns and presumed forces of order.[6]

The recipe metaphor, which promises a corporeally significant pay-off, is too strong for much of social life, which has more meandering and less transformative results. But a core idea in recipes of action, that of progressing towards an ending, captures a defining feature of all situated action. Whenever one is engaged in a kind of doing, one operates in anticipation of completion. Pre-visioning an ending to the doing at hand is not promise, much less reliable commitment. But it is a meaningful foundation for structuring each moment's behaviour.

The progression through behavioural recipes that constitutes social life can be delayed or aborted by any number of tangential involvements and emergent contingencies. Fascinations may be discovered in matters intrinsic to a given phase. Progressions towards completion may be put in pause through meditations, reveries, intoxications, sleep, or other losses of consciousness that will take the structuring of experience out of the bounds of situated social life. A phone call can get you out of the shower before you have finished that routine; still, the phone's ring is answered with an understanding that lifting the receiver is not embarking on a rest-of-life engagement. All doings foreshadow endings in the minimal respect of anticipating eventual, and event-occasioned, moments of moving on to other situations, even if the mode and timing of departure is as yet unspecified, and even if departure when it comes is not in fact marked as a departure.

An anticipation of moving on, literally of moving the body in space, is the basis for the temporal foundations of situations as units of social life.[7] The bodily changes in moving on create the dimly sensed but most universal feeling substructure of social life, the tenor that underlies what Schutz (1962) referred to as wide awake everyday life. Relative immobility of the body, dialectically related to an absence of traction and friction in moving over space mentally, distinguishes the various 'fantasy' worlds of reveries, witnessing in a theatre, dream life, and so on.[8]

Across their range, situations are narratives in that they have endings. More precisely, people make their lives social by starting lines of action with an understanding that the line of action will be ended. The 'ending' feature of the social situation is not necessarily more focal in awareness than is the moving-towards-death that is a part of all living, but it is always implicitly attended to in the way situations are entered. As turning on the shower anticipates turning it off, so starting to put on a shoe by picking it up anticipates walking away from the shoeing process.[9]

Any social situation minimally has a narrative character by virtue of some action premised on an ending. The situation-constituting action may be no more than a preparation for a beginning that never occurs, an enacted promise to start that is reneged upon, or a project aborted, like putting on a shoe that is then discarded in favour of the decision to go barefoot. The fundamental actualization of social life is not the-positive step of completion but something negative, a commitment to ending, whether through completion or abandonment. I may be engaged in doing something without knowing what my action will lead to, but I know something will come next. I progress through the project of putting my shoes on, not yet knowing where I will be going. My uncertainty about the future does not detract from the socially organized character of my experience in putting on my shoes.

In addition to the quality of orienting towards an ending, life is made social by action that unites multiple moments of action into related stages. Putting on shoes requires multiple steps. Even the most accommodating flip-flops require finding the things.[10] Slipping into them means doing separate sub-acts for each foot. And after slipping each foot into sandals, some adjustment is typically required to get the strap at the desired relationship to the toes. Only in cartoons do shoes simultaneously encase both of a character's feet.

We are specifying the narrative features that make action social. To put on shoes one must not only do a series of steps, and do each step as related to others, the steps must be done in a certain order. If only because of the certainty of ending involvement, there is directionality in the sequential arrangement of action. People almost invariably develop habits as to which foot they put in first, a meta-narrative of 'my way.' But in any case, on each occasion the person will put the first foot in as 'putting in the first foot,' knowing that the other foot is next in turn. The 'certain order' that is requisite is not left first, then right, nor vice versa, but first one, then the other. With one pair of shoes, the tongue may be pulled up before the foot is put in; with another pair the order may be reversed. But the sense of an obdurate world, of the need for strategy based on an understanding that action must be materially pragmatic, is acknowledged in the glosses of directionality given to various steps in the project. It 'matters' which order one follows because one acts in a physical world. Here is a first bit of resonance or sensual reflexivity, a first analytic step towards an understanding of how feelings arise and are patterned in social life.

We may note that here is a 'babushka' or nested quality to the sequential structure that makes action into behavioural units of social life. If putting on shoes is a project with several stages, each stage is itself a mini-narrative, for example, tying the laces. Tying laces is itself an ordered sequence. Each end of the lace is grabbed; the grabbing motion has a start and a finish. The tying of a knot requires following an ordered sequence: this end goes over and then around the other end of the lace, which then is pulled around the first, and so on.

Should a problem arise or should a special examination be engaged, any step may be broken into subunits. Still, a description of the typical experience of putting on shoes does not lead to infinite regress. In the routine of putting on shoes, commonly nothing structural intervenes to create internal stages between an attentive start to grasp and the grasping of the lace. If the lace is not found where an eye-guided hand's trajectory expects to find it, a corrective subunit will be devised. But commonly the move is a flow, requiring no sub-molecular unit of attention.

Narrative is meaningful as a concept for describing the social structuring character of action because it is empirically differentiating. At some point of deconstruction we reach the smallest narrative doll; the actor's production of demarcations typically is no more microscopic. We inspire and exhale; inspiration has a beginning and an ending; but between the start of inspiration at the end of the prior exhale, and before the ending of inspiration in the beginning of the next exhale, we commonly note no intermediary stages. There are flows in our action, smooth passages within stages that may be broken down into smaller units by biologists, or by oneself if for some reason one decides to pause to create a clear end of one phase before the beginning of the next. But the undifferentiated flows in behaviour are as natural and as vulnerable to attentive disruption as respiration is vulnerable to holding our breath. To a degree and to achieve a certain effect for awhile, what has been flow may be made into differentiated and ordered subunits, but as inspiration must give way to expiration, ending and continuity must both exist as constants in our social life.

As sociological description can find smaller sequences within the sequence of putting on shoes, so it can find that the project this time through is one of a series of similar projects, either experienced or imagined. Each time shoes are put on they are put on as variations of a generic action. Is this the first time you've put on this type of shoe or the nth occasion? The typification of the project this time through is also embodied, conveyed, or lived sensually; typification is naturally not an act of cognition but a kind of feeling. Putting on a 'new type' of shoe requires special attention, which is a certain tension of corporeal engagement. As the saying suggests, putting on 'an old shoe' evokes a familiar self.

In searching for the foundations of feeling, we have noted the evocative implications of orienting action towards ending, of ordering moments of action into stages as in a recipe, and of attention that gives strips of action narrative character as a certain instantiation of its type. We may also note that the narrative structuring of action is accomplished most immediately not as a direct focus on endings, not as a focus on typification, not as a focus on the recipe of which the action may be a constituent part, but as each action is related directionally to others in the situation. In the awareness of how doing this moment's action is a pushing off from a prior action or a pulling towards/setting up of a next action, there is a corporeal sense of how the relationship is being shaped. For example, to put on laced shoes, the grabbing of lace ends may be moved fluidly through and into a tying operation or the lacing through the eyelets may be adjusted to perfect the equality of the finger accessible endings. In the latter case the step of grabbing onto the laces is prolonged, occasioning a hesitation before the next step of tying the knot is begun. Or each step is done with the same emphasis as the prior and the next. Or a given step that completes a prior step – think of tightening a double bowknot – may be done in a manner that comments upon, perhaps celebrates, the completion of the sequence.

Describing the narrative structuring of action that creates the mundane situation of putting on shoes veers into vocabulary that could be used to describe a musical performance. A piece of music is given a certain feel as the component parts are marked by the performers as sub-narratives, and related to other parts in what is, despite the part-markings, a constant flow. Few people live to make music, but all social life is lived in musical ways. And as music gives rise to feelings, so does the prosody of each social situation. Perhaps in this morning's putting on shoes, the move from one step to the next is especially even and smooth; perhaps tomorrow it will be balky and awkward. There is feeling here, although we are reluctant to call it 'emotion.' An aesthetic feeling, perhaps: a matter of sensually experienced style that is part and parcel of the very doing of social life. A person putting on shoes is at once producing a colloquially recognizable identity and a sensate self.

We can now quickly move the analysis to appreciate the emergence of what will be more familiar as 'emotion.' Say the laces seem to be too short for a customary bow. Or maybe, even though the shoe is new, the laces break. 'Shit!' one might exclaim, referring to the breakdown of order and the messy release of the negative powers for which everyday rituals are prophylaxes. More interestingly for our purpose, one might also blurt out 'Stupid!' Stupid is a characteristic of a person, not a shoe. Falling out of involvement with the practical project, the person turns to recognize, emphatically if indirectly, that the shoe already is a social object. Someone, most likely some corporate set of people, made it. And in the design process they anticipated how people would put the things on. The user is enacting a version of a role that complements the manufacturer's script as presented to the user in the material of the shoe. 'Stupid!' is about the people who made and sold this thing.

It is more difficult, but for our objective more important, to appreciate the positive feelings that shoes can give rise to. Through practically using shoes the shoe buyer ties him or herself to the designer and manufacturer. As social analysts we are used to focusing on the status qualities laid on marketed objects, so that when they are satisfying to users, it may seem to us that the users are preoccupied with the artificialities of prestige structures. But putting on shoes requires craft; some high fashion boots require exceptional effort and trained dexterity. Accomplishing putting them on can confirm oneself as successfully connected to the others who made the shoes. Children know this and adults do not forget it. Those others may be inaccessible – anonymous, not present now or ever in one's life, collective, never envisioned as flesh and blood individuals – but even as the shoe is 'mine' it never exhausts its being in my possession. It connects me to 'them,' and even if I don't care about their prestige, even if I begrudge them the profits they are making, there can be a puzzle-solver's pride in getting the things to work smoothly as 'mine.' This appeal, a kind of-material seduction to a time-fragmented intercourse, works across the spectrum of society, from elaborately and creatively laced up 'ghetto' sneakers to designer boots gratuitously elaborated with function-less buckles and ribbons that circumnavigate the calf before ending in front-displayed bows. There are feelings, emotions, irrationalities here, but they are not necessarily related to advertised status distinctions. Getting into social objects and making them 'mine' is a way to confirm that I can connect with an invisible, transcendent community of others. For some that irrationality is religious in a way that advertising semiotics may not know. When the narratives for using bought objects work well, they complete a social act that was still fragmented at the point of purchase.

Putting Shoes on Another

We are tracing the emergence of emotions in social life within a pragmatist perspective. Emotions emerge in response to problems in the organization of conduct. The structure of conduct is in the first instance created by what the actor experiences as corporeally distinguished, sequential actions used in the course of getting something done. Taking the example of putting on shoes, we note that a sequence is anticipated in the design of shoes. In putting on shoes on any given occasion, a person may go through the course in different ways. He or she may follow the designed patterning of action, employ a customary but idiosyncratic approach, or stumble on details of materials or of the scenic context that are taken to call for a novel approach this one time. The project may run smoothly or become balky as the person moves from one phase to the next.

Some feeling is always involved. The practices that constitute social situations are somehow sensually appreciated. Acting in the world inevitably evokes some sense of self on a continuum of being merged naturally with and being artificially inserted into the world. Perhaps the repertoire is performed as a flowing motif in the background of thought and talk that are at the centre of consciousness. Perhaps the situation is lived through as a halting operation requiring repeated focus on the details of the operation. On occasion the little daily routine of putting on shoes provokes a more fully formed emotion. The practitioner may become irritated when focusing on some perceived fault in design, delighted in the totemic fit between self and world that is implied in proficient use, or caught up in self-recrimination as the process is taken to exemplify a general state of personal disorganization.

Note that interaction is already involved even though no one else is present. When putting shoes on another person – call the latter the 'wearer,' the former the 'aide' – the interaction in the project becomes more obvious. Think of putting shoes on a child, an invalid, or a customer in a store. Will the wearer remain passive, the aide active throughout? If not, who will do each of the necessary practical acts? Who will pick and pick up the pair of shoes? Who will guide each foot into each shoe? Who will do the buckling or lacing up? Who will adjust sock or stocking, if any is worn, to shoe? Will one or both define errors in the process, such as uneven lengths to lace ends, wrong match of left/right shoe and foot, tongue not pulled out, degree of fastening too loose or tight? Who will finalize the adjustment of foot and shoe? Perhaps the wearer in the initial steps of walking in the shoes, perhaps the aide by judging that the size or style is off and triggering a return to the start of the process with another pair.

Each of the two, wearer and aide, come to the process with narratives more or less in mind. And each will find that the pair of shoes applied this time requires some innovation of an unprecedented narrative structure, if only because each operates from an historically unique physical position. Theoretical differences may get implicated, as when the aide presumes that shoes should be tied but the wearer does not. The two must work out which narrative to use, who will do each part, and when each will do what. The aide may lift the shoe towards a foot, the wearer may then take over the stage of getting foot into shoe.

A coordinated single narrative will usually be worked out. We may gloss the action as 'the work of putting shoes on another,' or 'having another put on one's shoes,' but either formulation is a bit off because the process inevitably is collaborative. Each will give off and perceive the other as giving off expressions that indicate offer and acceptance of contributions to the collaborative process.

It is tempting to refer to the interaction, now occurring between two co-present individuals, as a 'conversation,' and then to rethink the action of putting on one's shoes alone as a silent conversation. Some claim that conversation is the fundamental or primordial form of social interaction. But children learn to negotiate patterned interactions with the world before and as a way into language use. For understanding the rise of emotions, 'conversation' must be appreciated as metaphor: it can mislead in a way that loses the phenomenon it would illuminate. Talk, or descriptions of expressive gestures, can be reduced to transcriptions, but transcriptions are irreducibly static and disembodied; the transcription process inevitably loses much of the corporeal reality that makes lived experience a three-dimensional reality.

If we are to understand the rise and fall of emotions in social life, we need to keep the moving line of intertwining between self and other (or world) at the centre of our investigation. If the wearer remains passive throughout, the aide will repeatedly cross a gap in touching the other through touching the shoe and foot. Conversely, if the aide supervises without laying on a hand, two worlds of experience remain at a distance. But as soon as the two actively interact, their movements enter an area of ambiguous overlap. The aide pushes the shoe on the wearer; the wearer moves foot into shoe. Interaction has become intercourse, a temporally meshed form of interaction that creates existential ambiguities about who leads, who follows, who owns the project.

In putting shoes on a child, the area of ambiguous overlap may be revealed to the adult aide in an unexpected protest: 'Let me!' In watching a clerk put on a pair of shoes, a customer may take over the lacing up in a way that may be defined as abrupt by the clerk even while it is appreciated by the wearer as considerate. These are not simply differences in the 'vocabularies' or 'scripts' engaged by each. In the practice of social life, emotions emerge in the inherently ambiguous overlap between his action and her reaction, which sequence is itself ambiguously preceded by her invitation, indifference, or alienation, and his response to that prior phase.

We have now specified two levels of analysis necessary to the description of how emotions arise in moments of social life. First we traced the practical social narrative of the wearer, as he or she interacts with the shoes. We find that shoes are not 'just put on,' they are put on through following a sequential logic of one sort or another, a recipe with discrete stages and transition strategies. The process entails following and editing a logic encountered as built into the shoes. Engaged in this little project of everyday life, feelings arise, usually more in a sensate, perhaps aesthetic, but not clearly emotional form.

When we examine a situation of co-present interaction such as putting shoes on another, a second level of sociological work appears. Now in addition to finding and following the social logic of the objects, one must collaboratively work out a meshing with the social logic perceived in the other's practices. The two must produce an effectively single narrative train through emitting and observing signs of who will do the next move.

For understanding how emotions arise in immediate interaction with another, the metaphoric vocabularies that are common in social interaction studies today are inadequate and misleading. The processes that give rise to emotions are not grasped by looking at the 'symbolic' aspects of the interaction. It is specifically the embodied interwinings that matter, the physically registered intercourse that occurs when one touches the other and when the two collaboratively produce trajectories of motion in which actions by one, say in pushing on a shoe, are met with a simultaneous reciprocating action such as pushing the foot in. What we call emotions are reflections on these embodied intertwinings.

From one to the other side of the transaction, and in ways that the participants may not themselves appreciate, the emotions being experienced may diverge. The wearer may think that both are experiencing the project as done crudely or rudely; the aide may imagine that both are appreciating a clockwork, mutually respectful collaboration in the event. The embodied, interactive coordination of individual contributions to the project is one thing. The emotional upshot of the process entails individual disengagement from the other and it may be quite different for each.

Interaction with another is inevitably three-dimensional. From moment to moment, in finely shaded degrees, each more or less gets traction from the other's actions. The phenomenon of traction is not a figure of speech or thought; it refers to the practical grounding of action. Your pulling up and tightening the laces makes it a more immediately accessible task for me to tie the bow.

We see that to get the science of emotions right, we have to go beyond received interaction vocabularies and we have to go beyond the notion of a mind/body binary. Emotions are not an alternative to or an enemy of thought. They arise and are perfected in thought-like reflections. In the shoe example, emotions may arise in a positive form, in recognition of the other's sympathetic consideration for what one can and cannot readily do, or in a negative form, perhaps as a perception of 'too much' passivity, or, conversely, as an arrogation of the narrative course. In any case, emotions will arise as the individual, in his or her existential autonomy, turns in interpretive isolation on the areas of ambiguous overlap in the process.

Situated Action and Its Transcendence

Using the shoe-dressing example, we have traced two ways that feelings arise out of making behaviour social by producing coherent narrative sequences. There is the recipe-like sequential coherence required to accomplish the project, a requirement that applies whether acting alone or with a co-present other. The structure of the sequence is created through changes in the embodiment of action. Pauses, transitions, problems, and shortcut solutions for getting from one stage to the next are all experienced corporeally.

When acting with another to put shoes on, the process requires that each work out an understanding with the other as to the relevance to a jointly executed recipe of one and the other's actions. The narrative of practical action must now be narrated: I have to indicate where I am in the process, my narration has to be monitored for effective comprehension, I have to register the other's indications of the other's offers to execute steps in the other's version of an effective narrative, and on these grounds each stage in the project is subject to misunderstanding, adjustment, repetition, and so on. I have to signal and monitor the reception of signals as to when the process begins, which foot I am first trying to fit, who pushes the foot in, when a sub-strip of incidental inspection of the foot's anatomy has begun and ended, what is and is not meant as a tickle, and so on. Not uncommonly the other will volunteer to complete parts of the recipe, perhaps grabbing for the second shoe, completing the tying of laces, or standing up to press a resistant foot into a possibly too-small shoe. If we are to collaborate in putting on the shoes, I must follow the other's mobilization of the sequential structure of the process, as the other may idiosyncratically understand it.

Now my actions and inactions are doubly embodied, in my own and the other's responsive/non-responsive body. At some moments, the other lends his/her body to complete my actions; the other's body becomes an extension of mine, and mine an extension of the other's. The line of action is now carried on by the integration of two bodies.

We must note another way that the social actions entailed in collaboratively putting shoes on another person differ from the solo project.

Putting on shoes with another requires an essentially negative reper-toire of expressive action. When I am putting my shoes on alone, I do not have to be concerned that the shoes remain committed to the project at hand. But when putting shoes on another, I and the other are both accountable in a Janus-like sense. Each of us has to shape his/her action so that it will be witnessable as produced for the shoeing situation that prevails here and now, which means manifestly avoiding, or in other words, positively negating personal involvements that transcend the situation.

In the collaborative situation I do not have to execute any particular positive action. With the other I may arrange any of a great variety of combinations of responsibilities defining who does which part of the necessary operations (finding the shoes, lifting the foot, adjusting laces, etc.). But when I am alone I must do all of the sequence. In this sense the solo situation requires more positive or constructive action. But should I wish to sustain continuous collaboration with another in the project of putting on shoes, I must not only do the positive narra-tive work of indicating where each of my motions is in the progression of the project, and the positive work of indicating my perceptions of where the other is in his/her understanding of the narrative's progress, I must also do negative work. I must also indicate that I am not too little involved, not 'away' on a reverie or otherwise so little engaged that the other must take up solo responsibility for completion; and I must avoid indicating I am too much involved in what is transpiring here and now, as might be the case were I to become so 'into' the project that it goes beyond the dressing narrative; for example, by suggesting a foot fetish.

When dressing alone, I need not be concerned to perceive in-dications that the shoes remain in the situation, that they have not abandoned the project. But when putting shoes on with another per-son, I know that the other's life simultaneously persists in other ongo-ing relations, the totality of which are unknowable to me; has a past and a future, both of which transcend the framework that is practically relevant to the project at hand; and has a realm of private meanings that I cannot access in the immediate situation. As I work out a com-mon narrative practice with the other, I will be responsive to signs that the other is 'away,' or desirous of pausing from the collaborative project, or giving it more meaning than as a practical dressing task. As I am putting a shoe on another person's foot, I may wonder whether her pause in pushing her foot in the shoe conveys an expectation that

I should push the shoe on, or means that she has abandoned the process of putting on this pair in favour of trying another, or indicates that her attentions have moved to some other area of concern, and so on. I attend to signs of a certain tension of consciousness – signs of an at-tention – that are consistent with a presumption that she is negating orientations that transcend the launched project of putting on the shoes at hand.

The contrast should not be overdrawn. While I do not need to be concerned to perceive signs that the shoes remain in the situation, when putting on my own shoes in private I will at a certain stage in the project need to be concerned to show to the shoes, in a manner of speaking, that I remain in the project. Shoes are social objects, made in ways that anticipate how they will be used. Once engaged, material objects differ in the demands on persistent attentions that they require. Shoes impose a notable if minimal constraint. Once engaged in the project to the point that one shoe is on, there are consequences for not continuing; one is in a more awkward position for walking than before the project began. If my mind wanders, the shoes will in effect call me back to finish or to reverse the project. As objects aiding motility, shoes make matters worse before they make them better. Shoes have not yet been designed to facilitate a thoroughgoing disrespect for their ontology. I must respect them in the sense that, once I introduce myself to the shoes and accept the willingness of one shoe to be put on, I will suffer if I do not negate concerns that transcend the dressing project until my feet are in both of the shoes.[11]

In effect, I have to show the shoes that I respect their ontology by limiting my transcending concerns until the project is complete. But I need not monitor whether the shoes are respecting my ontology; they will not go away on their own. In the co-present collaborative version of the project, there is a distinguishing symmetrical obligation for negating transcending concerns. When putting on shoes with another, the project requires that I manifestly negate my transcending concerns and also that I monitor whether the other is doing the same.[12] This doubly negative structure of co-present social action is the foundation for a rich array of emotions as they arise in the practice of everyday life.

Now we can return to the opening examples of lecturing in a college class. As when putting on shoes alone, there is a narrative logic that the lecturer presumes imposes demands on him or herself. The lecturer's talk is constrained to be arranged sequentially on a number of simultaneously sustained levels: any moment's utterances are to begin, complete, or advance the progress of sentence-like phrasings; such phrasings are to be interrelated into a manifest 'train of thought'; what is expressed in earlier parts of the hour is to be related to what comes later, and vice versa. By 'are to be' and 'is to be' I mean that each utterance is executed teleologically, in a manner that claims its emergent functionality in narrative structure: each moment's action is performed in a way that asserts the becoming of which it is a part and how it is a part of that becoming. The lecturer makes his/her action into behaviour by producing an expression accountable as a coherent advance in an emergent narrative.

Some of the lecturer's feelings are imposed by demands on persistent attention that are encountered as arising from the social form of the lecture. To isolate the feeling-evocative pressures that arise during a live lecture delivered to an audience, we can identify those that emerge in the lecturer's private rehearsals. In any instance of reviewing notes or rehearsing a lecture, the lecturer will register transitions, perceive gaps among segments, realize an awareness of unfulfilled promises and unannounced tangents, and so on, not necessarily in anything as abstracted, distanced, or self-contained as 'thought,' but through feeling the relationship between narrative structure and the action executed this time through. Perceived gaps, contradictions, unfulfilled introductory promises, awkward transitions, muddy passages, and so on, are registered not in stand-alone thoughts but in and as provocations to remediation. Seeing a problem in the narrative may not immediately throw up a solution, but no intervening thought is required to feel the need to do more. Something 'nags,' there is a source of disquiet, some part of the narrative does not feel right. A private reading of preparatory notes is already a corporeally implicated, feeling-evoking process. If when preparing lecture notes something seems wrong, the project cannot be freely abandoned. Like shoes, the lecture is a social form that once engaged is experienced as demanding that the user not abandon it for other concerns. That demand often appears as a haunting anxiety that more preparatory work is needed.

When delivered to a class, the lecturer will be constrained to do the class 'with' the audience. This means not only displaying that he/she is in the lecture situation and not taken up by transcendent concerns, but also monitoring that the correspondents are also suppressing transcendent concerns. The class, however passive it may seem, is still a correspondent in the production of the lecture. If on consulting the clock the lecturer appreciates that the moment to begin has come but no one has entered the room, she/he will be responsive to the fact. Indications that the audience is not playing a corresponding role that makes sense of continuing the lecturer's role may appear in question/answer phases, when hands are raised unexpectedly, or, most likely in today's college teaching environment, if the lecturer takes notice that many students appear preoccupied with web-searching activities that follow rhythms not connected to the lecturers. On such occasions the lecturer will take for granted that he/she must do the work of determining where the audience 'is at,' or the work of trying to ignore his/her concern about the matter. As the class time goes on the lecturer will be pressed to verify that the audience is still there as an audience.

Now, the negations required by the lecture as a live, correspondent social form are not just shared on both sides of the lectern, they are dynamically interactive. In order to keep the audience in the situation, the lecturer must do the work of manifesting that she/he is maintaining a lively consciousness to the situation. Pauses can go on only so long before they begin to undermine the audience's involvement. A monotonic reading may be adequate for timing in a rehearsal, but in a live lecture it will typically be replaced with a prosody that instructively dramatizes responsiveness to the instant narrative of the lecture; that is, that the lecturer him or herself is being taken by the talk as he/she expects the audience to be taken. A second generation of feelings emerges from the constraint to manifest a time/space specific collaborative posture; that is, a being in the situation, in order to keep the audience in the situation. Becoming a lecturer entails awakening to and developing a way of structuring a new order of sensibility.

In their debut lectures, Turner and Sarbin sustained the professional requirement that for all immediate appearances the show was going on unproblematically. Both not only performed the positive tasks of producing a coherent lecture neatly bounded by the duration of the class, both also avoided indicating problems with the transcendent meaning of the instant session. Both had a problem with the pre-class phase of the occasion; both came to understand that they had not prepared enough. Both came to understand the future implications of the particular challenge their first class meant, that they would have to prepare more for future sessions. As far as they understood, the students were unaware of their transcending occupational problems.

Where did the lecturers' realization of the problematic transcendent meanings of their situationally polished performances reside? Not in 'thoughts' but in emotions. As Sarbin flipped over his deck of index cards to restart once and then a second time, he continued to respond to the requirements for maintaining apparent narrative coherence in his talk. As Turner came to the end of the hour and realized he had expended all the preparation he had done for the course, his dilemma was not shared with the class. The lecturers' emotions arose in the crucible formed by the requirements of situationally specific, publicly witnessable, narratively coherent action, and their embodied manners of appreciating the transcendent meanings of this class session for the next, this 'first time teaching' for their teaching careers, and so on.

Lecturers will always experience something on the continuum that Sarbin and Turner dramatized at the extremes, although not necessarily in negative directions. At a given moment in a day's class, one may realize that preparation for the current lecture has more resources than anticipated, that there are multiple narrative lines to develop, only one of which will exhaust the current class session. As the current lecture is delivered, the awareness that less work will be necessary to set up future classes will be appreciated in some positive emotional form.

Emotions are distinctively three-dimensional experiences. Across their variety, emotions are characterized by feelings that pervade and recede from anatomically unbounded, more or less deep corporeal realms. This three dimensionality corresponds to the three dimensions along which transcendent meanings arise in socially situated conduct. In a temporal perspective, the novice lecturer senses what he did and did not do in the past, and the implications of that for future work. Spatially, the lecturer must stay visibly rooted in the here, even as his orientation may shift to situations located elsewhere, such as his study, other class sessions, and what he will make of the experience within family and friendship circles. A boundary between the public and private self emerges in such experiences, the lecturer's emotions serving as vehicles for an awareness that must be kept inner. Emotional expressions, such as joking, righteousness, professional élan, and intellectual passion, are themselves situation-shaped responses which leave hidden the lecturer's transcendent understandings; for example, that this is the nth re-telling of the joke, that righteousness works with this audience but not others, that passion expressed in a lecture hall is a low-risk variety, and so on.

Few lecturers could long sustain careers that suffer the volcanic emotional upshots of the novice's first-time experience. What happens as people repeatedly work through a given, initially intense emotional experience? They learn to manage tame, discipline, or civilize the emotional potential by developing a working aesthetic. Instead of pre-writing each word or leaving fate to situational inspiration, the lecturer will develop a preparation and a performance style. For guiding preparation, he/she will develop ways of interpreting nagging feelings of insufficient preparation. As the Turner and Sarbin horror stories illustrate, one learns to cultivate a useful disquiet, to distinguish between haunting feelings that are nuisances as opposed to practically significant warnings that should be heeded. For a performance style, the lecturer may adopt a strategy of relying on a small number of pre-planned stories that are to be delivered in an ordered progression, focusing in the classroom on 'hitting the mark' for each narrative component more or less at a certain time interval, leaving vocabulary and possible tangents to be worked out in the moment within this overall strategy. As strategy becomes style, emotions become largely a matter of occupational aesthetic. For first timers, a private awareness of these situation transcending, existential meanings will often be intensely emotional. Over time transcendent awareness commonly becomes mannered appreciation.

The Crucible

At some point in the transition from infancy to social competency, we move into a compelling stream of social situations. In wide-awake everyday life, we are virtually always 'doing something,' organizing our conduct so that it is part of an activity or project that is accountable to self as one or another typical narrative. The person may be doing the narrative ostensibly on his or her own, like putting on shoes in private, although indirectly, in ways emotions often will grasp before thought can reflect on the matter, the process will be one of interacting with shoe designers. Or the person may appear to be following a narrative that others have produced, like watching a TV show, in which case what a viewer attends to on the screen and in the audio track will be in some way unique, the process always a private editing of the script. Active or passive, behaving on our own or collaboratively with others, we shape our conduct from moment to moment so that at any time and in any place we are doing a version of something that routinely has a colloquially cognizant name. The most fundamental units of social life are formed through this giving of narrative meaning to corporeal movement. All meaningful action is felt because it is produced and grasped by discrete bodily action. It is the very work of structuring action into behaviour that is the crucible of emotions.

NOTES

1 This chapter has benefited from comments received when earlier versions were delivered at the Centre for Advanced Study in Behavioral and Social Sciences in 2001; the Emotions Matter workshop at Carleton University in 2009; and a conference of Italian ethnographers held in Bergamo, Italy, in 2009.

2 There are exceptions for ritual occasions. When 'prize' lectures are read, a lack of spontaneity sustains a double impression, of extraordinarily careful preparation and of the preciousness of each word. The former conveys reciprocation for the respect shown by the award committee; the latter affirms that the audience's deference is well deserved.

3 As objects of expression, emotions become flattened out. Paul Ekman (1982) has shown that people universally can identify several different emotions by looking at two-dimensional photographs. We can name emotions, but to characterize feelings as 'anger' or 'happiness' is to reduce a three dimensional experience to a metaphor-stripped semiotics that applies equally well to non-emotional self-descriptors. We can enact emotions so that others, correctly or not, infer what we are feeling. But as we feel, within our emotional experiences, we resonate with implications of what we perceive in ways that language always struggles to grasp, in ways that metaphors and audiovisual representations often convey better than does flatprose, and in ways that our enacted emotions may turn into two-dimensional masks. The study of how emotions are presented, dramatized, or shaped as managed performances leaves the experience of emotion off the research agenda.

4 Defence of the claim that the dialectic is ontogenetic requires examination of fetal and neonate behaviour and must await another writing.

5 Blumer (1969) persistently argued that social interaction is at the foundation of all behaviour. By social interaction he meant taking into account the response of others in the formation of one's own action. Following Mead, Blumer would understand that the narrative structuring of action is part of social action, whether others are present or not. Action is interactively formed when the actor, acting in solitary situations or in the presence of others, takes account of his/her own action from the standpoint of what he/she assumes is a collectively recognizable kind of doing. In picking up my shoe I am at the beginning of what I take for granted that others, were they present, would, were they to see the ensuing stages of the sequence I am launching, see as putting on my shoes (or cleaning my room, or swatting a fly . . .). But there

is social action even when one's solitary action, if observed by others, would
be incomprehensible as narrative construction. Thus to a peeping Tom I
may seem to be wandering aimlessly around my garden when I am in deed
systematically structuring my gaze in discrete strips, each strip of attentive
gaze internally structured to gauge the progress of previously noted pest
damage, to follow trajectories of plant growth that may be progressing
towards crowding, to witness novel light patterns as they emerge across
the landscape, and so on. In such solo experiences there is interaction, in
that each moment's observation implicates the meaning of the person's past
action (prior observations of pest damage, plant growth, and light patterns
set up the meaning of the current observation as disturbing, intriguing,
etc.) and next actions (time now to act or not, reason or not to continue the
exploration); but to call this 'social' interaction is tendentious or redundant
with the concept of interaction. More clearly the activity has narrative
structure.

6 There is no clear line between ritualistic and pragmatically required recipes.
Indeed, one youthful recipe for being antisocial is ritualistically rejecting
steps that others take for granted as practically necessary. Thus adolescents
who do not tie shoes create magically powerful ways of resisting the
embrace of the social; their untied shoes will drive some onlookers to mad
fantasies of tying them.

7 Adam Kendon's (1990, 2004) studies come the closest to theorizing the
relationship between body movements and the situated structuring
of social life. Body movement may consist of walking off, turning the
page, changing gaze, and so on; no particular region of the body need
be engaged, although in the responsive actions of others, the further
down the corpus the alteration occurs (compare eye gaze to head turn to
torso turn to walking away), the more effective it will be in shaping the
understanding of a co-present other than that the situation is ending. Much
of McNeil's (1992, 2005) work approaches the relationship from a direction
opposite to that taken in most interaction analysis, which, following
Blumer, sees body deployed in service of mind (anticipating how one will
be seen, one gives a movement a certain flair). McNeil finds that gesture
commonly precedes and shapes the thought to which it is related; body
gives rise to mind. I would add that it does so through the intermediary
step of invoking a situation.

8 See Schutz (1962) on multiple realities.

9 Someone who has never seen a shower might turn a handle, bringing the
water on, without anticipating or understanding that a counter-directional
turn will shut it off, but whatever that person is doing – perhaps turning an
obviously designed object to see why it was made – he or she is not 'turning
on a shower.' The nouns we use to designate objects in the social world are
shorthand references to narratives.

10 The pun is not simply rhetorical. Learning to walk is aided if one already
    knows how to interrelate moments of life as connected steps, and vice
    versa. For the young child, walking is initially a series of discrete narratives.
    The concept of steps, with which we populate the social world with
    differentiated doings, is laboriously and spontaneously, delightedly and
    painfully acquired.

11 The example of putting on shoes raises in a useful way the question
    of whether or to what extent the social world is all embracing. Is there
    escape? If we avoid commodity objects like shoes, can we declare our
    independence from social control? Not so easily. If one goes barefoot,
    it matters all the more the nature and condition of the materials on the
    ground one walks upon. Walking on paths will be a different experience
    than walking off-path. The very phenomenon of a path is a creation by
    others. How many have come before and moved over this space, with what
    weight, leaving what depressions and ridges, scattering what detritus –
    all that will matter even more. Walking on paths barefoot is an especially
    intimate way of being with anonymous others (Solnit 2000).

12 A caveat is necessary here. The contrast I have made between the
    interaction requirements that obtain when collaborating with co-present
    others and that constrain one when using material objects in private
    requires complex and historically changing qualifications. Over time,
    the material environment of work changes in its negative demands on
    users. Computers, for example, are evolving to minimize the constraining
    pressure of a given task to monopolize the user's attention. A few years
    ago, 'multi-tasking' was unknown; then for some years operating systems
    were at a state in which multi-tasking would risk 'crashing' the computer.
    Computer users were constrained not to be flaky. Now, working alone
    on a computer is a robust environment for jumping in focus from here to
    there, from work obligations to private indulgence, and among tasks at
    different stages of their evolution, whether the tasks are pursued on or off
    the computer. One can more reliably take for granted that the computer will
    hold as-yet-incomplete projections of the user's virtual self – where the user
    is in a digitally expressed task – in a steady state until he or she is ready
    to return. 'Ticklers,' alarms, and various reminders can be programmed in
    to minimize the scattering of attention. These strategies understand and
    respond to the increasingly flexible, costless ability to depart attention from
    and return at will to a situated project that has begun.But the progression
    towards a computer that can be thoroughly treated with disrespect is not
    complete. Even if, given the low level demands I make on my computer,
    Imay not have to limit my task-transcending concerns out of fear that the
    computer may 'freeze up.' I still must treat the computer like a flesh-
    and-blood work partner, as having a life of its own. The contemporary
    computer has a biography beyond my project that it might divert or

digress to attend to. It might pause my work for 'system maintenance' or to download software updates from the Internet. Depending on how I arrange my coffee around it and manipulate it, the computer may break down or otherwise effectively go away. Users are not yet free to disregard or disrespect the computer's ontology.

3 Sociable Happiness

SARA AHMED

Introduction

Emotions are quite sociable. We are moved by the proximity of others. Sociability can even be a feeling: when you feel sociable you want to be with others; you register the proximity of others as enjoyment. In this chapter, I consider happiness as a form of sociability. It is a truism that happiness is happiest when it is shared with others. And yet does happiness simply bring us together? A social bond might be created if the same things make us happy. In turn, those who are not made happy by the same things might threaten our happiness. If emotions are sociable, then sociability might need to be theorized in terms of the restriction as well as enjoyment of company.

Before thinking about happiness as a form of sociability I want to reflect on questions of methodology. How do I approach happiness? It might be useful to note that there is a body of research called 'happiness studies,' which is also widely referred to as 'the new science of happiness.' Much research in this field draws on the nineteenth-century tradition of English utilitarianism and is premised on the following beliefs: happiness is a good thing, and the task of government is to maximize happiness (cf. Ahmed 2008). One of the key figures in the recent science of happiness is Richard Layard (2005), often referred to as 'the happiness tsar' by the British media. Layard's important book, *Happiness: Lessons from a New Science*, begins as a critique of the discipline of economics for how it measures human growth: he argues that 'economics equates changes in the happiness of a society with changes in its purchasing power' (ix). Layard argues that happiness is the only way of measuring growth and advancement: 'the best society is the happiest society' (5). The science of happiness presumes that happiness is 'out there,' that you can measure happiness, and that these measurements are objective.

If the science of happiness presumes happiness as being 'out there,' then how does it define happiness? Richard Layard (2005) again provides us with a useful reference point. He argues that 'happiness is feeling good, and misery is feeling bad' (6). Happiness is 'feeling good,' which means we can measure happiness because we can measure how good people feel. So 'out there' is really 'in here.' The belief that you can measure happiness is a belief that you can measure feelings. Layard argues that 'most people find it easy to say how good they are feeling' (13). Happiness research is primarily based on self-reporting: studies measure how happy people say they are, presuming that if people say they are happy, they are happy. This model both presumes the transparency of self-feeling, as well as the unmotivated and uncomplicated nature of self-reporting.

It matters how we think about feeling. Much of the new science of happiness is premised on the model of feelings as transparent, as well as the foundation for moral life. If something is good, we feel good. If something is bad, we feel bad.[1] The science of happiness thus relies on a very specific model of subjectivity, where one knows how one feels, and where the distinction between good and bad feeling is secure, forming the basis of subjective as well as social well-being. Cultural Studies may have an important role to play in these debates by offering alternative theories of emotion that are *not* based on a subject that is fully present to itself, on a subject that always knows how s/he feels (see Terada 2001). Of course, I should note here that even the association of happiness with feeling is a modern one. One of my concerns is thus to track an association – to ask how feeling good becomes attached to other kinds of goods. To give happiness a history is to give a history to its associations.

We do have examples of happiness histories, such as the one offered by Darrin McMahon (2006). He describes his history of happiness as an 'intellectual history' (xiv) and suggests that his history is one history of happiness that should exist alongside others: 'there are infinite histories of happiness to be written' (xiii). He suggests that such histories would be told from more specific viewing points as 'histories not only of the struggles of the peasants, slaves, and apostates . . . but of early-modern women and late-modern aristocrats, nineteenth-century bourgeois and twentieth-century workers, conservatives and radicals, consumers and crusaders, immigrants and natives, gentiles and Jews' (xiii). Different histories, we might imagine, unfold from the struggles of such groups.

I have no wish to supplement McMahon's history with a history told from a specific viewing point, as a particular history within a general history. I want to think about how the intellectual history of happiness – as a history of an idea – can be challenged by considering what gets erased if we take this viewing point, where to see what is erased would change the view you see from this point. Just note how women appear or do not appear in McMahon's intellectual history. The index includes one reference to women, which turns out to be a reference to John Stuart Mill's *The Subjection of Women*. Even the category of 'women' returns us to philosophy as a white male European inheritance. If differences matter within the history of happiness, then they may trouble the form of its coherence.

If we take up happiness as an intellectual history, it is striking how consistent this history is on one point: happiness is what gives meaning, purpose, and order to human existence. As Bruno Frey and Alois Stutzer (2002) argue: 'Everybody wants to be happy. There is probably no other goal in life that commands such a high degree of consensus' (vii). Even a philosopher such as Immanuel Kant (2004), who places the individual's own happiness outside the domain of ethics, suggests that 'to be happy is necessarily the wish of every finite and rational being, and this, therefore, is inevitably a determining principle of its faculty of desire' (24). And yet Kant (2005) himself suggests, rather mournfully,'unfortunately, the notion of happiness is so indeterminate that although every human being wishes to attain it, yet he can never say definitely and consistently what it is that he really wishes and wills' (78).[2]

What if we refuse to wish this wish or to will this will? What if we were to suspend our belief that happiness is what we want or even that happiness is a good thing? In this mode of suspension, we can consider how happiness *participates* in making things good. Simone de Beauvoir's (1997) *The Second Sex* uses this technique of suspension. As de Beauvoir argues: 'it is not too clear just what the word *happy* really means and still less what true values it may mask. There is no possibility of measuring the happiness of others, and *it is always easy to describe as happy the situation in which one wishes to place them*' (28, second emphasis added). De Beauvoir shows so well how happiness translates its wish into a politics, a wishful politics, a politics that demands that others live according to a wish.

Feminist histories offer a different angle on the history of happiness. Or perhaps feminist histories teach us that we need to give a history to unhappiness. The history of the word 'unhappy' might teach us about the unhappiness of the history of happiness. In its earliest uses, unhappy meant 'causing misfortune or trouble.' Only later did it come to mean 'wretched in mind.'[3] We can learn from the swiftness of translation between causing unhappiness and being described as being unhappy. We must learn. The word 'wretched' also has a suggestive genealogy, coming from wretch, referring to a banished person, and is said to reflect the sorry state of the outcast. The sorrow of the stranger might give us a different angle on happiness not because it teaches us what it is like or must be like to be a stranger, but because it might estrange us from the very happiness of the familiar.

I offer a different account of happiness not simply by offering different readings of its intellectual history, but by considering those who are banished from it, or who enter this history only as troublemakers, dissenters, killers of joy. In this chapter, I explore how happiness offers a promise (the promise of the return for being sociable in the right way) before considering how happiness appears to those who are alienated from its promise, taking up two key figures: the feminist killjoy and the angry black woman.

Happy Objects

My starting point is not to assume there is something called affect (or, for that matter, emotion) that stands apart or has autonomy, as if it corresponds to an object in the world. I begin with the messiness of the experiential, the unfolding of bodies into the world, and what I call 'the drama of contingency' (Ahmed 2006), how we are touched by what is near. It is useful to note that the etymology of 'happiness' relates precisely to the question of contingency: it is from the Middle English 'hap,' suggesting chance. One of the early meanings of happiness in English relates to the idea of being lucky, or favoured by fortune, or being fortunate. This meaning may now seem archaic: we may be more used to thinking of happiness as an effect of what you do, as a reward for hard work, rather than as what happens to you. But I find this original meaning useful, as it focuses our attention on the 'worldly' question of happenings.

What is the relation between the 'what' in 'what happens' and the 'what' that makes us happy? Empiricism provides us with a useful way of addressing this question, given its concern with 'what's what.' Take the work of John Locke (1997). He argues that what is good is what is 'apt to cause or increase pleasure, or diminish pain in us' (216). So we judge something to be good or bad according to how it affects us, whether it gives us pleasure or pain. Locke suggests that 'he loves grapes, it is no more but that the taste of the grapes delights him' (216). So we could say that an object becomes happy if it affects us in a good way.

Note the doubling of positive affect in Locke's example: we *love* the grapes if they taste *delightful*. If the object affects us in a good way, then we have an orientation towards that object as being good. Orientations register the proximity of objects, as well as shape what is proximate to the body. Happiness can thus be described as *intentional* in the phenomenological sense (directed towards objects), as well as being *affective* (contact with objects). To bring these arguments together we might say that happiness is an orientation towards the objects we come into contact with. We move towards and away from objects according to how we are affected by them.

To describe happiness as intentional does not mean there is always a simple correspondence between objects and feelings. I think Robin Barrow (1980) is right to argue that happiness does not 'have an object' the way that some other emotions do (89). We have probably all experienced what I call 'unattributed happiness': you feel happy, not quite knowing why, and the feeling can be catchy, as a kind of brimming over that exceeds what you encounter. The feeling can lift or elevate any proximate object, which is not to say that the feeling will survive an encounter with anything. It has always interested me that when we become conscious of feeling happy or of a happy feeling (when the feeling becomes an object of thought), happiness can often recede or become anxious. Happiness can arrive in a moment, and be lost by virtue of its recognition.

I would suggest that happiness involves a specific kind of intentionality, which I would describe as 'end oriented.' It is not just that we can be happy *about* something, as a feeling in the present, but some things become happy *for us*, if we imagine they will bring happiness *to us*. Happiness is often described as 'what' we aim for, as an end-point, or even an end-in-itself. Classically, happiness has been considered as an end rather than as a means. In *Nicomachean Ethics*, Aristotle (1998) describes happiness as the Chief Good, as 'that which all things aim at' (1). Happiness is what we 'choose always for its own sake' (8).

We don't have to agree with the argument that happiness is the perfect end to understand the implications of what it means for happiness to be thought of in these terms. If happiness is the end of all ends, then other things (including other goods) become means to happiness. As Aristotle describes, we choose other things 'with a view to happiness, conceiving that through their instrumentality we shall be happy' (8). Aristotle is not referring here to material things or physical objects, but is differentiating between different kinds of goods, between instrumental goods and independent goods. So honour, pleasure, or intellect we choose 'with a view to happiness' as being instrumental to happiness, and the realization of the possibility of living a good or virtuous life.

If we think of instrumental goods as objects of happiness then important consequences follow. Things become good, or acquire their value as goods, insofar as they point towards happiness. Objects become 'happiness means.' Or we could say they become happiness pointers, as if to follow their point would be to find happiness. If objects provide a means for making us happy, then in directing ourselves towards this or that object, we are aiming somewhere else: towards a happiness that is presumed to follow. The temporality of this following matters. Happiness is what would come after. Given this, happiness is directed towards certain objects, which point towards that which is not yet present. When we follow things, we aim for happiness, as if happiness is what you get if you reach certain points.

The very possibility of being pointed towards happiness suggests that objects can be associated with affects before they are even encountered. Happy objects thus need to be re-thought beyond a sequential logic of causality. In *The Will to Power*, Nietzsche (1968) suggests that the attribution of causality is retrospective (294–5). We might assume that the experience of pain is caused by a nail near our foot. But we only notice the nail if we experience an affect. We search for the object, or, as Nietzsche describes it, 'a reason is sought in persons, experiences, etc. for why one feels this way or that' (354).

Once an object is a feeling-cause, it can cause feeling, so that when we feel the feeling we expect to feel, we are affirmed. The retrospective causality of affect that Nietzsche describes quickly converts into what we can call an *anticipatory causality*. We can even anticipate an affect without being retrospective insofar as objects can acquire the value of proximities that are not derived from our own experience. For example, with fear-causes, a child might be told not to go near an object in advance of its arrival. Some things more than others are encountered as 'to-be-feared' in the event of proximity, which is exactly how we can understand the anticipatory logic of the discourse of stranger danger. As I argued in *Strange Encounters* (2000), even if the stranger is conventionally understood as *anybody* we do not know, the stranger is also *somebody* we recognize as a stranger, as a 'body out of place.' Some more than others are recognized as strangers: the stranger as a figure is thus painfully familiar. We recognize strangers as the cause of danger in advance of their arrival.

We can also anticipate that an object will cause happiness in advance of its arrival; the object might enter our near sphere with a positive affective value already in place. Objects can become 'happiness-causes' before we even encounter them. This argument is different from John Locke's account of loving grapes because they taste delightful: I am suggesting that the judgment that some things are good not only precedes our encounter with things, but can direct us towards certain things. For example, the child might be asked to imagine happy events in the future, such as the wedding day, the 'happiest day of your life.' The very expectation of happiness might be what gives us a specific image of the future. To share happy objects is to pass certain things around, as if you are passing the cause of happiness.

The more happy objects circulate, the more they accumulate affective value, as signs of the good life. What happens when happy objects circulate? How do happy objects sustain their promise in the absence of happiness being given? Consider that the word 'promise' derives from the Latin verb *promittere*, suggesting 'to let go or send forth, to put forth,' as well as 'to promise, guarantee, or predict.' The promise of happiness might be what sends happiness forth. When objects are promising, they are sent out or sent forth; *to promise can mean to pass around a promise.*

Is happiness sent forth? Does the promise of happiness mean that happiness is passed around? If we were to say that the promise of happiness means that happiness is sent forth, we might also suggest that happiness is contagious. David Hume's (1975) approach to moral emotions rests on a contagious model of happiness. He suggests that 'others enter into the same humour, and catch the sentiment, by a contagion or natural sympathy' and that cheerfulness is the most communicative of emotions: 'the flame spreads through the whole circle; and the most sullenly and remorse are often caught by it' (250–1; see also Blackman 2008). A number of scholars have recently taken up the idea of affects as contagious in very interesting ways, drawing in particular on the work of the psychologist of affect Silvan Tomkins (Gibbs 2001; Brennan 2004; Sedgwick 2003; Probyn 2005). As Anna Gibbs (2001) describes: 'Bodies can catch feelings as easily as catch fire: affect leaps from one body to another, evoking tenderness, inciting shame, igniting rage, exciting fear – in short, communicable affect can inflame nerves and muscles in a conflagration of every conceivable kind of passion' (1).

Thinking of affects as contagious helps us to challenge what I have called an 'inside out' model of affect (Ahmed 2004:9), by showing how we are affected by what is around us. However, the concept of affective contagion does tend to treat affect as something that moves smoothly from body to body, sustaining integrity in being passed around. When Sedgwick (2003) argues that shame is contagious, for example, she suggests that proximity to someone's shame generates shame (36–8). The implication of such arguments is that affects are sustained in being passed around: shame creates shame in others, and happiness creates happiness in others, and so on. The concept of affective contagion underestimates the extent to which affects are contingent (involving the 'hap' of a happening): to be affected by another does not mean that an affect simply passes or 'leaps' from one body to another. The affect becomes an object *only given the contingency of how we are affected*. We might be affected differently by what gets passed around.

We can take the example of atmosphere. We might describe an 'atmosphere' as a feeling of what is around, which might be affective in its murkiness or fuzziness, as a surrounding influence which does not quite generate its own form. At the same time, in describing an atmosphere, *we give this influence some form*. We might say the atmosphere was tense, which would mean that the body that arrives into the room will 'pick up' tension and become tense as a way of being under influence. When feelings become atmospheric, we can catch the feeling simply by walking into a room, from a crowd or the collective body from being proximate to another.

Do we pick up feelings in quite this way? Consider the opening sentence of Teresa Brennan's (2004) book, *The Transmission of Affect*: 'Is there anyone who has not, at least once, walked into a room and "felt the atmosphere"' (1). Brennan writes very beautifully about how the atmosphere 'gets into the individual,' using what I have called an 'outside in' model, very much part of the intellectual history of crowd psychology and also the sociology of emotion (Ahmed 2004:9). However, later in the introduction she makes an observation, which involves a different model. Brennan (2004) suggests that 'if I feel anxiety when I enter the room, then that will influence what I perceive or receive by way of an "impression" (a word that means what it says)' (6).[4] I agree. Anxiety is sticky: rather like Velcro, it tends to pick up whatever comes near, such that anything that is proximate to us when we are anxious can become anxious (for a more detailed explanation, see Ahmed 2004:66). Anxiety is, of course, one feeling state amongst others. You might say we are always in a certain mood, even if we are not certain what mood we are in. Bodies thus never arrive in neutral; we are always moody in some way or another. What we will receive as an impression will depend on our affective situation. This second argument suggests the atmosphere is not simply 'out there' before it gets 'in': how we arrive, how we enter this room or that room, will affect what impressions we receive. To receive is to act. To receive an impression is to make an impression.

So we may walk into the room and 'feel the atmosphere,' but what we may feel depends on the angle of our arrival. Or we might say that the atmosphere is already angled; it is always felt from a specific point. The pedagogic encounter is full of angles. How many times have I read students as interested or bored, such that the atmosphere seemed one of interest or boredom (and even felt myself to be interesting or boring) only to find students recall the event quite differently! Having read the atmosphere in a certain way, one can become tense, which in turn affects what happens, how things move along. The moods we arrive with do affect what happens, which is not to say we always keep our moods. Sometimes I arrive heavy with anxiety, and everything that happens makes me feel more anxious, whilst at other times things happen which ease the anxiety, making the space itself seem light and energetic. We do not know in advance what will happen given this contingency, given the hap of what happens; we do not know 'exactly' what makes things happen in this way and that. Situations are affective given the gap between the impressions we have of others and the impressions we make on others, all of which are lively.

Think too about experiences of alienation. I have suggested that happiness is attributed to certain objects that circulate as social goods. When we feel pleasure from such objects, we are aligned; we are facing the right way. We become alienated – out of line with an affective community – when we do not experience pleasure from proximity to objects that are attributed as being good. The gap between the affective value of an object and how we experience an object can involve a range of affects, which are directed by the modes of explanation we offer to fill this gap.

We might feel disappointed. Disappointment can be experienced as a gap between an ideal and an experience that demands action. We can return to the example of the wedding day: the 'happiest day of your life.' What does it mean for such a day to be anticipated as being the happiest day when the day is actually happening? We might say that the day happens because of this anticipation of happiness. However the day happens, when it does happen, happiness is supposed to follow. As Arlie Russell Hochschild (1983) explores in her classic *The Managed Heart*, if the bride is not happy on the wedding day and even feels 'depressed and upset' then she is experiencing an 'inappropriate affect' (59), or is being affected inappropriately. You have to save the day by feeling right: 'sensing a gap between the ideal feeling and the actual feeling she tolerated, the bride prompts herself to be happy' (61).

The capacity to 'save the day' depends on the bride being able to make herself be affected in the right way or at least being able to persuade others that she is being affected in the right way. When it can be said 'the bride looked happy' then the expectation of happiness has become the happiness of expectation. To correct our feelings is to become disaffected from a former affectation: the bride makes herself happy by stopping herself being miserable. Of course, we learn from this example that it is possible not to inhabit fully one's own happiness, or even to be alienated from one's happiness, if the former affection remains lively, or if one is made uneasy by the labour of making oneself feel a certain way. Uneasiness might persist in the very feeling of being happy, as a feeling of unease *with* the happiness you are in.

The experience of a gap between the promise of happiness and how you are affected by objects that promise happiness does not always lead to corrections that close this gap. Disappointment can also involve an anxious narrative of self-doubt (Why am I not made happy by this? What is wrong with me?), or a narrative of rage, where the object that is supposed to make us happy is attributed as the cause of disappointment. Your rage might be directed against the object that fails to deliver its promise, or spill out towards those who promised you happiness through the elevation of some things as good. Anger can fill the gap between the promise of a feeling and the feeling of a feeling. We become strangers, or affect aliens, in such moments. An affect alien is one who is not affected in the right way by the right things. To be affected wrongly might be to commit a social wrong: to be wrong, or to be found as being in the wrong. As I will explore in the following sections, the distribution of affects is at once to the distributions of rights and wrongs in different bodies.

Killing Joy

If happy objects are passed around it is not necessarily the feeling that passes. So what are we sharing when we share happy objects? To answer this question, I will take as an example Rousseau's *Émile*, first published in 1762, which was crucial for how it redefined education and for the role it gave to happiness. This book is written in the first person by a narrator whose duty is to instruct a young orphan named Émile. Within this book, happiness plays a crucial role: the good man does not seek happiness but achieves happiness as a consequence of virtue. Rousseau offers a model of what a good education would do for his Émile, but also for Émile's would-be wife, Sophy, whom he introduces in the fifth book. In this book, happiness provides a script for her becoming. As Rousseau (1993) describes: 'She loves virtue because there is nothing fairer in itself. She loves it because it is a woman's glory and because a virtuous woman is little lower than the angels; she loves virtue as the only road to real happiness, because she sees nothing but poverty, neglect, unhappiness, shame and disgrace in the life of the bad woman; she loves virtue because it is dear to her revered father, and to her tender and worthy mother; they are not content to be happy in their own virtue, they desire hers; and she finds her chief happiness in the hope of just making them happy!' (431). The complexity of this statement should not be underestimated. She loves virtue, as it is the road to happiness; unhappiness and disgrace are what follow from being bad. The good woman loves what is good because this is what is loved by her parents. Her parents desire not only what is good; they desire their daughter to be good. So for the daughter to be happy, she must be good, as being good is what makes them happy, and she can only be happy if they are happy.

It might seem that what we can call 'conditional happiness,' where one person's happiness is made conditional upon another person's, involves a relationship of care and reciprocity as if to say, I will not have a share in a happiness that cannot be shared. And yet, the terms of conditionality are unequal. If certain people come first, we might say those who are already in place (such as parents, hosts, or citizens), then their happiness comes first. For those who are positioned as coming after, *happiness means following somebody else's goods.*

The concept of conditional happiness allows me to be more precise in thinking about what we share when we share an orientation. If my happiness is made conditional on your happiness, such that your happiness comes first, then *your happiness becomes a shared object.* Max Scheler's (2008) differentiation between communities of feeling and fellow feeling might help explain the significance of this argument. In communities of feeling, we share feelings *because* we share the object of feeling. We might share sadness, for example, if someone died whom we both loved. Fellow feeling does not depend on a shared object: it 'involves *intentional reference* of the feeling to the other person's experience' (12, emphasis added). I would be saddened by your loss because I love you, even if I did not share your loss. In the case of happiness, then, we would have a community of feeling if we were both made happy by the same thing (for example, we might both be happy as supporters of a football team if they won). In the case of fellow feeling, I would share your happiness, but my happiness would refer simply to yours, such that your happiness was the object of my happiness. (I might be happy when your football team wins, because their winning makes you happy, even if I don't support the team.)

I suspect that in everyday life these different forms of shared feeling can be confused because the object of feeling is sometimes, but not always, exterior to the feeling that is shared. Say I am happy about your happiness. Your happiness is with x. If I share x, then your happiness and my happiness is not only shared, but can accumulate through being returned. Or I can simply disregard x: if my happiness is directed 'just' towards your happiness, and you are happy about x, the exteriority of x can disappear or cease to matter. In cases where I am also affected by x, and I do not share your happiness with x, I might become uneasy and ambivalent, as *I am made happy by your happiness but I am not made happy by what makes you happy.* The exteriority of x would then announce itself as a point of crisis. In order to preserve the happiness of all, we might even conceal from ourselves our unhappiness with x, or try and persuade ourselves that x matters less than the happiness of the other who is made happy by x.

We have a hint of the rather uneasy dynamics of conditional happiness in Rousseau's (1993) *Émile*. For Sophy wanting to make her parents happy commits her in a certain direction. In one episode, the father speaks to the daughter about becoming a woman. He says, 'you are a big girl now, Sophy, you will soon be a woman. We want you to be happy, for our sakes as well as yours, for our happiness depends on yours. A good girl finds her own happiness in the happiness of a good man' (434). For the daughter not to go along with the parents' desire for marriage would be not only to cause her parents unhappiness, it would threaten the very reproduction of social form. The daughter has a duty to reproduce the form of the family, which means *taking up the cause of parental happiness as her own.*

It should be no surprise that Rousseau's treatment of Sophy was a crucial object of feminist critique. Mary Wollstonecraft (1975) in her *Vindication of the Rights of Women* spoke out against Rousseau's vision of what makes women happy. She comments wryly about his treatment of Sophy: 'I have probably had an opportunity of observing more girls in their infancy than J.J. Rousseau' (43). The struggle over happiness forms the political horizon in which feminist claims are made. My argument is simple: we inherit this horizon.

The figure of the feminist killjoy makes more sense if we read her through the lens of the history of happiness. Feminists might kill joy simply by not finding the objects that promise happiness to be quite so promising. The word *feminism* is thus saturated with unhappiness. Feminists by declaring themselves as feminists are already read as destroying something that is thought of by others not only as being good, but also as the cause of happiness. The feminist killjoy 'spoils' the happiness of others; she is a spoilsport because she refuses to convene, to assemble, or to meet up, over happiness.

In the thick sociality of everyday spaces, feminists are thus attributed as the origin of bad feeling, as the ones who ruin the atmosphere, which is how the atmosphere might be imagined (retrospectively) as shared. In order to get along, you have to participate in certain forms of solidarity: you have to laugh at the right points. Feminists are typically represented as grumpy and humourless, often as a way of protecting the right to certain forms of social bonding, or holding onto whatever is perceived to be under threat. Feminists don't even have to say anything to be read as killing joy. A feminist colleague says to me she just has to open her mouth in meetings to witness eyes rolling as if to say, 'Oh, here she goes.'

My experience of being the feminist daughter in a conventional family taught me much about rolling eyes. I recall feeling at odds with the performance of good feeling. Say, we are seated at the dinner table.

Around this table, the family gathers, having polite conversations, where only certain things can be brought up. Someone says something you consider problematic. You respond, carefully perhaps. You might be speaking quietly or you might be getting 'wound up,' recognizing with frustration that you are being wound up by someone who is winding you up. The violence of what was said or the violence of provocation goes unnoticed. However she speaks, the feminist is usually the one who is viewed as 'causing the argument,' the one who is disturbing the fragility of peace.

Let's take this figure of the feminist killjoy seriously. Does the feminist kill other people's joy by pointing out moments of sexism? Or does she expose the bad feelings that get hidden, displaced, or negated under public signs of joy? Does bad feeling enter the room when somebody expresses anger about things, or could anger be the moment when the bad feelings that circulate through objects get brought to the surface in a certain way? The feminist subject 'in the room' hence 'brings others down' not only by talking about unhappy topics such as sexism but by exposing how happiness is sustained by erasing the signs of not getting along. Feminists do kill joy in a certain sense: they disturb the very fantasy that happiness can be found in certain places. To kill a fantasy can still kill a feeling. It is not just that feminists might not be happily affected by the objects that are supposed to cause happiness, but their failure to be happy is read as sabotaging the happiness of others.

Of course, within feminism, some bodies more than others can be attributed as the cause of unhappiness. We can place the figure of the feminist killjoy alongside the figure of the angry black woman, explored so well by writers such as Audre Lorde (1984) and bell hooks (2000). The angry black woman can be described as a killjoy; she may even kill feminist joy, for example, by pointing out forms of racism within feminist politics. Listen to the following description from bell hooks: 'a group of white feminist activists who do not know one another may be present at a meeting to discuss feminist theory. They may feel bonded on the basis of shared womanhood, but the atmosphere will noticeably change when a woman of color enters the room. The white women will become tense, no longer relaxed, no longer celebratory' (56).

It is not just that feelings are 'in tension,' but that the tension is located somewhere: in being felt by some bodies, it is attributed as caused by another body, who thus comes to be felt as apart from the group, as getting in the way of its organic enjoyment and solidarity. The black body is attributed as the cause of becoming tense, which is experienced as the loss of a shared atmosphere. Atmospheres are shared if there is an agreement as to where we locate the points of tension. As a feminist of colour you do not even have to say anything to cause tension. We learn from this example how histories are condensed in the very intangibility of an atmosphere, or in the tangibility of the bodies that seem to get in the way. Some bodies are reminders of histories that are disturbing, which disturb an atmosphere.

Consciousness and Unhappiness

Some bodies become causes of unhappiness in order both to defend and restrict the sociability of happiness. Returning to *Émile*, it is interesting that the danger of unhappiness is associated precisely with women having too much curiosity. At one point in the narrative, Sophy gets misdirected. Her imagination and desires are activated by reading too many books, leading to her becoming an 'unhappy girl, overwhelmed with her secret grief' (Rousseau 1993: 439–40). If Sophy becomes too imaginative, we would not get our happy ending premised on Sophy being given to Émile. The narrator says in response to the threat of such an unhappy ending, 'Let us give Émile his Sophy; let us restore this sweet girl to life and provide her with a less vivid imagination and a happier fate' (441). Being restored to life is here being returned to the straight and narrow. Imagination is what makes women look beyond the script of happiness to a different fate. Having made Sophy sweet and unimaginative, the book can end happily.

Feminist readers might want to challenge this association between unhappiness and female imagination, which, in the moral economy of happiness, makes her imagination a bad thing. But if we do not operate in this economy – that is, if we do not assume happiness is what is good – then we can read the link between female imagination and unhappiness differently. We might explore how imagination is what allows women to be liberated from happiness and the narrowness of its horizons. We might want girls to read the books that enable them to be overwhelmed with grief.

Feminism involves political consciousness of what women are asked to give up for happiness. Indeed, in even becoming conscious of happiness as loss, feminists have already refused to give up desire, imagination, and curiosity for happiness. There can be sadness simply in the realization of what one has given up. Feminist archives are thus full of housewives becoming conscious of unhappiness as a mood that seems to surround them: think of Virginia Woolf's (1953) *Mrs. Dalloway*. The feeling is certainly around, almost as a thickness in the air. We sense the unhappiness seeping through the tasks of the every day. There she is, about to get flowers, enjoying her walk in London. During that walk, she disappears: 'But often now this body she wore (she stopped to look at a Dutch picture), this body, with all its capacities, seemed nothing – nothing at all. She had the oddest sense of being herself invisible; unseen; unknown; there being no more marrying, no more having children now, but only this astonishing and rather solemn progress with the rest of them, up Bond Street, this being Mrs. Dalloway; not even Clarissa anymore; this being Mrs. Richard Dalloway' (14). Becoming Mrs Dalloway is itself a form of disappearance: to follow the paths of life (marriage, reproduction) is to feel that what is before you is a kind of solemn progress, as if you are living somebody else's life, simply going the same way others are going. If happiness is what allows us to reach certain points, it is not necessarily how you feel when you get there. For Mrs Dalloway to reach these points is to disappear. The point of reaching these points seems to be a certain disappearance, a loss of possibility, a certain failure to make use of the body's capacities, to find out what it is that her body can do. To become conscious of possibility can involve mourning for its loss.

For Clarissa, this rather uncanny sensation of becoming Mrs Dalloway as a loss of possibility, as an unbecoming, or becoming 'nothing at all,' does not enter her consciousness in the form of sadness *about* something. The sadness of the book – and for me, it is a sad book – is not one expressed as a point of view. Instead, each sentence of the book takes thoughts and feelings as if they are objects in a shared world: the streets of London, the very oddness of the occasion of passing others by, a feeling of that oddness. The coincidence of how you coincide with others. As Clarissa goes out with her task in mind (she has to buy flowers for her party), she walks into a world with others. Each might be in their own world (with their own tasks, their own recollections) and yet they share the world of the street, if only for a moment, a fleeting moment, a moment that fleets.

If unhappiness becomes a collective impression, then it too is made up of fragments that only loosely attach to points of view. In particular, the proximity between Mrs Dalloway and the character of Septimus iswhat allows unhappiness to be shared even if they do not share their feelings; two characters who do not know each other, though they pass each other, but whose worlds are connected by the very jolt of unhappiness. We have the imminence of the shock of how one person's suffering can impact the lifeworld of another. Septimus suffers from shell shock. We feel his feelings with him, the panic and sadness as the horror of war intrudes as memory. His suffering brings the past into the time of the present, the long time of war, its persistence on the skin as aftermath, its refusal of an after. To those who observe him from a distance, those who share the street on this day, he appears as a madman, at the edge of respectable sociality, a spectacle. To encounter him on the street, you would not know the story behind his suffering. To be near to suffering does not necessarily bring suffering near.

Clarissa and Septimus, as characters who do not meet, thus achieve an odd intimacy: the not-just-private suffering of the housewife and the not-quite-public suffering of the returned soldier are interwoven. Importantly, their sadness is proximate but not contagious. They do not catch sadness from each other; their sadness is what keeps alive histories that are not shared, that cannot be shared, as they pass by on the street. And yet something is shared, perhaps those very things that cannot simply be revealed. It is Clarissa thinking of her 'odd infinities' with strangers 'she had never spoken to,' as she sits on the bus, who wonders whether the 'unseen part of us' might provide a point of attachment to others, and might even be how we survive through others, 'perhaps – perhaps' (Woolf 1953: 231–2).

Much of the book is about an event that will happen. For Mrs Dalloway is planning a party. To some feminist readers, it is the preoccupation with the party that makes the book disappointing. For Simone de Beauvoir (1997), Mrs Dalloway's enjoyment of parties is a sign that she is trying to turn her 'prison into glory,' as if as a hostess she can be 'the bestower of happiness and gaiety' (554). For de Beauvoir the gift of the party turns quickly into duty, such that Mrs Dalloway, 'who loved these triumphs, these semblances,' still 'felt their hollowness' (554). For Kate Millett (1970), Mrs Dalloway is a rather disappointing figure; she exposes Woolf's failure to turn her own unhappiness into a politics: 'Virginia glorified two housewives, Mrs. Dalloway and Mrs. Ramsey, recorded the suicidal misery of Rhoda in *The Waves* withoutever explaining its causes' (37). We might say that it is because Mrs Dalloway is planning a party that we do not have much revealed about her unhappiness, other than the sadness of recalling lost intimacies: with Peter and with Sally, who both turn up unexpectedly during her day,

in a way, it is implied, that does not just happen but bears some relation to Mrs Dalloway's own thoughts, 'all day she had been thinking of
Bourton, of Peter, of Sally' (280). Such lost intimacies become lost possibilities, hints of a life she might have lived, if things had not turned
out the way they did.

If Mrs Dalloway is distracted from the causes of unhappiness by the
party (and we can have some sympathy with the necessity of distrac-
tions), the party is also the event at which unhappiness comes to life.
For Mrs Dalloway, her party is life; it is how she can make things happen; it is a gift, a happening (Woolf 1953:185). What happens? That this
question is a question is a preservation of the gift. And something does
happen. For it is in the party that Septimus's life 'touches' Mrs Dalloway most directly:

> What business had the Bradshaws to talk of death at her party? A young
> man had killed himself. And they talked of it at her party – the Brad-
> shaws talked of death. He had killed himself – but how? Always her body
> went through it first, when she was told, suddenly, of an accident; her
> dress flamed, her body burnt. He had thrown himself from a window.
> Up had flashed the ground; through him, blundering, bruising, went the
> rusty spikes. There he lay with the thud, thud, thud in his brain, and then
> a suffocation of blackness. So she saw it. But why had he done it? And
> the Bradshaws talked of it at her party! She had once thrown a shilling
> into the Serpentine, never anything more. But he had flung it away. They
> went on living (she would have to go back; the rooms were still crowded;
> people kept on coming). They (all day she has been thinking of Bourton,
> of Pete, of Sally), they would grow old. A thing there was that mattered;
> a thing, wreathed about with chatter, defaced, obscured in her own life,
> let drop everyday in corruption, lies, chatter. This he had preserved. Death
> was defiance. Death was an attempt to communicate, people feeling the
> impossibility of reaching the centre which, mystically, evaded them; close-
> ness drew apart; rapture faded; one was alone. There was an embrace in
> death. (280–81)

Septimus's death becomes a question that takes Mrs Dalloway away
from the party. She attends to his death and wonders about it. She becomes a retrospective witness even though she was not and could not
have been there. The shudder; the sounds of it; the thud, thud, thud of
it; the ground that flashes; the rusty spikes. His death becomes material, becomes fleshy through her thoughts. His death announces not

only that sadness can be unbearable but that we don't have to bear it, that you can fling it away. And in this moment, when death intervenes in the life of the party, life becomes chatter, becomes what goes on – 'they went on living' – what comes and goes – 'people kept on coming.' Death comes to embody the suffering that persists when life becomes chatter.

What is striking about Mrs Dalloway is how suffering has to enter her consciousness from the edges, through the arrival of another, another who is an intruder, who has not been invited to the party. It is the suffering of an intruder that exposes the emptiness of life's chatter. Suffering enters not as self-consciousness – as a consciousness of one's own suffering – but as a heightening of consciousness, a world-consciousness in which the suffering of those who do not belong is allowed to disturb an atmosphere. Even when unhappiness is a familiar feeling, it can arrive like a stranger to disturb the familiar or to reveal what is disturbing in the familiar.

I want to think of consciousness of the 'un' in unhappy, as consciousness of being not. Consciousness of being 'not' or 'un' can be consciousness of being estranged from happiness, as lacking the qualities or attributes required for a happy state of existence. Consciousness of being not involves self-estrangement, you recognize yourself as the stranger. Note here that self-estrangement is already worldly if you are the one whose arrival disturbs an atmosphere. Audre Lorde (1982) dramatizes how becoming conscious of being a stranger involves a retrospective renaming of apparently random events as racism:

Tensions on the street were high, as they always are in racially mixed zones of transition. As a very little girl, I remember shrinking from a particular sound, a hoarsely sharp, guttural rasp, because it often meant a nasty glob of grey spittle upon my coat or shoe an instant later. My mother wiped it off with the little pieces of newspaper she always carried in her purse. Sometimes she fussed about low-class people who had no better sense nor manners than to spit into the wind no matter where they went, impressing upon me that this humiliation was totally random. It never occurred to me to doubt her. It was not until years later once in conversation I said to her: 'Have you noticed people don't spit into the wind so much the way they used to?' And the look on my mother's face told me that I had blundered into one of those secret places of pain that must never be spoken of again. But it was so typical of my mother when I was young that if she couldn't stop white people spitting on her children because they were Black, she would insist it was something else. (17–18)

An event happens. And it happens again. The violence is directed from the white body to the black child, who receives that violence by shrinking, shrinking away from its sound. But the mother cannot bear to speak of racism, and creates an impression that the humiliation is random. You learn not to see racism as a way of bearing the pain. To see events as racism you have to be willing to venture into secret places of pain.

Some forms of 'taking cover' from pain – from not naming the causes of pain in the hope that it will go away – are to protect those we love from being hurt, or even to protect ourselves from hurt, or at least might be meant as a form of protection. Happiness can also work to conceal the causes of hurt, or to make people the cause of their own hurt. In *The Cancer Journals*, Audre Lorde (1997) offers a powerful critique of the politics of happiness. She writes as a black lesbian feminist who is experiencing breast cancer. Lorde never refuses the power of 'writing as' nor assumes it can abbreviate an experience. Faced with medical discourse that attributes cancer to unhappiness and survival to being happy she suggests, 'looking on the bright side of things is a euphemism used for obscuring certain realities of life, the open consideration of which might prove threatening to the status quo' (76). Lorde moves from this observation to a wider critique of happiness as an obscurant: 'Let us seek "joy" rather than real food and clean air and a saner future on a livable earth! As if happiness alone can protect us from the results of profit-madness' (76). Lorde suggests that the very idea that our first responsibility is for our own happiness must be resisted by political struggle, which means resisting the idea that our own resistance is a failure to be responsible for happiness: 'Was I really fighting the spread of radiation, racism, woman-slaughter, chemical invasion of our food, pollution of our environment, and the abuse and psychic destruction of our young, merely to avoid dealing with my first and greatest responsibility to be happy?' (77). I think Audre Lorde has given us the answer to her question.

We can retrieve a model of false consciousness in critiquing claims to happiness. You would not be saying: 'You are wrong, you are not happy, you just think you are as you have a false belief.' Rather, you would be saying there is something false about our consciousness of the world; we learn not to be conscious, not to notice what happens right in front of us. It is not that an individual person suffers from false consciousness, but that we inherit a certain false consciousness when we learn to not notice certain things, or not to apprehend them in a certain way.

The familiar is that which is not revealed to those who inhabit it. I am suggesting that happiness is one of the ways in which the familiar recedes. Those who are strangers are thus estranged from happiness; and those who are estranged from happiness might be the ones to whom happiness is revealed. Of course, it has effects to do the work of witnessing (and for some, as we have seen, simply to arrive into a room is a kind of witnessing of a history that others prefer to forget). The sociability of happiness has costs that are revealed in such moments of witnessing but are not caused in such moments. In a way, the 'happiness' of happiness is protected by locating its costs in those who refuse its promise. Political struggles are often struggles against happiness, as struggles to reveal its costs. To struggle against happiness often means being framed as antisocial; to challenge who and what gathers under the sign of happiness is to trouble the very form of social gathering. You can cause unhappiness by revealing the causes of unhappiness. And you can become the cause of the unhappiness you reveal.

People often say that the struggle against racism is like banging your head against a brick wall. The wall keeps its place so it is you that gets sore. We might need to stay as sore as our points. Of course that's not all we say or we do. We can recognize not only that we are not the cause of the unhappiness that has been attributed to us, but also the effects of being attributed *as* the cause. We can talk about being angry black women or feminist killjoys; we can claim those figures back; we can laugh in recognition of the familiarity of inhabiting that place. There is solidarity in recognizing our alienation from happiness, even if we do not inhabit the same place (and we do not). There can be joy in killing joy. And kill joy we must, and we do.

NOTES

1 We can see the problems with such an approach when feelings become measures of rights and wrongs. Richard Layard (2006), for example, argues that what makes something wrong is that it makes people unhappy, or even offends people's feelings. For Layard, the science of happiness is 'inherently'

pro-poor and for the re-distribution of wealth, as inequalities increase unhappiness (120–1). Though the unfortunate implication of his argument is that if inequalities did not increase unhappiness, then he would not be against them. As he describes it: 'American slaves wanted their freedom, not because it would give them higher incomes, but because of the humiliation of being a slave. Slavery offended their feelings, and that is why slavery is wrong' (121). The idea that slavery was wrong because it hurt people's feelings shows us what is wrong with this model of wrong. It individuates and psychologises social wrongs. See Lauren Berlant's (2000) important critique of the conflation of pain and injustice, as well as my conclusion to *The Cultural Politics of Emotion* (Ahmed 2004) for a reflection on the relationship between social wrongs and hurt. Note in particular that one of the problems of the conflation of injustice with hurt is that it presumes access to the other's feelings. Any forms of wrong that are not accompanied by consciously felt suffering that can be spoken about to others would become invisible in such a model.

2 I will not be engaging with the substance of Kantian philosophy in this chapter. For a good discussion of Kant in relation to Bergson see Lefebvre and White, this volume.

3 These definitions and all subsequent definitions and etymological references are drawn from the *Oxford English Dictionary*.

4 Brennan (2004) explains this tension between these two aspects of argument by suggesting that even if I am picking up on an affect, 'the thoughts I attach to that affect, remain my own' (7). The distinction between feeling and thought used here suggests that if feelings are social or shared, then thoughts are individual and private. What if the distinction does not hold? Could affects sometimes be what are not shared, what we don't pick up on, and thoughts sometimes be what are shared? For example, we might come to an agreement about what x means, but feel differently about x. I think we can go further by unpacking not only this distinction, but also the model of the social implicit in this distinction. Note that the social becomes what is shared and transmitted. Perhaps we need to think about the social as an object of experience that is not shared, so that feelings of tension and antagonism become part of the fabric of social life rather than being understood as its failure or absence. My questioning of the model of the social implicit in the idea of contagion can also be related to other work written under the rubric of the sociology of emotion. Randal Collins (2004), for example, describes interaction ritual chains in the following way: 'processes that take place as human bodies come close enough to each other so that their nervous systems become mutually attuned in rhythms and anticipations of each other' (xix). I would not deny that emotional and bodily attunement can take place. But I want to suggest that the tendency to locate sociality in 'becoming attuned' means that we might miss out on some important dimensions. We need to ask for example how some proximities might be refused in the first place:

certain others might be designated in advance as strangers, as those with whom one cannot share a rhythm. The determination of what cannot be shared – and with whom – is part of social experience. We can also ask: how is it that some proximities engender attunement and not others? We need, in other words, an approach that can account for the uneven distribution of attunement and even the uneven distribution of contagion: the tendency to become attuned to the bodily rhythms of others or to pick up on affects might depend on points of identification with or disidentification from others that are exercised without even being revealed to consciousness. To use the example of happiness, we might be affected happily by proximity to some people's happiness, as a kind of bodily attunement, but not be affected happily by other others,' as a way of being or staying out of tune. What happens once proximity is given depends on how we already feel about others, or even how we feel in the situation in which we are thrown together with others. We are thus affected happily by proximity to another person's happiness depending on various conditions. Adam Smith (2000) comments dryly on the conditional nature of sympathetic emotion: 'it gives us the spleen, on the other hand, to see another too happy, or too much elevated, as we call it, with any little piece of good fortune. We are *disobliged even with his joy*; and, because we cannot go along with it, call it levity and folly' (13, emphasis added). For Smith, to be affected sympathetically is always dependent on whether emotions 'appear to this last, just and proper, and suitable to their objects' (14). To analyse the conditions in which feelings are shared is to consider the ways in which feelings are directed towards objects that will not be agreeable to all. My own work explores how disagreeable feelings come to be located in particular bodies. To come to an understanding of the sociality of emotion thus requires historical knowledge of how certain bodies come to the cause of disagreement (we would need to think of how histories get under the skin) that would not be visible if we simply took 'the situation' as the starting point for social analysis.

4 'Feeling a Feeling' in Emotion Management

CATHERINE THEODOSIUS

Introduction

This chapter explores neurophysiologist Antonio Damasio's (2000) hypothesis on emotion, consciousness, and self, and examines its significance to how emotion is managed. Whilst the emphasis is on the biological character of emotion, this is situated within the broader bio-psycho-social nature of emotion (Theodosius 2008). Understanding the neurophysiological function of emotion is critical to understanding the embodiment of emotion and its management, since if it is not included within an embodied approach, the body becomes a mere mechanistic vehicle that is inhabited by us, rather than being us. Feelings and emotions come from within, I argue, even when they are externally elicited. It is because they come from within that we know the feelings we have belong to us, representing our experiences of, and responses to, the natural and social world (Wentworth and Yardley 1994). Understanding the embodiment of emotion is filled with hidden pitfalls as it traverses traditional conceptual, methodological, and epistemological boundaries, confusing mind-body, subject-object dualisms.

Invariably, the mind is considered subject and the body an object 'either "in itself" or one that is "good to think"' (Csordas 1994:8); or the mind becomes a mechanistic object, its processes and functions minutely examined and the body becomes subject to 'sensation, experience and world'(8). Emotion sits uncomfortably within these different approaches that make conceptualizing its embodiment problematic. However, it is not possible to examine the intersubjective experience, sensation, and cultural difference of emotion whilst separating it from

the mechanistic processes through which the body and mind physiologically and anatomically work to produce and make sense of them.
Emotion is expressed and experienced within both mind and body, and
it is both the mind and body that enables and constrains that experience. In acknowledging this, it can be seen that individual embodiment
of mind and body cannot be separated from its material and sociocultural environment. Thus emotions are social and part of social interaction. To understand emotion management it is necessary to know
what is happening within the individual and between individuals, as
well as understanding the social context (see also Thoits, this volume).
For example, how does a nurse manage her emotions of frustration in
dealing with a patient with dementia caught up in a continuous loop
of anxiety due to short-term memory loss? To understand this emotion
interaction it is necessary to consider the physiological limitations of
emotion for the nurse who is healthy and the patient who is mentally
unwell, as well as the interaction that is occurring between them and
the social context in which it happens.

Damasio's hypothesis on emotion, feeling, and consciousness attempts to link internal body function with its external environment by
suggesting that emotion results in the evolution of consciousness so that
human beings might better communicate, develop, and express social
intelligence. Rather than emotions being the antithesis of reason, they
are fundamental and necessary to it. Damasio sees emotion as being
a bodily internal manifestation that feeds into homeostatic processes.
As such, emotion is unconscious. However, he suggests that human
consciousness is feeling the experience of self. He argues that neuro-
scientific evidence reveals that human consciousness has arisen from
the development of emotion, and claims that consciousness cannot
exist without emotion whereas emotion can be present without consciousness. The brain achieves this due to there being different levels of
conscious awareness of feeling. Thus, Damasio's hypothesis offers both
insights and challenges to current sociological understanding of the nature of embodied emotion and how it might be managed. This chapter
critically considers the significance of his hypothesis to Hochschild's
(1983) notion of surface and deep acting and Archer's (2000) notion of
the inner dialogue – each being concerned with emotion management.

Understanding how individuals carry out emotion management is
important to understanding its significance in social interaction, especially in the workplace. Hochschild, who first developed the term *emotion management/work* (see Hochschild 1975, 1979, 1983), suggests that

it is learned through socialization and takes work to achieve. In the workplace the way in which this is taught, monitored, and put into practice (the transmutation of emotion work into emotional labour) can result in the inauthenticity of emotion and the alienation of self from self and from work (also see Thoits, this volume; Walby and Spencer, this volume). Recently Erickson (2009) has made a direct link between stress and burnout amongst health care professionals and emotional labour, a core component of health care practice.

The act of emotion management/emotional labour usually takes place as a result of the elicitation of an emotion in response to a particular social interaction at a particular moment in time. It is externally elicited and is essentially linked to cognitive appraisal that assesses the emotion responses required. Thus, Hochschild's (1983) definition asserts that it is 'to induce or suppress feelings in order to sustain the outward countenance that produces the proper state of mind in others' (7). This process suggests that an individual has conscious control over his/her emotions in that he/she can actively suppress feelings and actively induce them as needed. Hochschild suggests that how individuals achieve this is through surface acting and deep acting. Surface acting is the 'ability to deceive others about how we are really feeling without really deceiving ourselves'; in deep acting, however, 'we deceive ourselves about our true emotions as much as we deceive others' (33). She states that the act of emotion management is one that draws on an integral source of self and that emotion may be elicited internally. Thus, she recognizes the importance of self-reflection and the experience of emotion to that in the relationship between the self who owns his/her emotions. What Hochschild finds difficult to do is conceptualize that relationship (Theodosius 2006, 2008). Thus her self ends up dividing into a 'true' and 'false' self that becomes alienated (Wouters 1989; Theodosius 2008).

Elsewhere, I have presented Archer's (2000) notion of the inner dialogue as being useful in understanding how self-identity and emotion management are connected (Theodosius 2008). Archer incorporates emotion into the inner dialogue by separating its elicitation from its management. Emotion elicitation is what she terms *first order emotion*. Second order emotions emerge through the reflexive inner dialogue when the individual becomes cognizant of them. This distinction conceptually allows for emotion elicitation to be unconscious and a result of broader relations than social ones. Thus, Archer argues that first order emotion is elicited as a result of body-environment (natural order), subject-object (material order), and subject-subject (social order) relationships. The significance of these emotions is determined by the individual experiencing them in respect to their inner dialogue, where they attempt to understand them in relation to their developing personal identity, what they are interested or involved in, and how they need to portray that through their social identity. Thus, personal identity is an achieved self that balances and coordinates all concerns of the continuous self from the past, in the present, and into the future. Social identity is tied to social role and context. Archer sees emotions as fundamentally reflecting on the concerns of the individual, elicited in response to what is being engaged with in the development of personal identity through the inner dialogue.

Awareness of the significance of emotion to the individual comes with the inner dialogue, a reflexive conversation between the 'I,' 'you,' and 'me.' Archer (2000) defines reflexivity as the 'ability to reflect upon emotionality itself, to transform it and consequently to reorder priorities within emotion sets' (222). Using Charles Sanders Peirce's different phases of the ego in dialogue, the 'I' of the present can address the future self through the 'you' by criticizing, ordering, or anticipating in relation to past experience, or present or future events. The 'me' (non-Meadean) represents a more overall sense of self held in the emotion memory: 'the "me"' is 'all the former "Is" who have moved down the time line of future, past and present' (Archer 2000: 229). The dialogue directly links emotions to rational cognitive processes and together they form a commentary on the concerns of the individual. The emotions emerging as a result of this dialogue constitute second order emotions (Theodosius 2008).

Archer (2000) suggests that an individual's personal identity is shaped and continuously developed and reflected on through their inner dialogue. The inner dialogue also comments on and works towards maintaining a balance between first order emotions elicited as a result of interaction with the social, material, and natural world. Second order emotion, which arises from the reflexive inner dialogic process, represents the process through which individuals manage their emotions. Thus, emotion management is directly linked to personal identity, aspects of which are acted out through social roles and identities to which emotional labour is connected (also see Thoits, this volume). Emotional labour not only draws on personal identity, it is dependent on it. Thus, emotional labour stems from the individual's continuous and constantly developing personal identity, of which a knowledgeable conscious awareness is created through his/her inner dialogue (Theodosius 2008).

To help analyse the significance of Damasio's hypothesis for emotion management and the inner dialogue, an overview of his argument is presented first, followed by a theoretical analysis of its application to Hochschild's notion of surface and deep acting and Archer's inner dialogue. The chapter concludes by juxtaposing the theoretical analysis with an empirical example. The empirical example is drawn from an ethnographic case study examining the relationship between emotion and emotional labour as experienced by registered nurses working on an acute surgical vascular ward in a National Health Service Hospital in the UK.[1] Short extracts are used from a larger narrative of a newly qualified staff nurse named 'Kate.' The complete narrative, constructed from her audio diary and interview, can be found in my book *Emotional Labour in Health Care* (Theodosius 2008).

Damasio's Hypothesis

Damasio (2000:133–67) argues that the brain evolved the capacity to distinguish between stimuli and organic responses to objects that are internal and belong to it, and those that are external and separate from it. This ability means that the internal body can respond to itself as if it too is an object, thereby recognizing the significance of its own internal mechanisms. The brain can do this because it considers 'thought' or 'emotion' to be an object, thus emotion and/or thought can elicit emotion. Consequently the brain can distinguish between emotion states and the sources of those emotions (internal and external), and simultaneously regulate its internal milieu. This ability is fundamental to an individual's embodied experience of emotion and her/his capacity to reflect meaningfully upon it. Emotion therefore is not just elicited in response to the body's external relationship to its environment, but also in response to its internal one. How the brain does this is important to understanding the embodied experience of emotion and how individuals manage it. This has implications for Archer's (2000) conceptualization of the inner dialogue, which separates the internal unconscious elicitation of emotion from its reflexive management.

However, Damasio argues that emotion is almost entirely unconscious. Drawing on Spinoza's distinction, Damasio distinguishes between *emotion* that is unconscious and present at all times, and *feelings* that represent an awareness and conscious understanding of emotion states. Archer (2000) does not distinguish between emotion and feeling, whereas Hochschild (1983) considers feelings to be a milder form of emotion and uses the terms interchangeably (244). For Damasio, the distinction is fundamental, for it is only when an individual comes to feel a feeling that emotion begins to emerge into conscious awareness. Human consciousness is the conscious feeling of feeling the experience of self. The central tenet of his hypothesis is that human consciousness developed and extended from feeling emotion. Understanding how he conceptualizes the relationship between emotion, feeling, and consciousness is vital when critically assessing the significance of his hypothesis to Hochschild's and Archer's representations of emotion management.

Damasio (2000) suggests that emotion's primary function is concerned with 'survival-orientated behaviours,' sensing emotions, the having of feelings that 'impact on the mind as they occur in the here and now.' Thus 'consciousness allows feelings to be known' and promotes the impact of emotion internally, allowing 'emotion to permeate thought process through agency of feeling.' Consciousness essentially 'allows the "object" of emotion and any other object' to be known (56). This enables individuals to respond adaptively, thus both emotion and consciousness are ultimately concerned with survival. This representation of the relationship between emotion and consciousness echoes that of Archer's (2000) in the emphasis she gives towards emotion reflexivity and cognitive process.

Damasio (2000) suggests that there are different levels/types of emotions: background emotions, primary and secondary emotions (all unconscious), and feelings (conscious awareness of emotions). Background emotions are constant and represent the internal condition ofthe body that arises from physiological processes and responses tothe body's interaction with its environment. 'These emotions allow us to have background feelings of tension or relaxation, of fatigue or energy, of well-being or malaise, of anticipation or dread' (52). Neither Hochschild (1983) nor Archer (2000) includes this definition of emotion, because they do not conceptualize the internal physiological significance of emotion to the maintenance/awareness of bodily function – a significant omission to developing understanding of the embodiment of emotion. Primary emotions refer to the six universal emotions of fear, anger, surprise, disgust, happiness, and sadness (Darwin 1872; Ekman 1973, 1982, 1984, 1992); and secondary emotions to social emotions such as embarrassment, shame, guilt, jealousy, and pride (Kemper 1987; Scheff 1990; Barbalet 1998). Unlike Archer (2000), Damasio (2000) does not include emotions elicited in response to the material world. Damasio claims that all emotions are concerned with 'the life of the organism and their role in assisting that organism to maintain life' (51). They constitute 'complicated collections of chemical and neural responses' that are 'biologically determined processes, depending on innately set brain devices, laid down by a long evolutionary history' that 'regulate and represent body states.' Emotions can be 'engaged automatically without conscious deliberation' and impact on the whole body system causing changes within the 'internal milieu, visceral, vestibular and musculoskeletal systems, [and] numerous brain circuits.' They 'occupy a fairly restricted ensemble of subcortical regions, beginning at the brain stem and moving up to the higher brain' (51). An emotion occurs and sends commands to other parts of the brain and throughout the body via the vascular system and through neural pathways. These commands either act on other neurons, muscular fibres, or on organs (such as the adrenal gland), which then release their own chemicals into the blood stream (67). This unconscious process affects a global change in the body with muscles, for example, in the face and elsewhere in the body immediately changing. 'These changes constitute the substrate for neural patterns which eventually become feelings of emotion' (67), which represent conscious awareness of them. Until conscious awareness occurs, when knowing an emotion by feeling a feeling takes place, the emotion remains unconscious. However, awareness of the minute changes that take place in the body is something that can be detected by others, and is more commonly termed *non-verbal communication*. The impact of the physiological manifestation of emotion has ramifications for Hochschild's (1983) notion of surface acting.

How does unconscious emotion emerge into a conscious awareness of self that is 'knowing' of its feeling state in a way that separates the brain's capacity to distinguish between something that simply belongs to itself, and mind, which has a complex consciousness and awareness of self? Damasio (2000:25) argues that the brain can distinguish between stimuli and organic responses that relate to objects and those that relate to the body. This is important to how the brain differentiates between its internal processes and things that are happening externally to it, but are equally relevant. Because the brain can respond to itself as an object, detecting the significance of its own internal mechanisms, this allows for 'thought' or 'emotion' to also be perceived as an object.

The brain achieves this by the emergence of a feeling of knowing. 'Consciousness begins as the feeling of what happens when we see or hear or touch,' 'it is the feeling that accompanies the making of any kind of image – visual, auditory, tactile, visceral'; 'ultimately these feelings are what allow us to say that such images belong to us,' argues Damasio (26). Feelings at a very basic level are the foundation of our 'sense' of self, and consciousness is the representation of knowledge of that sense of self – sense of self being an awareness of self derived from the senses and therefore 'sensed.' Damasio suggests that there are different levels of consciousness. The initial feeling of knowing is what he coins the *proto-self*. The proto-self is mostly unconscious; individuals have a feeling of knowing, and knowing that feeling belongs to them (a sense of knowing). The proto-self then extends to 'core consciousness' where neural and mental patterning occurs in a way that allows the brain to recognize the pattern of the organism and the object and the relationship between the two.

The brain does this by generating stories through images (based on visual, auditory, olfactory, gustatory, and somatosensory modalities inclusive of phonemes and morphemes) that reflect conscious knowledge of self and objects, internally and externally. Core consciousness, however, is transient and instant, whereas 'extended consciousness,' the next level, is 'everything core consciousness is,' only it is linked to 'past lived experiences and anticipated future ones' (Damasio 2000:197); the extended conscious sense of self is more robust and is autobiographical. It is therefore linked to the brains working emotion memory (LeDoux 1998), which represents organized records of past experiences (of objects, etc.), which are both explicit (conscious) and implicit (unconscious). The significance of emotion memory is in the development of the 'autobiographical self,' which has been influenced both consciously and unconsciously by many factors including intelligence, exposure to knowledge, the social and cultural environment, and personality traits and predispositions. 'The autobiographical self which we display in our minds at this moment is the end product not just of our innate biases and actual life experiences but of the reworking of memories of those experiences under the influence of those factors,' argues Damasio (2000:224). Hochschild's (1983) notion of deep acting and Archer's (2000) inner dialogue are predicated to varying degrees on an autobiographical self that can draw on emotion memory (Theodosius 2008). However, both conceptualize emotion memory as being conscious and explicit. In addition, neither acknowledges that emotion can be felt without being understood or have such a developed understanding of the degrees of consciousness and how either of these relates to emotion experience and its management.

Surface Acting

Damasio's (2000) hypothesis is complex, making emotion fundamental to consciousness and to cognitive process, while paradoxically being itself unconscious. Because the elicitation of emotion is unconscious, Damasio claims that 'we are about as effective at stopping an emotion as we are at preventing a sneeze' (49). He argues that it is not possible for us to prevent the expression of an emotion, only 'disguise some of its external manifestations.' This is because it is not possible to 'block the automated changes that occur in the viscera and internal milieu.' We can 'educate' our emotions but not suppress them entirely, 'the feelings we have inside' (49) representing this inability. This is because emotions are unconscious; therefore, the automatic physiological brain and body responses that result are impossible to prevent. Thus, Damasio disputes that emotions are manageable.

However, his emphasis on prevention suggests that the point of management occurs *prior* to the emotion's elicitation; thus, the act of management is one that prevents the emotion from being elicited in the first instance. This is difficult to achieve, because emotion elicitation is unconscious. In Hochschild's definition of surface acting, the point of management occurs *after* the emotion has been elicited. Surface acting is carried out in order to prevent the emotion from controlling the actor, and is intended to limit or manipulate the emotion in order to prevent it from wholly dictating. Hochschild uses the term *suppression* precisely because the emotion has already been experienced. In suppressing the emotion in surface acting, the actor recognizes that it is not possible to prevent it; rather his/her efforts are directed at stifling and covering it up. However, surface acting takes the act of management further. The reason the emotion requires suppressing is because it is considered socially inappropriate. The actor expresses a more socially acceptable emotion in its place. Surface acting is an act of management that aims to prevent emotion from controlling and overriding the individual's choice of how he/she presents him/herself to others. Not to do so would render every individual subject to his/her emotions, making social interaction extremely unpredictable. For example, being nervous due to an unknown situation may elicit physiological changes to my body that I cannot consciously prevent, such as sweaty hands, tremors, rapidly beating heart, feeling sick to my stomach, and suffering from a desire to go repeatedly to the bathroom. If I gave in to those feelings every time I was nervous, my life would be severely limited. Instead, I consciously suppress my anxiety and present a calm and confident face in the presence of others.

The difficulty with surface acting is that the suppression of emotion is not easy to achieve. Even if I manage to present a calm and confident front, as Damasio argues, my body will display physiological changes automatically triggered by the unconscious elicitation of anxiety. My whole being will embody my anxiety. This will impact on the degree of success my surface acting has with others because of the visible physiological presence of anxiety. Equally, because I embody my 'real' emotion state, my display of the more socially appropriate emotion will be less convincing because the physiological changes that accompany the release of that emotion won't be present. Thus despite my surface acting, I will embody the felt emotion and perform the simulated one.

The ability to suppress nervousness and present a calm and confident persona is not the only factor that impacts surface acting. The social context and the capacity and willingness of other social actors to accept, recognize, and interpret it also impacts on how the performance is received. The significance of emotion being unconscious in surface acting is not that it is not manageable, but that the emotion being 'hidden' will actually be physically visible. This impacts on how surface acting is consciously or unconsciously interpreted. However, because the felt emotion is being deliberately managed and another one expressed in its place, it is difficult for others to identify with any degree of accuracy what the managed emotion might be. In unconsciously picking up signals through another's body language, people may be confused as to the individual's actual feelings, or they may recognize the surface acting for what it is, either accepting it at face value or judging the actor accordingly, or they may even concoct an entirely different interpretation. Thus, socially, the interpretation of emotion expression is extremely subjective.

That emotion elicitation is unconscious has further ramifications on surface acting. Because surface acting takes place after the emotion has been elicited and because the simulation of a different emotion is required in its place, the actor needs to be sufficiently cognizant of the unwanted unconscious emotion in order to suppress it and display a different emotion. Because emotion elicitation is unconscious, it is possible that the actor might physiologically display an emotion they are not aware of having, or display the feeling of an emotion without understanding its significance. It is simply not possible to suppress an emotion that the actor is not aware of experiencing. Arguably, this is irrelevant to understanding the experience of emotion; however, it is relevant to understanding the relational character of emotion in social interaction because of the emotion's physiological manifestation. Equally, it is likely that suppressing 'feeling a feeling' is also difficult because recognizing its external manifestation requires some degree of knowledgeable awareness of the emotion experience, in the same way that those observing it find the physical presence of a managed emotion, as described above, difficult to interpret. Damasio's assertion that emotion and its elicitation is unconscious and his representation of its physiological function, therefore, both challenges and is challenged by understandings of surface acting.

Deep Acting

In deep acting Damasio's assertion that emotion is not preventable is more problematic. Hochschild (1983) argues that in deep acting the individual can induce or exhort emotion, or has previously learned the correct emotion response to the social situation. She argues that the act of management in deep acting is so deep that the individual is unaware that the emotion has been managed; rather the individual believes it to be his/her 'real' emotion. In this respect the point of management is at the point of elicitation, but Damasio argues that this cannot be the case because emotion elicitation is unconscious. However, Hochschild conceptualizes both surface and deep acting as involving deception because her representation of emotion management involves conscious, cognitive processes. In surface acting, the actor knowingly deceives others by his/her 'false' performance of an unfelt emotion, but in deep acting Hochschild believes the actor deceives him/herself. I have argued elsewhere that deep acting can be an unconscious or pre-conscious process (Theodosius 2008), and consequently is not about processes of deception. For example, learned responses to emotion triggers are remembered in the emotion memory, unconsciously eliciting the previously learned social emotion response to the trigger. In this sense, the emotion is truly elicited and therefore really felt.

Nevertheless, Hochschild's notion of deep acting includes emotion being consciously induced or exhorted, which Damasio (2000) would dispute. His assertion that it is not possible to prevent an emotion, however, contradicts his own assertion that the brain has the capacity to distinguish between objects, which include thought and emotion too. If this is the case, it must be possible for thought or emotion to unconsciously or consciously act as an emotion inducer. For example, when he writes about the stages involved in moving from emotion elicitation to feeling a feeling, stage one requires the 'engagement of the organism by an inducer of emotion, for instance, a particular object processed visually, resulting in visual representations of the object. The object may be conscious or not, and may be recognized or not, because neither the consciousness of the object nor the recognition of the object are necessary for the continuation of the cycle' (283). The particular 'object' could be visual, as in the example he gives here, but it could also be auditory, olfactory, gustatory, or somatosensory modalities such as phonemes and morphemes (the basic units of language – therefore representing thought), or even an emotion itself. If all of these constitute an inducer of emotion, then it is possible that an individual could purposefully use them to induce or exhort an emotion through the use of his/her senses such as sight, sound, taste, touch, or through thought processes. That actors do this is at the heart of Hochschild's (1983) concept of deep acting, which she bases on Stanislavski's method acting. As Damasio (2000) asserts here, it is irrelevant as to whether this is a conscious process or not. In deep acting it is possible to deliberately exhort an emotion in this way. In doing so, the emotion elicited is really released and felt; it is not fabricated, and so the individual does not deceive him/herself about his/her 'real' emotions.

It is also possible to provoke this process unconsciously, due to socially learned behaviour, psychological reasons, or pre-consciously through habit (Theodosius 2008). This is where unconscious process inputs into conscious process; for Damasio argues that implicit (unconscious) emotion memory can input into conscious process such as core consciousness, extended consciousness, and the autobiographical self. Again this lends itself to supporting Hochschild's suggestion that emotion memory can be used to induce emotion (Hochschild 1983; Theodosius 2008). However, to be able to induce emotion in this way, an individual would need to be knowledgeable about his/her emotions and emotion triggers. Such knowledge is tied to reflexivity and self-identity. Hochschild has difficulty conceptualizing the relationship between emotion and self. Archer (2000) achieves this by focusing on the relational element of emotions.

Feeling a Feeling and the Inner Dialogue

The relationship in Damasio's hypothesis between emotion, consciousness, and self is one that has significant implications for Archer's (2000) notion of the inner dialogue (Theodosius 2008). Archer's distinction between first and second order emotion allows emotion elicitation to occur independently from cognitive process, and acknowledges that it can be unconscious. However, in her notion of second order emotion, where the inner dialogue offers a commentary on its emotional state, Archer assumes that the (healthy adult[2]) individual has a knowledgeable awareness about what his/her emotions are. There is some debate within sociology and psychological disciplines about the distinction between emotion and feelings. As Turner and Stets (2005) note, most researchers 'would define feelings as emotional states about which a person is consciously aware' (286). This is also Damasio's stance. Archer, however, does not engage with the distinction between emotion and feeling; rather she distinguishes between first and second order emotions where the development of the reflexive inner dialogue, representing self-consciousness, brings cognitive awareness to the individual's emotion state. Like Damasio, she distinguishes between primary and secondary emotions as identified by Ekman (1982), Izzard (1977), and Plutchik and Kellerman (1980); but unlike Damasio, she includes emotions elicited in response to the external material environment, such as satisfaction, dissatisfaction, and frustration, which are similar to secondary emotions (Archer 2000). She argues that emotions are emergent to the relationship individuals have with the natural, material, and social world with which they interact continuously. The impact and importance of that interaction is known to us through our self-consciousness: 'by definition self consciousness means that we are necessarily reflexive beings' (201). For Archer, it is reflexivity that enables agents to act purposefully. She draws on Frankfurt's work on identification to reinforce her argument: 'Being conscious in the everyday sense does (unlike unconsciousness) entail reflexivity. It necessarily involves a secondary awareness of a primary response. An instance of exclusively primary and unreflexive consciousness would not be an instance of what we think of as consciousness at all. For what would it be like to be conscious of something without being aware of this consciousness? It would mean having an experience with no awareness of its occurrence. This would be, precisely, a sense of unconscious experience. It appears then that being conscious is identical with being self-conscious. Consciousness is self-consciousness' (Frankfurt, in Archer 2000:201).

Archer's stance on consciousness is substantially different from that of Damasio, who, as a medical scientist, argues that some individuals, due to injury or illness (e.g., head injury or epilepsy), can be conscious – even mobile and conscious – yet have no self-awareness. Equally, he sees consciousness as being fluid, as something that continuously changes as it moves forward in time. Thus, Damasio suggests that it is possible to retain a sense of self from the instance before to the instant we are moving into – and have an understanding of self that has a long time biography, yet can move forward and be challenged as life continues. These different emotion memory feats are functionally and physiologically distinct. Archer's use of Charles Peirce's 'I,' 'you,' 'me' in the inner dialogue recognizes this movement; yet her notion of consciousness itself is more static because it is more dualistic, with unconsciousness (un-reflexive) at one end and consciousness (reflexive) at the other. Conscious awareness of the unconscious primary instance appears to occur immediately. Thus, as Frankfurt argues, consciousness is self-consciousness. Thus in the morphogenic articulation and re-articulation process of the inner dialogue, Archer conceptualizes this as always being progressive, thereby resulting in second order emotions that are readily recognizable and manageable. This does not allow for emotion to impede cognitive processing (Theodosius 2008). Consequently, Archer's dialogue does not allow for an individual to go over and over and over again in his/her mind the same dialogue, unable to move forward, held stationary by a welter of emotions that can inhibit and confuse. In some cases, that confusion arises because the feelings that overwhelm are not readily identifiable. Rather the individual is feeling the feeling(s) continuously without the ability to reflexively make sense of them.

Whilst this might be the case, in healthy adults normal life continues, and though they may not be able to reflexively move forward within the inner dialogue on this particular issue, their inner dialogue can still function and progressively comment on other emergent emotions in response to other events and everyday activities. In this sense, self-consciousness is continuous. There is a dichotomy within the mind, therefore, between the continuous reflexive self, and one that can feel without having a conscious awareness of the significance of that or be able to reflect upon it.

Damasio (2000:217) argues that 'the seemingly changing self and the seemingly permanent self, although closely related are not one entity but two.' The changing self is 'transient and ephemeral' and is based on core consciousness. He suggests that it is not so much that it changes, but 'that it needs to be remade and reborn continuously' because working memory is concerned with the *connections* between each instance of experience. The permanent self, however, draws on long-term working memory, also supported by core consciousness, but based on extended consciousness and the autobiographical self where the connections between experiences have already been established into an understandable narrative. Here, the working memory is based on long-term repository of both implicit and explicit memory (LeDoux 1998). These memories, however, come initially from core consciousness; they require sorting, the development of a narrative, such as that which the inner dialogue provides. Thus, the autobiographical self is influenced consciously and unconsciously by other factors such as personality traits, knowledge, and cultural and social experience in the working and reworking of memory. Effectively, an individual has the capacity to experience emotion she/he is not knowledgeable about yet is aware of, through feeling a feeling – and can manage, using surface acting, that feeling. At the same time, the individual's ongoing inner dialogue can be unsuccessfully attempting to make sense of that feeling, in a continuous negative feedback loop, *and* at the same time manage successfully other emotions emerging in response to ongoing interactions as they occur.

Essentially, an individual can experience an emotion and be aware by feeling a feeling in the proto-self that that feeling belongs to them. Core consciousness develops an 'image' through the senses or/and somatosensory modalities, that pulse the feeling into conscious awareness in an instant. This process can keep reoccurring, with the emotion that is felt but not known also impacting through an embodied awareness (through physiological changes which occur in the body in response to its release) and with the brain's conscious (but unknowledgeable) recognition of it. Until extended consciousness can, through the working memory, develop a narrative (made up of consecutive and connecting sensory and somatosensory modalities), which links to the autobiographical self (connecting the past self to the present and anticipating the future), the emotion remains unknown, but felt. Thus, 'feeling a feeling' impacts the inner dialogue that attempts to make sense of it. That the brain has this capacity is essential, or it would not be possible for emotions to become known; they would either remain unconscious or automatically be consciously known. At the same time, because the brain has the capacity to distinguish between different objects, core consciousness can pulse in images representing the actual instant being experienced that make sense to working memory in the extended consciousness and to the autobiographical self (consciously and unconsciously) in the carrying out of everyday working life. Thus, the inner dialogue's ongoing commentary reflexively monitors emergent emotions, thoughts, and other sensory modalities in response to what is currently being experienced and require managing in the presentation of self in everyday life.

Embodied Emotion, Emotion Management, and the Inner Dialogue: The Case of 'Kate'

In order to consider the significance of Damasio's hypothesis for Hochschild's notion of emotion management and Archer's inner dialogue to emotion embodiment in social interaction, I now juxtapose the theoretical analysis with an empirical one in the case of Kate. Kate has been the victim of bullying by her colleagues, whose actions imply she is a poor nurse. Throughout her audio diary, how she felt, reacted, experienced, and made sense of the bullying emerged as a strong narrative thread. To begin with, Kate expressed a great deal of anger (a primary emotion) although she does not directly link this to the bullying. She also expresses a strong sense of shame (a secondary emotion), self-doubt, and inadequacy. She complains of feeling tired, unhealthy, and miserable (background emotions). During the course of the diary Kate comes to realize that she is a good nurse and overcomes the actions of the bullies. The diary reflects some of her inner dialogic workings in how she does this, providing an interesting insight into how she managed her emotions in the short and long term. It is important to remember that while the diary represents glimpses of Kate's private emotion processes, throughout each day she had to maintain her relationships with her colleagues while carrying out her duties. The emotion management she carries out in order to do so is what I term collegial emotional labour (CEL). The purpose of CEL is to facilitate effective communication in the administration of nursing duties, to assert status rights over one's colleagues and to acknowledge one's place in the immediate hierarchy (Theodosius 2008:182).

Over a 10-day period, during which Kate records her (audio) diary, this process comes to a culmination: ' I've just done two long days. I was as miserable as sin, basically because of the people I was working with. I cannot work a whole day with some people, and if it hadn't been for them, being immature, loud, being stupid around the desk, I just, I can't work in those conditions. So basically I just shut down and ignored them totally, for maybe the last two-thirds of my day shift.' Here, Kate suppresses her feelings using surface acting. In so doing, she 'effectively' carries out successful CEL. It was 'effective' because she suppresses unknown emotions of felt feelings unconsciously elicited as a result of the bullying. The suppression of these feelings is socially expected because it is inappropriate for her to express them due to her low place in the hierarchy. Her CEL was successful because it was accepted by the others. However, despite her emotion management, on the elicitation of the emotions, her body physiologically changed in response. Thus, while her display attempts to cover her feelings, they are still visibly present in, for example, the way she carried herself, the shape of the line creases in her face, in the non-verbal communicative processes of her body due to the automatic impact of her emotions on the internal milieu and viscera of the body. The visible presence of her actual emotion state (even if it is not recognized by Kate) is significant to the other nurses because it evidences the effectiveness of their actions.

Although at this stage Kate does not recognize what her emotions are/represent, their presence is felt, making her feel miserable and unwell; this conscious feeling is an awareness of the unconscious emotion of unacknowledged shame elicited as a result of the bullying. Kate does not recognize it as such; rather she states that she is feeling miserable: 'I really wasn't feeling very good, I was totally miserable about being at work and I just wanted to go home.' In order to help her manage and make sense of her feelings, Kate stokes and successfully induces anger (deep acting).

At the same time that she induces her very understandable anger, Kate also suppresses it because the nurses behaving badly are the ones who are bullying her and have a higher place in the hierarchy. In her interactions with them Kate has to suppress her anger in acts of CEL. However, some of the minute physiological changes that the anger unconsciously produces will also be displayed because this induced

Figure 1: Workplace Bullying (Cartoon by Jo Rice, © 2008)

Kate (audio diary): I could quite happily have left yesterday because I am not part of the crowd that are there, and I most of all don't wish to be part of it. I don't find it very nice; I don't find it very professional. I don't find it professional sitting on the nurses' station trying to get the loudest fart to ripple along and to make the loudest noises. If anybody did that in a shop they would be sacked. Because it's a hospital these people think that they can get away with it and I think that it is disgusting.

emotion has really been elicited. Thus, Kate carries out effective CEL through surface acting, and displays in a non-conscious way her real emotion state that represents unknown 'hidden' feelings of shame and anger induced through deep acting. That Kate can be experiencing and managing different sets of emotions (or as Archer would term them, 'clusters of emotions') is significant for interpreting the social interaction. If Kate was not able to simultaneously do this, then the bullying would not have been successful, because the bullies would not be able to see the impact that they were having. Thus, being able to express their 'different interactional rights,' by evaluating Kate's work, pointing out her flaws, having their opinions count, and in doing 'something more important' in their games, the bullies exclude Kate and demonstrate their higher status (Clark 1990:306). Kate's CEL actively embodies her subordinate place amongst her colleagues.

The ability to simultaneously induce, express, and suppress emotion is essential to this act of CEL. The non-conscious physical expression of anger and her unacknowledged feelings of shame are just as necessary to the social interaction as her conscious suppression, socially acted out through her CEL. The value of Damasio's neuro-scientific approach is that it draws attention to the physical presence of felt emotions that have been managed for social purposes, and thus their significance to social interaction can be considered. It also contributes to understanding the complex feelings involved in the embodied experience of emotion, the brain's capacity to distinguish between different sets of emotions, and the degree to which they are consciously recognized. Despite Damasio's negative assessment of an individual's ability to manage his/her emotion because the emotions are unconscious, his hypothesis actually lends support to Hochschild's differentiation between surface and deep acting. The significance of emotion being unconscious and the different degrees of conscious awareness is also relevant to the inner dialogue because it is difficult to manage an emotion if the individual has no conscious knowledge of it.

For example, although Kate's CEL was socially effective, she was not cognizant of her entire emotion state. She was consciously aware in 'feeling a feeling' that things were not right, but she was unable to define her emotions or express what they represented. Rather, she had a conscious awareness of feeling emotional all the time. However, a turning point arrived following an emotional outburst, when she lost the ability to manage her emotions at all: 'This is me after night duty. I didn't realize how upset I was about the people I have been working with. Because quite out of the blue in the middle of handover, we were just generally chatting about the way people behave on the ward and I just burst out crying. I thought I was angry, I didn't know I was that upset. I really thought I was more angry than upset.'

Following this outburst, Kate realizes that she is feeling differently. The outburst is elicited as a result of a trigger. That trigger is a discussion about the people who have been bullying her. The disapprobation of the other nurses towards those who have been bullying her enables Kate to generate a conscious connection between the bullying and her belief in her nursing abilities and the shame and distress this has elicited in her. Kate realizes that she does not have to accept the evaluation of the bullies about her nursing abilities. Subsequently, she recognizes that how she perceives herself and her feelings has changed: 'This will be my last report. I feel that I have turned a corner at work. Maybe I've had a "Ward" to shed, maybe my blow out has helped me. But the most positive thing I have realized in the last week to 10 days is that

I can do my job. And a little while ago I doubted myself, I wasn't sure that I could do it. I think that it was because I was feeling less confident myself for obvious reasons already mentioned before this, and I know I can do this job because I have been doing it and I do, do it, and I know that I am not perfect and I'm a human being and I have times when some days I do the job better than others depending on how I feel.'

It would appear that Kate's extended consciousness has made a narrative link, allowing her to acknowledge the impact the bullying had on her, making sense of the feelings this produced. Several months later, this emotion trajectory has resulted in a stronger narrative that links these events to her maturing personal identity (autobiographical self). Kate then goes on to recognize the significance of her emotions to her physical well-being. In her interview, she states:

> KATE: I felt physically sick before I went into work, I felt very emotional all the time. Very sort of wobbly as well, you know where you feel like you have got butterflies in your stomach all the time. It was like I was the new girl every single day for about two and half months. I shouldn't be feeling like this! I was questioning myself all the time. But physically I felt sick and it wasn't until I burst out crying in the middle of a hand-over, which embarrassed me quite a lot, that it actually came to a head. I was getting unhealthy as well. I was getting quite bad skin and my eyes were really dark all the time; I had permanent bags under my eyes. I was sleeping like there was no tomorrow. I was sleeping, sleeping, and sleeping, and I was struggling to get up in the morning, which is a sign of depression actually, isn't it, if you don't want to get up and all you want to do is go to sleep? And I was just walking around knackered all the time. And I think that was due to the fact that I was having such a hard time at work.
>
> CATHERINE: And that was mostly due to relationships with colleagues?
>
> KATE: Yes. Definitely, and the way they were condescending and just implying that I wasn't doing my job properly um, sideways, bang on, head on, they were at it all the time . . .

Because 'knowing a feeling requires a knower subject' (Damasio 2000:285), feeling is fundamental to cognitive process, to the inner dialogue; this is why the recognition of emotion and feelings is often considered to be the culmination of, or the pinnacle of, the narrative – the point at which the individual can move forward. However,

Archer's inner dialogic commentary is one where the individual is predominantly cognizant, able to knowledgeably label and interpret the significance of his/her emotions. Damasio's hypothesis suggests that consciousness can move from one of simple embodied awareness of feeling to one that requires a knower subject who embodies their emotions within their autobiographical self. These stages are evident in Kate's narrative, where prior to her outburst she experienced feelings that made her aware of a change in her inner state, but not in a way that she had knowledge of (proto-self). However, she was at the point of knowing she had feelings, and this precipitated her into adapting to them by responding, considering, and reflecting on what they meant (core consciousness). Kate needed to act in a way that enabled her survival in that environment and defended her sense of self. This was carried out through her acts of CEL using both surface and deep acting. In her CEL she actively suppressed her known anger and feelings of misery. In the act of not expressing it, Kate displayed her low place in the hierarchy, and their higher place. If Kate had really been able to manage her emotions, her anger would not have been visible/felt at all and the action of the bullies would have been meaningless. At the same time as this was occurring, Kate became acquainted with her emotion state and considered what it meant to her (extended consciousness). This was precipitated when two central factors brought sudden recognition and conscious acknowledgement of her emotion state. First was the physical expression in the crying outburst that took place during 'handover' when she acknowledged how upset she was feeling; second, following this, in her inner dialogue which traversed the time period during which she was bullied and beyond, Kate made the connection between feeling unwell and miserable, to the bullying, and the loss of confidence and self-esteem that she experienced as a consequence and in her inner dialogue goes on to demonstrate how good a nurse she is in the recognition that she had doubted her ability (autobiographical self). Further, when recalling her experiences and her understanding of those emotions using herautobiographical self, she can remember the feelings without re-experiencing the physiological changes that they elicit. Damasio (1995) terms this the 'as if body loop,' where the body can create the 'feeling of the body-state without there being any actual change' (Ellis and Cromby 2009:328). This multi-layered process represents an embodied experience, awareness, and burgeoning understanding of emotion and its management in respect to both a sense of self and personal identity.

Conclusion

Damasio's (2000, 1995) hypothesis unwittingly provides scientific weight to Hochschild's distinction between surface and deep acting in managing emotion. However, due to the unconscious elicitation of emotion, Damasio argues that there are physiological limitations to the degree of control an individual has over emotion. Rather than simply contributing to the autonomy of emotion over cognition argument, his explanation of how and why this is the case when applied to the act of emotion management, highlights the visible presence of 'hidden' managed emotions in social interaction, broadening the significance of embodied emotion in understanding group interaction.

More significantly, Damasio's hypothesis about the relationship between emotion, consciousness, and self, when critically synthesized with Hochschild's (1983) and Archer's (2000) sociological representations of emotion and its management, offers interesting insights into how brain function constrains and facilitates how emotion is experienced and managed in the experience of sensing self, and within personal and social identity. He identifies the brain's capacity for different levels of consciousness and its ability to generate a multi-layered inner dialogue, representative of emergent emotions that are both consciously known and those that are merely felt, in a way that is representative of the individual's embodied self and its immediate and continual presence within the material and social environment. This synthesis tentatively moves beyond traditional mind-body and subject-object dualisms and conceptualizes emotion experience and emotion management as embodied within a sense of self and personal and social identity. This transcends the incongruity between Hochschild's notion of surface and deep acting, acts of emotion management which happen in the instance required, and Archer's inner dialogue which represents personal identity which reflexively makes sense of the significance of emotions to individuals as they traverse through life. The inner dialogue is also essential to how the individual draws on his/her personal identity in acts of surface and deep acting in the performance of social identity. This is because the embodiment of emotion represents the self in situations that can be both present, emergent, and congruent, and present, emergent, and incongruent in an instant and through the passage of time. We experience emotion and manage it in transient moments of time in ways that resonate with our sense of self, without necessarily losing a more comprehensive understanding of personal identity that develops and changes in response to the collation of experience, personal maturity, and the expression of social identity.

NOTES

1 The data comprised 14 months of participant observation, 15 audio diaries recorded by the nurses, and 15 interviews that included a discussion about their diaries. The aim of these methods was to observe emotion and emotional labour as practised (through the observation), to capture intense emotion that was experienced and felt but not necessarily displayed and to uncover private emotion commentary (through the diaries), and to retrospectively consider the significance of those emotion experiences in respect to their wider identity (through the interviews).
2 The reference to a 'healthy' adult is because physical (e.g., head injuries, epilepsy, tumours, autoimmune diseases, even flu) or mental (e.g., depression, psychosis, dementia) disorders may affect the physiological, anatomical, and biochemical nature of emotion, thereby impacting on how such an individual 'perceives' and manages his/her emotion experiences and expressions. The reference to adult is because children are not considered to be sufficiently physiologically, psychologically, or socially developed, thus their circumstances are not comparable.

5 Illegitimate Pain: Introducing a Concept and a Research Agenda

J. SCOTT KENNEY AND AILSA CRAIG

Introduction

We all experience pain to various degrees and in different ways. Pain is mundane. Pain is universal. But pain is also variable and it is not transparent. Pain is often felt so physically and individually that it is hard to conceive as socially constructed or contingent. Yet some forms of pain are more hidden than others. Indeed, many have noted the ways that pain is private, subjective, or individual (Ahmed 2004; Bendelow and Williams 1995a, b). Scarry (1985) observes that physical pain is inexpressible by its very nature, noting that 'pain comes unsharably into our midst as at once that which cannot be denied and that which cannot be confirmed' (4). But there are reasons other than ineffability for pain to be hidden. Pain may be disguised or veiled *for fear of possible consequences*. It is this latter type of pain that we discuss in this chapter, a form of suffering we term *illegitimate pain*. Even though pain is often physical in its experience (and this includes both emotional and more directly physical pain), it is important to understand the socially contingent nature of suffering (Bendelow and Williams 1995b). Just because an unpleasant feeling is socially illegitimate, it is no less real in its consequences. We maintain that attending to such lived experiences can have important implications for understanding behaviour in a number of sociological subfields.

It is our contention that 'illegitimate pain,' although hinted at in earlier literature, has yet to be theorized with adequate depth. To address this, we will first discuss how existing literature contributes to an understanding of this form of pain. We then propose a theoretical conception of 'illegitimate pain' that is grounded in that literature but moves beyond it in order to hone the concept into a sharper analytical tool. We further elaborate this concept through an initial application of it to understanding some of the pain experienced by lesbians and gay men. This illustrative case helps highlight the kinds of research possibilities the concept of 'illegitimate pain' brings to the foreground. Our aim is not only to point out the existence of an under-explored aspect of emotional and social life, but also to extend that vision and provide a conceptual definition that opens possibilities for detailed analysis and future research. By applying the concept of 'illegitimate pain' to our understanding of 'coming out' and other pains associated with lesbian and gay experiences, we articulate the connections between the subjective realm of emotions and more external realms of social life (e.g., relationships, organizations, institutions, and culture). Indeed, with 'illegitimate pain' in our conceptual toolkit, possibilities and interpretations emerge that can be developed in a wide variety of contexts and sociological areas of study.

Prior Literature: Hinting at the Illegitimate

A range of work in the sociology of emotions has anticipated and informed our theory. For example, there has long been a normative focus on the organized parameters surrounding feeling and expression. Clark (1987) discusses the social organization of sympathy, arguing that suffering individuals are entitled – or disentitled – to sympathy depending on adherence to norms of 'sympathy etiquette' (303–13).[1] Those who breach 'sympathy etiquette' may find themselves lacking the support they desire, or even face stigmatization (291). Similarly, Hochschild (1990, 1983) contends that people manage emotions in line with feeling and expression rules through both 'surface' and 'deep' acting (1990:118–22). Building from this, Thoits (1990) argues that if emotions deviate from norms, or emotion management fails, the result is 'emotional deviance' (181; see also Thoits, this volume).

While a normative emphasis largely investigates suffering from the 'outside in,' phenomenological work like Denzin's (1990, 1985, 1984, 1983) stresses the need to study emotion from the inside out (1985:224). Denzin emphasizes: (1) the social interplay between inter *and* intra personal interactions (1984:54–7), particularly inhibited social acts, subvocal thought, interpretations, and self-conversations in social action; and (2) the role of the *'lived body'* as the point of reference for 'modes of emotion' that may ratify, reveal, or transform the reality experienced in

relation to interpretive resources. This phenomenological stress on social subjectivity and lived embodiment adds depth to our understanding and suggests that 'illegitimate pain' fosters thought, revelation, self
transformation, perhaps even social change – thereby resonating with
current interest in emotion in social movements (see, among others,
Flam 2005; Robnett 2004; Schrock, Holden, and Reid 2004; Gould 2002;
Aminzade and McAdam 2001).

Finally, Freund (1998) adds a dramaturgical focus on how boundaries are unequally manipulated/enforced in relation to social structure and power. Depending on social position and the performance
demands made, feelings can encourage one to be open to others or to
close off boundaries; that is; emotions can prompt one to adjust the
space of conscious embodied experience (275). This means that the more
subordinate one is, the more likely one is to close oneself off and engage
in dramaturgical displays to maintain social decorum – however, feelings may 'leak' out somatically (277). Freund contends that minorities,
subordinates, and those who negotiate stigma by 'passing' as 'normal,'
fear that their 'inner' selves are visible to more powerful others, and
the only outlet for embodied, dramaturgical stress is somatic (283–4).
This is consistent with research in the sociology of emotion and health
(Leventhal and Patrick-Miller 2000; Williams 2000).

Theory Building: Defining the Range of Illegitimate Pain and Sufferers' Responses

While the literature makes clear there is space for further analysis of
suffering that is not legitimated, simply pointing out the existence of
this form of suffering is insufficient for the creation of a theoretical
concept that can more incisively understand the relations between the
lived, phenomenological aspects of unrecognized pain and the social
relations and structures that shape its existence and experience.

Drawing upon the above, and the examples that follow, we define
illegitimate pain as pain that involves suffering: (1) that is unrecognized and/or socially neglected by society, one's social group, one's
significant others, or by the self; (2) that may be stigmatized as devi-
antor deserved, or involve cultural misunderstandings either about
appropriate ways to respond to it or its etiology; and (3) that can be
understood as existing on a continuum of legitimation. Generally, illegitimate pain is related to broader interpretive standards and structured power relations in society, yet mediated through one's social

interactions and relationships. In other words, illegitimate pain is the suffering brought about when individuals internalize, subject themselves to, or are subjected to, moral codes that are in conflict with embodied emotional experiences. This conflict between lived experience and social expectations makes it socially inappropriate for others to express sympathy or compassion, and this, in turn, exacerbates suffering. Our theorization of illegitimate pain clearly resonates with the concept of disenfranchised grief (Doka 1989, 2002), whereby '[people] incur a loss that is not or cannot be openly acknowledged, publicly mourned or socially supported' (1989: 4). Importantly, the concept of disenfranchised grief has been usefully employed to understand bereavement within LGBTQ communities (see Green and Grant 2008). This resonance bolsters our claim that pain and suffering is, at least in part, experienced differently depending on how it is woven into (or disconnected from) social expectations and contexts, and that LGBTQ lives provide insight into the construction and experience of illegitimate pain. While the two concepts share a deep affinity, the concept of disenfranchised grief can be understood as existing beneath and providing support to the broader theoretical umbrella of illegitimate pain, which includes but is not limited to understanding bereavement and loss.

As in Ahmed's (2004) discussion of shame, we see illegitimate pain as rooted in sociality, a sense of failure before an idealized other, and an affective cost of not following the scripts of normative existence. Yet illegitimate pain is broader than shame, just as it is broader than disenfranchised grief, and it potentially includes other emotions such as loneliness, anger, or types of prior physical suffering that receive short shrift from medical professionals. Indeed, our concept is also broader than stigma, which is but one of the above-noted grounds for illegitimacy. While our concept can be related to Scheff's (2000:97) discussion of shame as involving a threat to the social bond, and while we agree that illegitimate pain, like shame, is often hidden from others, we do not so readily claim that all its varieties are so hidden from the sufferer (Scheff 2000). Illegitimate pain also shares an affinity with Katz's (1988) analysis wherein forms of crime centre on the ways vulnerability to humiliation is unevenly distributed in our social structure. Again, Katz's focus remains narrower than what we present here.

It may be hypothesized that the more legitimate one's pain is perceived to be in relation to structural, normative, and cultural frameworks, the more likely one is to express than somatize it. After all, if one is seen as a legitimate victim, if peers have received congruent compassion training, and if one follows standards of sympathy etiquette, one's suffering implicitly calls for sympathetic response, though its extent and quality can vary widely depending on factors such as social standing and interpersonal closeness (Berlant 2004; Holstein and Miller 1990; Clark 1987). If an individual's suffering is misunderstood (rather than stigmatized or sanctioned), it may still be expressed by sufferers to some degree, but will evoke few tangible responses. As with crime victims (Kenney 2002b), family members, friends, and others may feel sympathy for a victim in pain, but misunderstand how to appropriately respond, and therefore avoid interaction. As a result, sufferers' social circles may shrink, or they may learn to hide their feelings. Still other types of pain may be neglected, considered relatively unimportant, and be given little attention. Examples of pain being neglected or deemed unimportant include: the grief of families of death row inmates (Jones and Beck 2007), the treatment of the homeless in emergency wards (Jeffery 1979), and attitudes towards male victims of domestic disputes (George 1994). Such sufferers face institutional neglect, scarcity of services, or are constrained by gendered scripts, and quickly receive the message that their suffering is unimportant.

Key to the development of 'illegitimate pain' is our contention that illegitimate pain exists on a continuum. In any given historic, social, and political context, the legitimacy of pain is relative and ranges from legitimate pain (i.e., suffering seen as sympathy worthy) at one end; through to less severe forms of illegitimate pain where individuals' suffering is misunderstood, neglected, or considered unimportant; to the far extreme of illegitimate pain where individuals are stigmatized – often to the point that their pain is viewed as 'just punishment.'

Examples along this continuum can be found in the literature. First, there is the pain of those whose initially understandable pain persists too long, as seen in 'complicated grief' (Johnson et.al. 2009). Second, there are those whose emotional expressions are defined as emotionally deviant (Thoits 1990) – for example, expressing grief at a wedding. Third, there is the suffering experienced by members of highly stigmatized social groups. Examples of such illegitimate pain include the intense pain experienced by heroin addicts and alcoholics or the difficulties faced by ex-convicts seeking to reintegrate into the community (see Schwartz and Skolnick 1962). It is a reasonable assumption that the greater the relative degree of stigmatization, the greater will be the somatization, the lived embodiment of pain. This somatization of pain may result in individuals being unable to function efficiently or effectively, and, when coupled with the leakage (Freund 1998) of feelings of the lived body (Denzin 1985), can thereby contribute to theproduction of 'evidence' for negative stereotypes (Shilling 2003) by making such people more visible to us (Scarry 1985). We see, then, that understanding the dynamics of illegitimate pain can help us understand informal, or even formal labelling, as well as the invocation of various social control practices and ideologies, particularly medicalization of conditions that could be better understood as resulting from social interactions and context.

However, this continuum should not only be understood as a continuum within which different categories of sufferers are necessarily placed at different points on a spectrum. That is, someone with fibromyalgia is not necessarily linked to a predetermined 'ranking' of illegitimate pain. Instead, as noted in relation to compassion, actors' experiences of illegitimate pain may shift along the continuum depending on the social and historical context at hand (Berlant 2004; Bendelow and Williams 1995b). Indeed, gaining control over the context of one's experiences is central to the options, rooted in deviance literature, which we contend actors may adopt when they respond to the dramaturgical stress of managing illegitimate pain. These options include, but are not limited to: (1) adopting a negative self-concept or deviant identity through self-labelling of one's painful feelings, but without deviant acts or a deviant role to support it (Rubington and Weinberg 2005:385).[2] This may also involve individuals 'passing' as 'normal' (Charmaz 2000; Goffman 1963), and needing to carefully manage information while suffering in silence; (2) when 'passing' is difficult, relying on others' active efforts that attempt to preserve the appearance of 'normal' interaction (Rubington and Weinberg 2005); (3) engaging in rationalizations and justifications relative to dominant moral codes (Scott and Lyman 1968; Sykes and Matza 1957); (4) getting involved in a subculture and gaining self-esteem and recognition through participating in subcultural activities (Rubington and Weinberg 2005; Cohen 1955; Lemert 1951); and/ or (5) transforming deviant identity by engaging in 'tertiary deviance' (Rubington and Weinberg 2005; Kitsuse 1980), which involves protesting against the current moral regime and attempting to validate oneself or one's group through political action and activism. Here, our model has suggestive links with Scarry's (1985) discussion of the cultural implications of pain's mandated inexpressibility. The first and third of these responses for managing illegitimate pain (suffering in silence and rationalizations) can be understood as mechanisms *within the victim* that participate in what Scarry defines as the 'unmaking' of an actor's world by the regimes and contexts that wield normative power, while the fourth and fifth can be seen as creative social acts that Scarry argues emerge to work against pain.

An Illustration and Elaboration: 'Illegitimate Pain' and Lesbian and Gay Experiences

In order to clearly illustrate the concept of illegitimate pain, we now use it to explore the pain from stigmatization of same-sex desire or sexual behaviour, and/or from how openly individuals express lesbian or gay sexual orientation. Examples of pain that lesbian and gay people encounter include (but are not limited to) the pain of being disowned because of one's sexual orientation, being held distant by family and friends, being physically or sexually assaulted, losing employment or housing without due cause, and, finally, the pain that comes from *fearing* any of these things happening. That fear can result in the necessity or choice to live a 'double life,' and can contribute to a deep sense of shame. Clearly, leading a 'double life' is an example of the conflicted and difficult emotional work that Freund (1998) suggests leads to 'dramaturgical stress,' and that is often an unrecognized and illegitimate pain.

We call the illegitimate pain of lesbians and gay men the 'pain of the closet,' understanding that this is not a homogeneous type of pain, but can result from a variety of causes, experiences, or contexts. Indeed, part of the reason we choose this example is to highlight the ways that the continuum of illegitimate pain is socially, historically, and geographically contingent. The case of lesbian and gay pain is also particularly illustrative because different aspects of the 'pain of the closet' meet all the components of our definition of illegitimate pain: the pains of the closet are unrecognized or socially neglected; homosexuals' pain is often stigmatized as being deserved because of their presumed deviance; the pain of lesbians and gay men can result from cultural misunderstanding about appropriate responses to pain, or from misunderstandings about the root of the pain; and the pains of the closet can be understood as existing on a continuum of legitimation.

Changing historical and political contexts provide one example of how illegitimate pain exists on a continuum. The legalization of same-sex marriage in Canada as well as active lesbian and gay rights campaigns that extend the argument beyond that of access to the institution of marriage, have helped to alter what was once largely considered illegitimate, even 'deserved' pain. Rather than same-sex desire being deemed punishable, it is now more often seen as part of human sexual diversity, and acknowledgement of the 'pain of the closet' is more likely than has been in the recent past – at least in some circles. Indeed, the LGBTQ rights movement in North America has helped build an institutionally complete subculture capable of providing participants with a deep sense of moral self-worth vis-à-vis heterosexist culture. In the personal and social questioning this movement has encouraged, it has enabled a movement that works to replace heterosexist moralism with affirmation of sexual diversity. This changing historical and political situation is part of the context within which people 'come out' – a process often understood as one of identity formation where the shackles of shame are dropped and acceptance of or pride in one's sexual identity is taken up – though conscious politicization is not mandatory to the process.

Much work[3] has been done on the process and experiences of lesbian and gay identity formation (i.e., 'coming out'). There have been models suggested to help better understand this life transition,[4] and studies of how the process and experience of coming out differ according to race, gender, age, ability, class, historical period, and nation.[5] Research has also examined the effect coming out has on the families of lesbians and gay men,[6] as well as the effects it may have in the workplace or classroom.[7] Additionally, research has examined the role of the Internet or the importance of place in the coming out process.[8]

What connects much of the research on coming out is its individual-level focus. Coming out is most often seen as a deeply personal transition that individuals can experience as self-discovery, realization, confession, or life-changing choice. Alongside the individual process of coming out is the process of telling others. This is shown in the many narratives that make a distinction between 'coming out to myself' and 'coming out to the world' (Wolfe and Stanley 1980). Indeed, there are many people who are involved in same-sex relationships, but do not divulge their sexuality to those outside of an LBGTQ context. Also, there are those who do not hide their sexuality, but choose not to politicize that aspect of their lives. This highlights the fact that coming out is not always a politicization of LGBTQ identities. Yet even when lesbians and gay men do *not* come out in a public or political way, the transition of coming out is still central to LGBTQ experience. Given the personal nature of this transition, as well as individuals' choices regarding public expression of orientation, it is unsurprising that much of the literature has concentrated on an individual level of analysis.

Interestingly, individuals in the process of coming out react and make choices that fit well into the options we suggest are possible for those experiencing illegitimate pain: they may (1) choose to stay closeted, 'pass' as straight, suffer in silence, and in so doing nurture a negative self concept; (2) rely on heteronormative accommodative actions that preserve the appearance of conventional heterosexual interaction for all concerned; (3) engage in rationalizations for homosexuality that do not question the dominance of heteronormativity (e.g., 'I can't help who I love' – with the unspoken message being that if one could, one would not be lesbian or gay); (4) get involved in an LGBTQ subculture that helps nurture self-esteem and positive identity through recognition – yet which still may not challenge the dominance of heterosexism outside the bounds of the subculture; and/or (5) become politically active by making claims for legitimizing and acknowledging the pain of the closet, thereby working to challenge heterosexism and homophobia.

The continuum of legitimacy concerning the pain of the closet is not, however, solely a matter of an individual progressing through stages of 'development' to a more positive sense of self or to being someone more likely to engage in activism. As Sedgewick has noted, the closet is a metaphor that has wide-ranging effects (Sedgewick 1990), and one therefore does not need to be 'in the closet' to experience unacknowledged suffering that results from the social and cultural dynamics of the closet. Violating the norms of heterosexism through being identifiably lesbian or gay – through being 'out' – can be the impetus for painful acts of homophobia. That is, one can be 'out,' and have a positive self-image, and that very openness can result in heterosexist assumptions or homophobic attack. Indeed, no matter how 'well-adjusted' an individual may be, that will not assure the recognition and legitimacy of their pain.

While the individual focus in research on coming out has led to work that 'gives voice' to the pain of the closet, by being rooted in social developmental models, the connections between institutions, structures, and social contexts are not sufficiently highlighted. One notable exception is Evans's (2002) work on negotiating sexual identity in the classroom, and the emotional work required by teachers negotiating disclosure or nondisclosure of sexuality. Here, Evans highlights the connection between social-structural position and emotion work, noting that those who live on the margins must perform qualitatively different emotional work (32). Other work that *does* highlight context or institutions often focuses on place and space in the coming out process (Weston 1995; Valentine and Skelton 2003). The argument is that urban spaces provide helpful resources for affirming sexual diversity – so much so that becoming an urbanite is often deemed central to forming lesbian or gay identity (Aldrich 2004; Weston 1995). Cities have a large and varied population, and businesses can therefore benefit from catering to specific subcultural markets. That is, given the prevalence of heterosexuality, a bookstore or bar that is intended for lesbians and gay men is not a feasible business venture in a rural place with a limited population.

Furthermore, while rural spaces often do not have a large enough LGBTQ community for there to be community meeting spaces, they also provide fewer sexually diverse role models, and fewer potential partners. Indeed, the city has long been understood as a place that provides the anonymity, population density, and variety that makes sexual freedom possible more generally – not only for lesbians and gay men. While consideration of urban/rural differences is important for understanding the role of place in the social construction of sexuality because of the opportunities that each provide and preclude,[9] it also provides examples of how the illegitimacy of pain may be geographically contingent and how place may be a variable in the continuum that can act fairly independently of other factors. That is, while shifting historical and political contexts have great effects, and the lived experience of coming out is connected to the relative legitimacy of the pain of the closet, the differences between urban and rural spaces can quickly change one's place on the continuum of illegitimacy for the pain of the closet, regardless of where one is in the coming out transition. In other words, being sensitive to the concept of 'illegitimate pain' opens alternative ways of understanding the question: Why do lesbians and gay men often gravitate to urban centres? Why? Because it *hurts* to stay in rural areas,[10] even if those areas are 'home,' and it hurts in ways that overshadow the influence of recent political change and historical advances for lesbian and gay rights and recognition. It hurts in ways that cannot be attended to or solved or absolved through a lesbian or gay person's stage of homosexual identity development. It hurts because of the current social and cultural characteristics of rural areas – the place itself contributes to the illegitimacy of some people's suffering, and this is not attributable solely to the beliefs of the dominant population (who may have heterogeneous – even positive – views on homosexuality). Not only does the sensitizing concept of 'illegitimate pain' have the potential to support tentative conclusions that rural spaces are presumed to be heterosexual spaces (Little 2003), and to provide further nuance to our understanding of sexual migration, it could also help us understand how the connections between subjective, embodied motivating factors and external structural factors effect migration patterns for other groups as well.

Furthermore, through employing the concept of 'illegitimate pain,' coming out can be seen as a continuing navigation of the factors that affect the legitimacy of the pain of the closet. Rather than simply being understood as a process of internal self-recognition, journey towards enlightenment, or progression towards political activism, coming out can be seen as an ongoing negotiation of the continuum of legitimacy. Coming out is more than a life transition, and is instead an ongoing relationship of negotiating power between the margins and centre of a complex system of sexual stratification (Rubin 1993). In this way, the concept of illegitimate pain allows us to better account for the apparent contradiction between the fact that 'coming out' is both a stage of lesbian and gay life, and something that lesbians or gay men 'never stop doing.'

Conclusion

Illegitimate pain, as a new concept, is implicit in a diversity of earlier, more narrowly focused work on shame, grieving, humiliation, and stigma. However, by integrating work from the normative, phenomenological, and dramaturgical traditions in the sociology of emotions, we present a concept with the potential to comprehensively unite and bolster previous work on pain, grief, shame, humiliation, and stigma, and the ways they are connected to social structures, contexts, and norms. We have shown the concept to be applicable – even evocative – of further research in the important area of LGBTQ experiences. Indeed, it is suggestive of further research in several other broad areas of sociological study.

Thus, pain that is perceived as illegitimate at one point in time, or in one culture, may be seen as legitimate, even sympathy worthy in another. In at least some circles, this is the case with lesbians and gay men in North America in terms of the pain that can be associated with coming out of the closet. As with compassion (Berlant 2004), since attributions of illegitimate pain are not static, it is important to investigate how illegitimate pain is constructed by society across both time and space. Despite the folk perception of unified development or 'progress' as we move forward in history, time is not a unifying standard, and variation in attributions of legitimacy exist both within and between different social contexts, locations, and time periods. As well, areas of future research where the concept of 'illegitimate pain' may be fruitful emerge in examination of the many writers who have built upon Spector and Kitsuse's (1977) work on the emergence and social construction of social problems through claims-making, which itself updates and extends the earlier work of Howard Becker (1963). Particularly suggestive in this respect is the work of Loseke (1993), who argues that a social problem in the making is an issue in search of a victim. Indeed, this idea may be deepened by suggesting that a social problem in the making is an issue requiring evidence of legitimate pain, or claims-makers fighting for recognition of illegitimate pain as socially legitimate.

As outlined above, actors experiencing illegitimate pain face several choices. By understanding the factors that constrain and enable different choices in the face of illegitimate pain, we can therefore approach the development of social problems with further analytical clarity. Rather than simply observing that social problems are issues in search of victims, we are better equipped to understand the social processes that contribute to the formation of social selves and relations that bolster claims for recognition. Indeed, Emilio Viano's (1989) four-stage model of the emergence and struggle for social recognition of various forms of victimization may also be reinterpreted in this way. Nevertheless, it will be important to supplement such relatively pluralistic approaches with other, more recent work on emotion and the emergence of social movements that considers structural and power relations in the emergence and evolution of social categories, problems, and norms. Finally, it will also be important to consider the role of embodied emotion in revealing new meanings or interpretations for social action and social movements.

A second area for further research employing our concept of 'illegitimate pain' is the related concern that the relative legitimacy or illegitimacy of pain depends upon the perspective of the people in question. What may be legitimate pain, deserving of sympathy, concern and redress to one may be perceived as illegitimate, even deserved, by another. Hence, in addition to the conceptual utility of 'illegitimate pain' in understanding identity-based movements for social change, it will also be important to consider the potential role played by illegitimate pain in social conflict. For example, Holstein and Miller (1990) speak of 'victim contests' over who is the 'real' or the 'biggest' victim in conflict situations (113–15), and Kenney and Clairmont (2009) have noted offensive and defensive use of victim rhetoric in their observations of youth restorative justice sessions. Indeed, it may be possible to consider broader social conflicts related to the sociological trinity of race, class, and gender as, at least in part, imbued with the implicit issue of the legitimacy/illegitimacy of a groups' suffering. Thus, the concept of 'illegitimate pain' can also help us understand reaction and/or resistance to social movements that are born of legitimacy claims related to the experience of pain. Indeed, this concept adds phenomenological depth and an embodied aspect to our understandings of social movements and resistance.

Third, and in conjunction with the above-mentioned areas of social movement and social conflict, it will be important to investigate the dynamic, embodied aspects of illegitimate pain. While Denzin and Freund's formulations incorporating phenomenological and bodily concerns are welcome from a theoretical standpoint, it will be necessary to do in-depth qualitative investigation of socially illegitimate pain.[11] While it may be difficult to access and gain the trust of groups or individuals whose pain is stigmatized, Thoits's (1990) suggestion of the four structural conditions under which emotional deviance is more likely to be reported may prove a helpful starting point for the recruitment of participants, and could also prove useful in the initial stages of coding and analysis by providing a possible range of structural forces that may unite and divide participants.

Even with the difficulty presented by the task of recruiting participants, gaining a phenomenological understanding of illegitimate pain will be a significant step in advancing sociological understandings of emotion, the body, health, and identity-based social movements. Illegitimate pain, if left unattended, may hypothetically be expressed in angry behaviour, such as interpersonal violence or other forms of criminal behaviour, as reflected in studies of humiliation (Katz 1988) and of offenders' condemnation narratives (Maruna 2001). Similarly, illegitimate pain may lead to secondary victimization (Kenney 2002b) whereby one adopts the victim role in the face of social reaction to or neglect of one's pain.

In summary, we suggest that the concept of illegitimate pain may be of particular use in understanding the following three areas: (1) the emergence of social-problems, claims-makers, and development of social movements; (2) the formation and nuance of social conflicts in reaction or resistance to identity-based social movements; (3) the variable effects and relations concerning the range of embodied, lived pain, particularly in relation to literature on the sociology of the body, health, and deviance. However, this is not an exhaustive list, and we suspect that the concept could be applied in many different settings. Deri's work in this volume, for example, could possibly use the concept to understand how sensing potential loss in the emergent pain of jealousy is understood and acted upon in polyamorous relationships.

Ultimately, future research must incorporate but move beyond normative external concerns such as the need to adhere to the rules of 'sympathy etiquette' (Clark 1987), to 'manage' one's emotions in line with 'expression' and 'feeling rules' (Hochschild 1990), and must also avoid attributions of 'emotional deviance' (Thoits 1990). It will also be important to consider the etiology of illegitimate pain in any given society or social situation. Certainly Thoits's reference to structural variables such as multiple role occupancy, subcultural marginality, normative and non-normative role transitions, and rigid rules governing ongoing roles and ceremonial rituals provide useful ideas for research sites, as does her suggestion to consider self-help and protest groups (188). Similarly, Freund's (1998) suggestion of studying subordinates with imposed and stressful emotion work, minorities, as well as those who must cope with a social stigma and 'pass' as 'normal' (281–2) is useful. Indeed, this vein of work we propose is in line with a longstanding literature in the sociology of health indicating a link between socially structured inequality, socially structured ambiguity, and physical/mental health problems (Clarke 2004; Stolzman 2000).

Again, other avenues of research may well present themselves. Indeed, 'illegitimate pain,' with its phenomenological attention to the lived body, may well be a central component of what Shilling (2003:8) refers to as the 'absent presence' of the body in social theory and research. Yet, to neglect illegitimate pain is to fail to step outside ourselves and take up a sociological vision that digs beneath our commonsense assumptions and understandings: just because forms of socially organized pain are perceived as illegitimate, does not mean that they should be neglected in sociological analysis – indeed, this kind of socially and culturally sanctioned neglect could prove to be an important social force in its own right. Nevertheless, by attending to this idea and using it as a sensitizing concept (Blumer 1969), we hope to shed light on a number of key areas of sociological inquiry. In this sense, at the very least, we can question whether we must continue to conceive of pain as a zero sum game, where one person or group's legitimated pain infringes upon the claims made by others, and we can also explore how even unrecognized pain is woven into our social fabric even in spite of – or indeed *because of* – its illegitimacy.

NOTES

1 These interpersonal norms include: (1) do not make unwarranted claims; (2) do not claim too much sympathy; (3) do not reject sympathy; and (4) reciprocate gifts of sympathy (Clark 1987:303–13). A broader approach is set out by Berlant (2004), where emotions in operation, like sympathy and compassion, must be placed in the broader context of inequality and political economy, along with current debates about things like 'compassionate conservatism.' Berlant's normative and aesthetic reading considers that people are taught to feel *appropriately* compassionate (11). Variation in compassion training 'emerg[es] at historical moments . . . [is] shaped by aesthetic conventions, and tak[es] place in scenes that are anxious, volatile, surprising and contradictory' (7). As such, 'the word *compassion* carries the weight of ongoing debates about the ethics of privilege – in particular about the state as an economic, military, and moral actor that represents and establishes collective norms of obligation, and about individual and collective obligations to read a state of distress not as a judgment against the distressed but a claim on the spectator to be an ameliorative actor' (1).
2 These options are not exhaustive. Kenney (2004:244–9) notes how individuals in similar situations may choose, learn, or innovate responses based on awareness of informational resources and orientation to past behavioural patterns or the synthesis of innovative responses. While one may still suggest that options may be narrowed relative to, for example, the visibility of stigmatizing attributes (Charmaz 2000; Goffman 1963), the availability of significant subcultural contact or differential illegitimate opportunity structures (Cloward and Ohlin 1960), one cannot dismiss the possibility of further varieties of innovative responses on the part of reflexive, self-aware individuals.
3 Citations of previous work on the coming out process are illustrative, not exhaustive.
4 See Johns and Probst 2004; Chirrey 2003; Floyd and Stein 2002; Esterberg 1997; Levine 1997; Morris 1997; Eliason 1996; Cox and Gallois 1996; Kitzinger and Wilkinson 1995; Phelan 1993; Rust 1993; Cass 1984a, b; McDonald 1982.

5 See Parks, Hughes, and Matthews 2004; Li and Orleans 2001; Bhugra 1997; Bohan 1996; Jackson and Brown 1996; Savin-Williams and Diamond 2000; Lynch 2004; Jones and Nystrom 2002; Sherry 2004; Samuels 2003; Appleby 2001a, b; Mallon 2001; Watzlawik 2004; Ryan 2003.

6 See Cohler 2004; Herdt and Koff 2000; Lynch and Murray 2000; Oswald 2000.

7 See Ward and Winstanley 2003; Taylor and Raeburn 1995; Schneider 1986; Raissiguier 1997.

8 See Heinz et al. 2002; Munt, Bassett, and O'Riordan 2002; McKenna and Bargh 1998; Holt and Griffin 2003; Valentine and Skelton 2003.

9 See Little (2003) for one examination of how heterosexuality is affected by gendered and sexualized understanding of space and place.

10 This example helps clarify the relation between affect, feeling, and sense. If emotion may be seen as a physical sense that transmits information to the self (Hochschild 1983), then emotionally *sensing* potential claims to the illegitimacy of one's sexual orientation in rural areas, including the probable stigmatization of one's significant yet hidden desires should they become known, results in an *evaluative* response in relation to self, a devaluing of who one is. In a slightly different way, this could operate through the 'somatic sensation of society' at the heart of Shilling's (1997) discussion of Durkheim. This devaluation is manifested both cognitively and in embodied affect. Indeed, given the need to wall oneself off and engage in dramaturgical displays discussed by Freund (1998), it may manifest unpleasantly in the various modes of feeling relative to the lived body discussed in Denzin's (1985) phenomenological account.

11 The methods employed by Theodosius in this volume could prove particularly helpful as an example of how to better capture subjective experience in relation to social contexts.

6 Religion within the Bounds of Emotion Alone: Bergson and Kant

ALEXANDRE LEFEBVRE AND MELANIE WHITE[1]

> Religion, being coextensive with our species, must pertain to our structure.
> – Henri Bergson, *The Two Sources of Morality and Religion*

Introduction

There are several reasons, perhaps nowhere so concentrated as in their treatment of religion, to see Bergson and Kant as opposed. And yet, as is typical of disagreement, this opposition springs from a shared insight: both Bergson and Kant envision human beings as endowed with an overreaching faculty of reason which distorts and even imperils human life. Religion is a privileged site to examine emotion, particularly the relation between reason and emotion. Of course, these terms require specification; but, as a starting point, we see that philosophy and theology alike have widely assumed religion to be the paradigmatic case for opposition between emotion and reason. On the one hand, religion has been dismissed as 'anthropology disguised as theology' (Feuerbach), 'ideology and false consciousness' (Marx), 'infantile neurosis' (Freud), 'the nonsensical expression of feeling, diffused by metaphysicians without poetic or musical talent' (Carnap), and a 'category mistake' (Ryle) (see de Vries 1999:2–3). On the other hand, from Luther to contemporary evangelism, faith and belief have been upheld as the only way to reach a God 'incomprehensible and inaccessible to human reason' (Luther 1969:330; see also Connolly 2008:39–68). In short, these positions represent an antinomy (i.e., a shared presupposition developed in antagonistic directions). Starting from a shared opposition between reason and emotion, one position claims that religion will vanish if reason masters emotion, and the other position claims that religion will endure if faith asserts its autonomy from reason.

Kant and Bergson are valuable to a sociological study of emotion precisely because they criticize and avoid this antinomy.[1] As we shall see, Kant argues that far from opposing emotional excess, extravagant use of reason solicits it.[2] And Bergson argues that the purpose of emotion is to check the demoralizing and dissolvent tendencies of reason. It is this shared refusal to oppose reason to emotion and to instead explore their entanglement that informs the purpose of this essay: to use Kant and Bergson's discussion of religion to assess the nature, function, and source of emotion and its relationship to reason.

We propose to cut into Kant and Bergson's treatment of religion, hence their treatment of emotion and reason, through their respective visions of the potential fanaticism internal to reason. To make this shared vision clearer, we begin with a remarkable passage in which Stanley Cavell (1979) comments on Kant's major work regarding religion, *Religion within the Bounds of Bare Reason*: 'Here, as is typical of Kant's procedures, he goes beyond an expected Enlightenment battle that takes up the cause of reason against irrationality on the most famous field of the irrational [i.e., religion]. The collection of sections called General Observations, one of which concludes each of the four parts of Kant's volume on religion, together constitute what I think amounts to a general theory of irrationality, a systematic account of what turns out, on this theory, to be a whole class of phenomena, each of them involving a particular distortion of human reason. Kant calls the four members of this class fanaticism, superstition, delusion, and sorcery' (455).

Cavell frames his praise on this ground: Kant is remarkable for having shown us the specific deformations reason threatens to impose upon itself. We propose to extend the spirit of Cavell's remark. In the first section we elaborate how, for Kant, reason can elicit reckless emotion which can take the form of passion (*Leidenschaft*) or enthusiasm (*Schwärmerei*).[3] In the second section we turn to Bergson's discussion of 'static religion,' in which instinct and emotion counteract the demoralizing and dissolvent power of the intellect. In the third, and last, section we turn to Bergson's difficult discussion of love in 'dynamic religion.' Love is of fundamental importance to *Two Sources of Morality and Religion*. It is the emotion that not only saves us from our instinctive tendency to wage war, but it also serves as a counter to our intellectual tendency to separate us from both God and the world. As we seek to define a concept of creative emotion in Bergson, one constitutively engaged in limiting the intellect, our discussion centres on love and (perhaps hardheartedly) specifies criteria to identify its function. We propose the following two contributions. First, to provide a concrete analysis of emotion by contrasting a conception of religion that accords priority to reason over emotion (Kant) with one that accords priority to emotion over reason (Bergson). And second, to provide an original interpretation of Bergson's *Two Sources of Morality and Religion* as organized by a simultaneous extension and criticism of Kant's philosophy of religion.

Kant: The Fanaticism of Reason

In the preface to the first edition of *Religion within the Bounds of Bare Reason* [1793], Kant makes clear that religion is the product of morality, not the other way around. Indeed, he maintains, 'morality in no way needs religion . . . rather, through the power [*vermöge*] of pure practical reason [morality] is sufficient to itself' (2009:3). Absolute and unconditioned, pure practical reason commands our will without needing an external (religious) purpose to learn one's duty or to impel its performance. Nevertheless, Kant does establish a direct and necessary relationship between morality and religion. This relationship is rooted in the fact that morality is not indifferent to its realization in the world. Indeed, it is a duty to bring about a union between morality and its empirical existence. Kant calls this union the highest good. But seeing as the realization of the highest good depends on circumstances beyond the control of finite individuals, we are led to presuppose – but merely as a principle or idea of reason (Kant will say a 'reflective' presupposition [52]) – 'a higher, moral, holiest, and all-powerful being that alone can unite the two elements of this good' (5). Religion, therefore, is a natural and necessary product of pure practical reason. In short, Kant stresses two points: first, morality is the foundation for religion; and second, religion is not an accidental or contingent phenomenon but arises to meet an inherent moral need, that is, the realization of the highest good. In a word, 'morality leads inevitably to religion' (8).

The point can be rephrased in language evocative of Bergson: reason alone should be the source of both our conduct *and* the content of religion. It is, however, a standing possibility that reason should fail to determine either of these. In other words, conduct and religion are free to adopt sources besides reason. This possibility is crucial for Kant. It represents nothing less than the condition for the two kinds of grief specific to human beings: evil and fanaticism. On the one hand, the source of evil lies in the adoption of a maxim that determines the will by sensuous nature and not by the moral law. On the other hand, the source of fanaticism lies in the creation of ecclesiastical rules and practices unsupported by pure practical reason. We take each in turn.

Evil

It is fundamental for Kant that evil is rooted in freedom of choice. He thus opposes two major traditions. Against Christian doctrine, Kant argues that we are not evil by fact of birth or original inheritance. For him, such an approach would vitiate responsibility for evil by placing it in acts that cannot be attributed to us (2009: 40). Second, contrary to Stoicism, evil does not reside in the senses or natural impulses as such. This approach too would eliminate our responsibility for evil, this time by grounding it in our natural constitution (57–9). Kant's position is not that we should deny our sensuous nature (which includes not only basic needs but also emotions), but that we should put it in its proper place. It is only when we elevate sensuality to the status of a maxim for conduct that we are properly called evil. And so, for Kant a moral human life consists of striking the proper arrangement between reason that determines conduct and the natural needs and emotions subordinate to it. As Arnold Davidson (1993) writes, 'To place [sensuous nature] in this role is to create the proper human life, to give appropriate structure to the link that hangs us between the animal and divine. Our choice of proper structure is our choice for humanity' (83). The point we emphasize is that while the temptation to substitute a moral with a pathological maxim may be ineradicable – hence Kant's claim that human evil is endemic or 'radical' (32) – moral or rational life does not require release from natural needs or emotion. We need only keep them in their proper place.

Fanaticism

While the problem of evil opens *Religion within the Bounds of Bare Reason*, it becomes clear that Kant is equally preoccupied with a more insidious danger. This danger is taken up in the General Remarks that conclude each of the four parts of the book. Here, Kant addresses ideas that, while not constitutive elements of rational religion, arise in order to resolve moral problems raised by our evil nature: 'Reason, conscious of its incapacity to deal adequately with its moral need, extends itself to extravagant [or transcendent: *überschwenglich*] ideas that might compensate for this lack, without appropriating them to itself as part of an expanded possession. [Reason] does not dispute the possibility or actuality of the objects of these ideas; it just cannot admit them into its maxims of thought and of action' (2009:52).

In a letter written more than a decade before this passage, Kant remarks on the 'endless religious madness to which people in all ages are inclined' (Kant 1967:83). We might say that the General Remarks flesh out the three species of madness: grace (Remarks 1 and 4: belief in practices to propitiate the supernatural); miracles (Remark 2: belief in events that contradict the law of experience); and holy mysteries (Remark 3: belief in concepts unfathomable to reason). On the one hand, Kant admits that these ideas are valuable to clothe or dramatize concepts of pure practical reason. As we will see in a moment, they respond to a moral need. But on the other hand, all too often (perhaps inevitably: 'in all ages') these ideas of reason are mistaken for positive insights into the supernatural. Properly speaking, it is this mistake, not the ideas themselves, that perverts reason. And it is this mistake that gives the General Remarks their deep unity. Whereas on the surface they enumerate three distinct religious delusions, they are in fact reducible to a single cause: the failure to preserve pure practical reason as the sole source of religion. The rest of this section is taken up with two questions. First, how is it that reason engenders the delusions characteristic of religion? And second, in what ways does reason excite the fanaticism it should instead check?[4] These two questions anticipate our discussion of Bergson, who, in persistent dialogue with Kant, also charts the complex internal connections between reason and moral need, and delusion and fanaticism.

We begin with the mistake at the root of delusion and fanaticism. Throughout his critical writings, Kant acknowledges our human need to correlate concepts with sensible intuitions or concrete examples. This correlation goes by different names depending on which interest is at stake: 'schematism' for theoretical reason (Kant 1996a:A137–B176); 'typic' for pure practical reason (Kant 2002: 67); and 'symbolization' for aesthetic judgment (Kant 1987:58). Religion is no different; in fact, this need is pressing: 'Because of the natural need of all human beings to demand for even the highest concepts and grounds of reason, something that *the senses can hold on to*, i.e., some experiential confirmation and the like (a need which one does actually have to take into account if the intention is *to introduce* a faith universally), some historical church faith must be employed, which one usually also finds to be already at hand' (Kant 2009:110, translation modified).

Kant (2009) argues on two levels. On the historical level, he claims that for a new religion to gain acceptance – even Christianity, the rational religion *par excellence* (127) – its teachings must take recourse in sensible examples, even if these appear to contradict its rational core (miracles, for example). The hope is that once accepted, rational religion will set aside its sensible aids (152). But on a deeper or universal level, sensible exemplification of pure practical concepts is a human need as such. To become comprehensible, moral concepts must undergo schematization. Christ, for instance, is a sensible example used to illustrate the idea of a human being morally pleasing to God. By bridging divine and human worlds, Christ models the exemplary life for Christians (63–6). Such an example is perfectly acceptable, even desirable, so long as we remember that these examples are *illustrations* of pure practical concepts. They are not only necessary but also salutary and give moral concepts vivid expression.

Examples, however, pose a unique danger: they might be mistaken for the concept they are meant to represent. The risk is that we invert the order of priority between concept and intuition, such that the latter becomes primary. Inherent to religious schematization, therefore, is the possibility that we treat the illustrations of a moral concept as if they were a predicate of it. This slip leads us to claim positive knowledge of the supersensible: 'This way of conceiving [pure practical concepts through sensible examples] is the *schematism of analogy* (for elucidation), which we cannot dispense with. But to transform it into a *schematism of object-determination* (for expansion of our cognition) is *anthropomorphism*, which – for a moral aim – has in religion the most dangerous consequences' (2009:65, emphasis added). In theoretical cognition, this problem does not arise.[5] Sensibility does not impede or limit human knowledge but defines it. But for practical reasons, sensibility poses a double threat: first, we may adopt sensuous nature as the basis of our maxims (evil); and, second, we may transform the schema into a determination of the object itself (delusion). This latter temptation of reason, at once natural and perverse, is the source of religious illusion. By virtue of its inherent tendency to seek the unconditioned and get to the bottom of the supersensible, *reason engenders delusion by taking the sensible schema of pure practical concepts* (which by right has only a heuristic function) *as cognition of the supersensible*. It remains now to be seen how reason can inspire fanaticism and passion.

We can approach this question through Kant's (2009) discussion of biblical interpretation. Recall that the basis of religion is morality (i.e., pure practical reason). As such, all religions are roughly equivalent: they each consist of a rational core developed through various illustrations and narratives. Certain religions are more faithful to this core but all consist in this core (111) It follows for Kant that the key to Scriptural exegesis is pure practical reason: '[Rational] interpretation, in view of the text (of the revelation), may often seem forced, and may often actually be forced; and yet this interpretation must, if only the text is capable of bearing [*annehmen*] it, be preferred to a literal interpretation that either contains within itself absolute nothing for morality, or perhaps even acts counter to morality's incentives' (110). Pure practical reason is doubly recommended for decoding scripture. First, it is moral and enables edifying study. And, second, it is universally shared and secures public discussion and argument (see Rawls 1989/1999). But what happens when the schema intended to represent religious concepts eclipses their rational foundation? Kant's reply is that empirical faith and subjective feeling become the basis for scriptural interpretation. Without a core of pure practical reason, biblical interpretation becomes based, as Kant (1996b) observes, on 'a certain (indemonstrable and inexplicable) *feeling [Gefühl]*' (Ak 285; see also de Vries 2002:67–87). The direct object of Kant's (2009) criticism is Luther, for whom no criterion beyond faith is required to read scripture. Kant criticizes this function of feeling as an 'illumination' that threatens to introduce every kind of arbitrariness and fantasy into religion (83).

We have so far seen two instances in which reason loses its relative priority: (1) Revelation and not reason furnishes the substance of religious concepts (*delusion*); and (2) Feeling and not reason grounds religious interpretation and practice (*fanaticism*). Kant's genius, if we can put it this way, is to have shown the internal connection between delusion and fanaticism. Faith in revelation cannot be rational, for we would then be asked to believe that an empirical event provides knowledge of the supersensible; any religion that privileges it will transform faith into felt conviction. Or, in other words, when a natural moral need (to sensibly illustrate pure practical concepts) is taken as positive knowledge of the supersensible (*delusion*), faith forfeits its rational basis (for it now attaches itself to revelation and not morality) and adopts feeling as both a cognitive and practical means to access the supersensible (*fanaticism*). Kant's further accomplishment is to have clearly described the disastrous consequences of this connection between delusion and fanaticism. On the one hand, religious communities become closed (literally parochial) for they are grounded merely on convergent feelings privately held by their members. On the other hand, faith turns into intense passion because it has replaced argument with assertion. The fanaticism of reason is such that by assuming positive knowledge of supersensible concepts – something we cannot know and morally do not need – feeling paves the way for a religious enthusiasm that cannot but dogmatically insist upon its faith and practice.

Bergson: The Dissolvent and Demoralizing Intellect

In several respects, Bergson could not be farther from Kant. As Anne Sauvagnargues (2004) puns, he is the 'anti-Kant' (155; see also Merleau-Ponty 1960:288). Gilles Deleuze also observes that Kant serves as a 'point of reference' [le rôle de repère] for Bergson, from which he repeatedly gauges his distance (2004:166; 1991:23). In important respects this is true, and we will articulate Bergson's fundamental opposition to Kant on two issues. First, for Bergson the origin of morality and religion is biology. Indeed, Bergson's *Two Sources of Morality and Religion* is the pre-eminent work on the sociobiology of religion (Ansell-Pearson and Mullarkey 2002:37). Second, for Bergson neither religion nor morality takes place within the limits of reason alone. Instead, both constitutively involve emotion. Yet, despite these differences, we will argue that Bergson's *Two Sources* renews central insights of Kant's philosophy of religion. Specifically, we identify a Kantian debt in Bergson's identification of the illusions and dangers internal to reason that solicit and combine with emotion.

Bergson's *Two Sources* opens with a sustained engagement with Kant, one that provides us an opportune sketch of the principal line of argument in the book as a whole. Throughout his practical writings, Kant isolates a particular group of emotions he calls rational emotions. These are special for Kant because they arise spontaneously from the performance of our duty. Feelings of humiliation, sublimity, respect, and awe are our characteristic experiences of a moral law that subordinates our sensuous nature without any incentive outside of reason (see Saurette 2005). Bergson (1977) begins his critique by charging Kant with a 'psychological error': Kant can attribute such a stern inflexible aspect to moral obligation because he assumes that those exceptional moments of struggle with our desires are our ordinary experience of it (20). The trouble for Bergson is that this approach traces the transcendental nature of obligation from occasional empirical experiences of it. As such, it explains neither the origin nor the essential nature of obligation.

What then is the nature of obligation? Bergson's (1977) rule of thumb is to approach any faculty – moral, cognitive, or pragmatic – by asking how it helps the creature endowed with it to survive and flourish. In a word, the function of obligation is to integrate the individual into the social group and thereby ensure its health and cohesion. It is crucial to notice that, unlike Kant, Bergson does not confine obligation to human life insofar as 'it ranks among the most general phenomena of life' (29). And so, it is with keen irony that Bergson imagines the following situation: 'If we want a pure case of the categorical imperative, we must construct one *a priori* . . . Let us imagine an ant who is stirred by a gleam of reflection and thereupon judges she has been wrong to work unremittingly for others. Her inclination [*velléités*] to laziness would indeed endure but a few moments, just as long as the ray of intelligence. In the last of these moments, when instinct regaining the mastery would drag her back by sheer force to her task, intelligence at the point of relapsing into instinct would say, as its parting word [*en guise d'adieu*]: "You must because you must"' (25).

We see three significant reversals of Kant. First, where reason commands duty for Kant, here intelligence is the condition for asocial behaviour. It is when the ant reflects, and only as long as that reflection endures, that it questions the need of its attachment and duty to the group. Second, instinct drags the individual back to his/her social duty. Against Kant, for whom sensuous and instinctive nature is self-regarding, for Bergson it is instinct that reasserts itself over and against the temporary egoism intelligence counselled. Third, intelligence supplements or backs up instinct. Intelligence plays on both teams, as it were: it is the cause for the initial crisis of individualism, but then, once the individual is reintegrated into the group, it contributes a discursive and categorical command which effectively doubles the force of instinct. With this, Bergson effectively reverses the priority Kant gives to reason by according to the intellect a secondary role in enacting obligation.

Of course, ants are one thing and humans another. But Bergson's point is that both actualize obligation according to their specific makeup. The social structure of insects such as bees and ants is given directly by their instinctive constitution. Here, the pressure obligation exerts is instinctive. As Bergson (1977) claims, social life is immanent in instinct (27). Now consider human beings. Obligation in humans responds to the same problem as in ants: how to integrate the individual into the group. But given that we are endowed with intelligence, obligation takes a unique form. At once a general phenomenon of life, it is differently actualized according to the specific being in question. Borrowing a beautiful phrase from *Creative Evolution*, obligation in insects and humans 'represent[s] two divergent but equally elegant solutions to one and the same problem' (Bergson 1998:143, translation modified).

What form does obligation take in humans? Bergson's (1977) reply is decisive: habits. According to Bergson our social lives consist of a series of interlocking obligations to different groups; for example, family, profession, church, state, and so on. These obligations are made concrete and quotidian by their embodiment in habits. Actualized by habits, obligation is less a force that bears down upon us than it is the weave or texture of life: 'When it has become fully concrete, [obligation] coincides with a tendency, so habitual that we find it natural, to play in society the part which our station assigns to us. So long as we yield to this tendency, we scarcely feel it. It assumes an imperative [*impérieuse*] aspect, like all deep-seated habits, only if we depart from it' (19, emphasis added, translation modified).

A series of remarks on this passage will bring us directly to religion. First, when Bergson (1977) observes that habits are as if natural, he is being deceptively literal. It is not just that effective habits resemble instinct in their unthought performance. Bergson's claim is stronger. Habit is the form instinct assumes in beings endowed with variability and intelligence (28). Habit accomplishes the work of instinct in the animal kingdom: it actualizes obligation and assures group solidarity. Habit and instinct, therefore, are varieties of obligation that establish continuity and difference between human and animal societies.

Second, whereas animal instincts are fixed (thus the societies they generate are predetermined), habits are radically contingent. So too, therefore, are human societies. As one interpreter puts it, 'Bergson by no means affirms that social and political forms of organization are biologically determined or determinable' (Marrati 2006:595). The only necessity Bergson (1977) insists upon is the habit of contracting habits (26). No human society could exist without them, for it would forfeit moral obligation as such. With this, Bergson establishes the limits of unsociability. Intelligence may counsel egoism and break any particular habit or obligation, but it is inconceivable for intelligence to challenge habit as such. Like Kant who denies that humans are diabolically evil and can contradict the form of the moral law, Bergson insists that even if intelligence denies any specific obligation, it is impossible for intelligence to challenge the form of obligation. Third, obligation and duty are fundamentally passive for Bergson. To be moral, all we must do is ease ourselves into the grooves of habit that society has worn for us. Indeed, according to Bergson, it takes much more effort and activity to resist habit and morality than to submit to them. Inverting Kant, we might say that for Bergson humans are ineradicably good, a fact that testifies not to their rectitude but to their indolence.

Let us summarize the foregoing. The origin of obligation is not reason but biology. Obligation, in both animals and humans, responds to the vital need to integrate the individual into the group. Humans stand out because they are endowed with intelligence. This endowment poses unique risks: intelligence threatens the social order by dissolving bonds of duty. Habits may mitigate this threat by serving as a proxy for instinct; nevertheless, it is a standing possibility that intelligent beings break obligations as it suits them. It is at this juncture that Bergson introduces religion. In a word, religion is a quasi-instinctive function that protects human beings from their own intellect. Bergson (1977) begins his analysis of religion on a decidedly Kantian note: 'The spectacle of what religions have been in the past, of what certain religions still are today, is indeed humiliating for human intelligence . . . But there is nothing for it, facts must be faced. *Homo Sapiens*, the only creature endowed with reason, is also the only creature to pin its existence to things unreasonable' (102).

In addition to the experience of humiliation, a decidedly Kantian emotion, Bergson agrees that the very condition for superstition and error is the existence of a rational being. That animals are not superstitious is a fact that marks humans out as the irrational (not the arational) animal. The problem for Bergson (1977), therefore, becomes to explain 'how beliefs and practices which are anything but reasonable could have been, and still are, accepted by reasonable beings (103). A further point of agreement between Bergson and Kant is their vision of religion (and religious error) as a 'general structure of human thought,' one that they refuse to confine to a distant or primitive past (104). Writing against Lucien Lévy-Bruhl, who postulated a difference in kind between primitive and Western minds (1923), Bergson insists that if we look inward – especially in moments of shock or distress – we may recover insight into original and enduring superstitions that accompany intelligence as such.

But now we come to a decisive difference. For Kant, reason must criticize or check its own overextension, one that illumination and passivity encourage. Reason is the critical limit. By contrast, for Bergson superstition itself is the salutary check that mitigates the dangers of the intellect. Superstition, therefore, is the critical limit. Such is Bergson's surprising conclusion we must reconstruct. A good place to start is to list the dangers posed by the intellect: (1) it counsels egoism (it is dissolvent); (2) it knows we will die (it is demoralizing); and (3) it only imperfectly predicts the future (it is anxious). Two Ds can summarize these dangers: the intellect is at once a *dissolvent* and *demoralizing* faculty (Bergson 1977:205). And so, if intelligent beings are to thrive, life must provide a solution for the specific problems intelligence poses:

> If intelligence threatens to breakup [*romper*] social cohesion at certain points – and if society must carry on – *there must be a counterbalance, at these points, to intelligence.* If this counterbalance cannot be instinct itself, for the very reason that its place has been taken by intelligence, the same effect must be produced by *a virtual instinct* . . . [This virtual instinct] cannot act directly, but, since intelligence works on representations, it will call up 'imaginary' ones, which will hold their own against the representation of reality and will succeed, through the agency of intelligence itself, in counteracting the work of intelligence. This would be the explanation of the *myth-making function* [*la fonction fabulatrice*]. (1977:119, emphasis added, translation modified)

The myth-making function – what Bergson calls fabulation – is the heart of religion. Its purpose is to provide representations that check those tendencies of the intellect that are pernicious to action and survival. As one interpreter puts it, 'Fabulation is an action of the intelligence, yet its basic function is to counteract tendencies that are inherent in intelligence itself' (Bogue 2006:204). Bergson (1977) is subtle in his description of fabulation; it is, as it were, an intellectual or *virtual instinct*. At once instinctive and intellectual, the essence of fabulation is to create representations (fictions, myth, narratives, hallucinations, etc.) able to 'thwart [*contrecarrer*] our judgment and reason' (109; see also Lapoujade 2005).[6]

To conclude this section, we sketch three dangers posed by the intellect along with the myth or representation fabulation invents to foil them. We also identify emotions either created or reinforced by religion.

Because for Bergson religion is a feature of the mind as such, these emotions are characteristic of human existence in all times and places. In short, religion engenders vast regions of our emotional life.

Egoism

For Bergson (1977), it is intelligence and not instinct that is pathological because: '[intelligence] would counsel egoism first' and overrides the instinct that privileges the group (122). To counter egoism, our myth-making faculty produces an illusory perception or recollection: 'Just now, before the open gate a guardian appeared, to bar the way and drive back the trespasser. So now some protective deity of the city will be there to forbid, threaten, and punish' (122). Religion, therefore, doubles social obligation with a divine power that prohibits, judges, and punishes conduct. In this role, fabulation intensifies those emotions that provide for the durability of the group such as duty, loyalty, compulsion, fear, guilt, sanctimoniousness, and so on. Once religion posits a watchful deity, a whole spectrum of human feeling is entrenched and intensified.

Death

Humans know we will die because we alone have an intellect that enables us to reflect on the death of others and to generalize it to our own case. For Bergson (1977), such knowledge is an obstacle to survival. It is demoralizing and paralyzes action; nothing is more useless to an animal than the awareness it will die (130). Once again, fabulation comes to the rescue: 'To the idea of an inevitable death [nature] opposes the image of a continuation of life after death; this image, flung by her into the field of intelligence, where the idea of death has just become installed, straightens everything out again. This neutralizing of the idea by the image simply expresses the equilibrium of nature, saving herself from slipping' (131). Religion, therefore, furnishes a defensive reaction against the intelligence. And with the notion of an afterlife comes feelings of assurance, calm, hope, fear, zeal, uncertainty, doubt, and disbelief. These are specific and direct contributions of religion to our psychic life.

Uncertainty

Perhaps the main gift of the intellect is that it allows us to anticipate the future. But by the same predictive capacity that allows insight into the future, we are made aware of how uncertain it is. This is an acute case of the more you learn the less you know: 'There can be no reflection without foreknowledge, no foreknowledge without inquietude, no inquietude without a momentary slackening of the attachment to life' (Bergson 1977:210). Whereas knowledge of death is certain, knowledge of the future is uncertain. And yet, both grip us with anxiety and discourage action. Here, fabulation steps in to imagine a supersensible or tutelary causality (call it theism) that guides our actions and watches over the future: 'A representation will accordingly arise, that of favorable powers overriding or occupying the place of the natural causes' (140). In this case, it is less that religion comes to check intelligence, and more that it allows us to be in the world with intelligence. It relieves us of paralyzing incertitude and replaces it with confidence, gratitude, and peace.

Bergson and Dynamic Religion: Love

We have just claimed that fabulation creates emotions that define the human. But while fabulation produces emotions, Bergson reserves the name of 'dynamic religion' to a phenomenon that *is* emotion. This emotion – and so too this religion – is love. Of course, to equate religion with love ties Bergson to a Christian identification (see Marion 2007:221–2). But to appreciate Bergson's (1977) interpretation of thisidentification, it is perhaps best to begin with the famous (and famously difficult) concluding lines of *Two Sources*: 'Whether we choose small measures or great, a decision is forced upon us. Humanity lies groaning, half crushed beneath the weight of its own progress. Men do not sufficiently realize that their future is in their own hands. Theirs is the task of determining first of all whether they want to go on living or not. Theirs the responsibility, then, for deciding if they want merely to live, or intend to make just the extra effort required for fulfilling, even on their refractory planet, the essential function of the universe, which is a machine for the making of gods' (317, translation modified).

We can work backwards. It would be accurate to say that fabulation is a machine for the making of gods: its purpose is to create precisely those representations that thwart the intellect. But Bergson's sense in this passage is very different. The gods he is talking about are *us*, that is, human beings. This astonishing claim is bound up with Bergson's (1977) cosmology and philosophy of time and evolution. We will try to put it as simply as we can. The essence of life for Bergson is creativity. As we have seen in our discussion of obligation in insects and humans, different species represent nothing other than creative solutions to problems posed by survival. But while the coming into being of each species marks a creative effort or act, it is also a relative stop or immobilization of evolution. The activity of each new species runs 'indefinitely in the same circle' (209). Ants will be ants. Humanity, however, is different; it is not stuck in the same rut or loop by necessity. Borrowing an apt expression from Deleuze (1986), humans alone are able to undergo a 'conversion' and apprehend creativity and the production of the new (7; see also Lefebvre 2008:89–90). Or, in other words, humans alone are capable of thought, experience of time (or duration), and evolution (life in time).

But we are capable of more. It is possible for us to not only apprehend and adequately think time and life, but also to extend and renew the creative activity of life itself. This is dynamic religion. It does not represent the whole in ways that comfort us (as does the 'static' religion of the preceding section), nor is it satisfied to adequately contemplate the whole (as does philosophy); rather, dynamic religion makes of life what it should have been had it not been burdened by the species that immobilizes it: an open and creative whole. Bergson (1977) thereby inverts the doctrine of grace: rather than receive God's succour and favour, human beings unblock divine creativity. We have the potential to become '*adjutores Dei,*' helpers of God: 'God needs us, just as we need God' (232, 255). The concluding lines to the *Two Sources*, however, tell us that our divine vocation remains a potential, and not a necessary capacity. As with Kant, who firmly grounds the distinction between good and evil in human choice, here too Bergson anchors his text in decision and responsibility. To turn to a Kantian phrase, we must make ourselves worthy of our creative privilege through an extra effort.[7] Only then will we be 'capable of loving and making [ourselves] loved' (255).

We arrive at love. As we have said, it is not merely an emotion associated with dynamic religion; rather, it is the entire content of it. Where there is love, there is religion. The challenge becomes, of course, to specify what Bergson means. Seeing how tempting it is to speak abstractly about love, our procedure errs on the hardhearted side. We identify six criteria that make up Bergson's understanding of it. It is important, however, to note that Bergson does not claim his writings on love to be original. He takes himself to report the mystical tradition: 'God is love, and the object of love: herein lies the whole contribution of mysticism' (1977:252). The value of mysticism for Bergson is that it experiences and enacts this association of love with God (see Cariou 1976). To see what is enacted, we turn to our criteria.

Objectless

As with Christianity, divine love is not partial or preferential. It does not attach to the beloved. Indeed, divine or mystic love outstrips even the Christian injunction to love thy neighbor. It would not be misleading to associate it with what Romain Rolland called the oceanic feeling: 'The sentiment of being present here and now in a world that is itself intensely existing . . . of essential co-belonging between myself and the ambient universe' (Hadot 2009:8). Bergson (1977) is strict that mystical love does not depend on content; it certainly extends to humans, animals, and all of nature, but 'not one of these things which would thus fill it would suffice to define the attitude taken by the soul, for it could, strictly speaking, do without all of them' (38). As the essence of life is not an object or species but a tendency towards creativity, the essence of love is not of a thing or even humanity. It is incorporation and participation in the vital creativity of life (see Ansell-Pearson and Mullarkey 2002:37).

Embodiment

While love exceeds attachment to any particular thing, Bergson insists that it is always embodied in specific individuals, that is, mystics. As Bergson (1977) puts it in Christian phraseology, 'In all times there have arisen exceptional [individuals], *incarnating* this morality' (34, emphasis added). Love, therefore, has a complex relationship to embodiment. On the one hand, it is incarnated, literally made into flesh, by singular individuals. The lover is always of flesh. On the other hand, love is of the vital or creative tendency within any of its corporeal actualizations. Love is not of the flesh. But we must be careful not to conflate Bergson with Platonic or Christian metaphysics: love is not of the beyond but of this world. As Deleuze (1989) might put it, dynamic religion is 'belief in this world;' it is conviction in and affirmation of the openness of every existent as of the whole (172).

Call

'If a word of a great mystic . . . finds an echo in one or another of us, may it not be that there is a *mystic dormant within us*, merely waiting for an occasion to awake?' (Bergson 1977:100, emphasis added). The word Bergson repeatedly uses to characterize the relationship to a mystic is *appel*, which in French means both appeal and call (34, 84, 100, passim). And, as he puts it in another context, 'it is to these [mystics] that men have always *turned* for that complete morality' (34, emphasis added). This language is obviously theologically loaded: our relation to the mystic is one of conversion (i.e., to turn) and of a calling. But we must be attuned to what is being called: to follow a mystic is not to reproduce his example, but is instead the means to access one's own love and joy. In another context, Ralph Waldo Emerson ([1849] 2000) will say that the value of another great individual is utterly and only to discover one's own genius (132–3). Relationship to a mystic, whether lived or indirect, is at once impersonal and intimate: on the one hand, the mystic is merely an occasion to discover one's own singular capacity; but on the other hand, an encounter with a mystic redirects our love to a tendency everywhere present but exemplified by the mystic, with whom we share special fellowship.

Attraction

Bergson (1977) is fond of calling the mystic a new species: 'The appearance of each one of them was like the creation of a new species, composed of one single individual [*d'un individu unique*], the *élan vital* culminating at long intervals in one particular [individual] (95, translation modified). No doubt, Bergson intends an irony: the most germinal individuals are evolutionary dead ends, a species of one unable to procreate.[8] It is not that mystics constitute a unique species (which could breed); rather, each mystic is him/herself a species. How then do they reproduce? Bergson's answer is that mystics exert attraction over us, an 'irresistible attraction' in fact (96). And so here, as in his concept of the call, Bergson at once preserves and modifies the ordinary criteria of love: attraction and procreation. With the call, we attach ourselves to the mystic only to discover ourselves. With attraction, we fall for the mystic's irresistible example, and, in so doing, we are reborn.

Transformation

That love knows no bounds may be a platitude. But in Bergson's (1977) hands it becomes a transcendental and cosmological proposition: '[Love] is the *élan vital* itself, communicated whole [*communiqué intégralement*] to exceptional men who . . . by a living contradiction [*contradiction realisée*] change into a creative effort that created thing which is a species, and turn into a movement what was, by definition, a stop' (235, translation modified). Love knows no bounds; it is without obstacles. It can accomplish – with an ease unthinkable to anyone out of love – anything. So too for Bergson. Mystic love accomplishes nothing short of a transfiguration of the human species. Or, in other words, that human beings are a stop of evolution is not a problem for mystics. In fact, the entire purpose of mysticism is to transform the human species such that it becomes adequate to the thought, experience, and activity of duration. For the moment, this must appear abstract. But we will develop this further in the conclusion to the chapter when we examine two ways that the mystic transfigures humanity: by checking our war-instinct and by overcoming our intellectual denial of duration.

Divine

A profoundly Spinozist dimension of Bergson's writing is that we experience divine joy and love. Whereas Spinoza argues that our joy in adequate ideas is equal to God's joy, and that we 'feel and experience [*sentimus experimurque*] that we are eternal,' Bergson claims '[that] by going deeply into [mystic love], we should find a feeling [*un sentiment*] of coincidence, real or imaginary, with the generative effort of life (Spinoza 2002:374; Bergson 1977:54, translation modified). When Bergson asserts that we have experience of God's love, he does not mean it in the received sense. It is not that we experience God's love for us (his favour or grace), but rather, by renewing the creative impulse of life, we participate in divine joy and affirmation. If, as Bergson says, the universe is a machine for the making of gods, then divine love is our own.

Although these six criteria barely scratch the surface of Bergson's treatment of love – much less of mysticism and dynamic religion – we have tried to show how he both preserves and transforms its ordinary meaning. Love is objectless but attaches to the living world; love is embodied but outstrips corporeality; love is an intimacy by which we rediscover ourselves; love is attraction to a being too singular to join; love completes the human by transfiguring the species; and love is divine in that we love as gods. The title of our chapter – 'Religion with the Bounds of Emotion Alone' – is intended, of course, to contrast Kant with Bergson. We have seen that for Kant, rational religion checks our propensity to extend reason beyond what we can know and to elicit passions all too ready to combine with it. Our discussion of Bergson was split according to the division Bergson establishes between static and dynamic religion. Static religion is defined by a myth-making instinct that limits the dangers to which humans are exposed by virtue of their intellect. Dynamic religion is defined by mystic love. What binds Kant and Bergson is an acute sensitivity to the illusions and dangers brought on by reason. Furthermore, they reject any straightforward opposition between reason and emotion, and instead explore their mutual intensification and coupling. Last, both are committed to a critical philosophy of religion that assigns to each faculty its place and limit so that life may be peaceable if not happy. But, among their many differences, we have isolated one: Kant and Bergson do not agree on which faculty is in charge. For Kant, it is reason that checks emotion. For Bergson, whether in static or dynamic religion, the intellect must be limited so that humans may thrive, either by superstition (static) or love (dynamic).

To conclude, we sketch two instances in which Bergson urges love to adopt a critical role to keep the intellect within its proper limits. Or, put negatively, we examine the cost of two denials of love by the intellect, one that separates us from God and the other that separates us from one another. Throughout his writings, Bergson attends to the intellect's denial of time and duration. Intelligence, like all our faculties, is a product of evolution. Its principal function is to predict the future; as such, it conceives of time as an external frame in which events occur and can be calculated (Bergson 1998:ix–x). All of this is pragmatically necessary. But Bergson's point is that the intellect negates duration; it denies creativity and unpredictability to time. In the context of his earlier writings, the denial of duration falsifies psychical experience (*Time and Free Will* [2001]) and evolution (*Creative Evolution*). In *Two Sources*, however, the denial of time is, strictly speaking, a (intellectual, experiential, and practical) denial of God. To adapt Spinoza's formula, *Deus sive Tempus*: God *or* time, substance *or* temporality. Or, as Deleuze (2004) remarks, God is a movement and not a being (185). It seems safe, therefore, to claim Bergson's *Two Sources* as a critical work: it delimits the proper place for the intellect as pragmatic action, and it elaborates the costs of its overextension. This cost is separation from the substantiality of time, hence from substance itself. What, then, checks the intellect? Bergson's response is intuition, '[it] is what attains spirit, duration, pure change' ([1938]1974:33, translation modified). Although we cannot elaborate this difficult concept nor trace its history, we claim that *Two Sources* advances a major reinterpretation of intuition. Love in *Two Sources* represents Bergson's final development of intuition: 'Intuition was turned inward; and if, in a first intensification, beyond which most of us did not go, it made us realize the continuity of our inner life, a deeper intensification might carry it to the roots of our being, and thus to the very principle of life in general. Now is this not precisely the privilege of the mystic soul?' ([1932]1977:250). Mystic love, therefore, has both a negative and positive function. On the one hand, it checks the denial of time by the intellect, and, on the other hand, it opens access to the real, whether that is called life, time, or God.

Despite the importance of the intellect's denial of time, Bergson is occupied with a more pressing problem: war.[9] To summarize his discussion of the 'closed society' in *Two Sources*, Bergson ([1932]1977) claims that human beings instinctively form determinate and exclusive communities (whether families, tribes, societies, etc.). Love in closed societies, therefore, is altogether different from mystical love: it involves choice and exclusion and does not exclude hatred (39). As Bergson puts it, 'the two opposing maxims, *Homo homini deus* and *Homo homini lupus* are easily reconcilable. When we formulate the first, we are thinking of some fellow countryman. The other applies to foreigners' (39). The intellect, however, loses sight of the difference in kind between the two loves. All it sees is that love appears to expand indefinitely: from love of family to love of nation, to, so it concludes, love of humanity. 'It will see in these three inclinations one single feeling, growing ever larger, to embrace an increasing number of persons' (38). For Bergson, this is an illusion; it falsely groups together irreducible kinds of love. Closed love cannot indefinitely expand; its very condition is the maintenance of a determinate group through exclusion. From the perspective of closed love, we catch a 'sudden chill at the idea that [we are] working "for mankind." The object is too vast, the effect too diffuse' (36). The consequences of this intellectualist illusion are disastrous. Writing at the same time as Carl Schmitt, Bergson too anticipated that human rights are effective only within a determinate community willing to back them.[10] The error of the intellect is to believe that love and protection of the human can grow from closed societies. It is against this danger that mystical love takes on urgent political import. On the one hand, clear presentation of its nature will distinguish it from closed love and avoid intellectualist confusion of the two. And, on the other hand, objectless and affirmative mystical love may work to circumvent our instinct towards exclusion and war. The tendency towards closure may be 'ineradicable [*indéracinables*]' as Bergson says, but, like Kant, he holds hope that we may always choose against it (288).

NOTES

1 This chapter is dedicated to Beatrice, who did not exactly help but definitely made everything more fun.
2 For a useful study of Kant and emotion, specifically his concern with the similarities between extravagant reason and the passions as a pathology of will, see Caygill (2006). And for a sociological discussion of Bergson's attempt to upset the conventional opposition between reason and emotion, see Game's (1997) use of Bergson's creative emotion to contribute to a 'passionate sociology' that cultivates wonder, love, and joy in knowledge practices (398). See also Power's (2003) discussion of creative emotion as a qualitative multiplicity that affirms new ways of living and being together in freedom (70).
3 The delicate distinctions between emotion, affect, passion, and enthusiasm in Kant are complicated by issues of translation. For example, affect [*Affekt*] is often indiscriminately rendered as passion, emotion, and affection (for a discussion, see Caygill 1995:56–9, 313–14). Schematically put, we use passion to designate an emotion that has become pathological and potentially destructive in its disfigurement by the overextension of reason. This usage is particular to Kant. For an interesting discussion of the emergence of the concept of emotion as a secularization of passion and affect, see Dixon (2003).
4 For a discussion of Kant's positive appreciation of enthusiasm and *Schwärmerei*, which appears mostly in *Critique of Judgment* and *Conflict of the Faculties*, see Gailus (2006:28–73) and Lyotard (2009).
5 Better put, it does not arise in this way. In theoretical reason, dialectical illusions arise when we leave the limits of possible experience. In pure practical reason, delusions arise when we substitute sensible examples for the ideas they are intended to represent.
6 In our usage, affect is a higher order term that includes dispositions such as laziness, passivity, and indolence, which are not adequately termed 'emotions.'
7 Bergson provides a vivid example of fabulation in recounting William James' reaction to the San Francisco earthquake of 1906. James' immediate impulse was to characterize the earthquake as an intentional, personal, and irascible force. Bergson (1977) comments: 'Intelligence, impelled by instinct, transform[s] the situation [and] evokes the reassuring image [i.e., of an intentional rather than mechanical force]. It lends to the Event a unity and an individuality which make of it a mischievous, maybe a malignant, being, but still one of ourselves, with something sociable and human about it' (158). This picture indeed thwarts judgment and reason, but it does so in the service of a rational end: to overcome fear and paralysis.
8 See also Deleuze (1990), who speaks of the need to make ourselves worthy of the event (149).

9 Indeed, Bergson (1977) verges on the sardonic inasmuch as he qualifies his age as one of overpopulation and hedonism ('Sex-appeal is the keynote of our whole civilization' [302; see also Lawlor 2003:91–7]).

10 Although Bergson's argument addresses the transcendental conditions for war in instinct and intelligence, we should not lose sight of the fact that *Two Sources* was written in the early 1930s. Furthermore, we should not forget Bergson's active participation in international politics and the establishment of the League of Nations (see Soulez 1989).

11 See Lefebvre (2011, 2012) for an exploration of Bergson's argument for theorizing human rights.

7 Humanitarianism as a Politics of Emotion

LAURA SUSKI

Introduction

When we witness human suffering and pain, emotions like compassion, pity, anger, and sadness can be evoked. Early philosophers of morality, most notably Adam Smith, saw the potential of what Nancy Sherman (1998) labels 'imaginative transport'; they note how the act of imagining another's experience of suffering can inspire moral action to respond to that suffering. Belief in the power of emotion to move us speaks to the etymological source of 'emotion' in the concept of movement. Emotion can stir or agitate us. We can be 'moved' to tears when we view human suffering. Emotional moments are powerful because they destabilize the very terrain on which emotions are felt. The ability of emotions to move us also suggests a kind of vulnerability to the emotional moment as we are being put in motion by the force of a feeling that may be out of our own control.

Eighteenth-century thinkers such as Adam Smith pointed to the ability of sympathy to function as a humanitarian emotion and compel action in the name of suffering. However, cultural historian Thomas Laqueur (2009) notes that a feeling of sympathy for the suffering of others produces a 'strange moral geography' (33) in which sentiments for humanity can equally produce indifference as they can relief, and, thus, the sentiments themselves carry no 'moral gyroscopes' (35) that lead the 'feeler' in one direction and not another. Sympathy has become quite suspect in the contemporary political landscape. Sympathy is often conceived of as capable of building an ethical connection, while at the same time maintaining a relationship of power that prevents a 'real' social connection between humanitarian and sufferer. 'Bleeding hearts' may be meaningful to those who experience them, but they do not inherently bring justice to those who suffer exploitation.

As Brown and Wilson (2009) note, the politicization of humanitarian sentiments lies most centrally in questions of mobilization. How, when, and why do emotions *move* us to ethical action? Inspired by these larger questions, this chapter aims to analyse the emotional models we might use to elaborate this mobilization process. My goal is to problematize the way in which emotions like sympathy and empathy are often conceived as *fuels* or *triggers* for humanitarian action. I argue that this 'trigger model' of political action privileges certain emotions over others, and can lead us to position the emotional as existing prior to the political. When emotion is positioned as a trigger, its political character is defined solely by its ability to elicit political action.

The chapter begins with a brief intellectual history of the concept of humanitarianism. I respond to the historical emphasis on sympathy as a particularly humanitarian emotion. The contemporary critiques of the apparent limitations of the sympathetic encounter have led to an embracing of empathy as an emotion more likely to elicit solidarity. In such a reading, empathy is positioned as the best emotion for a humanitarian project since it purportedly can offer a 'real' identification with the humanitarian victim. But how is it that empathy can configure a radically different social connection than emotions such as anger or sadness? The second half of the chapter attempts to answer this question. I use Ahmed's ontology of emotion as a framework for understanding the nature of emotional attachment. Ahmed (2004) argues against both an 'inside-out' model of emotions that sees emotions as moving from within a self outward, and an 'outside-in' model that sees emotions as cultural practices that come from outside the self and then move inward. She sees emotions as neither in the individual nor in the social, and instead as producing 'the very surfaces and boundaries that allow the individual and the social to be delineated as if they were objects' (10). By exploring an alternate model of emotional connection, I hope to offer some insight into the complex, and often imperfect, space of the humanitarian endeavour.

Humanitarian Emotions

As a political, social, and philosophical idea, humanitarianism is a rather vague concept. It is loosely associated with charity and philanthropy. It is popularly used to describe the actions of organizations, states, and individuals. When positioned as a broader social movement, humanitarianism can be described as a secularized or 'left over' religious response in the modern era, as a motivation borne out of the welfare state, or as part of a third sector or civil society. Humanitarianism applies to a spectrum of social actors ranging from those who donate to international charities, to those who intervene on the part of states to end human rights abuses, and even sometimes to those who show humane feelings towards animals. The concept of humanitarianism appears in only a few dictionaries of philosophy and political thought. In these rather few entries, it is defined by its central focus on 'the centrality of human values,' and by its 'emotional dedication to social reforms' (Dunner 1964:245).[1]

Humanitarian organizations and institutions began to flourish in thepost-Second World War era. These organizations continue to have a rather ambiguous relationship to the political, and, similarly, to the emotional. An organization such as the International Committee of the Red Cross emerged specifically as a politically neutral organization able to offer aid during times of war. The field of international humanitarianism became more professionalized and more institutionalized since the end of the Cold War. In turn, the purpose of humanitarianism has become more politicized. Older agendas to provide relief have been replaced by more overtly political agendas to eliminate the roots of conflict (Barnett 2005). Now the defence of human rights is the more likely humanitarian mantra, and vague obligations of charity and stewardship have been discarded by more radicalized international organizations. However, while the intellectual histories of humanitarianism and human rights overlap, particularly in the contemporary space of international humanitarianism, they also have quite distinct histories that require some 'careful disentanglement' (Wilson and Brown 2009:5).

The emergence of humanitarian movements requires a belief in the possibility of human agency to end suffering, however distant that suffering may be. Laqueur locates this shift in eighteenth-century fiction such as realist novels, and in medical writing such as autopsies and clinical reports. For Laqueur (1989), the new and key element of this body of writing was that it detailed human suffering and exposed lines of 'causality' between readers and those suffering, in turn presenting a moral imperative, although often selectively applied, for social action: 'Someone or something did something that caused pain, suffering or death and that could, under certain circumstances, have been avoided or mitigated' (178). By presenting a script of causation alongside 'habits of feeling,' the alleviation, reduction, and ultimately prevention of suffering becomes possible, and humanitarians become the agents in the process.

Humanitarianism's emergence in the eighteenth century can also been traced to the development of moral philosophy and sentimental literature of the period. In these historical discourses, and indeed in many contemporary social and political discourses, humanitarian sentiments are largely associated with the most 'mobile,' 'active,' and 'social' of sentiments – the moral emotions. Published before his famous *Wealth of Nations*, Adam Smith's *Theory of Moral Sentiments* tries to come to terms with how benevolence could be compatible with market structures run by an economy of self-interest. For Smith (1984), sympathy works by allowing a spectator to imagine himself in the position of others. In doing so, the individual need not be part of the sufferer's community in order to act on his/her behalf. 'In the breast of every attentive spectator,' writes Smith, 'an analogous emotion springs up' at the thought of the situation of others (10). Hume (1949) also argued that morality had a source in the passions. This relationship is stated strongly in Book II of his *Treatise on Human Nature*: 'Reason is, and ought only to be the slave of the passions, and can never pretend any other office than to serve and obey them' (415).

In the early discourse of sentimentalism, the objects of sympathy are rather predictable groups of 'unfortunates': the poor, the imprisoned, and the enslaved. The expression of humanitarian sentiment in the eighteenth century seems to rely on the existence of race, class, and gender differences. It is a state of social inequality that appears topermit a humanitarian expression of sympathy. As John Mullan (1988) reminds us, the instinct to benevolence in the sentimental novel was being celebrated as a 'rare and delicious moment' and not as a 'universal phenomenon' to elicit social reform (146). Nonetheless, the new way in which the sentiment of compassion was being described, and the way in which pain was considered remediable by human efforts, set in motion the development of 'public compassion.' In distinction to earlier forms of charity and later forms of the welfare state, explains Sznaider (1998), the public compassion that would come to characterize movements like the abolition of slavery 'de-legitimized earlier values and practices' as 'morally reprehensible' and 'cruel' (120). Still, the expression of humanitarian sentiment is selective. While the eighteenth-century sentimentalists embraced the passions and shed tears for the poor, that form of sensibility could easily coexist alongside larger forms of social cruelty (Todd 1986:132). Mee (2000) notes that sad, sentimental stories of the eighteenth century spoke of real social concerns such as child labour, but they often merely offered the opportunity for polite readers to 'exercise their sensibility' (404). However, some work, like William Blake's late-eighteenth-century *Songs of Innocence* and *Songs of Experience*, demonstrated a keen awareness of the fact that pity could be empty and shallow if it did not incite active sympathy. Thus, while sentimental literature can be characterized by its indulgence of emotion, this characterization did not preclude attention to the analysis of a more active human sympathy.

Some scholars note a heightened sense of ambivalence in the sentimental literature of the period. Audrey Jaffe's (2000) work on sympathy gives a particularity to the way in which sympathy is intricately aligned with middle-class identity. She argues that many of the visualized narratives of the Victorian novel serve to create 'primal scenes' where the middle class is precariously poised between 'dread' and 'fantasy.' For Jaffe, 'the objects of Victorian sympathy are inseparable from Victorian middle-class self-representation precisely because they embody, to a middle-class spectator, his/her own potential narrative of social decline' (9). The core of the sensibility that informs 'vicarious suffering,' notes Julie Ellison (1999), is 'alienated and guilty from the start' (122). In reference to colonial history, she argues that the 'real politics of colonialism' exhibits a powerfully ambivalent wish: that it was 'actually possible to conquer and to spare' (147). Kennedy's (2004) more recent work on international humanitarianism entitled *The Dark Sides of Virtue* uses a similar vocabulary to describe the possibilities of a new humanitarianism. Imagine a humanitarianism, he asks, that 'exercised power not as humanitarian knowledge imprinting itself on the real, but with all the ambivalence and ignorance and uncertainty we know as the human' (354).

Humanitarian emotions, however, also work to 'constitute some others as legitimate objects of emotion' (Ahmed 2004:191). The power of any humanitarian appeal relies on some assessment of how important or worthy we deem the suffering of those who appeal for our help. Humanitarianism has strong narrative and representational dimensions. It compels action through the ways that social and political actors witness or read literal testimonies and visual images of human suffering (Brown and Wilson 2009). The abolition of British slavery is often cited as one of the first and most important international humanitarian movements because it required political action to end a form of suffering that was distant and out of view. The suffering of slaves, however, is constructed and reconstructed in different historical and social contexts. In reference to the American abolition of slavery, Kellow (2009) notes how antislavery arguments came in many competing forms. The aftermath of independence saw some Americans confronting the conflict between slavery and values of American freedom. Some Americans upheld the property rights of slaveholders arguing for the compensation to slave holders for the release of slaves, and others embraced a categorical rejection of slavery itself (133–4).

International humanitarianism has also garnered its own power as an 'ism': once a practice restricted to emergency assistance and merely palliative, it now has an expanding scope and scale such that it is a key player in 'helping to reproduce a geopolitical order' (Barnett 2005: 723–40). Many see international humanitarian intervention as the extension of the foreign policies of the Northern states. Examples such as the 2003 bombing of the Baghdad offices of the International Committee of the Red Cross suggest that many share this view. The line between politics and humanitarian relief has been severed. Latouche (1996) reads the proliferation of non-governmental and charitable organizations as obeying the same logic of colonial advance: 'world domination' (31). Suspicious of certain versions of Western humanism, Latouche wonders if the nostalgia for universals propels the West into 'innumerable snares of bogus universality' (122). The only 'true universality' denotes an 'authentic dialogue between cultures' (125).

Latouche's commentary reads humanitarianism as a form of social discipline. Like those who join Foucault in seeing the unfolding of modern society as the emergence of often more subtle and sophisticated forms of power, the emphasis of the analysis is on the conflict and social control that humanitarian narratives represent in modern society (Sznaider 1998). Emotions, too, are part of the practice of social regulation (see Hunt, this volume; Wouters 2007). Arlie Hochschild's important work in the sociology of emotion also shows that emotional labour requires a suppression and regulation of emotion, at great cost to the labourer (see Theodosius, this volume; Walby and Spencer, this volume). Similarly, Eva Illouz (2007) stresses the way in which emotional life is informed by economic regulations and exchange. Modern capitalism, she claims, means that the 'private' emotional lives of individuals are publically 'performed and harnessed' to the 'discourses and values of economic and political spheres' (4).

This conceptualization of the humanitarian as a social and political actor is affected by the way in which suffering itself is constructed. Morgan and Wilkinson (2001) argue that sociology as a 'moral science' still has difficulty with the meaning of suffering.[2] There remains an 'unresolved problem of theodicy' when 'suffering confronts the limits of rationality' and 'impresses upon us the need for other-worldly (magical, religious, ecstatic) meanings for experiences which cannot be explained pragmatically' (204). How can the idea of rationality and progress, ask Morgan and Wilkinson, be sustained against the historical record of the twentieth century? They argue that sociology can offer a 'sociodicy' for our times if it is able to study its pain. While articulating experiences of pain and 'thinking with suffering' is difficult, it is absolutely necessary to what they see as a project of exploring the 'decivilizing tensions within modernity' and breaking down the distance between 'rationally ordered structures of economic and social progress' and apparently irrational violence and suffering (Morgan and Wilkinson 2001:210).

Clearly, the shift to modernity is a critical part of the analysis of emotion and its regulation. We need to analyse our social relationship to the suffering of others by examining the movement away from traditional, community relationships towards de-personalized, industrial ones. Still, we should not assume that such a shift necessarily represents a reduction in an overall humanitarian 'other-orientation.' Some sociologists read this shift as positive because it ushers in a kind of morality which is better able to deal with difference and the forms ofsuffering that are not 'community' based. In Turner's (2002) model of 'cosmopolitan virtue,' for example, the contemporary moment of sociological inquiry is one of discomfort. Images of the modern intellectual as the 'revolutionary hero' who is 'passionately committed to social and political causes' are no longer appropriate to a 'fragmented and diverse global culture' (59).

One of the moral implications of 'feeling for' distant others in the contemporary space of the global continues to be the selective nature of the humanitarian emotions. Our reactions to global suffering must also be set in relation to the selective presentations of human suffering in both the popular media and international development campaigns (see Butt 2002; Lidchi 1999; Tester 2001). Even if driven by claims touniversal humanism, not every humanitarian impulse is acted upon. The humanitarian impulse seems to be strengthened when we encounter the testaments of individual suffering (Wilson and Brown 2009), but rarely so profoundly invoked by stories of large-scale suffering. Using the example of the Gulf War, Hendrickson (1999) speaks to this selectivity when he explains that 'something odd happens to the humanitarian sentiments' when they are delivered through military intervention:

'Intense moral concern over two-dozen Kuwaiti babies deprived of their incubators easily passes to moral indifference over a million Iraqi babies deprived of food and clean water' (234). The humanitarian impulse seems to continue to sit in a very tense position 'between the liberal ideal of universal sympathy and specificity of particular identifications' (Jaffe 2000:22). In turn, it sits in a very dynamic and often problematic relationship to the social. Our understanding of humanitarian sentiments relies heavily on how we map its transformation from an individualized emotion to a self-reflective or other-reflective emotion.

Configuring the Social

Contemporary philosophers such as Martha Nussbaum and Richard Rorty have argued for the potential usefulness of models of political emotions. Others, most notably Hannah Arendt, warned against emotional politics, in particular what Arendt called 'a politics of pity.' Current scholars, it seems, feel much more comfortable in a language of moral emotions that emphasizes the ethical importance of empathy. This shift, at its most basic level, suggests a shift from the sympathetic claim 'I recognize your pain' to the empathetic claim 'I feel your pain' (Wilson and Brown 2009:2). On these terms, empathy can offer a more politically comfortable vocabulary, as it becomes short form for a more egalitarian, more politicized, and, ultimately, more social identificatory emotional politics than sympathy and pity. The comfort with a politics of empathy parallels a new demand in humanitarian ethics to demonstrate solidarity with victims and to engage in the restoration of their dignity (Barnett 2005:733). Contemporary scholars in international development, for example, speak of a new model of post-development that is not driven by a charitable aim to end large-scale poverty, but rather embraces new forms of participatory, local, and sustainable development (Sachs 1992). Lilie Chouliaraki (2010) charts this shift by exploring how humanitarian communication has utilized different aesthetic models to engage emotional connectivity between humanitarian spectator and sufferer. Earlier models relied heavily on realist 'shock effects' in which guilt and shame became pivotal emotions. Later development campaigns relied more on positive images that attempted to restore dignity and agency to the sufferer. Despite the differences, Chouliaraki notes that both communication regimes have failed to 'sustain a legitimate claim for public action on suffering' (109). 'Shock effect' imagery of human suffering may be particularly problematic when it leads to compassion fatigue, or a feeling of powerlessness on the part of the spectator.

One of the many ways in which emotions are categorized is to draw a distinction between basic emotions such as joy, fear, or sadness, and self-conscious emotions such as guilt or embarrassment. Among the unique features of self-conscious emotions are that they require self-awareness, they facilitate the attainment of complex social goals, and they emerge later in childhood than basic emotions (Tracy and Robins 2007:6–7). Self-conscious emotions such as shame are moral emotions because they provide the 'motivational force' to do good or bad (Tagney, Stuewig, and Mashek 2007). Positioning an emotion like empathy as self-conscious offers some analytical use for drawing out some of the uniqueness of the moral emotions, and for exploring the different relationships between thinking and feeling. As Michael Lewis (2007) notes, feeling empathy means that we 'feel an emotion *and* we are aware that we are feeling this emotion' (36). It is because of this complex relationship between thinking and feeling that it is difficult to predict which social context or experience will elicit such emotions. The complexity of these 'self-conscious' aspects of emotions, however, is also linked to the complexity of the social connections of morality.

The shift from a sympathetic claim to recognize pain to the empathetic claim to feel pain is neither easy nor simple. In the case of empathy, we have often assumed a kind of equation between emotions and political actions by suggesting that empathy is inherently tied to a solidarity model of politics, and, similarly, sympathy to a pity politics. A politicized humanitarianism, however, must speak to the dynamic ways in which emotions are, to use Ahmed's language (2004; 2004a), about 'attachments' to people, places, signifiers, the individual, the social, the psychic, and the collective.

Even a socially powerful emotion such as empathy is not able to overcome the scenario of inequality that such an emotion confronts. Can any emotion felt by the humanitarian overcome the fundamental gap of alterity between those helping and those being helped? Some forms of pain cannot be shared empathetically (Ahmed 2004). Here, the connected histories of colonialism, imperialism, race, and gender inequality are lurking. According to Kozol (2008), we often distinguish the passive looking at violent spectacles, such as the everyday footage from Iraq, from conceptualizations of 'witnessing' human suffering. She argues that even the assumed 'ethical vision' of empathy must not 'ignore' its own 'political investments.' 'Human rights scholars and activists,' she asserts, 'need to recognize visual witnessing as enmeshed inthe historical problematics of neocolonial spectacles of power and dominance' (68).

Ahmed's reflection on economies of emotions is extremely useful here. By asserting that emotions are not a 'private matter' and that they do not 'come from within and move outward,' she positions emotions as moving, as 'non-resident,' and as 'doing things' (2004a:117). While she is not particularly focused on the examination of the moral emotions, I argue that her analysis of how emotions work to both 'attach' us to things and to put us 'in motion' is instructive for humanitarian sentiments: 'What moves us, what makes us feel, is also that which holds us in place, or gives us a dwelling place. Emotion may function as a *contingent attachment*' to the world . . . Contingency is linked then to proximity, to getting close enough to touch another and to be moved by another. So what attaches us, what connects us to this or that place, or to this or that other, *such that we cannot stay removed from this other*, is also what moves us, or what affects us such that we are no longer in the same place' (2004b:27).

Humanitarian emotions work to configure us in social and political spaces. I use the concept of configuration because it maintains the importance of ethical connection to the mobilization of humanitarianism. Again, as Laqueur (1989) and others have emphasized, connection allows for humanitarians to see themselves as implicated in the lives of others. The notion of configuration suggests connections that include many elements. We can conceptualize an emotion such as empathy as moving between the individual and the social, and the private and the public.[3] Humanitarian emotions *mobilize* by not only attempting a connection between the humanitarian and sufferer, but by profoundly altering the terrain on which such a connection is built. As Ahmed (2004) stresses, struggles against injustice are not about the quality of feelings; they are not about 'good' or 'bad' feelings. As she puts it, 'they are about how we are moved by feelings into a different relation to the norms we wish to contest, or the wounds we wish to heal' (201).

This conceptualization requires a re-visitation of the dominant 'trigger model' of political emotions. Such a model positions certain emotions as political because they trigger political action, and others as apolitical or anti-political, because they do not. The best example of the 'trigger model' is anger. Humanitarians are rarely associated with this more negative, and more politically passionate, emotion. By thinking of emotion as configuration, we focus less on how a so-called irrational emotion like sadness should be managed, and dwell more on how it may situate us in social and political contexts.

Woodward (2004) argues that the economy of emotions is shifting in the contemporary period. A central part of this uniqueness lies in the fact that we are witnessing in our media-saturated culture a kind of 'flattening' of emotions in which we experience emotion as 'sensation,' rather than more deeply or intensely (also see Hunt, this volume). Woodward also notes that at the same time we are seeing an increase in an individual's emotional repertoire, particularly for men. Even political male figures like former U.S. president George W. Bush can be 'compassionate conservatives,' and apparently feel other people's pain. This tension in contemporary emotion is felt even more acutely in humanitarian politics, where the relationship between experience and performance is central to the process of mobilization. If we experience humanitarian emotions like sympathy on a surface level, or if we simply attach compassion to an ideological stance, we do not fully embrace the sociality of suffering, and we may instead succumb to a kind of self-centred experience of emotion (see Illouz 2007; Wouters 2007). Chouliaraki (2010) signals this danger as a 'removal of the moral question' from the contemporary humanitarian emotional landscape whereby a private, and often narcissistic, emotional sensibility 'renders the emotions of the self the measure of our understanding of the sufferings of the world at large' (121). Perhaps, then, the promise of a more radical humanitarianism is a humanitarianism that can confront itself by 'moving' the humanitarian into a different emotional relationship to injustice.

Conclusions

When we watch one of the many commercials pleading for us to help children suffering from famine and disease, and find ourselves moved but not helping, we must ask: Where does the emotion go? There is something ephemeral about the humanitarian sentiment. As it configures the space between the individual and the social, the public and the private, so too can it be lost. This ephemeral quality is another reminder of the complexity of the emotional response to human suffering and the difficulty of predicting which emotional responses configure political actors. Emotions, it seems, are far less like the *fuel* for the political that we may have imagined them to be, and much more like the political itself. They are a critical part of the project of uncovering injustice precisely because injustice inserts itself into the space of emotion, whether we can feel it or not. Hochschild (2007) was right to suggest that from 'feeling we discover our own viewpoints on the world' (88). The mobility of humanitarian emotions is not located in some kind of trigger moment, but instead in the social space of ethical connection itself.

I began this chapter with the question of how humanitarianism is mobilized, and readers may conclude that I am not much closer to answering the specific questions of why the suffering of some humans compels humanitarian action, and the suffering of other humans goes unaddressed. We can begin to answer these questions by paying close attention to humanitarian narratives, and to the social and political construction of victims and suffering (Brown and Wilson 2009). In this chapter, I have argued that the analysis of the model of emotion also has something important to offer to the project of understanding emotional mobilization. If we can reflect on the ways in which humanitarian emotions work to attach us and to put us in motion, we may deepen our understanding of humanitarian action and indifference. The answers to the questions of mobilization seem to rely less on identifying a particular emotion as *having* political potential, than they do on addressing how humanitarianism puts us into a space where the political relationship between injustice, suffering, and emotion is configured.

Sociologists of emotion may find themselves in the strange position of arguing that emotions are inherently and fundamentally social, while at the same time noting that the analysis of emotion has not always figured prominently in sociology. This strangeness is particularly awkward for the analysis of the moral emotions, given that sociology often stakes its claim as a 'moral science.' Sherman (1998), for example, claims that empathy or imaginative simulation is 'a basic feature of occupying a social world, however extended that social world may be' (113). Sociology clearly has much to offer to the project of addressing the social dynamics of humanitarian sensibilities.

The emotional space of humanitarianism has become quite messy, nothing close to the space of moral guidance we might wish it to be. Empathy is only one among many of the emotional routes a contemporary humanitarian might take. When confronted with the pain and suffering of others, we may feel fear, anger, disgust, or sadness, and these feelings can lead to a range of actions, and indeed inaction. The only certainty of the humanitarian encounter is that we fail to fully comprehend the suffering of another if we simply imagine it as our own

(Nussbaum 2001). In this way, the emotional space of the humanitarian is necessarily social: it must be occupied by the presence of both the self and the other. So too is this emotional space necessarily mobile; the bleeding heart is never still.

NOTES

1 Humanitarianism demands its position in the realm of morality precisely because it is an act that is 'other-regarding,' and, similarly, seems to lose this intrinsically moral position if the act of 'other-regarding' serves the pursuit of self-interest (Badhwar 1993), as in the claims by some thinkers in international relations that foreign aid could never be deemed humanitarian. Its 'other-regarding' nature situates it more squarely in the sociological, rather than the economic, because the economic subject is assumed to always act in self-interest (Wolfe 1998).

2 The analysis of humanitarianism does not occupy a larger role in sociological inquiry, but there are a few references in passing. Becker (1968) used the word 'humanitarian' when he wrote that there was no reason to suggest that sociologists should choose between being scientists and being humanitarians: a person can be both 'passionately convinced of the dire need for actual, applied scientific control' and 'devote his [sic] efforts to the pursuit of *that* ultimate value and still be a humanitarian who subjects his [sic] work in that role to the requirements of "the men of good will"' (302). Sociology stakes its claim as a 'people-oriented' discipline. Yet, as Berger (1963) once noted, a 'benevolent interest in people could be the biographical starting point for sociological studies,' but a 'malevolent and misanthropic outlook could serve just as well' (2).

3 This analysis carries on a dialogue with the work of those feminists interested in ethics of care, such as Tronto (1993), who emphasized how care is 'devalued conceptually through a connection with privacy, with emotion, and with the needy' (117). An ethics of care offers an alternative to classical models of international relations and justice because it departs from the emphasis on the liberal values of rationality and autonomy. It offers an account of the self as inherently social, and therefore rejects the abstract individualist view of self and of community common to much liberal theory (Friedman 1993; Held 1999). Illouz (1997, 2007) also has much to say about liberalism and its role in the analysis of 'public' and 'private' life.

8 The Civilizing Process and Emotional Life: The Intensification and Hollowing Out of Contemporary Emotions

ALAN HUNT

Introduction

I arrived at an interest in emotions by a circuitous route. I had been engaged for some time in seeking to understand how groups and activities come to be acted upon by varieties of moralizing politics. It became evident that social anxieties played a significant role in stimulating projects of moral regulation; my concern was with social, shared, or collective anxieties, as distinct from individual states of anxiety. It became necessary to try and conceptualize anxiety as an emotion.

As I engaged with the emotions literature, it was apparent that much of it had its intellectual roots in psychology and presumed that emotions were manifested in individual mental states, affects, or feelings. My initial question was whether it made sense to think in terms of 'social or collective emotions.' I formed the view that the most fruitful way to distinguish a sociological line of inquiry about emotions was to insist that emotions have histories, and that engaging with the history of emotions provided the space for a sociological, rather than a psychological perspective. A major thrust in the history of emotions has been the concern to identify periodizations of emotional features of historical epochs, captured by the use of such concepts as 'emotional styles,' 'emotional regimes,' or 'emotional climate' – as illustrated by Stearns' contention that an emotional style of 'American cool,' characterized as 'impersonal, but friendly,' emerged in the United States in the 1920s (Stearns 1994). This chapter will offer an analysis of the contemporary-emotional climate of advanced capitalist societies (also see Bookman, this volume; Suski, this volume), which I characterize as exhibiting a tension between two distinct processes, one that manifests an intensification of emotionality and the other that yields an emotional climate that is distinctively hollowed out, flattened, or shallow.

I approach the periodization of emotions through the deployment of Raymond Williams's (1977) treatment of 'structures of feeling' and Norbert Elias's (1978) analysis of 'civilising processes.' These two traditions offer the necessary components of a fully social sociology of emotions. Williams links emotions to social structure with an emphasis on the plurality of emotions as a cluster of emotions rather than as discrete individual emotions. Elias makes available a link between emotions and social practices.

Raymond Williams

A fruitful avenue for addressing emotions is provided by the Marxist cultural historian Raymond Williams (1977), who suggests that lived experiences can be explored through the transformations that take place in what he calls 'structures of feeling' that capture the 'meanings and values as they are actually lived and felt' as well as their interaction with systematic beliefs (132). Williams adopts 'feelings' to avoid such alternatives as 'world-view' or 'ideology.' Structures of feeling are 'structures' in that they have specific internal relations that both interlock and are in tension. A structure of feelings grasps these shared elements and the interconnections that can be found both in specific generations and in different classes. Williams does not have much to say about generations, but there is a case to be made for the contention that generations share a structure of feelings as major harbingers of changes in emotional paradigms. A generation embodies its collective identity in response to formative events (Eyerman and Turner 1998:96); for example, the participation by Canadian and Australian forces in the First World War was formative for their respective national identities. A generational structure of feelings produces a distinctive range of body styles and performances, fashions, and emotional currents; thus the generation of the 1960s shared significant cultural and political markers that provided an emotional orientation that stimulated the sexual revolution.

Williams (1977) presents a structure of feeling as involving 'a specific structure of particular linkages, particular emphases and suppositions, and, in what are often its most recognizable forms, particular deep starting-points and conclusions' (134). Such structures are not unitary;he stresses the need to take account of the complex relations of differential structures associated with the feelings of different classes. We are accustomed to thinking of moods as a summary form for the variety of emotions that an individual experiences; I extend the notion of 'moods' to refer to diffuse emotional states as a workable summary version of the more abstract concept of structures of feelings of social aggregates. More generally, social configurations exhibit what might usefully be termed 'emotional climates' or 'emotional regimes.'

There may be merit in extending Williams's ideas by looking beyond the emotional shifts arising from cultural-class configurations to explore the extent to which state agencies may act as emotional agents; for example, state welfare in the twentieth century promoted not only the discourses of 'social citizenship' but engendered emotions about participation that differed from the older model of citizen as a 'subject' of sovereignty. T.H. Marshall's (1963) influential account of the genealogy of the rise of political, economic, and social rights invites us to look at emotions from above, for example, the emergence of sympathy for the poor or the unemployed; but it may also be fruitful to explore the responses from below, such as resentment against inequality. The significant implication being that it becomes fruitful to view social policy issues through the lens of emotions. Denzin (1984) stresses that emotionality, the capacity for emotional responses, is a key dimension of lived consciousness and the 'self-feeling' involving inner moral feelings and intersubjectivity. Emotionality lies at the intersection of the individual and collective experience; people are joined to their societies and to others through both self-feelings and collective structures of feeling.

Norbert Elias

Elias's major thesis associates 'civilization' with practices of an advancing 'social constraint towards self-constraint' (1994:443), which results from competitive struggles between social classes that originated first within aristocracies who had been subjected to practices of restraint imposed in court society (1978). The civilizing process resulted in the inculcation of practices of a wide range of emotional restraints, such as affected relations between the sexes, eating practices and the like, that became a matter of habit and resulted in changes to the personality structure associated, for example, with the privatism of familialism and of marital sexuality. 'The prohibitions supported by social sanctions are reproduced in the individual as self-controls,' writes Elias

(1978:190). Elias pays little attention to specific emotions (aside from some significant attention to the role of shame) since his concern is with the internalization of self-control over what might loosely be termed negative emotions. He provides an account of the managed decontrol of emotions that is exemplified in the restraints on aggression and anger and their displacement; for example, into sport where aggression is subject to rules and subject to an enforcement mechanism (referees, umpires, etc.), and, at the same time, is excluded from other fields of social activity. In the absence of formal controls in everyday life, the relaxation of control over emotions is possible only when mechanisms of self-restraint are sufficiently widespread and strongly enough internalized.

Elias is at pains to stress that the civilizing process takes different forms during the course of modernization as wider sections of the population are drawn into relations that are both more extensive and that develop specific dynamics. As the lower orders become drawn into these longer chains of interdependence (during the course of which mechanisms of self-restraint become more or less automatic), short-term impulses become subordinated to the commands of an acquired long-term perspective. The implication is that the civilizing process is characterized by tensions and contradictions. Individuals experience tensions or strains as they negotiate the challenges posed by their individual desires and passions alongside the normative expectations of self-restraint; in this process they experience the anguish that results from shame and embarrassment. Modern social life emphasizes the tensions involved as individuals negotiate their relationship with themselves and with others such that there is an increasing emphasis on differences between individuals (the 'I') as opposed to shared commonalities (the 'We'). In modernity, there is an increasingly equalized balance of power between classes and genders, such that all members of society are required to behave civilly towards one another. The increasingly sharp tensions of modern life mean the individual faces a unique series of pressures that arise from greater social differentiation, specialization, and heightened competitiveness. The pressures for self-restraint are such that individuals may give in to spontaneous impulses. These structural pressures of differentiation and individualization impose stress on the individual such that he/she is no longer able to securely regulate his/her impulses; since these drives can no longer legitimately be acted on in society, they may be inflected internally to manifest themselves in anxiety and other disturbed and disturbing conditions. Such tensions may result in dilemmas over patterns of so-cial behaviour about such matters as the degrees of sexual familiarity and appropriate levels of informality.

A characteristic feature of contemporary social life is the prolifera-tion of varied forms of offensive behaviour; such behaviour is gener-ally not unlawful but causes distress to others, and, when persistent, can be threatening to social order. Such behaviour is exhibited by adults (driving whilst using electronic devices, dumping litter from their vehicles, etc.), but most interest has focused on conduct exhibited by young children who behave aggressively towards teachers, senior citizens, shopkeepers, and others, leading to an increasing experience of social disorder that results in an undermining of the experience of community. Such children are often beyond the control of their parents, or their parents are unwilling to attempt to exercise the traditional ex-pectation of parental control (Field 2003). The first point to be made is that it is necessary to amend Elias's assumption that the achieve-ment of self-control is a process that the individual achieves alone. But it is necessary to stress that the process involves what Elias views as both internal and external constraints. Children typically acquire self-restraint through relations at home and at school. If a significant pro-portion of children do not acquire the self-control that is necessary to sustain viable relations with the communities in which they live, this will have implications for the emotional lives of communities and their wider societies.

Elias is careful to avoid equating the 'civilizing process' with 'self-control.' While Elias has been criticized as implying a smooth advance of the civilizing process, he himself was clear that both civilizing and decivilizing trends coexisted, such that barbarism arises in contexts where there is a declining restraint on emotional expression. He in-sists that the civilizing process is not smooth or easy; it is a two-edged weapon. Its spurts are not necessarily pleasant or convenient for those involved.

Elias identified a contemporary trend towards informalization that requires more than the effective internalization of social norms; more important is a widely dispersed capacity that has become almost au-tomatic by which individuals are able to select the appropriate level of formality-informality in a wide range of interaction scenarios. I confess that I would rather not have sales staff, whom I have only just met and will never see again, using my first name; this only goes to show how rapidly the practices of informalization have developed.

The question that I raise in connection with Elias is: How are we to understand the transformations in the structure of personality in the civilizing process that made it possible to relax controls over emotions without at the same time giving rein to spontaneous and dangerous surges of impulse? Elias's key contribution can best be characterized as proposing a 'controlled decontrolling of emotions,' in which the civilizing process is manifest in a generalized way such that an internalized self-control has been firmly established in a way that emotional spontaneity no longer poses any risk to civilized conduct. Such a controlled decontrolling of emotions characterizes contemporary heterosexual relations, which permit a considerable degree of familiarity between the sexes, while, at the same time, the reality of sexual aggression and harassment reminds us that the decontrolling of emotional constraints is always unstable. A key feature in this transformation is a change in the balance between externally imposed constraints on the individual's impulses and constraints that spring from a constant and rigorous self-control. But Elias resists the idea that the civilizing process simply involves an even extension of self-control. It is important to a comprehension of his life work to recognize that he was preoccupied with understanding the dynamic spurts of both civilizing and decivilizing processes. This was central to his engagement with the history of Germany, which grappled with an attempt to understand the rise of Nazism (Elias 1996). It is now time to harness these resources to explore the development of the emotional history of contemporary society.

The Contradictions of Emotions Today

The predominant feature of the contemporary emotional regime is the coexistence of a contradictory presence of an intensification of emotionality alongside a flattening of emotional experience. There is agreement that by the end of the nineteenth century a new emotional style was developing rapidly. This new style is perhaps best captured by Warren Susman (1984) as a transition from character to personality. This involved a shift from externally defined rules of correct (masculine) demeanour (stiff upper lip, straight back, walk on the outside of the sidewalk when accompanying a lady, and many more) and a distinct set of prescriptions for females organized around the theme of modesty. The shift to personality involved the quest for individualism made up from an autonomous, authentic, and distinctive set of emotional and behavioural characteristics. The world of personality was less rigidly gendered than that of character, but in the early part of the twentieth century personality was a predominantly masculine trait. The rise of personality involved a shift from externally defined behaviour rules to an injunction that the individual construct a more or less coherent sense of the self by putting together a consistent set of emotional practices and dispositions. Given the significance of generating an emotional figuration it followed that the expression of emotions, rather than the prior preoccupation with the control of the emotions, played a significant part in the performance of subjectivity. This did not mean that emotional self-control disappeared, but rather that the focus shifted to concerns with emotional management.

Practices of self-control change over time and across cultural contexts. In the twentieth century some nineteenth-century standards have been intensified; for example, those surrounding personal hygiene have generated a widening set of restraints and major expansion of consumerism; also intensified have been restraints on such disparate practices as personal violence and punctuality. But other nineteenth-century themes have waned, including formal rules of etiquette and manners. In the twentieth century there have been fewer detailed rules (e.g., a retreat of strict gendered division of emotional practices, and a decline of concern for posture). Change has also been evident in child-rearing practices that have become more informal and less disciplinary. An array of more detailed ways of manifesting personal discipline has expanded in both range and specificity (e.g., restraints on food intake, weight, smoking, drunkenness, etc.).

The shift from character to personality constituted a significant historical change in the formation of the individual. How are we to understand why this change occurred when it did? Two factors are of significance. First, there was the rise of consumerism, as a result of which the importance of choice came to the fore, thus requiring that the consumer make active selections in pursuit of the goal of social distinction – a phenomenon analysed by Bourdieu (1984) in his study of distinction. In the same way, the individual had to make choices in the elaboration of his/her personality. Consumerism was further stimulated by the new prospects that confronted the expanding middle classes. They no longer had access to a sufficient level of economic capital to promote the socio-economic circumstances of their children; they had insufficient resources to provide for inheritance between generations, so it became increasingly important that parents help their offspring develop the illusive goal of personality. Education increasingly became the way in which either general cultural capital or economically relevant skills were acquired. Demographic changes manifested themselves, such that the middle classes raised fewer children. Parents devoted increasing time and energy to their children. There was declining reliance on the disciplinary promotion of obedience. Not only did parents engage in more emotional relations with their children, but in doing so they sought to stimulate their capacity for self-command along with a personality and skills that fitted them for the specific roles appropriate to an ever more complex social division of labour. Not only did these processes stimulate the self-formation of individuals, but they also contributed to the collective formation of an increasingly self-confident middle-class ethos, a self-conscious middle class that was concerned with distinguishing itself from the urban working classes. The resulting culture of self-control was both powerful and assertive.

A major focus of this new middle-class ethos was strongly focused on a novel orientation to the economic realm that was different from the concern with accumulation of the nineteenth-century middle class; less preoccupied by the goal of wealth, the new middle class was orientated to the construction of successful careers. It would be interesting to explore the history of the transformations of the idea of a 'career' during the various stages of the formation of the middle classes. The 'career' involved the pursuit of a long-time commitment, often spanning the whole working life, focused on internal advancement through the increasingly formalized mechanisms of 'promotion.' Such a long-term commitment required stable emotional self-command, identification with the enterprise, and cooperative competition with fellow employees. At an earlier time, particularly from the 1880s, such employment was viewed as a considerable challenge. The neurasthenia craze brought the relationship between the middle classes and work into focus for the first time by presenting the hectic pressures of 'modern' work as a source of stress and as a general threat to health and mental well-being (Beard 1972; Gijswijt and Porter 2001). By the end of the twentieth century, work stress had again reached epidemic proportions (Wainwright and Calman 2002).

These processes in the formation of the middle classes gave rise to a changing configuration of emotional life. The emphasis on the maintenance of emotional control declined, and the behavioural problem was no longer keeping the passions in check. The key requirement becomes the selection of appropriate emotional responses for specific social situations; the concept of emotional management captures this style of emotional conduct and manifests itself in working and domestic life.

Emotionality in the Workplace

From the late nineteenth century, psychological approaches provided means to address human subjectivity via new languages for the running of schools, prisons, factories, and in particular the workplace (Rose 1989; Illouz 2008). The workplace became a key site for the reconfiguration of the emotions; while the discouragement of anger had long been a concern, between the two world wars attention was increasingly directed at producing configurations of emotions that facilitated cooperative relations that would stimulate efficiency – although there was always a tension between rational efficiency and job satisfaction.

The emotional configuration in the workplace was never smooth and integrated. Rather, it was marked by a paradox between a hierarchical ordering that required emotional conformism and obedience and thus required high levels of self-restraint, and, simultaneously, the self-motivation of employees. The disciplinary practices led to increasing levels of surveillance over workplace conduct. However, there is a realm of work-life in which workers strive to evade the surveillance of management, and when lack of restraint with respect to many of the operative emotional codes had free play; 'escape attempts' seek relief from routine and monotony at work, some being mere breaks while others are more transgressive and resistant (Cohen and Taylor 1992). Subordinate groups come to speak in two different voices, the hidden and the public (Scott 1990). It would be interesting to explore further the emotions of insubordination, which are to be found not only in workplace, but also in the school and other institutions. Much attention has been paid to the routinized transgression in early modern societies that provided relief from the strictly hierarchical social order. Christopher Hill (1972) refers to 'waves of feelings' that temporarily 'turned the world upside down' and freed the common people from the authority of the church, state, and social superiors (see also Hobsbawm 1959).

An important feature of the intensification of emotional discipline is that emotional issues have become increasingly viewed as appropriate matters for intervention. Significantly, there has been an expansion of formalized disciplinary codes in the workplace, accompanied by a similar enlargement of human resources personnel who provide a quasi-judicial framing of such projects exemplified in procedures around anger and violence. The most prominent fields of action have been with regard to 'equity' issues that began with matters of race, but have grown to incorporate other arenas of 'difference.' Prominent have been the disciplinary engagement with gender relations encompassing issues of harassment and discrimination.

At the same time as the workplace imposed emotional restraint, the twentieth century saw a rising current of informalism. Hierarchical distance was weakened. Often this was unplanned, as in the spread of the use of familiar names between differently located people; but there are usually well-understood rules about how far hierarchical formality can be displaced. While it has become increasingly common to use familiar names for immediate superiors, this has not granted permission for such informality with higher-ranking persons. There have also been planned moves towards informality at work that seek to stimulate cooperation, as exemplified by the gradual disappearance of segregated dining rooms and the introduction of activities promoting sociability that range from wilderness adventures to trips to the bowling alley.

The informalizing tendencies are not in contradiction with the processes of intensification, but rather should be understood as facilitating the dominant emotional paradigm in such a way as to yield an ever more complex framing of everyday life that calls upon individuals to acquire levels of self-regulation, making these more intensified emotional demands liveable. Informalization does not abolish or even weaken hierarchies. It manifests itself in displacing the requirements of formal acknowledgment of social hierarchy and social difference. It is most evident in informal modes of address and practices between differently situated individuals: between students and teachers; between generations; between the sexes. These shifts have taken place with few, if any, articulated rules. It is no longer compulsory for males to open doors for females; but the question of when it is appropriate to do so is now much more unclear and creates endless possibilities for making mistakes. To live as we all do within these shifting relations requires a subtle balance between a variety of opposing motives and behaviours such as directness and tactfulness, simplicity and sophistication.

Difficult though it is to intuit these unarticulated norms, most people succeed in doing so with great skill and have internalized the new forms of emotional expressivity and restraint. As Elias (1994) observed, 'as more and more people must attune their conduct to that of others, the web of actions must be organized more and more strictly and accurately' (445). We should add, this has to be achieved without there being anyone to do the organizing. Elias's own solution to this difficulty is less than satisfactory, since along with conscious self-control, he invokes 'an automatic, blindly functioning apparatus of self-control [that] is firmly established' (446). This misses the remarkable skill with which people negotiate the complexity of everyday social life. Thus, it is important to stress that informalization places increased demands on the mechanisms of self-restraint; these are not 'decivilizing' processes, but rather they involve a change in the form of the civilizing process from external constraint to internal self-restraint.

Informalizing processes coexist with currents that may be viewed as instituting a 'reformalization.' Over the last century, the formalization of emotional restraint existed in the form of semi-formalized systems of etiquette and manners. While etiquette as a system of formal rules of conduct has faded from much of social life, manners have acquired a somewhat more formalized existence. Manners were historically buttressed by practices of social exclusion. Today, important areas of emotional sensitivity are guarded by institutionally supported rules of political correctness that impose a restrained emotionality. This requires strong internalization and self-checking mechanisms that are particularly evident in language rules, for example usage that requires the suppression of 'girl' and the substitution of 'woman,' or the suppression of 'Inuit' and the requirement to remember the currently approved label. In addition to strong internalization, there is a strong external moralization in contrast to the customary conventionalism that sustained the rules of manners, and, in addition, there are significant sanctions that meet breaches of the speech and behaviour codes. To offend can result in acquiring culturally and politically significant labels such as 'racist' or 'sexist' that are important mechanisms of social exclusion.

Collective Emotions

The paradox of contemporary emotional life requires that individuals exhibit both expressivity and restraint, which requires a careful balancing of the culturally approved emotional standards and an awareness of the everyday reality of emotional practices. Complex though such an emotional life is, much of the time we succeed with a fair degree of spontaneity in 'carrying it off' with respect to many frequently encountered emotional contexts in which we have a reasonably clear appreciation of what emotional dispositions are expected of us and the permissible range of emotional display or practice.

There is a second and deeper form of the paradox of emotions. My discussion thus far has been located within the conventional framework that treats emotions as either individual experiences or as affects involved in interpersonal relations. It is in this context that most of the work that has described itself as a sociology of emotions has been undertaken. It is characterized by the concern to chart the social context of interactions that manifest emotional features. For present purposes, Hochschild's (1983) study of the commercialization of the emotion work of flight attendants exemplifies this approach. What she does so well is to reveal the socio-economic context in which conventional signifiers of politeness are mobilized in the context of self-conscious self-control within a work situation. There is, however, an inherent limitation to any such 'social context' approach to emotions in that it sets up two domains – one of emotions and the other of the social environment in which they exist. Thus, for example, Hochschild's work does not inquire where the emotions deployed on board an aircraft come from; the emotions are taken for granted as the common sense emotions that 'we all know about' – anger, jealousy, and so on – as if these were 'natural' endowments of humans. What happens is that managers and others in authority can call upon employees to exhibit commercially appropriate emotions. What is needed is a social theory of emotions that starts out from the proposition that emotions are an integral component not only of relations but also of the structures within which those relations are located. For example, love may be an individual sentiment shared between two persons, but it is also a structural feature of social relations in societies in which 'love' is a structure of feeling, understood and desired by most, if not all, people.

One of the most distinctive manifestations of the profoundly social nature of emotions is located in the importance of collective or shared emotions. Collective emotions arise where people share an emotional response without necessarily being in direct contact with one another. Thus, a collective emotion does not necessarily involve a situation in which people are together in a shared location or social context, such as a crowd. More interesting are those circumstances in which disparate individuals in significant numbers experience the same emotional and politico-moral reactions. The emotion is shared when people reveal the same evaluation of a situation, share collective emotional standards, and agree on the appropriate range of responses to the situation. A further dimension of collective emotion is the experience that Durkheim ([1912]1961:241) termed 'collective effervescence' – something that occurs typically in religious rituals, as a result of which the participants are themselves changed, but more importantly change their relationship with those with whom they share that experience. When the assembled individuals feel themselves dominated by some external event, they begin to think and act differently from normal times; this is particularly important in events that constitute shared generational experiences, such as collective action against the Vietnam War or the demonstrations against the World Trade Organization in Seattle in 1999.

One classic and important instance of a collective emotion that serves to illustrate a wider category of collective emotions is that of *ressentiment*. The use of the French word is justified in order to distinguish it from the more passive connotations of the English word 'resentment,' and also because a long line of debate has focused on ressentiment. What is significant about this collective emotion is its close links to forms of social (and often political) action. Ressentiment is not simply a sentiment or feeling linked to an individual's sense of self; rather, it imports an element of objective social structure since it seems always to be an expression of different positions in one or more social hierarchies and is thus always capable of collective social action.

When Nietzsche ([1887]1989) christened the concept of *ressentiment*, his concern was with the distinction between noble and slave morality in the context of his critique of the historical linkage between Christian and bourgeois morality. He emphasized the passivity of slave morality (forgiveness, turning the other cheek). As the concept was subsequently developed, it acquired a wider range of nuances. Max Scheler's (1961) consideration of ressentiment differed slightly from Nietzsche's, as his version focused of the repression of the feelings of slave morality that expresses itself in impotent hatred, envy, and a desire for revenge, which can find no expression in an alternative culture but secretly craves the values that it denies. This form is characteristic of societies in which a hierarchical order has broken down, yet inequality and envy remain rife. Ranulf ([1938]1964) links ressentiment to what he called 'disinterested moral indignation' that demands the punishment of criminals. His notion is associated with the presence of a lower middle class that has been subjected to high degrees of self-restraint, and thus is subject to frustration of its own desires and the experience of misery. The resentment of such a class can be deployed against any social group or class that is perceived as violating these self-imposed norms. Ranulf's 1938 study viewed German fascism as a key instance of lower-middle-class indignation.

Ressentiment makes it possible to understand how structural features – in particular, forms of inequality, disadvantage, and ethnicity and class – stimulate socio-political action via the intermediation of the negative emotions that are attached to undeserving and unworthy others. Barbalet (2002) makes the important point that emotions link structure to agency. He goes so far as to insist that all emotions are related to differences of power and status between actors.

Further complexity and variation can be added by distinguishing between different forms of indignation of differently located groups and classes, for example, by distinguishing between rising and declining classes (Barbalet 2002b). Thus, the political and emotional content will be different when advancing classes of merchants are denied access to privileged social spaces of a declining aristocracy who can no longer afford the display that had previously sustained their class self-confidence. A very common form of ressentiment is deployed against groups who violate these projected standards of self-control. I recall that as a child in small town England after the Second World War, every year people we called 'gypsies' travelling in horse-drawn caravans would set up camp on the edge of town. During their stay, the residents believed that you needed to buy the clothes pegs that the gypsy women sold door-to-door because if you did not, bad things would happen, such as the theft of produce or animals. The gypsies were feared and resented; their unsettled form of existence and the mess they always seemed to leave behind led to the shared feeling that 'someone should do something.' While the local policeman was sympathetic to complaints, he would insist there was nothing he could do. One of the interesting features of this example is the co-presenceof desire for action ('Someone should do something.') and a fatalism ('Nothing I can do.').

It is characteristic of ressentiment to mobilize spontaneous truth-claims ('Gypsies are thieves.') that generally encounter little resistance, or, when there is resistance, the commitment to the shared values is passionate and organized – as in the case of the genocide in Rwanda in 1994 when the sentiments mobilized were so strong that they were directed not only against ethnic Tutsis, but also against moderate Hutu. The concept of ressentiment helps in understanding a variety of social movements that range from relatively mild forms of prejudice through to some of the most atrocious acts of genocide. Typical manifestations of ressentiment can be illustrated by the nineteenth-century American prohibition campaigns and by today's anti-smoking campaigns.

Gusfield (1963), in dissecting prohibition did not use the concept of res-sentiment, but it fits perfectly with his account of the declining status of rural Protestantism in the USA pitted against the less self-controlled manners and habits of immigrants from Southern Europe. It is the de-monstrable evidence of an inability to exercise self-control that today fuels resentment against smokers and justifies imposing restrictions on smokers while at the same time displaying the self-control and re-spectability of the non-smoker (Brandt 2007). It is interesting that Peter Stearns (1999), having stressed the importance of the struggle for self-control, misses its other side: the ressentiment at those who either fail to, or, even worse, celebrate their lack of self-control.

An emergent form of ressentiment has recently targeted obesity. Pre-viously, individuals varied in size and weight; but now that we have 'obesity' as a medico-moral category (and we should also factor in class), we have a collective, 'the obese,' who can be resented because of their 'life-style' with its palpable lack of self-control. A general form manifests itself in distress that is occasioned by the belief that some third party has gained an undeserved advantage (for example, the al-location of a second seat to an obese passenger). It is important to dis-tinguish this from envy, which is the desire for benefits that others are believed to possess (Barbalet 1998:137). Ressentiment may also focus on the shame that arises from a failure to succeed in a legitimate distribu-tional system, as a result of which collective anger is directed against those who benefit unfairly without following the rules. This is a very common form of current ressentiment against immigrants. The emo-tion of ressentiment is significant in that it reveals a more general fea-ture of emotion as the unintended and generally unreflexive response of people to structural features of their social circumstances; in brief, emotions provide a link between subjective experience and objective circumstances. It is worth noting that new forms of ressentiment con-tinue to emerge. Of particular interest is what may be called the 'new ressentiment,' which is exhibited by the socially marginalized (often referred to as 'the underclass'), who display extreme forms of aggres-sive and unrestrained hostility that is closely linked to the antisocial behaviour discussed above. Another new form of ressentiment is found in the significant role of media figures, typified by Rush Limbaugh, who articulate widely dispersed sentiments of ressentiment which may stimulate forms of collective political action.

It is instructive to compare the emotions of hate and ressentiment. There is much overlap between ressentiment and hatred in that ressentiment is likely to involve sentiments of hatred towards the target of the negative sentiments. But there is a significant difference. Hatred may be both individual and collective, while ressentiment can only be experienced in some collective form. I may hate someone while at the same time recognizing that others do not share my sentiment, but that a collective 'we' may hate some other individual or social group.

Cultural histories reveal waves of ressentiment and of social hatreds. Contemporary emotional currents are buttressed by widely acknowledged social anxieties and fears, perhaps not so strong as ressentiment, but collective nonetheless. It is not only socially legitimate to admit one's fears and anxieties, but it becomes almost expected that one confesses these existential emotions. Parents reveal their commitment to the project of parenting by revealing their anxieties about their children, whether it addresses their safety, their education, or their physical or mental health. In the early years of the twenty-first century, this is so familiar that we need to be reminded that probably no more than two generations ago such anxieties would not have been so readily expressed. This trend is further amplified by the way in which security consciousness, which is primarily manifested in emotions of fear and anxiety, creates an emotionally charged climate that is primarily expressed via the relationships between individuals and the wider society. Indeed, anxiety and fear have become predominant emotions of our epoch.

Insufficient attention has been paid to the fact that emotions may exhibit both individual and collective forms. Emotions change their form not only between cultures, but also across time. An interesting case is that of grief. Grief varies between cultures; the subdued tears and muffled sobs of Northern Europe contrasts with the vocal and physical manifestations in the Middle East. More interestingly, I suggest that grief confirms the important contention that emotions have histories which undermine any lingering suggestion that emotions are natural and invariant physiological responses to external stimuli (Stearns 1993). Grief has undergone a significant historical shift, one that involves an expansion of its collective manifestations. Grief has long had distinctively group manifestations. In many cultures, bereaved kin gather to weep as a form of collective effervescence at a funeral or other death ritual (Ariès 1985). Such mourning often takes extensive expression in terms of the numbers involved and their spatial separation, particularly when the person being mourned has an institutional status, such as a monarch or a religious leader. But more recently grief has become

particularly interesting because in the West a significant new phenomenon is the expression of collective grief in the absence of any personal
or institutional contact between those that grieve and the departed. The
prime instance is the continuing cult of Princess Diana and other celebrities including Elvis Presley and John Lennon. Such manifestations of
sustained and indeed institutionalized grief closely approximate to the
'collective effervescence' that Durkheim ([1912]1961) identifies at the
core of religious experience and are part of the wider phenomenon of
the 'culture of celebrity' (Schickel 1985).

One important corollary of taking account of the historical variation
exhibited by emotions is that it should shift attention away from emotion management, without in any way implying that the practices of
emotional self-control are unimportant. I make no claim to have demonstrated that all emotions exhibit this characteristic. Yet, it is important to remain attentive to the fact that emotions embedded in specific
historical and cultural contexts may be subject to processes of both restriction, by management or self-control, and to enhancement, in situations in which the display of emotions is encouraged.

That emotions are subject to historical change is hardly surprising.
What is more interesting is to address the question: Why do emotions
change when they do? Why do they change in one direction rather than
another? One available approach is to examine the biographies of individual emotions; important work has been undertaken on anger (Stearns and Stearns 1986), jealousy (Stearns 1989), disgust (Miller 1997),
and fear (Bourke 2005). This approach runs the risk, however strong
the intention to avoid it, of treating individual emotions as isolated entities. The alternative approach is to seek to capture the emotional climate of a people or a nation in some specific epoch. Many outstanding
social and cultural histories succeed in presenting a rich and nuanced
image of a society; for example, one can have the feeling of 'knowing'
nineteenth- and early twentieth-century France from Theodore Zeldin's account (1973). The most explicit attempt to capture an emotional
culture is Peter Stearns's 'American Cool' (1994). His account depends
very much on what we understand by 'cool,' since his definition of
twentieth-century American culture as 'impersonal, but friendly' could
just as well describe a number of other contemporary Western societies, each with significantly different inflections. His account is centred
on the triumph of emotional restraint, but his argument is significant
in that he succeeds in capturing the coexistence of emotional restraint
with the parallel requirement for emotional openness and expressivity.

Emotions and Personal Relations

The other realm of social life in which there has been an expansion of emotionalization is that of personal relations. This development is closely connected to the major changes in the position of women in society. The nineteenth-century marriage was conceived in terms of a contractual, gendered division of labour with the male as breadwinner and the female as homemaker. The twentieth-century marriage was increasingly conceived in terms of the 'companionate marriage' (Lindsey 1927; Collins 2003), in which both parties were enjoined to aspire to emotional closeness and mutual sexual satisfaction. In the early part of the century there occurred a major expansion in the various forms of advice literature – literature that was influenced by the concern with rising divorce rates that created widespread professional and personal anxiety. Perhaps most significant was the expansion of marital advice literature; but there was also the beginnings of marital expertise dispensed by a variety of therapeutic counselling methods. At the same time, discourses that constructed marriage as problematic were widely diffused throughout popular culture.

There were considerable tensions and controversies surrounding the place of emotions within marriage. On the one hand, there was concern that the weakening of paternal authority should not unleash uncontrolled emotions in which wives rejected the injunction to wifely obedience enshrined in the promise to 'love, honor and obey' (Stearns and Stearns 1986). The problem was posed in terms of promoting 'restraint' rather than obedience. Yet, at the same time, the new emotionalism within the companionate marriage had to create spaces for emotional expression. Some of the advice literature came to permit the expression of marital anger; Cancian and Gordon's (1988) study of twentieth-century women's magazines reveals the permission given to wives to express anger while being warned against lapsing into hysteria and tears. A major innovation in the new discourses on the companionate marriage was the valorization of 'communication,' in which the controlled expression of emotions was encouraged. The new therapeutic expertise granted couples permission to acknowledge conflicts in which anger arose from lack of communication. To achieve communication, individuals needed to learn to express their emotions, but at the same time to maintain emotional control. This focus created a new opportunity for marriage counsellors to formalize their role as mediators between spouses. Hochschild (1990) astutely notes that the permission for emotional display gave rise to the need for 'expression rules.' The implication of this quest for communication in marriage makes it more necessary that the parties develop the skills necessary to discharge this unveiling of 'feelings.' To have feelings as the lived experience of emotions has become a fundamental manifestation of subjectivity.

There is an elusive but significant slippage from 'emotions' to 'feelings'; it is not a sharp break, but it is characteristic of the contemporary discourses of the emotions. Nietzsche ([1887] 1989) was characteristically blunt: 'I am opposed to the pernicious modern effeminacy of feeling' (20). Emotions generally take the form of distinguishable and categorized forms; they are ordered into positive and negative emotions. There are a few ambiguous emotions that do not fall neatly into a simple positive and negative classification, such as nostalgia, suspicion, and possibly boredom, although this tends to fall on the negative side. Emotions carry names, and even though their meanings are not necessarily precise, it is generally possible for there to be some agreement about what they designate; there is a common sense intuition that 'we' know what we are talking about when we refer to jealousy, hate, or loneliness. In contrast, 'feelings' lack the same degree of definition. I can report feeling sad or happy and these feelings are considered equivalent to the same named emotions; but I can also have feelings that I cannot put names to. The result is that a culture of feelings is one in which individuals are expected to have feelings, and there is a certain sense in which any and all feelings are legitimate expressions of our self-identity.

The Search for Intimacy in an Age of Pure Relationships

One of the most pervasive elements of contemporary emotional discourse is that of intimacy. It is a goal much sought after. Yet, like other contemporary elements of emotional discourse, it is far from clear exactly what intimacy requires. While the twentieth-century marriage aspired to companionship, today the benchmark for a successful relationship is an intimacy that requires a mutuality of closeness, openness, and trust that sets the bar very high. This is the age of Anthony Giddens's 'pure relationships,' whose hallmark is the very strange form of quasi-contractualism: both parties consent to enter the relationship on terms which allow either party to leave if the relationship no longer satisfies their needs. Thus, intimacy is more than a desired goal to be aimed at, but is the very condition of the survival of the relationship. Eva Illouz (2008) is correct to pose the problem as being 'the tyranny of intimacy' (105).

Intimacy has been extended to wider familial relations, in particular between parents and children. The quest for familial intimacy is interestingly captured in the phrase 'quality time.' It is not so much the content of the relation, but the fact that sufficient time should be set aside from the busy lives of modern parents to devote to their children. At the same time 'love' is no longer an adult emotion grounded in sexual attraction, but rather plays a significant role in the parent-child relation with both parents and children regularly needing to confirm their love. Here there is evidence of the paradox of emotions; love stands at the emotional apex and yet it has become an everyday ritual to be displayed whenever parent and child part for even a short time. Thus, there is a routinization of love that can detract from its emotional import.

Meštrovicÿaa (1997) seeks to capture this trajectory by means of his concept of the 'post-emotional.' I don't like the term *post-emotional* since 'post' suggests that society is no longer emotional. But what he succeeds in capturing is the coexistence of a hyper-emotionality, a quest for emotional intensity, with a routinization of emotions that strip them of any real content. This is the emotional configuration that I seek to capture with the idea that today emotions are increasingly 'hollowed out.' By this I mean that while modern social life requires that emotional practices play a more pronounced part in personal life, the emotions deployed tend to have less depth or intensity. This is most evident in the expectation today that everyone should 'be nice' at the expense of real emotions. In the new etiquette books, 'being nice' becomes ritualized and routinized, and is a primary form of the demand for emotional self-command, such that the emotions are no longer policed by the injunction for 'emotional control'; rather, emotional display is to be modulated in such a way that no possibility arises of giving offence or of raising the emotional temperature of social interactions. The devaluation of emotions is epitomized in the rise of the greeting card industry that makes possible a quasi-emotional act whose content is sentimental and conventional; and more significantly, sending a card frees the purchaser from any need to express an active or personalized emotion. This devaluation of emotions is also manifest in the infantalization of Valentine's Day – no longer an expression of young love, the occasion has moved into a children's realm in which it is compulsory to send a card to everyone in the class. This is part of the commercialization of emotions, epitomized by the routinization of bunches of flowers for Mother's Day; and in a world of gender equality Father's Day had to be invented – although my hunch is that many people have seen through the fabrication and ignore it. So, rather than the descriptor 'post-emotional,' these processes constitute a move to a world of synthetic emotions.

A significant component of synthetic emotion is the group that maybe termed 'vicarious emotions.' These have become of increasing importance as the expansion of popular culture provides endless opportunity to experience emotional stimulation vicariously. One of the most commonly encountered forms is provided by TV soap operas in which the viewer is invited to share the emotional responses of fictional characters. The joys and sorrows of the daily lives of the characters provide endless opportunities to not only empathize with the fictional others, but for their emotions to pass across the boundary of virtual reality and become the viewers' own emotional experiences. This is evident in the subsidiary material of soap opera magazines and on-line sites in which the division between characters and actors is blurred and the viewer comes close to direct participation in the real-fictional emotions. In another form provided by TV, talk-show audiences are invited to engage with the displayed emotions of the participants who are selected precisely to provide emotional dramas; the audience is expected to take sides and thus to participate in the emotions on display. This public display of emotions provides an extraordinarily direct display, not only of specific emotions, but, more significantly, of a composite of the emotional style of the wider cultural configuration. Individuals exposed to such an emotional lexicon are provided with a tutorial guide to socially recognized or appropriate emotional responses without having to experience the emotions themselves. One might speak of the emotional ideology of the period in the sense that soap operas and talk shows provide a full display of the emotional contexts that are typical of the period. Jock Young (2007) provides a delightful illustration. While in the neighborhood that is represented in the long-running soap *East Enders*, he goes into a local pub where passive spectators are watching one of the episodes; they don't interact with each other but they participate vicariously in the emotional diet being played out (183). The culture of celebrity similarly provides an invitation to participate in the emotional context of the distant but so close lives of the celebrities (Friedman 1999).

Distant Suffering

A significant contemporary manifestation of synthetic emotions is the exponential increase in our exposure to distant suffering. The video camera ensures that the news media is suffused with images of distant suffering, epitomized by images of starving children in far-away refugee camps, and of natural disasters, plane crashes, and the like. It is probable that the high profile in the media attests to a lack of conviction about what constitutes news, with the sense of the irrelevance of what constitutes matters of public and political importance. Distant suffering has come to fill the vacuum. But from the standpoint of emotions, this is significant because it mobilizes sentiments of pity, sorrow, and anguish while rendering viewers passive because there is little or nothing that they can do; or at best we can reach for our chequebooks or put a few coins in a collection box. The passive viewer is incited to an emotional response to distant suffering, but the response can only be plastic because there is such separation between the viewer and the reality of distant suffering. Thus, although appearing to be a form of emotional expressivity, its all too frequent shallowness suggests that it is a manifestation of the hollowing out of emotions (also see Suski, this volume).

However, there is a further paradoxical dimension that arises from distant suffering. It has become all too common that whenever a local incident involving death or injury occurs the institution in question offers counselling to help people presumed to be emotionally affected by the event. This clearly is a manifestation of the self-interest of counselling professionals, but such a response also expands the category of victims to any degree of proximity. It constructs people as emotional while ignoring the capacity of people to cope through their own resources with the ordinary difficulties of everyday life. This is even more evident with respect to larger-scale events such as earthquakes and floods, when the counselling teams are on the ground only just behind the emergency forces. The complexity of contemporary responses to distant suffering is further illustrated by the increasingly common phenomenon of 'strangers' exhibiting emotions and practices of grief and mourning aimed at celebrities with whom their relationship is merely virtual; the long-lived emotionalism exhibited after the death of Princess Diana is the classic instance of this response.

Conclusion

I have sought to harness the theoretical resources provided by Norbert Elias's concept of 'civilising process' and Raymond Williams's idea of the 'structure of feelings' to give a historical framing to this engagement with a sociological account of the formation of the emotional configuration of contemporary Western societies that has revealed the paradoxical nature of the emotional currents that course through society. The argument has been developed that we persistently encounter a tension between an endorsement of an increasingly expressive emotional display between intimates, of which the highly charged emotionality of parent-child relations is the exemplar, and, on the other hand, emotionality by its ubiquitous display across a wider range of relations tends to have less depth or intensity, that I have characterised as an emotional hollowing-out. Nowhere is this more evident than in the way in which the 'love' emotion, which had long been elevated to the apex of interpersonal intensity, now figures in a wide range of relational dispositions. It may of course be that we need to take account of the fact that emotions do not have a fixed content and that 'love' is today a much broader category referring to a range of positive sentiments. If this is the case, it nevertheless underlines the contention that there is a continuing hollowing-out of emotional experience.

The ways in which emotions figure in everyday practices demarcate the distinctive civilizing and decivilizing features of modern societies. Emotions are much more than the internal feelings and behavioural practices of individuals; rather emotions form the structures of feelings through which social relations are lived and contested. What I have not addressed is the bigger question of how we might explain the historical trajectory of the emotional culture that I outline. A few reflections may be in order. Changes in emotional culture cannot be independent of wider changes in modern social formations. There does seem to have been a surprisingly strong reaction against the core rationalism of the Enlightenment, which takes the form of a widely diffused anti-intellectualism associated with increasing uncertainty about progress. One of its strongest manifestations is an increasing skepticism about the natural sciences whose most visible manifestation has been the reaction against evolutionism, which, leaving aside the battles over 'intelligent design,' speaks to a deeper current against objectivism one of whose major manifestations is a wider sympathy for non-rational, non-evidentiary forms of thought illustrated by the popularity of alternative medicine and alternative therapies. This has found popular expression in a turn towards subjectivism, which finds expression in the ready resort to hollowed-out emotions that embody a narcissism that refuses an engagement with the real difficulties of building and sustaining viable social relations.

9 Emotions In/and Knowing

ANDREA DOUCET AND NATASHA S. MAUTHNER

Introduction

This chapter focuses on how emotions matter in our knowing processes. It is rooted in a two-decade-long research program where we have explored interconnections between relationality, reflexivity, and inter-subjectivity in knowledge construction processes at intertwined levels of nitty-gritty methodological processes and epistemological conceptualization (e.g., Mauthner and Doucet 1998, 2003; Doucet and Mauthner 2002, 2006, 2008). Across several cross-cultural qualitative research projects, we have been grappling with emotions: our own, those of our research respondents, and those that reverberate through our fieldwork practices and epistemological thinking. Building from the perspective promulgated in this book that emotions matter, our argument is that they matter profoundly in knowledge construction processes. More specifically, we centre this piece around two questions. First, how can we bring emotions into our methodological practices? Second, how do we do this without veering into what Bourdieu terms 'narcissistic reflexivity'?

Our chapter is structured into three sections. We begin with a brief background on our theoretical approach to emotions in research, while also providing some detail on how emotions have been taken up in qualitative research practice. We then explore selected ways of working with emotions in research practice. Finally, we address the issue of if, and where, a sustained attention to emotions in research leads to 'narcissistic reflexivity.'

Background and Definitions

Our reflections on emotions draw on cross-disciplinary influences, including anthropology, sociology, philosophy, geography, and psychosocial studies. In brief, we maintain that emotions in research are embodied (Rosaldo 1980; Holland 2007; Denzin 1984), involve issues of judgment and rational thought (see Nussbaum 2001), and are eminently relational, thus constituting 'embodied, interdependent human existence' (Burkitt 1997:42; Davidson, Smith, and Bondi 2005; Davidson and Smith, this volume). We also posit a strong link between epistemology and emotions, which is grounded in a view that emotion constitutes a way of knowing our social worlds (Game 1997). Furthermore, our particular focus on narrative analysis in research draws together the issue of knowing others and their stories through empathetic connection (Nussbaum 1990). Finally, we draw on British geographer Liz Bondi's work on emotional geographies and her argument that knowledge construction involves attending to the emotional connections between researchers and their research subjects (Bondi 2005; Knowles 2006; Holland 2007; Davidson and Smith, this volume). We agree with Bondi (2005) that emotions are inter-subjective, rather than intra-subjective, and should 'be approached not as an object of study but as a relational, connective medium in which research, researchers and research subjects are necessarily immersed' (433; see also Hollway 2008a, b).[1]

As detailed throughout this book, the field of the sociology of emotions has burgeoned in the past decade; its articulation within the more specific field of qualitative methodologies has also received much attention for several decades, especially by feminist researchers. Much of this attention, however, has focused on emotions during fieldwork or data collection. One of the most well-recognized instigators of this long conversation is Anne Oakley's (1981) classic article published nearly 30 years ago on woman-to-woman interviewing and the importance of establishing good rapport and good emotional relations with research respondents.

Challenging the masculine assumptions of 'proper interviews' that dominated the sociological textbooks of the time, Oakley (1981) suggested that contrary to an objective, standardized, and detached approach to interviewing, the goal of finding out about people through interviewing was 'best achieved when the relationship of interviewer and interviewee is non-hierarchical and when the interviewer is prepared to invest his or her own personal identity in the relationship' (41).

Drawing on her interviews with mothers, she maintained that her own identity as a mother came to act as a leveller against a power hierarchy in the interviewee-interviewer relationship: 'Where both share the same gender socialization and critical life-experiences, social distance can be minimal' (55; see also Finch 1984; Rheinharz 1992). Although Oakley did not explicitly use the term *emotions* in her work, the tenor of what she was expressing relates explicitly to how particular types of methods promote emotional connections and conversely enhance a research relationship where 'social distance can be minimal.'

While Oakley's work was celebrated and embraced by many feminist researchers, her argument about connectivity and shared emotions on the basis of gender soon came to be viewed as overly naïve and essentialist. A decade later, such perspectives were being criticized and deconstructed by many feminist researchers who argued that emotional connections in research relations are also fraught with inevitable relational distances and barriers between researchers and the researched. Sociologists were particularly vocal on this issue of the potential dangers associated with trying to be 'friendly' in interviews. Pamela Cotterill (1992), for example, drew attention to the 'potentially damaging effects of a research technique which encourages friendship in order to focus on very private and personal aspects of people's lives' (597; see also Stacey 1991). Ironically, in what could be seen as a 360-degree turn, many feminist researchers began to note that striving for greater emotional connection did not always have straightforwardly positive results. As noted more recently by Gesa Kirsch (2005): 'It is perhaps ironic, then, that scholars are discovering that methodological changes intended to achieve feminist ends – increased collaboration, greater interaction, and more open communication with research participants – may have inadvertently reintroduced some of the ethical dilemmas feminist researchers had hoped to eliminate: participants' sense of disappointment, alienation, and potential exploitation' (2163).

Along with these discussions on how emotions should be invested in research, researchers have simultaneously recognized the potential dangers of such investments, and developed other lines of investigation on the subject of emotions in fieldwork. For example, there is a large body of research on the emotional exhaustion of fieldwork (Wolf 1996; Hubbard, Backett-Milburn, and Kemmer 2001) as well as on managing one's own emotions in interviews and/or fieldwork (Chong 2008; Coffey 1999; Kleinman and Copp 1993). In relation to the latter, researchers have pointed to how they have engaged in 'emotion management,' which Karen Ramsay (1996) called 'learn(ing) not to cry or laugh in the field,' and which Hochschild (1983, 1998) termed, more widely, 'surface' and 'deep acting.'

Perhaps the most extensive treatment of this issue is found in Kleinman and Copp's (1993) aptly titled *Emotions and Fieldwork*. While written nearly 15 years ago, it remains highly relevant to a discussion of emotions in knowing processes. The crux of their argument is that qualitative researchers tend to emphasize mainly positive emotions, including relational connection, towards their research subjects. In contrast to a rosy rendering of research relations, these authors encourage fieldworkers to acknowledge a wide range of feelings that they experience in the field and to take these feelings into account in data analysis. The strength of their work lies in Kleinman and Copp's emphasis on emotions in *both* fieldwork and data analysis, a point that is especially important given that there has been relatively less attention given to the latter.

Our own work coalesces with that of Kleinman and Copp and their plea for greater attention to emotions in data analysis (e.g., Mauthner and Doucet 1998, 2003). Yet, while this point that emotions matter profoundly in data analysis and knowledge construction processes is now a fairly well accepted one, the question of *how* to identify and work with emotions in our research practice is one that requires further attention. We begin to take up this challenge below.

Working with Emotions in Our Knowing Processes

Over the past two decades many researchers have found ways of grappling with, managing, and writing about emotions in fieldwork. Psychosocial researchers, for example, draw on psychoanalytic concepts, such as transference and counter-transference (see Bondi 2005) and the 'defended subject' (Hollway and Jefferson 2000; Hollway 2008a) to conceptualize ways of working with emotions in research (Lucey, Meldody, and Walkerdine 2003; Walkerdine, Lucey, and Melody 2001, 2002; Hollway and Jefferson 2000). Another prominent group of scholars seeking to incorporate emotional ways of knowing into research practice are relational researchers, who have been developing and using the Listening Guide, an approach to fieldwork and data analysis that focuses detailed attention on emotional inter-subjectivity (Brown and Gilligan 1992; Mauthner and Doucet, 2012). This approach is useful for sociological and other scholars seeking to work with emotions in research in meaningful ways, but who have no training in psychoanalytic theory or practice (see also Bennett 2009).

In this second part of our chapter, we draw on our ongoing development of the Listening Guide approach to qualitative research in order to explore three ways of working with emotions in knowledge construction processes. These are: (1) field notes; (2) linking fieldwork and data analysis processes; and (3) group-based data analysis (including memory work). We begin with a brief overview of our version of the Listening Guide.

The Listening Guide

The Listening Guide, also referred to as the voice centred relational method, is an 'emergent method of social research' (Hesse-Biber and Leavy 2006), which was developed over several years by Lyn Brown, Carol Gilligan, and their colleagues at the Harvard Project on Women's Psychology and Girls' Development at the Harvard Graduate School of Education. Its theoretical roots are in clinical and literary approaches, interpretive and hermeneutic traditions, and relational theory (e.g., Belenky et al. 1986; Brown and Gilligan 1992; Gilligan 1982, 1988; Miller 1976, 1986). Since its inception, it has been used, extended, and adapted in diverse multidisciplinary projects within psychology, sociology, education, and social work across several countries (e.g., Brown 1998; Doucet 2006; Halbertal 2002; Gilligan et al. 2006; Mauthner 2002; McCormack 2004; Tolman 2002; Way 1998, 2001).

We first used the Listening Guide as doctoral researchers working with Gilligan at Cambridge University in the early 1990s, with Mauthner further deepening her understanding of it as a postdoctoral student of Gilligan's at Harvard University (1995–6). While using the method under the guidance of Gilligan, we also simultaneously began to develop our own version of it. In the ensuing decades, we have further refined this interpretive guide with each subsequent research project that we have taken on, drawing on other methodological approaches which complement it, especially recent innovations in narrative analysis (see Doucet and Mauthner 2008). While respecting its history, our version of the Listening Guide is a more critical sociological one which relates to our broad interest in theoretical and empirical understandings of reflexivity, feminist approaches to methodologies and epistemologies, questions about what constitutes 'data,' and theoretical debates on subjectivities.

If there is a recurrent core to the Listening Guide approach, especially as articulated in our recent work, it is an integrated set of themes that rely on a relational ontology, inter-subjectivity in knowing, a deeply reflexive approach to knowledge construction, and an emphasis on narrative and narrated subjects. While its initial innovation is found in how it gives particular attention to the detailed processes of how to analyse qualitative data, and how to 'do' reflexivity, it also provides a reminder of the critical importance of the deeply engaged researcher involved in all stages of the research process, through open and receptive interviewing processes, reflexive field notes, and group-based analysis. We explore each of these below.

Field Notes

While taking field notes is standard practice in ethnography or in anthropological research (e.g., Clifford 1990), detailed field notes can act as an important part of our knowing processes in sociological research projects and as vehicles for linking emotion, observation, interpretation, and analysis. According to Kleinman and Copp (1993), when we 'immerse ourselves in the setting and feel like real fieldworkers there is a tendency to record voluminous notes as "recorded facts," as proof that we were there, and to "downplay our reactions and feel like good social scientists"' (19). We concur with their argument that avoiding negative emotions about the research process and its participants can lead to us to put off our analysis and to miss crucial observations that may lead to alternate explanations that build on those same negative emotions. We also suggest that field notes can act as an important emotional bridge between data collection and data analysis, and that doing one's own data collection allows for a greater possibility of the link between emotions felt while being in the field and those that resurface in analysis and writing. This has led us to argue for a critical approach towards the increasing tendency for more established researchers to delegate fieldwork to more junior research team members (Mauthner and Doucet, 2008).

The issue of how to *do* field notes, however, remains somewhat of a 'secret' in qualitative research texts (but see Wolfinger 2002). The question thus remains: How do we utilize field notes in ways that record some of the emotions that may matter in our knowing processes?

Guidelines for writing field notes are found, either implicitly or explicitly, in writing on the Listening Guide. Two points can be mentioned here. First, as the Listening Guide is focused on *listening* and attending to the emotional quality of the sound and tone of the voices that we record on our tape recorders, we recommend that, where possible, researchers listen again to their interviews and begin to jot down initial interpretations and responses. This allows for a weaving of emotional and intellectual responses to our research subjects and the narratives being told and heard (see also Hollway and Jefferson 2000; Hollway 2008b).

Our second point about field notes in relation to the Listening Guide approach to research is that they can provide the beginning of a first, 'reflexive' reading of interview data; that is, data analysis *begins* in the field notes as we re-engage with our research subjects and as we document our initial thoughts and feelings about our encounter and our interpretations of the many layers of evolving narratives (see also Somers 1995; Doucet and Mauthner 2008). While, as described below, the Listening Guide advocates several systematic readings of interview transcripts, its first reading combines insights from narrative research and literary theory, which translate into an integration of narrative analysis (see Riessman 2008) combined with reader response (Radway 1991). This highly subjective and intuitive reading can be started even before interviews are transcribed from talk to text in the form of initial recorded reflections in field notes.

In the projects in which we are currently engaged,[2] some of our most important insights have emerged in the emotional space of field note writing immediately after we leave the interview setting – in coffee shops, in our home office, on the bus or train, or in our cars. Sister approaches to the Listening Guide, such as the burgeoning field of psychosocial methods, take a slightly different approach to field notes, attending to how the fantasies and defences of researchers affect fieldwork, analysis, and writing (Walkerdine, Lucey, and Melody 2002; Lucey, Meldody, and Walkerdine 2003); as recently described by Wendy Hollway (2008b), psychosocial researchers may also utilize psychoanalytic insights to record field notes about embodied expressions of research participants.

Connection between Data Collection and Data Analysis

A second way of working with emotions during our research processes is to emphasize a continuous flow between fieldwork and data analysis; as discussed above, this can be achieved partly through documenting our emotional responses in field notes. It is also important to note that emotional connections may, and often do, occur out of a sense of 'being there' in the field (see also Geertz 1973, 1988). While a seemingly simple point, its radical nature is revealed when we consider current academic climates where more and more team research is being conducted and where grant holders and lead researchers may do less and less of their own fieldwork (see Mauthner and Doucet 2008). An excellent depiction of the importance of this view, while 30 years old, still strikes us as powerful and worth repeating. In the words of anthropologist, Rosalie Wax (1971):

> There were many times when I found sitting in the classrooms or driving many miles to call on Indian mothers so tiring and time-consuming that I was tempted to stay home and busy myself with 'analyzing my materials' and letting the younger research assistants do the hard, dirty, and sometimes very depressing legwork. But circumstances forced me to do much of the observation and quasi participation myself. When the time came to write our report, I was intensely grateful that I had done this, for there were all manner of statements and remarks in our field notes (and the fill-in interviews) that we would otherwise have been unable to understand. Somehow, by sitting in so many Indian homes . . . I, consciously or unconsciously, had picked up the cues that helped us to 'understand.' And we picked up these cues, not through introspection or by extrapolation from someone else's notes, but by *remembering what we saw and listening to what we heard.* (266–7, emphasis added)

Regardless of their career stage, researchers can benefit from conducting their own interviews, as these constitute 'privileged moment(s)' of knowledge construction (Bourdieu et al. 1999:615). If, as argued above, emotions in research are embodied, relational, and inter-subjectively constituted between researcher and researched, then research 'data' must be conceptualized as much more than textual residues encapsulated in interview transcripts. Our argument here is that the emotions gleaned during data collection, and tapped back into during data analysis, can lead us towards knowing particular forms of understanding of social phenomena. This is, moreover, part of a larger epistemological issue of constantly challenging 'the curious divide of the theory and practice of field research' (Wacquant, personal correspondence, 2009; see also Wacquant 2009a). Loic Wacquant (2009a) articulates this particularly well in his explanation of the difference between 'egological' and epistemic reflexivity (121–? see also 2009b): '   epistemic reflexivity is deployed, not at the end of the project, *ex post*, when it comes to drafting the final research report, but *durante*, at every stage in the investigation. It targets the totality of the most routine research operations, from the selection of the site and the recruitment of informants to the choice of questions to pose or to avoid, as well as the engagement of theoretic schema, methodological tools and display techniques, at the moment when they are implemented' (2009b: 147).

Group Analysis

Group analysis of interview transcripts can also provide a further venue for working with emotions in our knowing processes. While the Listening Guide employs multiple and successive 'readings' of interview transcripts, a first reading focuses on a narrative reading combined with a reflexive reading that attends to a wide range of re-sponses, including emotional ones. The latter part of this first reading involves reading oneself in the text, and watching for how we respond to being back in the research relationship. Providing a way of maintain-ing a sustained relationship with research subjects as well as a concrete way of 'doing reflexivity,' this approach offers the excellent suggestion of using a 'worksheet' technique for this reading; that is, the interview transcript is transformed into a working document where the respon-dent's words are laid out in one column and the researcher's reactions and interpretations are laid out in an adjacent column (Gilligan, Lyons, and Hanmer 1990; Brown and Gilligan 1992; Mauthner and Doucet 1998; see also Norum 2000). This technique enables the researcher to examine how and where some of her own assumptions and views – either emotional or theoretical – might affect her interpretation of the respondent's words, and in turn how she later writes about the per-son. As described by Lyn Brown (1994): '. . . the first listening or read-ing requires the listener/interpreter to consider her relationship to the speaker or text and to document, as best she can, her interests, biases and limitations that arise from such critical dimensions of social loca-tion as race, class, gender and sexual orientation, as well as to track her own feelings in response to what she hears – particularly those feelings that do not resonate with the speaker's experience' (392).

This 'reading' of interview transcripts can be done individually or in small groups with trusted colleagues. In the first research projects where we used the Listening Guide, along with Carol Gilligan and a small group of doctoral students at Cambridge University, we spent an intensive period of about 17 months collectively analysing each other's interview transcripts and building emergent explanations and theoretical analysis out of that group work (Mauthner and Doucet 1998). Working within the context of a group was extremely useful, because, having read extracts from our transcripts, others were able to point out where we might have missed or glossed over what they regarded as key aspects of the interview narrative. This made us acutely aware of how our emotional responses mattered in knowledge construction, as well as our control in choosing or ignoring particular lines of inquiry and explanation. That is, working with other colleagues highlighted how 'people have more than one way to tell a story and see a situation through different lenses and in different lights' (Gilligan, Lyons, and Hanmer 1990: 95).

Another kind of group work that works with subjectivity and emotion is the small but burgeoning field of 'memory work.' Rooted in the work of German feminist theorist Frigga Haug (1987) and her theories on self-development, memory work has mainly been taken up by researchers in the United Kingdom (see Holland 2007; Crawford et al. 1992; Thomson and McLeod 2009) who have further developed innovative approaches to bringing out researcher emotions. Working mostly in teams, researchers use memory work in varied ways to explore emotions in relation to research topics and research respondents, and to reflect on how emotions may affect knowledge production. Memory work has been effectively employed in research on sensitive or emotionally laden topics – such as motherhood, fatherhood, sexual violence, and transitions into adulthood. The value of memory work is well expressed by Thomson and McLeod (2009) who have recently written: 'We have engaged in memory work as a complementary research practice for ten years, with regular memory work becoming a vital part of communication within research collectives, feeding into the accumulation of a reflexive understanding of our investments in our topics of research, or connections with and differences from each other as well as directly into methodological and theoretical development' (16).

As with many methodological approaches, there is no one particular way or recipe to undertake memory work. Its recent iterations have been based in group-based approaches (Crawford et al. 1992; Gordon, Holland, and Lahelma 2000; Thomson and Holland 2005) or in individual approaches (Kuhn 2002, 2007), and with differing emphases on

textual journaling or the use of photography. In spite of its continuing
diversity within research practice, memory work can nevertheless be
called a methodological 'family' (Thomson and Holland 2009:29) and
an important means of working with emotions in our knowing processes.

Narcissistic Reflexivity

Taking an approach to knowing that involves attending to our emotions through field notes, an integrated approach to emotional work
in data collection and data analysis, and group analysis and memory
work, leads us to the question of how much emotional work needs to be
done in order to achieve 'good' knowing, or what philosopher Loraine
Code (1991) has referred to as 'responsible knowing'(132). On the other
hand, is there a possibility that, by taking emotions into account in our
knowing processes, we might inadvertently veer into what Bourdieu
(2003) called 'narcissistic reflexivity' (281)?

Bourdieu's concept of 'narcissistic reflexivity' is part of his larger
'obsessive insistence on reflexivity' (Wacquant 2006:11; emphasis added),
which is, in turn, part of an extensive body of writing that spans several decades. In brief, Bourdieu (2003) describes this concept in the following way: 'Scientific reflexivity stands opposed to the narcissistic
reflexivity of postmodern anthropology as well as to the egological reflexivity of phenomenology in that it endeavours to increase scientific-
ity by turning the most objectivist tools of social science not only onto
the private person of the enquirer but also, and more decisively, onto
the anthropological field itself and onto the scholastic dispositions and
biases it fosters and rewards in its members' (281).

Bourdieu's work with Wacquant helps to explicate even further his
conception of narcissistic reflexivity; he writes: 'This is to say that the
sociology I argue for has little in common with a complacent and in-
timist return upon the private person of the sociologist or to look for
the intellectual *Zeitgeist* that animate his or her work . . . I must also
dissociate myself completely from the form of 'reflexivity' represented
by the kind of self-fascinated observation of the observer's writing and
feelings which has recently some fashionable among some American
anthropologists'. . . who, having apparently exhausted the charms of
fieldwork, have turned to talking about themselves rather than their
object of research (Bourdieu and Wacquant 1990:72; see also Bourdieu
2003). Bourdieu (2003) is thus concerned not to turn the lens 'onto the

private person' and to avoid being taken in by 'the "diary disease,"[3] an explosion of narcissism sometimes verging on exhibitionism' (282); elsewhere, he urges researchers to draw a distinction between the "epistemic individual" and the "empirical individual" (Bourdieu 1988), and he cautions against being taken in by the "biographical illusion"' (Bourdieu 1987, cited in Bourdieu and Wacquant 1992:207). In light of these points, our question is: In reflecting upon the emotions that matter in our knowing processes, how can we ensure that we do not get trapped into research processes which constitute a 'self-fascinated observation of the observer's writings and feelings,' and which encourage 'a thinly veiled nihilistic relativism' as opposed to 'a truly reflexive social science' (Bourdieu and Wacquant 1992:72).

Drawing again from Bourdieu and Wacquant, we argue that this achievement of a 'truly reflexive social science' can be done by attending not only to the personal and biographical positioning of the researcher but to his/her positioning within theoretical, disciplinary, institutional, political, and cultural locations that impact on their knowing processes (Doucet and Mauthner 2003, 2008). In this vein, we agree with Bourdieu (2003) that epistemic reflexivity must attend not only to'the recording and analysis of the "pre-notions" (in Durkheim's sense) that social agents engage in the construction of social reality; it must also encompass the social conditions of the production of these pre-constructions' (282). As Wacquant (2006) puts it, there needs to be systemic attention to 'the personal identity of the researcher: her gender, class, nationality, ethnicity, education, etc.,' but also '(h)er location in the intellectual field,' including 'disciplinary and institutional attachments' (11). Put differently, this means that the objects of study or 'social phenomena [are] to be found, not in the consciousness of individuals, but in the system of objective relations in which they are enmeshed' (5).

Thus a key point for this discussion is to appreciate Bourdieu and Wacquant's argument that efforts to be self-reflexive in our knowing processes can indeed translate into 'narcissistic reflexivity' when this reflexive thinking remains focused only on the 'private person of the sociologist.' Nevertheless, we posit that there is a means of working with emotion and memories in ways that can have epistemological weight. For example, in her work on primary caregiving fathers, Doucet (2006, 2008) reflected on how a dream came to her while she was midway through her data analysis and she realized that a childhood memory about a single father who lived across the street from her childhood home was, in fact, the instigating point for her sympathetic openness to the narratives of lives of fathers who were primary caregivers of children.

Did Doucet fall into the trap, which Bourdieu (2003) clearly scorns, of shamelessly promoting 'the biographical particularities of the researcher or the *Zeitgeist* that inspires his (her) work' (282)? While this danger is, indeed, a possibility, we would argue that it does not necessarily emerge from this rather intimate approach to reflexive thinking. As argued by Amanda Coffey (1999), '[t]he boundaries between self indulgence and reflexivity are fragile and blurred' so that there 'will always be the question of how much of ourselves to reveal' (133). Our view is that any attention to memories, emotions, and dreams as instigators or critical parts of our research must always hold a sustained focus of inquiry towards *why and how* they matter to the knowledge being produced. What is thus required is detailed attention to how these emotions, memories, or dreams – whether analysed individually or within a group – lead us down a particular avenue of analysis, explanation, and knowledge construction (see also Gordon 1996; McMahon 1996). If they alter the general direction or tenor of the knowledge being produced, then they may indeed be useful to reflect on and to possibly write up as part of our 'audit trail' (Seale 1999).

We also want to point out that Bourdieu himself, in his last published work (2008), quietly argued that there is a way to turn the 'private person of the sociologist' and their 'intuition' into a form of research 'capital':

'This kind of experimentation on the work of reflexivity . . . shows that one of the rarest springs of the practical mastery that defines the sociologist's craft, a central component of which is what people call *intuition* is perhaps, ultimately, the scientific use of a social experience, which, so long as it is first subjected to sociological critique, can, however lacking in social value it may be in itself . . . be reconverted from handicap into a capital. As I have said elsewhere, it was no doubt a banal remark of my mother's . . . that . . . triggered the reflection that led me to abandon the model of the kinship rule for that of strategy.' (86)

This admission of Bourdieu that a 'banal remark' from his mother 'triggered' an important theoretical line of inquiry strikes us as both radical and somewhat contradictory to his earlier remarks on the dangers of narcissistic reflexivity. This admission is not the only one in which he reflects, in a subdued manner, on how his own biographical history and his emotional connections played a role in motivating particular theoretical interests.

Two other examples of his attention to biographical influences are Bourdieu's rambling reflections on how his father praised the young Bourdieu in his rebelliousness and 'stubbornness' against authority at school. The first is in a passage that begins with: 'Rediscovering a photograph in which I was walking alongside my father . . . I remember what he once said to me, when coming out of the lycée, I related one of my latest clashes with the school administration' (2007:89–90). A further instance are his thoughts on how '(t)he experience of boarding school no doubt played a decisive part in the formation of my dispositions' (2008:90). Such reflections open up the possibility of considering Bourdieu as an ally, albeit a cautious one, in work that argues for the importance of emotions in knowing. As we have argued elsewhere in our work on reflexivity, it is a matter of *how* it is done; it is a matter of 'degrees,' and of recognizing the necessary limits of knowing all that matters to our knowing (Mauthner and Doucet 2003). We thus argue that there is indeed a possibility that attending to emotions in research and in our knowing processes can veer towards 'narcissistic reflexivity.' What matters, then, is how this work is accomplished so as to balance biographical and emotional influences with a sustained attention to the demands of a larger conception of epistemic reflexivity. According to Henri Bernard (1990), Bourdieu 'has shown how ethnography can be reflexive without being narcissistic or uncritical' and offers 'a way out of the cul-de-sac that ethnographers and theorists of ethnography have created for themselves' (58, 71, cited in Bourdieu and Wacquant 1992:41). We concur that this remains a challenge for researchers who want to take emotions seriously in their knowing processes.

Conclusions

In this chapter, we have highlighted cross-disciplinary writings, particularly by feminist sociologists, emotional geographers, and psychosocial researchers, on the critical importance of taking emotions into account in processes of knowledge construction. As attested throughout this book, the field of the sociology of emotions is burgeoning; nevertheless, less attention has been given to how to work with emotions in our research practice and our knowing processes. Rooted in a two-decade-long immersion in extending the Listening Guide approach to qualitative research, we have laid out several practical strategies to identifying and utilizing emotions in ways that matter to our knowledge production. Specifically, we discussed field notes, an integrated approach to emotional thinking in data collection and analysis, and group analysis and memory work. Finally, building on selected insights of Bourdieu and Wacquant, we explored the issue of how researchers can work on emotional terrain in their reflexive thinking and practices without veering into 'narcissistic reflexivity.'

Our approach underscores the importance of the inter-subjective emotions that occur between researcher and the researched in fieldwork, field notes, and analysis. We also noted the value of psychosocial methods in excavating emotions in research while simultaneously concurring with Bennet (2009) that social scientists with no training in psychoanalytic methods are less well placed to bring such insights into their field notes and analysis. A final point on emotions in our knowing processes relates to the retelling of stories and to the knowledge outputs that are eventually produced. In our view, an additional key challenge for researchers who work with and write about emotions is how to convey, even partially, a small degree of the rich sensuousness of being in the field with people – embodied subjects who enter into a brief relation with us as they tell their stories in voices that register a wide array of emotions and with gestures that convey more than texts. That is, with Wacquant (2008b), we maintain that it is critical to work towards a sociology of emotions in methodological writing that seeks 'to expand textual genres and styles so as to better capture the taste and ache of social action' (101).

NOTES

1 We recognize that there is a complexity of work on the differences between emotions and feeling, and emotions and interpersonal processes, distinctions that are dealt with in other sections of this text (see also Turner and Stets 2005).
2 Doucet is currently writing a book on mothers who are primary breadwinners in Canada and the United States, while Mauthner is conducting a cross-cultural research project on academics and their work.
3 Bourdieu (2003) is drawing here on Clifford Geertz (1998:89), who is drawing in turn on Roland Barthes (1980:532).

PART II

Emotions and Empirical Investigations

At the conceptual level, many authors argue that emotions play a crucial role in shaping human interaction (see Turner and Stets 2005; Probyn 2005; Lupton 1998). Until recently, however, research regarding emotions in sociology was methodologically underdeveloped. This section briefly maps out some of the methodological trends in the sociology of emotions.

The entire tool kit of social science is now open for the study of emotion (Planlap 1999), which is a blessing and a curse. The opening of emotions for analysis by social scientists is a blessing, since, for a few decades, emotions were primarily an object of inquiry for cognitive and neurological science, black-boxing the relational aspects of emotions. The opening of emotions for analysis by all social scientists is also a curse since coherent theoretical understandings of emotions remain few and far between, which can result in methodological disarray. Up to this point in *Emotions Matter*, the chapters have focused on theoretical issues, addressing a lacuna concerning concepts and ontological commitments. The latter half of this volume now turns to empirical investigations, demonstrating how a relational approach to emotions can actually inform the craft and techniques of social scientific research. The prominent American sociologist C. Wright Mills was hesitant to use the idea of 'social science' and preferred the idea of 'social studies,' relevant here since the particular methodological and epistemological commitments required to study emotions as relational cannot be construed as scientific in an abstracted empiricist sense.

Robinson, Clay-Warner, and Everett (2008) argue that there are two methodological trends in the sociology of emotions in the United States. First, there has been a qualitative and descriptive methodological approach concerned with context. Katz and Hochschild are key amongst the scholars contributing to this trend. Second, there has been a quantitative and predictive trend using formal modelling techniques. The volume by Clay-Warner and Robinson (2008) puts these two methodological trends into dialogue. While several of the chapters in *Emotions Matter* dwell on structural issues, our volume does not follow the trend towards quantitative and predictive methodologies, for two reasons. First, a relational approach to emotions is skeptical of attempts to predict understandings of emotions or outcomes of interaction. A relational approach to emotions studies emotions in action, assuming that there is a creativity or contingency in action that cannot be predicted. Second, we question the objective of trying to predict understandings of emotions or outcomes of interaction as well as the use that such predictive knowledge might be put to. For instance, in the field of criminal justice, the goal of trying to predict understandings of emotions is tied to preventative policing of so-called 'antisocial behaviour' and an extension of the authority of criminal justice institutions.

Of note here is that the trend towards quantitative and predictive methodologies is not one that has been followed by Canadian sociologists. In Canada, sociologists and related scholars have a tendency to draw more from social and cultural theory coming from the United Kingdom as well as the qualitative and descriptive research trend in America.

Several of the following chapters engage in studies of emotions in situ, using numerous methodological techniques. Studying emotions in situ implies particular methodological and epistemological commitments that are contrary to structuralist but also psychological approaches to emotions. On the one hand, structuralist accounts ignore phenomenological, interactionist, and corporeal elements of emotions as the experience of social relations. For instance, despite his critical focus on stratification and power, the model of emotions proposed by Turner (2010) tends towards a structuralism that ignores interaction and corporeality. Yet psychological approaches to emotions often abstract emotions from interaction and phenomenal and corporeal experience (and from other emotions as well) in order to treat them asindicators or variables in (primarily) quantitative studies. We are critical of experimental approaches to research on emotions, where interaction is cut out from naturalistic settings and reduced to static behaviourism in a laboratory setting. Psychological theories of emotions can be reductionist in separating the analysis of emotions from a larger gestalt of the self (see also Sartre 1949). Not all psychological research is as adamantly positivist as we suggest, but we have construed psychological research this way to make it clear that a relational approach in sociology and related disciplines requires an attempt to conduct research on emotions at the interface of the self and social structure. The outcome of a relational approach, whatever methodological form it takes, should be a de-reification of emotions.

Methodological strategies reflective of this relational approach include participant observation used in conjunction with interviewing, and historical sociology or a historicization of emotions. Whereas an historical approach to emotions (similar to what Hunt and Suski attempt in this volume) does not so much examine emotions in situ, this method does place emotions in temporal context, examining how designations of emotions at the intersection of self and social structure change over time. Participant observation used in conjunction with interviewing (similar to what Walby and Spencer, Deri, as well as Bookman attempt in this volume) can allow for investigation of emotions in situ, though we want to stress the magnitude of long-term ethnographies as well as the tendency towards qualitative realism and subjectivism that can emerge in qualitative research that is not properly patient and designed. With these comments on method, we are not suggesting that the sociology of emotions become myopic as it regards the way we do research. We are arguing that a relational conceptual approach to emotions entails methodological and epistemological commitments. As Doucet and Mauthner put it in their chapter, our understanding of emotions as relational must feed back into our understanding of the research encounter itself. Although the chapters that follow are suggestive of how to study emotions as relational, more innovation in the field of qualitative research is required to achieve this goal.

10 How Emotions Matter: Objects, Organizations, and the Emotional Climate of a Mass Spectrometry Laboratory

KEVIN WALBY AND DALE SPENCER

Introduction

How do relations with objects matter for the trajectory of organizations and the people who work in them? There is a small literature on this topic. For instance, Suchman (2005) explores the capacities of objects to link human workers in organizations. Knorr-Cetina (1997) has argued that sociality with objects has become a primary form of sociality. In organizations today there has been a shift away from solely human worlds towards thinking of 'objects as relationship partners or embedding environments' (25). Objects play an important, almost pivotal, role in organizations. Objects are vital, like partners, to scientists as well.

Although there is a growing literature on objects and organizations, this has yet to be fully linked to the sociology of emotions. Emotions can be conceptualized as the experience of relations with others (Barbalet 2002). Up until recently, there has been a dearth of empirical research on emotions in organizational studies (Sturdy 2003). One consequence of this underdevelopment concerning theoretical and methodological approaches to emotions in organizational studies is that the significance of emotions as it regards relations with objects has been ignored. Scholars in organizational studies have now begun to assess the way emotions provide a sense of belonging, attachment, and solidarity in organizations (Miller, Considine, and Garner 2007; Landri 2007; Rafaeli and Worline 2001). Coupland and colleagues (2008) argue that the way people tell stories about emotions signals acceptance and/or dismissal of organizational practices. Yet scholarly depictions of people experiencing emotions at work in organizations are a new invention in organizational studies (Sturdy 2003; Ashford and Humphrey 1995; Fineman

1993). In this chapter, we demonstrate how the study of emotions in relation to objects can supplement the way we understand practices, rules, and status in organizations.

We discuss organizational practices regarding a mass spectrometer located in the Earth Sciences Department of one Canadian university. University science departments and their laboratories can be thought of as organizations since they operate in a shared material setting, with a shared set of practices, rules, and understandings (Schatzki 2006, 2005). Our case study supplements debates regarding emotions in organizations (Fineman 2000; Sandelands and Boudens 2000) by demonstrating how emotions in relation to objects matter to organizations. We draw on Barbalet's (1998) notion of 'emotional climates,' which refers to social sharing of emotions at the group level, to show how emotions matter in three ways. First, emotions provide an orientation towards objects and other people in the organization. Second, emotions at the group level, in the form of an emotional climate, provide a mechanism for binding those who are part of the lab relations amongst themselves. Third, emotions matter insofar as the micro-politics of maintaining the emotional climate and governing organizational practices regarding the central object affect how group members become valued and gendered.

The mass spectrometer object we discuss, referred to as 'Shiri' by the earth scientists, is used to produce mass spectrums of rock samples and determine their composition. Shiri's name initially came from the side of a carton that was atop the box the spectrometer arrived in when sent from the manufacturer. The scientists' experiences of sociality with this object fashion a trajectory for the organization and create a shared narrative among lab members. Objects do not always do what scientists want (de Laet and Mol 2000). Natural scientists are always dealing with 'a continuous resistance in their objects' (Czarniawska 2004:53). Law and Singleton (2005) argue that it is the aleatory capacities of objects, as opposed to their immutability, which makes them crucial to organizations, since some solution to the contingency posed by the object must constantly be sought after. We define 'aleatory capacities' as the tendency for objects to produce unanticipated effects that generate emotions for humans who are enmeshed in relations with the object. These aleatory capacities of Shiri affect the formation of an emotional climate in the organization. As humans try to standardize the performance of the spectrometer, they experience and narrate joy and frustration. The circulation of joy and frustration, especially concerning the small successes laboratory leaders achieve in working with the object, creates the emotional climate. Emotions are socially shared in particular contexts since they cannot be restricted to any particular individual (Ahmed 2004). The emotional climate arises from the sharing of joy and frustration related to attempts at managing the capacities of the spectrometer object. We examine scientists' talk about emotions as evidence of attempts to stabilize Shiri's capacities for producing contingent results. We also analyse the rules for governing the work of scientists, and the effect that scientists' deviant actions have on the maintenance of the emotional climate.

This chapter is organized into four parts. First, we discuss the centrality of objects to the experience of work in organizations. Second, we make an argument concerning how emotions matter in science department laboratories as organizations. After a note on method, we present our case study of Shiri and the emotional climate of a mass spectrometer lab by discussing how the aleatory capacities of the spectrometer influence the scientists' orientation to the object and to each other, and how this leads to the formation of an emotional climate. We discuss what maintenance of the emotional climate means in terms of the gendered micro-politics of emotions, which are constitutive of the organization's trajectory and the lives of workers in the organization. Experience of frustration compared to joy marks one's place in the status hierarchy of an organization (Clark 1990). Maintenance of the emotional climate of the lab is frustrating work, but it is also devalued, feminized labour. We argue that consideration of emotions related to object-centred sociality is a significant method of understanding gender subordination in organizations. Attention to the role of objects in forming emotional climates concerning science work is a contribution to understanding organizations, since the focus on emotions as the experience of relations with humans and with objects supplements understandings of how organizational practices are experienced.

Objects and Organizations

Understanding the capacities of 'objects' is key to appreciating how emotions related to objects matter to organizations. The way that researchers in science and technology studies have conceptualized objects is useful for informing how we conceive of the relationshipbetween objects and organizations. As some of the first scholars interested in objects and organizations, actor network theorists have conceptualized objects as 'actants' and 'immutable mobiles' (Latour 1996; Callon

1986). 'Actants' are material quasi-objects with their own capacities. 'Immutable mobiles' are versions of such quasi-objects that stay stable and are made use of by those trying to enroll others into world-making projects (Lynch and Woolgar 1988; Latour 1987). Knowledge networks form like eddies around objects, drawing other actants to the project. The object is thought of as an effect of network relations (Law 2002).

Earlier discussions of actor network theory (ANT) were limited insofar as they tended to operate with preconceived notions of what an object is, instead of asking ontological questions of the objects themselves (Law and Singleton 2005). In saying X is an object, an ontological claim about what X is and what X can do is posited, which works to 'fix' the object as singular and unchanging. It is crucial to keep 'a willingness to push the boundaries of what an object is, or could be' (Law and Singleton 2005:340). In other words, objects are 'fluid' (de Laet and Mol 2000). Objects are open to change in terms of what they are materially composed of and how people relate to them.

We conceptualize Shiri the spectrometer as a fluid object since this object is always being taken apart and added to, and since the way people in the laboratory establish the significance of the spectrometer is open to change. The boundaries and the meanings of the spectrometer are understood by earth scientists themselves as in flux, which influences how earth scientists in the lab approach the object, sometimes with careful technique, sometimes with attributions of superstition. As Ahmed (2006) puts it 'objects do not only do what we intend them to do' (47); their capacities are aleatory, which means our orientation to the object and the other people related to the object is contingent. The success of people working with the spectrometer can only be a matter of degree. We also comment on the gendered meanings that objects can be imbued with as a result of their aleatory capacities.

Knorr-Cetina's (1997) work on sociality with objects provides insight as to how objects become central in organizations. She argues objects are not simply commodities or instruments. Contemporary organizations are characterized by 'an increasing orientation towards objects as sources of the self, of relational intimacy, or shared subjectivity and social integration' (9). Solidarity emerges from this sociality with objects. Solidarity refers to how emotions bind members to the project of the organization and to one another.[2] Science laboratories are best conceived as organizational sites where relations with objects, relations between workers, and relations with other laboratories are ongoing. Following Knorr-Cetina, our case study of an earth sciences department examines how the spectrometer object becomes pivotal in narratives regarding emotions, work, and the future of the organization.

How Emotions Matter

Emotions are commonly conceived of as hardwired as opposed to embedded in social contexts (Coupland et al. 2008). Yet emotions need not be taken as idiosyncratic drives. Instead, 'the emotion is in the social relationship' (Barbalet 2002a:4). The sociology of emotions theorizes emotions as relational and investigates emotions not as an abstract category but in their specificity (Probyn 2005). The question of what emotions 'are' is displaced to focus on what emotions 'do' and how people talk about emotions (Ahmed 2004a). However, whereas much of the literature has conceived of emotions as experienced purely in relation to humans (Kemper 2004; Burkitt 2002; Williams 1998), we conceive of emotions as the experience of relations with humans *and* with objects.

The relationship between science and emotion is not one of science existing in scientists' heads. We think of science as a set of organizationally based material and relational processes involving scientists in groups, as a form of organizing (Thagard 2002). Barbalet (2002a) has argued that it is necessary to go beyond treating science in terms of individual brilliance, the politics between rival organizational groups, or even the passion for knowledge that scientists exhibit, to examine instead how emotions matter in lab settings. Emotions matter to an understanding of laboratories cum organizations in three ways.

The first way that emotions matter is in providing an orientation towards objects and other people (also see Ahmed, this volume; Katz, this volume). Ahmed (2006) argues that emotions are crucial in our orientation towards objects insofar as emotions are a particular way of turning towards an object and forming a definite sense of it. Objects can be viewed and worked with in any number of ways; orientation is always in flux. Yet the particular way we view and work with an object at any time is a matter of the emotions we experience in our relations with that object as well as with other people. Objects are shaped by our orientation towards them. Yet, in having their own capacities and their own persona, objects also shape our orientation. The possibility of relations with humans and objects depends on a basis for experiencing those relations; emotions are the basis (Collins 2004). Below, we describe how joy and frustration provide an orientation towards objects and humans in the organization, but also how this orientation is generated out of relations with the spectrometer object.

Emotions are the basis for experiencing relations with humans and objects, but this experiencing happens somewhere, and, over time, in a specific context (also see Davidson and Smith, this volume; Bookman, this volume). The second way that emotions matter is by providing a mechanism for binding together those who are part of the organization's social group (in our case, members of a lab). The 'emotional climate' concept signals emotional experiences that are collective, at the group level, related to the maintenance of the group as acting together on shared and specialized projects (Barbalet 1998). Emotional climates include patterns of experience not experienced by non-members. Participation in the group need not be equal, as each member contributes differentially to the emotional climate of the workplace. Though an emotional climate can be organized around any cluster of emotions, below we delimit the emotions discussed in our case study to joy and frustration. According to Ahmed (2004a), 'emotions *do things*, and they align individuals with communities . . .' (119). Not only do emotions provide an orientation towards objects and other people in relations with that object; emotions experienced at the group level also demarcate the parameters of the group and can orient humans to those outside the milieu. Below we discuss the formation of the emotional climate, but also the rules that steady the emotional climate by governing the actions of scientists. We focus on how Quimbanda, the laboratory leader, and Nell, the lab manager, contribute differentially to the lab's emotional climate.

Third, emotions matter insofar as the micro-politics of emotions influence the way work is organized in the lab. Our case study demonstrates one example of how relations between what Knorr-Cetina (1999:221) calls incipient and full-fledged scientific persons are mediated through emotional micro-politics that mark status. We define status as 'a position in some system or pattern of positions . . . related to the other positions in the unit through reciprocal ties, through rights and duties binding the incumbents' (Goffman 1961:85). Attention to the micro-politics of emotions in organizations – how people narrate their frustration, indignation, resentment, and so on, in relation to others in the organization – can signal how subtle gender disparities operate and how these disparities are experienced. In laboratories, the tendency is to relate to one another with a sense of 'mono-gender' insofar as everyone is treated as a scientist (Knorr-Cetina 1999: 232). Czarniawska (2006) conceptualizes gender subordination as an organizational practice, and in our case study we examine the experiencing of certain emotions in relation to objects and other people as a marker of status subordination. The work of gendered subjects can be devalued depending on their relationship to an object in an organization. Below we consider the work of Nell – the Earth Sciences Department mass spectrometry lab manager – in terms of emotions, status, and gender.

Case Study Methods: Opening the Black Box

Revealing the complexities as well as contradictions of living and organizing, case study research investigates events with a focus on context (Flyvbjerg 2006; Yin 2003). Analysis of only a few participant narratives from interviews is justified using the case study method since understanding the context, not staking universalizing claims, is the purpose. With an understanding that workers in organizations have multiple senses of self and offer multiple interpretations of any event (Halford and Leonard 2006; Sims 2005; Czarniawska 2004), we asked interviewees a series of open-ended questions about their emotions concerning laboratory work. We sampled graduate students and professors in order to maximize the range of experiences. Early interviewees were located by soliciting participants online in the departments of biology, chemistry, physics, and earth sciences. Entirely consistent with the method of selection proposed by case study researchers (Flyvbjerg 2006; Ruddin 2006), after completing an initial set of interviews in the various departments, the Earth Sciences Department was selected for a case study since our analysis of the spectrometer's centrality to lab operations demonstrates how emotions in relation to objects matter in organizations. A year after the initial interviews, we returned to our respondents in earth sciences and discussed changes in lab relations and organizational practices. Interviews were supplemented by observations of scientists' work processes in the labs.[3] We substitute pseudonyms for respondents' names.

Law (2004) writes that as social scientists, events and processes 'necessarily exceed our capacity to know them' (6). Research methods produce the reality they understand, rather than discover it. The same goes for emotions. Knowledge workers such as scientists are always burying traces of their constructional activities and black-boxing their methods (Law 2004). Since emotions are an important part of scientists' orientations towards objects, scientists might be wary of speaking about lab emotions. We are thus influenced by the methodological principles of actor network theory, but with a twist. The foundational position of actor network theory (ANT) is that we study science in action, not ready-made science (Latour 1987). It is not 'science' per se but the work of organizing and constructing 'facts' that is the focus. We are interested in black-boxed facts, but also in black-boxed emotions.

Discussing the lack of attention given to methodological issues concerning emotions in organizational studies, Sturdy (2003) argues 'emotion does not speak for itself' (83). Emotion is difficult to know in any definitive form. Although narrative analysis allows researchers to move beyond the 'tick box' measurement approach to understanding emotion (Fineman 2004), post-hoc emotion narratives can mask the relations that generated the experience (Sandelands and Boudens 2000; Fineman and Sturdy 1999; Ashford and Humphrey 1995). We focus on joy and frustration as prominently narrated emotions within the emotional climate of the earth sciences department. Whereas joy is thought to be a primary emotion, and frustration is thought to be a tertiary emotion derivative of anger, we are less interested in what these emotions 'are' than how scientists narrate a sense of them in relation to their lab work and the spectrometer object. We demonstrate how joy and frustration are generated from the contingency of success and failure in science work. As per Sturdy's (2003) comments on the limits of knowing emotion through interview-based research, we are reflexive about the claims we make using the emotion narratives of respondents.

Our rationale for pulling back from a more ANT-oriented study of the lives of objects in organizations is that such analyses, which insist on indeterminacy between humans and objects, while innovative, can miss how subtle forms of (gendered) subordination operate at work. Though it is crucial not simply to assume women are subordinated in organizations because of gender (Alvesson and Billing 1992), gender and emotion were for a long time ignored in organizational studies (Halford and Leonard 2006; Sturdy 2003; Linstead 2000). Our analysis demonstrates how maintenance of the emotional climate depends on subtle gendered subordination of status in the hierarchy of science, and how this subordination occurs vis-à-vis relations with the lab's central object: the mass spectrometer.

The Emotional Climate of a Mass Spectrometry Laboratory

Orientation towards the Object

Earth Science is interdisciplinary insofar as it draws from geology, geography, geophysics, chemistry, and mathematics. Earth sciences departments develop specific niches depending on the expertise they offer and the types of objects they work with. The Earth Sciences Department in our case deals with mass spectrometry. We toured the earth sciences department, viewing the rock crushing room, the microscope rooms, the rooms for chemical rock alteration and sample construction, as well as the mass spectrometry lab itself. As mentioned earlier, lab members refer to the central lab object – the mass spectrometer – as 'Shiri.' It is not unusual for scientists to name the objects they work with, said Dr Quimbanda, the most senior and experienced scientist in the lab: 'I know other laboratories where a lot of the instruments have names . . . major research instruments . . . I can think of other labs, it is people names, it is not calling them Archetypteryx or something like that, but people names, I know of one called Oliver. I guess it is because we work with them so much and they display personalities.'

By naming Shiri and placing the object at the centre of their lives and work, Shiri becomes a part of the relational milieu of the lab. Our connection with objects is central to working life and home life (Turkle 2004). The salience of the attribution of *persona* (Maffesoli 1996) cannot be understated, since the persona of Shiri creates an orientation towards the object for scientists within the group. Orientation 'describes a kind of affective investment we have in others' (Probyn 2005:13). The scientists' reliance on Shiri's capacities, to perform efficiently and accurately, facilitates an orientation towards the object and one another insofar as all lab sociality centres around Shiri.

Shiri's technical capacities are known and esteemed. Orientation towards the object reflects a readiness for anything to happen. Shiri's capacity to affect the scientists' work, through slowing it up or throwing off precision of analysis, is acknowledged:

> If something goes wrong with her the whole department shuts down. We can still crush rock or make samples or clean the lab, but can only go for so long. A month ago there was something wrong with Shiri. For three weeks her findings were way off, and everyone's research was coming out

with totally unexpected results. Useless. So our wonderful professor who works with Shiri, he was trying to fix her and could not. Everyone was frustrated. [Another university] has a mass spectrometer, it uses argon gas. The [other university's] spectrometer has been down for six months. Graduate students and professors are not able to do their work, because what is needed is a little piece called an ion multiplier. They are really frustrated. (Suzie, graduate student)

The slowing up of work is not Shiri's fault per se for all members of the lab. Blame is attributed to ancillary mechanical parts inside to spare Shiri of culpability, as if blaming Shiri would encourage another contribution to the frustrating scene. Indicative of the scientists' orientation towards the spectrometer, Shiri is anthropomorphized while the component parts that can be swapped out and upgraded retain a status as mere bits. Made up of multiple other objects (casing, vacuum chambers, filaments, fiber optic cables, sediment), Shiri is subject to various interpretations, since if the object is unpredictable 'so too is what makes it work' (Law 2002:98; see also Whitley and Darking 2006). The way that the earth scientists work with one another is influenced by the affiliative feeling between them and their mutual dependency on the spectrometer. Objects affiliate humans to each other in organizations in ways that are binding (Suchman 2005; Collins 2004). The affiliative feeling also extends to the object at the centre of sociality in this context.

Capacities of the Fluid Object

Objects do not have minds of their own, but they do not always perform in the way we want them to. Sometimes objects do things we think they are incapable of. Objects are thus 'fluid' insofar as objects can physically change and the meanings we impute to objects also change (de Laet and Mol 2000). To be a relationally situated object in an organization is to be subject to what we call 'capacity stabilization attempts.' Humans try to get the object to work the way they want them to. The object is changing conceptually and materially, but the humans wish it not to do so. Human reaction to failures during capacity stabilization contributes to the attribution of a persona to the object. Narratives regarding Shiri's persona vary depending on how one is situated in the milieu of the lab. The narrative of Suzie, a graduate student, demonstrates that some scientists have a closer relationship with the spectrometer than others: 'She knows when her master [Quimbanda] is in the room because as soon as he leaves the room, Shiri will conk out. I have to call Quimbanda at home and say "something is wrong with Shiri."' Suzie relies on Quimbanda to manage the aleatory capacities of the object, to keep the spectrometer running. Quimbanda is the 'laboratory leader' (Knorr-Cetina 1999:221), who selects personnel and has a significant relationship with the central lab object. Quimbanda's narrative regarding Shiri's persona reflects his status in the lab and orientation towards the object: 'We get into this silly business: people think the mass spectrometer is possessed by a spirit. There are jokes about if things did not work probably it was a new moon or a full moon. This is interesting in the context of an instrument called Shiri, referring to the moon. We have a good atmosphere down here and there is a lot of joking that goes on.'

Meisiek and Yao (2005) argue that 'silly business' makes sense in organizations as much as humour in the social sharing of emotion is binding, relieves tension, and creates meaning for group members. When testing procedures do not go as planned, the scientists sometimes point to contingencies outside the laboratory to explain Shiri's defiance, be it supernatural possession or astronomical forces. Quimbanda is never bored with Shiri, and says, 'Sometimes you wish it was a little more boring, you wish there was not as many problems to deal with.' These 'problems' are the capacity of the fluid object to act in an aleatory manner. Objects with an aleatory character are bestowed a persona by humans but also have the capacity to contribute to their own persona.

The name of the object stays the same, but the object signified by invoking Shiri is in constant flux. Every time a repair is made, parts are being swapped in. Software is upgraded. New samples are constantly being loaded on to the filament. Shiri is one of only a handful of spectrometers in Canada, and this makes the object especially important to scientists involved in spectrometry. When we asked if people go to other laboratories when Shiri's circuits or software act up, Quimbanda responded:

> They just have to wait until she gets fixed. So far we have not had any serious problems. Knock on wood. We had one outside the warranty period, last summer. It was not Shiri herself but an auxiliary unit . . . Everything was fine, except the current was running but not all the way to the filament. We would put the samples in, pump it down, and a couple hours later we would have results, except the results were all off . . . We could not figure out what it was. It was going though the motions but not doing the real job . . . I spent the first month of my sabbatical thinking it was a severe

technical problem, talking to the manufacturer, trying to track down information, that was frustrating . . . If you do not count my time, my salary, it only cost us five dollars to fix the bloody thing. The components were a couple of power transistors.

Quimbanda knocked on wood several times during interviews, indicative of his hope that he can, through various attempts, stabilize the capacities and persona of the spectrometer. Talk about Shiri's 'moods' is talk about the fluidity of the object, Shiri's capacity to change and be unpredictable. The relationship between objects and humans in the laboratory is put through constant repositioning (e.g., back to the drawing board) due to the aleatory capacities of the object, where failure results in frustration experienced by the scientists. One piece of ancillary equipment started giving us some trouble about two years ago. We limped along with it for a year, with it breaking down fairly frequently, once every two months . . . that has really been a frustration' (Quimbanda). The fluidity of the object extends to the users of the object (de Laet and Mol 2000) because their orientation towards the object must be variable rather than durable.

Formation of the Emotional Climate

As de Laet and Mol (2000) put it, objects need a community to keep up and running. The object is part of the community, since the organizational practices of the community are formed in relation to the object. In the words of Knorr-Cetina (1997), 'object worlds . . . make up the embedding environments in which expert work is carried out, thus constituting something like an emotional home for expert selves' (9). Relations with Shiri generate an emotional home or climate for the earth scientists in the lab. However, the relationship of Quimbanda is the most important here, because, according to everyone in the lab, he has the 'golden touch' (Knorr-Cetina 1999:229) that keeps Shiri running the way the lab needs if the lab is to be operational.

   The talk of earth scientists about emotions oscillates between narratives of joy and narratives of frustration. Earth scientists report that the most joyful part of their work, the part where they consider themselves successful, is when they get some publications out. For Quimbanda, the most enjoyable part of his work with Shiri is 'getting good results for a project. Having results that make some sense.' Success here can only be a matter of degrees since capacity stabilization attempts are often bound to failure. The most frustrating part of research in spectrometry is when the object fails. Quimbanda attributes failure to poor training of graduate students, the size of the samples, and contamination during sample construction or sample loading. The sharing of joy and frustration leads to formation of the emotional climate, though Quimbanda's relationship with Shiri is central in establishing an emotional tenor. As Nell, the lab manager, puts it: 'We all know isotopes, we can all run a mass spectrometer when it is working, but only Quimbanda can fix her. We need him. He has a magic touch, which of course he denies . . . he is the only one who can make Shiri sing. If something goes wrong he instinctively knows how to fix her. That is a skill none of the rest of us have. Not even the technicians. He waltzes in and says something bizarre and goes to some menu no one has ever seen before, presses a few numbers and it works again.'

To stabilize the capacities of Shiri, Quimbanda employs techniques only he seems to possess. Over time, there is a built-up attentiveness between Quimbanda and Shiri. Generated in this long-term interaction are mutual focus and closeness. This is what Collins (2004) calls 'emotional entrainment,' insofar as confidence is built between partners in ongoing interaction, which, in the case of Shiri and Quimbanda, is recognized by members of the organization. We extend the conception of emotional entrainment, which signals effervescence built up over the course of a relationship, to include objects. This enhances the argument of Collins, which otherwise conceptualizes emotions as concerning only humans. Compared to the narratives of incipient scientists, Quimbanda's narrative regarding Shiri is characterized by the emotional entrainment characteristic of intimacy. The emotional climate of the lab, with its circulating joy and frustration, builds around this pivotal relationship between Shiri and Quimbanda.

Maintenance of the Emotional Climate

There is a micro-politics to emotional climates inasmuch as emotions serve to mark one's status in relation to others in a given context (Clark 1990). Micro-politics of emotions are constitutive of the organization's trajectory and the lives of people working in organizations. Whereas the formation of the emotional climate in this case has to do with the ability of the laboratory leader to create some success for the organization in relation to the aleatory capacities of the object, the maintenance of the emotional climate – evident in the relation between Shiri and

Nell, the lab manager – evinces this connection between emotions, status, and gender in organizations.

Quimbanda does most of his work directly with the spectrometer. Nell, the lab manager, does most of her work with the numerous other scientists interested in Shiri. Nell has worked in spectrometry labs all over Europe as well as with supply companies, but is an 'incipient scientist' (Knorr-Cetina 1999) insofar as she has not experienced upward mobility in the hierarchies of science organizations. There is resentment on Nell's part when she says, 'I used to be right at the front of my research area,' but is now unable to chase her passion (despite her qualifications) due to a gendered division of labour both in her own home and her second home with the Shiri group. Nell must not only carry on her position in the lab, but also take care of her newborn child, often having to bring the child into the lab. Nell's job is to stock the lab with supplies, complete the bookings, and manage the finances. 'I do all the little things that need to be coordinated by a person,' she said, and, though it can be hectic, 'two days a week is right for me. I cannot be right at the front of my research area here because I do not have a faculty position and I do not have the emotional energy, I am overloaded with family responsibility.'

Nell's position in the lab is as crucial as Quimbanda's though it is attributed less status. Nell takes pride in her job as scientist-administrator, finding some parts joyful: 'There is satisfaction for me in knowing the lab is speeding along. Everything is smooth, ordered, samples are not getting held up, the accounts are in order, the feeling that the work I have to do is all done, so the lab appears to run itself, so Shiri is singing . . . I help people and meet their needs, I anticipate peoples' needs, helping them get the work done, making peoples' life easier because they are all stressed and busy . . . plus times when I am running the machine and we make a breakthrough or make her work really well or we overcome problems. That feels really good.'

The 'singing' of Shiri is a euphemism for optimal performance of the lab. When there is a sense of order and Shiri is 'singing,' Nell experiences the joy of helping other members of the emotional climate. Care for others, aiding others in completing their tasks, gives a sense of satisfaction to Nell. Such a characterization of the lab challenges quotidian conceptions of the uncaring, impersonal pursuit of truth and reveals the emotional effervescence integral to the relational milieu of the laboratory (Gherardi, Nicolini, and Strati 2007).

Nell's job is not so much to manage the aleatory capacities of the spectrometer as much as the unforeseen events imposed upon the lab by members who want access to the spectrometer. Nell said life in the lab is characterized by frenetic action and frustration. The most frustrating part of her job is people who do not 'play by the rules':

> I have tried to set up a smooth system, for instance with booking the machine. They have to put the request in by 9 a.m. Thursday morning to use Shiri the next week. But there are two people in the lab who are completely incapable of meeting the deadline. And then they wonder why there is no time for them or they go and ask Quimbanda, but Quimbanda does not know the schedule . . . that is my job, it is not his job. It makes life immensely complicated. I send out a form at the end of the month for people to pay for usage. The same person will never pay on time, she never has the money, I spend my time chasing her on stupid things. It is a job that should get done quickly. Yet one or two people always come in and screw it up. It gets difficult and frustrating. She wants a lot of time because she has a lot of samples to run, but she does not play by the rules.

Lower in the organizational hierarchy, it is Nell's job to rope in the rule-breaking of other scientists, which creates frustration. Nell is frustrated that so much of her time is wasted. When Nell took a medical leave, lab relations broke down. As Quimbanda put it, students 'want to put the samples in and get the numbers, so maintaining quality control under those circumstances is another aspect of not having the lab manager around at the moment, because she kept a pretty good eye on that sort of thing . . . [Nell] can keep an eye on them . . . there are things [students] could do to make quite a mess down there. Cause a fair bit of trouble.' Devoid of the aid Nell provides in managing the organizational practices of the lab, the sociality formed in relation to the object degenerates. Because of her position as manager in this milieu, Nell is treated not as a scientist but more as a caregiver. Caregiving is thought of as 'feminized labour' in most workplaces (Halford and Leonard 2006), meaning that the work is attributed less status. As Brewis (2006:499) argues, there is still a tendency to think of women in academic organizations as providing a service role.

Following Collins's (2004) discussion of emotions in groups, Nell is carrying away less effervescence from the context of lab interactions than she is contributing (134). These micro-politics of emotions relate to

status asymmetries in the organization. Despite her academic creden-
tials and serving as the veritable oil that keeps the lab cum organization
in working order, Nell does not acquire the symbolic capital that would
be granted to her if she had an academic position. Nell must deal with
the personnel-related issues of the organization rather than the 'more
serious' business of spectrometry and scientific fact construction that
Quimbanda is afforded through his status, reflecting a longstanding
separation of femininity from technical work in organizations (Brewis
2005; Linstead 2001). Nell is very busy with her work as a mother at the
same time she is meant to manage the lab. This double bind acts as a
dividing practice, placing Nell in a subservient position in the organization. The existing gendered order serves in effect to maintain Nell as
a lab manager. Status asymmetries in science labs and technical departments are often gendered in this way (Knorr-Cetina 1999:232; Alvesson
and Billing 1992).

Nell is pivotal to ensuring that situated and mundane organizational
practices will be completed, which, consequently, makes her central to
the maintenance of the emotional climate. Nell wrote a training manual
instructing scientists on how to work with Shiri and conduct themselves in the lab. The stakes are too high for deviation. Rule-breaking is
disallowed. According to Nell,

> . . . the more users we get, it is like a thoroughbred, and if you get people
> treating her badly, even if they do not realize they are doing it or it is the
> way they were doing it in another lab or elsewhere with an older machine,
> you end up breaking it. The samples have to be run very consistently. Each
> time we run a magazine of samples we run a standard. We know what
> the number should be. You should try to use the same conditions, so you
> know you are getting reproducibility. I was looking at the log of standard
> data and the way some people are running it and thought, 'Oh my God.'
> The status of the reproducibility of the lab becomes questionable if peo-
> ple do what they like or do not follow the guide. It screws up everyone
> when the lab's reproducibility is off, because people ask what the standard
> results are and I show them this mishmash of dirty printouts, which is
> no good. And then their data does not stand up to scrutiny when they
> publish.

Rule-breaking related to Shiri is 'emotional deviance' (Thoits 1985) as
a display of emotion by the rule-breaker and an experience of disruption for the rule-makers and followers (also see Thoits, this volume).

As with Sims's (2005) research on indignation formed in response to grievances in organizations, Nell's frustration is generated out of dealing with scientists who rush too much and do not pay attention. Meant to prevent degradation of the spectrometer's precision, guidelines are incontrovertible descriptive accounts of what is supposed to be going on in the lab, and present all members subject to the guidelines with the imperative of accountability (Amerine and Bilmes 1990). Accountability and reproducibility are the basis by which action is judged as in need of normalization.

Scientific laboratories have to be concerned about whether their projects and standards measure up against the projects and standards of other laboratories (Knorr-Cetina 1999; Latour 1987). The log of the standard is reproduced as a printout or a graph and shared in the research community. Nell is concerned about goings on inside the lab, but she is equally concerned about the reputation of the lab amongst outsiders. As Nell explains, the log of the standard is vitally important in promoting the status of the lab and enrolling other scientists to conduct spectrometry there:

> When you publish data you want to make sure it is comparable to the data of others. You say I have these numbers from this area and I will plot this data over here and you want to put them all on the same diagram and if they are different those differences are real, not just because analysis was wrong and just 10ppm off in one direction. Standards are how we keep our lab reproducible and know we have the right numbers. You have to know your data is real and you only do that by running standards and measuring things correctly, and running duplicates to ensure you get the same results. You cannot generate any old number to six decimal places. You have to say how you crushed things, leached them, dissolved them, measured them, what the standard reproducibility of the lab is, so people can judge whether they can believe your results.

Enrolment is the end product of an incitement or enticement to the organization based on strength perceived to arise through the reliability and validity of the results produced by the object when it 'sings.' The log of the standard represents Shiri's capacities to a wider audience of could-be members of the lab. Just as certain rules are meant to stabilize Shiri's aleatory capacities and limit the fluidity of the object, other rules steady the emotional climate by aligning the actions of some scientists with the organizational practices of the lab so as to prevent the detrimental effects that deviancy could have for relations with the broader earth sciences community. It is crucial that the emotional experience of inter- and intra-lab relations be of confidence, so that scientists will be continually enrolled in the lab's projects. Again, when Nell took a medical leave, lab relations broke down and very little research was carried out. As Quimbanda stated, 'since her absence there has been basically no one in the lab . . . the machine is sitting down there most of the time not being used.' In the absence of Nell, no one can manage the site, leaving the future of the laboratory-cum-organization more open-ended than the scientists, especially Quimbanda, would like.

Discussion

The lab cum organization becomes an emotional climate formed through each scientist's relationship to the spectrometer. The micropolitics of emotional climates occur through the marking of status in relation to the central object. Barbalet (1998) argues not every group member experiences the same emotions or the same intensity of emotions in the emotional climate. Nell carries away less effervescence than she contributes to the emotional climate, and experiences more frustration than joy because of the position she has been allocated in the organization. Nell's position in the lab is lesser than the position of Quimbanda. Positioning Nell in a service role has the consequence of reproducing her incipient status in the organization. Nell is treated as support staff despite her expertise, which amounts to a gendered economy of emotions and organization (Kerfoot and Knights 1998) in Nell's attempts at managing the lab. Maintaining the emotional climate of the lab is feminized labour, which is devalued despite its centrality to the organization.

Gender subordination at work in contemporary organizations occurs vis-à-vis particular tasks and activities (Erickson, Abanese, and Drakulic 2000; Gherardi 1994), and in our case study, those tasks and activities relate to the management of relations with an object. What happens when the black box of emotions related to objects in organizations is opened? Gender subordination in organizations can be demonstrated through consideration of how emotion narratives are indicative of one's status in a particular context (Knights and Surman 2008). Our discussion supplements existing conceptualizations of gender subordination as an organizational practice (Martin 1990; Czarniawska 2006) by showing how organizational practices oriented towards sociality with objects can lead to the gendering of incipiency in science.

Conclusion

Using the example of laboratory work, this chapter has considered the relationship between emotions and objects within organizations. The organizational studies literature has hitherto ignored how emotions are generated in relation to objects and how these emotions matter to the work conducted in organizations, which has been our rationale for this research. The work of lab science is accomplished through relations between objects and human scientists as well as larger research communities. We have sought to show that emotions concerning objects are integral to the work done in science organizations as far as they influence the formation and maintenance of emotional climates. The emotional climate of the spectrometry group is shaped by Shiri's capacities and Quimbanda's attempts at stabilizing them. The process of capacity stabilization attempts is frustrating due to persistent failure. Small joys emerge when success is achieved in any degree. Object-centred sociality in lab work is riddled with failure and so brings with it the same vacillating emotional experience as human-centred sociality (Suchman 2005; Orr 1996). Not everyone in the lab shares the same level of emotional involvement with Shiri as does Quimbanda, nor do all the group members experience the emotions of joy and frustration in the same way. Overall, the group feeling generated in the dynamic interaction of different objects and humans leads to a collective effervescence. Maintenance of the emotional climate, however, involves a frustrating set of tasks, such as time managing other scientists who disregard the organizational practices and protocol of the lab. The emotional climate can dissipate, and organizational practices can come to a halt when group members integral to maintaining these lab relations are absent.

We have told a story about the relationship between emotions and objects in organizations using scientists' narratives as it regards their work. Storytelling and use of metaphors are a rich source of creating meaning as it concerns work in organizations. Consideration of the stories and metaphors that workers share about their work also allows organizational studies scholars a method of analysing workplace gender subordination (Czarniawska 2004). 'Shiri' is a fluid object, an object that is always changing in terms of how people relate to it. Even the scientists' narratives concerning Shiri oscillate in and out of anthropomorphism, and the object is imbued with gendered meanings as a result of its aleatory capacities. The emotional climate of the lab is always in flux because of the aleatory capacities of this object. Yet 'Shiri' is also a metaphor for the relational research context of the lab, the organizational practices that group members must align themselves with, and how the work of scientists is allotted status.

NOTES

1 We thank Seantel Anaïs, Mike Mopas, Chris Hurl, and Robyn Smith for their comments.
2 Our position, that emotions are the experience of relations with objects and humans, is contrary to depictions that describe relations with objects as perverse. Williams (1998) argues that being lost in relations with cyber objects is 'the depth of emotional experience, warmth and understanding which comes from embodied gestures such as being "touched" by another human being through face-to-face contact and physical co-presence in the real world' (128). Setting up a false dichotomy between humans and the technological, Williams eschews how humans relate with objects, and the emotions experienced therein.
3 Field notes were gathered by shadowing the earth scientists at work (McDonald 2005; Bruni 2005). Fineman and Sturdy (1999) argue that shadowing is a solid method of researching emotions in action. Going through the various earth science labs gave us insight into organizational practices we otherwise may have not adequately understood.

11 Emotional Deviance and Mental Disorder

PEGGY A. THOITS

Introduction

Some time ago I developed the concept of 'emotional deviance' (Thoits 1985, 1990), extrapolating from Hochschild's (1979, 1983) seminal work on emotion norms and emotion management. Hochschild studied instances in which persons failed to feel or express an emotion that was socially appropriate for a particular situation (for example, losing one's temper with a customer when one should remain pleasant), and she described the strategies people commonly used to reduce 'emotive dissonance' (1979:565), that is, the mismatch between their feelings or displays and the situational emotion rule. It was only a short step from Hochschild's notion of emotive dissonance to the concept of emotional deviance. Emotive dissonance generally refers to a transitory discrepancy between a feeling or expression and a situational norm, a discrepancy that typically can be reduced using emotion work strategies. Emotional deviance refers to persistent, repeated, or intense violations of societal feeling or expression norms, where emotion management efforts are often ineffective.

In developing this concept, I was attempting to address an unresolved problem in the labelling theory of mental illness (Scheff 1966), namely, what types of norm violations are classified as symptoms of mental disorder. Scheff had argued that persons labelled as mentally ill had violated 'residual' rules, by which he meant norms that were not etiquette, moral, or legal norms, but social rules so taken for granted that they were not recognized as norms until they were violated (e.g., not making eye contact with an interaction partner). After reading Hochschild's work, it struck me that 'residual' norms might not be residual at all: some might be classifiable as feeling and expression norms. After all, the onset of mental illness is often characterized in emotional terms: having a nervous breakdown, becoming emotionally disturbed, losing emotional control. Consequently, I suggested that an important subset of mental disorders might be defined by emotional deviance, that is, recurrent or intense violations of feeling or expression norms (Thoits 1990).[1]

This argument, however, has lacked both theoretical development and empirical evidence. My purposes in this chapter are to establish the normative basis of judgments of disorder made by psychiatrists and clinical psychologists, and to marshal evidence that clinicians, community mental health researchers, *and* laypersons identify a substantial proportion of mental disorders by the presence of emotional deviance. Then I extend this normative argument to consider the persistent problem of diagnostic disagreements among clinicians. Because judgments of emotional deviance depend upon the ideological frames that individuals hold (Hochschild 1983), I suggest that diagnostic disagreements may be traceable to ideological differences among clinicians.

The Problem: How Do We Recognize Mental Disorder?

Psychiatrists and clinical psychologists tend to view mental disorders as real, by which I mean existing, observable, and measurable phenomena which have etiologies, characteristic symptoms, typical courses, expectable outcomes, and, for some disorders, effective treatments. I must immediately clarify that I believe that psychological disorders[2] are real. I have no intention of arguing that mental illness is a myth, that is, a misleading medical term applied to persons who are simply grappling with difficult 'problems in living' (Szasz 1960, 1994). Although problems in living (stressors) can indeed precipitate psychological distress and mood, anxiety, and substance-use disorders (Thoits 1995), severe mental illness, characterized by serious impairments in functioning, is both qualitatively and quantitatively distinct from reactions to stressors (Kessler et al. 2003; Payton 2009). This may be due to underlying psychological, biological, and/or genetic vulnerabilities.

Despite agreeing with clinicians that mental illness is real, sociologists (myself included) tend to view mental disorders as less definite, for lack of a better word, than most clinical practitioners and psychiatric researchers do, for several reasons. First, like anthropologists, sociologists are mindful that the nature, types, and definitions of disorders vary from culture to culture (Kleinman and Good 1985; Shweder 1994) and over time within cultures (e.g., Jutel 2009; Kirk and Kutchins 1992; Kleinman and Kleinman 1985). Second, sociologists emphasize that assessments of disorder are often far less reliable than measures of many physical conditions, and psychiatrists frequently disagree substantially about which diagnoses apply to patients depicted in standardized case histories or videotaped interviews (Aboraya et al. 2006; Garb 1997; Kirk and Kutchins 1992). Third, sociologists are aware that the inclusion, exclusion, and reclassification of disorders is done by experts in committees, who frequently are lobbied about proposed alterations by powerful interest groups such as insurance companies, gay rights groups, military veterans groups, and feminists, among others (Figert 1995; Kirk and Kutchins 1992; Mayes and Horwitz 2005). In short, social scientists return repeatedly to the idea that mental disorders are shaped, negotiated, or constructed through social or political processes.

These negotiation and construction processes are most obvious when one reads through successive versions of the *Diagnostic and Statistical Manual of Mental Disorders,* or DSMs, published by the American Psychiatric Association in 1952, 1968, 1980, 1987, 1994, and 2000 (1987 and 2000 are revisions of DSM-III and DSM-IV, respectively). Many changes are of note: neuroses have been dropped from the manuals' terminology; numerous disorders have been renamed; the diagnostic criteria for all disorders have been much more carefully delineated; multiple subtypes of major disorders have been distinguished; homosexuality has been eliminated as a form of psychopathology; many disorders have been added, including Post Traumatic Stress Disorder (PTSD), caffeine- and nicotine-related and pathological gambling disorders; contributing committees and their members are now listed in the manuals; and tentative new diagnoses are described at the backs of recent editions. Meanwhile, contentious debates go on in both the popular and professional press regarding the pros and cons of proposed changes. Due to the fact that the DSM is the clinician's 'Bible,' it is clear that what are considered mental disorders are periodically being refined, re-conceptualized, and reconstructed over time. To repeat, I am not arguing that psychopathologies are 'only' social constructions. Yes, the *boundary* around the broader concept of mental disorder can expand or shrink and the *boundaries* around various disorders are renegotiated (Jutel 2009). But most sociologists accept that there is something inside those boundaries that is real and problematic and cannot be dismissed as a mere social construction (see also Williams 2000).

The boundary-setting process, then, is crucial to understand because people who display the same cognitive, emotional, or behavioural symptoms may be classified either as well or ill depending on where the lines have been drawn between normality and abnormality (Erikson 1966). Dramatically different personal and social consequences can flow from such categorizations due to the stigma attached to mental illness (Corrigan 2004; Erikson 1966; Link and Phelan 2010; Scheff 1984; Wahl 1997). The key sociological question becomes: What determines where the boundaries are drawn? Putting it another way, how do professionals and laypersons decide that an individual is exhibiting a psychological disorder or not?

The usual answer to this question, from clinicians and laypersons alike, is that the person is behaving abnormally (and there is no discernible physical cause for that behaviour). So what is abnormality? A simple answer is: a deviation from what is normal. And what is normal? A cautious answer is that it depends on the cultural norms of the group within which the person's behaviour occurs.

Norms refer to expected or appropriate behaviours in specific situations (Gibbs 1965). Their existence can be discerned through verbal references to behaviours that are 'appropriate,' 'proper,' 'expectable,' 'normal,' and the like (and their converses), and by statements involving what one 'ought,' 'should,' 'must,' or 'have a right' to do (and their converses) (Gibbs 1965; Hochschild 1979). Norms essentially provide cultural standards against which individuals can evaluate their own and others' behaviours (Gibbs 1965). Although norms vary in the degree to which they are consensually held within a culture or subculture and in the severity of the informal and formal sanctions that are imposed when they are violated, when individuals egregiously, repeatedly, or persistently break the taboos, the moral norms (mores), or the conventions (folkways) of a society, observers perceive abnormality – that is, serious normative deviation – and entertain the possibility that it represents mental illness (Foucault 1965; Scheff 1966; Thoits 1985).

A connection between normative deviation and mental illness is in fact implicit in the guiding definition of mental disorders found in DSM-III (APA 1980) and repeated in the subsequent three versions of the manuals (APA 1987, 1994, 2000): '. . . [E]ach of the mental disorders is conceptualized as a clinically significant behavioural or psychological syndrome or pattern that occurs in an individual and is associated with present distress (e.g., a painful symptom) or a disability (i.e., impairment in one or more important areas of functioning) or a significantly increased risk of suffering death, pain, disability or an important loss of freedom. . . . in addition, *this syndrome or pattern must not be merely an expectable and culturally sanctioned response to a particular event, for example the death of a loved one . . .'* (APA 2000:xxi–xxii, emphasis added). So a person who has a set of symptoms that are expectable or normative responses to a major life event does not have a mental disorder. Conversely, then, if the symptoms are *not* expectable or normative responses, they may indicate a mental disorder. The manuals hasten to add, 'Neither deviant behaviour (e.g., political, religious, or sexual) nor conflicts that are primarily between the individual and society are mental disorders unless the deviance or conflict is a symptom of a dysfunction in the individual, as described above' (APA 2000:xxii). In short, normative violations that cause individuals distress, functional impairment, or substantial risk of personal harm are mental disorders.

The normative foundation of judgments of mental disorder becomes clearer when one looks at the language that appears throughout all texts of the *Diagnostic and Statistical Manual of Mental Disorders*, beginning with DSM-III (APA 1980) when criteria for diagnoses were first explicitly specified. These are a few examples from DSM-IV-TR (emphases added):

Hyperactivity may be manifested by fidgetiness or squirming in one's seat . . . by not remaining seated when *expected* to do so . . . by *excessive* running or climbing in situations where it is *inappropriate* . . . by having difficulty playing or engaging quietly in leisure activities . . . by appearing to be often 'on the go' or as if 'driven by a motor' . . . or by talking *excessively* . . . (APA 2000:86)

The essential feature of Selective Mutism is the persistent failure to speak in specific social situations (e.g., school, with playmates) where speaking is *expected*, despite speaking in other situations . . . (APA 2000:125)

At some point during the course of the disorder [Obsessive-Compulsive Disorder], the person has recognized that the obsessions or compulsions are *excessive or unreasonable.* (APA 2000:457)

The essential features of Bulimia Nervosa are binge eating and *inappropriate* compensatory methods to prevent weight gain. In addition, the self-evaluation of individuals with Bulimia Nervosa is *excessively* influenced by body shape and weight . . . A binge is defined as eating in a discrete period of time *an amount of food that is definitely larger than most individuals would eat under similar circumstances.* (APA 2000:589)

The point here is not that these judgments are subjective and prone to possible errors or wide interpretive variations, although one certainly can see why inter-subjective agreement among clinicians is often far from perfect. Instead, the point is a normative one: professionals diagnose mental disorders on the basis of shared cultural standards or norms. When individuals behave in normatively 'unexpected,' 'inappropriate,' 'excessive,' or 'unreasonable' ways that are distressing, impairing, or harmful, they are exhibiting symptoms of psychiatric disorder.

Emotional Deviance

Note that the above examples describe behavioural norm violations. But as Hochschild (1979, 1983) argued several decades ago, social norms not only govern behaviours, they guide feelings and emotional expressions as well.[3] Collectively, these rules are termed 'emotion norms,' which can be subdivided into subsets of 'feeling norms' and 'expression norms' (Hochschild 1979). Feeling norms govern private, subjective experiences of emotion in specific situations. For example, we are expected to feel sad at a funeral, happy at a success, and anxious before a test. Expression norms, or display rules (Ekman 1984), regulate outward, public expressions of emotion in particular circumstances. For example, we are not supposed to cry if we are big boys, we should smile at our customers, and we should show gratitude for a gift even if it was not what we wanted. Feeling and expression norms also specify the acceptable range, intensity, and duration of emotions in specific circumstances (Hochschild 1979) and the actors towards whom certain feelings should or should not be directed (Thoits 1985). Hochschild (1979, 1983) demonstrated that for a number of structural reasons individuals frequently do not feel or exhibit the emotions that they should, so they use a variety of coping strategies to bring their emotions back in line with the norms. She termed these coping efforts 'emotion management' or emotion work (see also Theodosius, this volume).

When a person experiences or shows inappropriate emotion, or when his/her emotion work fails to evoke, suppress, or transform unacceptable feelings into acceptable ones, the person exhibits emotional deviance (Thoits 1990, 2009). Deviant emotions, when intense, repeated, or prolonged, play a major, but usually overlooked, role in the identification of mental disorder. This claim can be substantiated by returning to the content of the *Diagnostic and Statistical Manual of Mental Disorder*. If one scrutinizes the DSM manuals from 1980 onward, one finds countless references to emotional deviance in the text. For example, drawing from DSM-IV-TR (2000, emphases added):

> Individuals with Conduct Disorder . . . may be callous and *lack appropriate feelings of guilt or remorse.* (96)

> The individual with Schizophrenia may display *inappropriate affect* (e.g., smiling, laughing, or a silly facial expression *in the absence of an appropriate stimulus*), which is one of the defining features of the Disorganized Type. (304)

> The intensity, duration, or frequency of the *anxiety and worry* [an essential feature of Generalized Anxiety Disorder] *is far out of proportion* to the actual likelihood or impact of the feared event. (473)

> The essential feature of an Adjustment Disorder is a psychological response to an identifiable stressor or stressors that results in the development of clinically significant emotional or behavioural symptoms . . . indicated either by marked *distress that is in excess of what would be expected* given the nature of the stressor or by significant impairment in social or occupational (academic) functioning . . . (679)

Once again the normative bases of these judgments are clear. A lack of appropriate guilt, excessive smiling or laughing, disproportionate anxiety, and excessive distress are violations of emotion norms. In these examples, the emotions are outside the acceptable range or the acceptable intensity of emotions that a person is culturally expected to feel or display. A skeptic, however, might point out that these excerpts are descriptions that are found in the explanatory text of the manuals. To what extent are deviant feelings or expressive behaviours used as *essential defining criteria* for psychiatric diagnoses?

A Content Analysis of DSM-IV Diagnostic Criteria[4]

To answer this question, I began with the list of diagnoses found in Appendix F of the DSM-IV-TR (APA 2000). There are 351 listed Axis I and II disorders, excluding codes for 'other conditions that may be a focus of clinical attention' (N = 40) and codes for 'no diagnosis' and 'diagnosis deferred' (N = 4)[5]; 351 may seem an astoundingly high number, but many major diagnoses have several subtypes, each with its own name, code number, and diagnostic criteria. For example, there are seven types of Schizophrenia (code 295) and 23 types of Bipolar I Disorder, Most Recent Episode (code 296). These subtypes are included in the count of disorders.

In editions III and IV of the diagnostic manual, the essential defining features of each disorder and subtype can be found in a box or a section that is set off from the accompanying text. The box or section summarizes the criteria that must be met in order for a diagnosis to be assigned by a clinician. Criteria are listed as points A, B, C, and so on. I coded a disorder as defined primarily by emotional deviance if at least one of the required criteria for the disorder described an inappropriate emotion or an intense, repeated, or persistent emotional state. Usually a normative standard of comparison was mentioned in the criteria with terms such as *excessive, unusual, inappropriate,* and so forth, as in the quoted text examples above. However, for a few disorders, normative standards were unstated. For example, criterion A for dysthymia is 'depressed mood for most of the day, for more days than not, as indicated either by subjective account or observation by others, for at least 2 years' (APA 2000:380). Because daily depression for a prolonged period of two years would clearly be an unconventional emotional experience in the eyes of most cultural members, I coded dysthymia as defined by emotional deviance. Finally, DSM criteria sometimes consisted of lists of several possible symptoms, only some of which referred to emotions. As an example, here are the criteria for Oppositional Defiant Disorder, a childhood diagnosis (APA 2000:102, emphases added):

A A pattern of negativistic, hostile, and defiant behaviour lasting at least 6 months, during which four (or more) of the following are present:
   (1) *often loses temper*
   (2) often argues with adults
   (3) often actively defies or refuses to comply with adults' requests or rules
   (4) often deliberately annoys people
   (5) often blames others for his/her mistakes or misbehaviour
   (6) is *often touchy or easily annoyed* by others

(7) is *often angry and resentful*

(8) is *often spiteful or vindictive*

Note: Consider a criterion met *only if the behaviour occurs more frequently than is typically observed in individuals of comparable age and developmental level.*

B The disturbance in behaviour causes clinically significant impairment in social, academic, or occupational functioning.

If half or more of a listing of symptoms involved deviant feelings or emotional displays, I coded it as a disorder defined by emotional deviance. In this case, four of the eight symptoms listed under criterion A are emotional ones. Note that the symptoms had to occur more frequently than is typically observed in children of similar ages and developmental levels – this is an explicit reference to normative standards in the diagnostic criteria.

Using these guidelines, a second rater and I independently coded all 351 diagnoses, with 84 per cent agreement between us. All disagreements were resolved by discussion. Analysis revealed that 107, or 30.5 per cent, of all disorders had emotional deviance as an essential defining feature.[6] Although it may not seem particularly striking that almost a third of all disorders are characterized and identified by the presence of emotional deviance, there are two considerations that make this figure more impressive. First, as seen in Table 1 (below), no other types of disorders in the diagnostic manual occur as frequently. Thus, a substantial minority of all currently defined disorders are identified by individuals' emotional deviations (Table 1, below). Second, and more importantly, the 30.5 per cent figure does not indicate the prevalence of emotional deviance in the general population, and therefore understates the social and clinical significance of these types of disorders. For estimates of prevalence, it is necessary to turn to the findings of three large-scale epidemiological studies of mental disorders in the general population: the Epidemiological Catchment Area Studies conducted in the early 1980s (Robins and Regier 1991), the National Comorbidity Survey conducted in the early 1990s (Kessler etal. 1994), and the National Comorbidity Survey-Replication which occurred in the early 2000s (Kessler et al. 2005). These studies used DSM-III and DSM-IV criteria to assess the most severe and the most frequently occurring psychiatric disorders in the community-residing U.S. adult population.

Table 1
Types of Disorders in DSM-IV-TR (APA 2000)[a]

Disorders defined by emotional deviance	30.5% (107)
Substance-related disorders	15.1 (53)
Disorders of infancy, childhood, adolescence	11.7 (41)
Delirium, dementia, amnestic, other cognitive	10.0 (35)
Schizophrenia and other psychotic disorders	9.1 (32)
Disorders due to a general medical condition	.9 (3)
Other disorders[b]	23.6 (83)
Total	100.0 (351)

[a] Disorders defined by emotional deviance are not counted in other groups of diagnoses.
[b] "Other disorders" include somatoform, factitious, dissociative, sexual, gender identity, eating, sleep, impulse control, adjustment, and personality disorders.

Table 2 (below) summarizes the two most common disorders among individuals with *any* disorder in the past six or 12 months. (About 25 to 30% of the adult population had a psychiatric disturbance in the past six to 12 months, depending on the survey.) The vast majority of persons with a disorder had an anxiety or mood disorder. The second most common psychiatric conditions were alcohol- or drug-related disorders, and these were noticeably less frequent. Disorders characterized by emotional deviance are *the* most common psychiatric disturbances among persons who have clinically diagnosable mental health problems. Not surprisingly, these are also the most prevalent disorders found among individuals in outpatient mental health treatment (Katz et al. 1997). In sum, for psychiatrists and clinical psychologists, emotional deviance is a central defining feature of a substantial subset of mental disorders, including those which are the most prevalent in the adult population.

Mental Health Screening in Community Studies

Community mental health researchers also rely on emotional deviance to identify psychological disturbance. Community studies typically assess the prevalence of 'non-specific' mental health problems. Non-specific means that particular psychiatric disorders are not measured

Table 2
Among Those with Any Psychiatric Disorder in the Past Year (Ages 15–55)[a]

Epidemiological Catchment Area Study, Robins et al. 1991 (6-month prevalence):

68% had an anxiety or mood disorder

40% had alcohol or drug abuse/dependence

National Comorbidity Survey, Kessler et al. 1994 (12-month prevalence):

78% had an anxiety or mood disorder

37% had alcohol or drug abuse/dependence

National Comorbidity Survey-Replication, Kessler et al. 2005 (12-month prevalence):

84% had an anxiety or mood disorder

18% had alcohol or drug abuse/dependence

[a] Because these surveys sampled respondents within differing age ranges, figures here are based on ages that are common to all three studies.

in these surveys. Instead, researchers assess the presence of *any* mental health problem in a given time period or the frequency with which individuals experience common psychological symptoms in a stated time frame. Investigators use either screening questions or scores on screening scales to indicate the presence or degree of non-specific mental health difficulties.

Across community surveys, the two most commonly used screening questions are, 'Have you ever had a nervous breakdown?' and 'Have you ever seen a professional for a personal or emotional problem?' (e.g., Brown 1978; Veroff, Kulka, and Duvan 1981). Note the terms 'nervous' and 'emotional' in these screening questions. Researchers use these terms because they are widely understood by laypersons to refer to mental illness or psychological difficulties (Gove 2005). Similar questions are used in contemporary epidemiological surveys such as the National Comorbidity Survey and its replication (Kessler et al. 1994, 2005).

Scales are employed far more often in community studies than single-item screening questions. Widely used scales include the Beck Depression Index (Beck et al. 1961), Spielberger's State and Trait Anxiety scales (Spielberger and Sydeman 1994), and the Centre for Epidemiological Studies-Depression Scale, or CES-D (Radloff 1974), among others. The most frequently assessed symptoms in these scales are those of depression and anxiety (e.g., feeling sad, feeling blue, feeling no interest in things, feeling tense, feeling nervous for no obvious reason, worrying constantly). Symptoms of depression and anxiety are highly correlated, and, when assessed together in the same instrument, indicate a state of generalized psychological distress (Mirowsky and Ross 2003). Depression, anxiety, and distress scales ask how often over the past week, month, or six months the respondent has experienced each symptom. Responses (e.g., never, sometimes, often, very often) are then summed into total symptom scores, running from low depression/anxiety/distress scores to high. Prolonged feelings of depression, anxiety, or distress represent moods, that is, emotional states that increasingly become unrelated to their initiating situational stimuli over time. Emotional states that appear unrelated to the person's present circumstances will be perceived by others as deviant. In essence, community mental health researchers are measuring emotional deviance when they estimate the prevalence of non-specific mental health problems in community samples.

How Laypersons Recognize Mental Illness

Not only clinicians and community mental health researchers recognize emotional deviance as an indicator of mental disorder, but laypersons do as well. In the 1996 General Social Survey (GSS), a nationally representative sample of 1,444 adults were read one of five randomly assigned vignettes which described individuals exhibiting DSM-IV symptoms of schizophrenia, major depression, alcohol dependence, cocaine dependence, or typical emotional reactions to ordinary life troubles. The sex, race/ethnicity, and educational level of the vignette characters were systematically varied across vignettes. The schizophrenia, cocaine, and alcohol vignettes did not refer to emotional states, while the depression and troubled person vignettes did (see Link et al. 1999 for exact wording). Among a number of questions, respondents were asked how likely it was that the person in the vignette was experiencing mental illness. The vignettes and survey questions were replicated 10 years later in the 2006 GSS with a sample of 1,518 respondents. Table 3 (see below) reports the percentage of respondents in each survey who said it was somewhat or very likely that the character was experiencing mental illness. Not surprisingly, respondents recognized mental illness in the character with schizophrenia, who displayed cognitive deviations (he/she thought people were spying on him/her, heard voices telling him/

Table 3
Percentages of General Social Survey Respondents Who Believed the Vignette Character Was Experiencing Mental Illness[a]

	1996	2006
Vignette Character:		
Schizophrenia	88.1	93.7
Alcohol Dependence	48.7	50.9
Cocaine Dependence	43.5	n.a.
Major Depression	69.1	75.2
Ordinary Troubles	21.5	29.9
Total N	1356	1373

[a] Percents summarize respondents who thought it was 'somewhat likely' or 'very likely' that the vignette character was experiencing mental illness.

her what to do) and behavioural deviance (he/she retreated from work and family, spending most days in his room) for a prolonged period of time (six months). It is also clear in Table 3 that survey participants were uncertain whether alcohol and cocaine addictions should be classified as mental illness. Of central importance, the percentages show that respondents distinguished sharply between the depressed and the troubled vignette characters.

The depressed character felt down for two weeks, had a flat, heavy feeling all day, felt no pleasure even when good things happened, could not concentrate, was constantly tired, could not sleep at night, felt worthless and discouraged, and had pulled away from his family for the past month. The troubled character sometimes felt worried, a little sad, and had trouble sleeping at night, believed things bothered him/her more than they do other people, was sometimes nervous or annoyed when things went wrong but, in general, enjoyed being with other people and was getting along with his/her family. Clearly, the negative affect of the depressed character was prolonged and unresponsive to positive changes in his/her life while the troubled character was only intermittently worried, annoyed, or sad in response to life changes.

Despite the fact that survey respondents heard the description of only one vignette character (so they could not make comparisons among characters' symptoms), they recognized the persistent negative emotions of the depressed character as deviant, indicating probable or certain mental illness, and evaluated the less intense and short-lived emotions of the troubled character as conventional or normal. Corroborating this interpretation, respondents were also asked how likely it was that the vignette character was 'experiencing part of the normal ups and down of life.' Among those who heard about the depressed character, 38 per cent and 25 per cent in 1996 and 2006, respectively, said the experience was 'very likely' part of life's normal ups and downs. In contrast, among those who evaluated the troubled character, 67 per cent and 62 per cent in the two surveys said it was very likely the character was experiencing normal ups and downs. These differences strongly suggest that lay observers' judgments were influenced by the degree to which vignette characters' symptoms deviated from emotion norms.

In sum, for clinicians, for community mental health researchers, *and* for laypersons, excessively intense, inappropriately prolonged, oddly flattened, unusually absent, or situationally unexpected emotions (as well as delusions, hallucinations, and bizarre behaviours, of course) play an important role in the identification of mental disorder.

Ideological Variations in Emotion Norms

Assuming that emotional deviance does play a central role in the recognition of psychological disturbance by professionals and laypersons, there is a further point to be made: what is viewed as emotional deviance depends on individuals' underlying ideological orientations or frames. As noted earlier, norms vary across societies and across subgroups within a society. This is because social groups differ in their cultures, or more specifically, in their cultural ideologies. Ideologies can be viewed as systems of ideas (assumptions, beliefs, values, and attitudes) that are shared by collectivities or interest groups (Purvis and Hunt 1993; Hall 1986; Swidler 1986). Drawing from Gramsci, Hall (1986:22) points out, 'There is never any one, single, unified and coherent "dominant ideology" that pervades everything,' but instead there are many systems of thought promoted by political, religious, economic, class, racial, ethnic, and other interest groups within societies. Ideologies guide practical activities and are manifest in individual and collective life (Hall 1986:20). Social norms are integral aspects of ideologies because norms are *beliefs* about what is valuable and appropriate for individuals to think, feel, or do in everyday life. It follows that emotion norms, and

therefore assessments of emotional deviance, will depend on the ideo
logical frames that individuals bring to situations (Francis 1997; Hochschild 1989, 1990; Taylor 1995, 2000; Thoits 2009). Hochschild (1990)
offers a useful example: men and women who are traditional in their
gender-role ideology believe a woman's place is in the home even if she
has to work, and a man's place is in the labour force even if he has to
help out at home. Traditional women who identify with and love their
jobs and traditional men who enjoy childcare tasks regard their feelings as socially inappropriate. In contrast, such feelings are regarded
as entirely appropriate by women and men who hold nontraditional,
egalitarian gender ideologies.

Data from the Emotions Module of the 1996 GSS allows a demon-
stration of the effects of ideology on assessments of emotional deviance
(Thoits 2009). The Emotions Module was a battery of questions about
emotions, particularly anger, administered to a random subset (N = 1,460)
of the GSS sample that year. Respondents were asked to recall a recent incident in which they felt 'really angry, irritated, or annoyed'; 77 per cent
(N = 1,125) recalled and described an event to the interviewer. A series of
closed-ended questions then were asked about that incident, including
towards whom the respondent felt angry and how intensely and how
long he/she felt angry. Among the follow-up questions was an item assessing emotional deviance: 'Did you feel like your reaction to the situation was appropriate, or did it seem wrong to you somehow, for example,
too intense or the wrong emotion for the occasion? On a scale that runs
from 0 as completely right to 10 as completely wrong for the situation, tell
me whether your feelings were right or wrong for the situation.' Among
respondents who described a social situation evoking anger (N = 966), the
mean score was 3.7 (st.d. = 3.3), indicating that the average respondent
regarded his/her anger as appropriate rather than inappropriate in the
circumstances.

Interestingly, women and men did not differ significantly in their ratings of emotional deviance, despite the existence of broad American
beliefs that anger is more permissible for men than women to feel and
display (Kring 2000; Simon and Nath 2004). This, it turned out, was because respondents' perceptions of emotional deviance were dependent
on their gender-role ideologies. I subdivided survey participants into
those holding traditional versus nontraditional attitudes on the basis
of their agreement or disagreement with statements about men's and
women's roles (e.g., 'It is more important for a wife to help her husband's career than to have one herself'; 'Both the husband and the wife

should contribute to the household income'). I also subdivided them into non-feminists and feminists if they replied no or yes, respectively, to the question, 'Do you consider yourself a feminist?' Table 4 (below) shows the mean emotional deviance ratings that respondents gave to their angry feelings by gender and gender-role ideology. Women who held nontraditional gender role beliefs were significantly *less* likely than other groups to see their angry feelings as inappropriate or wrong. Feminist-identified men perceived their anger as significantly *more* deviant and feminist women rated their anger as significantly *less* deviant compared to males and females who did not claim a feminist identity. Thus, individuals' evaluations of their angry feelings were contingent on their gender-role beliefs, supporting the idea that ideology frames the meaning and normative appropriateness of individuals' emotional experiences (Hochschild 1989, 1990). The patterns in Table 4 hint that persons who adopted egalitarian beliefs may have taken special pains to reject a quintessentially male-typed emotion in gendered ways – women by embracing their anger as a legitimate, acceptable feeling to have, men by regarding their anger as too stereotypically masculine or aggressive and therefore socially unacceptable.

Obviously, these kinds of findings can generalize to other social groups. For example, *clinicians'* gender, race, class, religious, and/or political ideologies could influence their assessments of the relative presence or absence of emotional deviance in their clients and thereby affect the diagnoses that they assign. However, clinicians' ideological beliefs usually are not measured in studies of diagnostic judgments, so their effects must be inferred from patterns of diagnostic errors. A classic example can be found in the work of Kleinman and Kleinman (1985) who studied the puzzlingly high prevalence of neurasthenia (somatization disorder) coupled with a low prevalence of major depression in psychiatric patients treated at Hunan Medical College in China. They showed with diagnostic interviews that patients with neurasthenia (chronic pain or illness without biological cause) were actually suffering from depressive disorders. They reasoned that both patients and psychiatrists focused on somatic complaints and overlooked emotional symptoms for ideological reasons: it was politically dangerous at the time of these studies (in the 1980s) for patients to be depressed (i.e., withdrawn, alienated, and in despair) in response to the upheavals and deprivations in their lives caused by the Cultural Revolution. To have physical ailments (headaches, insomnia, stomach problems, fatigue, etc., which are also depressive symptoms) was far more acceptable

Table 4
Mean Emotional Deviance Scores by Gender and Gender-Role Ideology

	Men	Women
Traditional Gender-Role Ideology	3.9	3.8
(St.d.)	(3.3)	(3.3)
N	267	279
Nontraditional Gender Ideology	3.9	**3.3***
(St.d.)	(3.3)	(3.4)
N	126	291
	Men	Women
Non-Feminist Identity	3.8	3.7
(St.d.)	(3.2)	(3.3)
N	341	415
Feminist Identity	**4.7***	**3.3***
(St.d.)	(3.4)	(3.4)
N	52	155

a Standard deviations in parentheses.
* Asterisk indicates that this group differs significantly from the other three.

both socially and politically. The political ideology of the era framed the meaning of patients' symptoms.

Studies of gender, race, and social class biases in clinicians' judgments also hint at the influence of ideological beliefs. A careful literature review by Garb (1997) showed that symptomatic individuals' status characteristics do not sway clinicians' judgments when they are assessing the patient's need for hospitalization, the need for involuntary commitment, or the severity of illness (see also Thoits 2005; Thoits and Evenson 2008). Social status biases become evident, however, when clinicians assign specific diagnoses (Garb 1997; Loring and Powell 1988; Dixon, Gordon, and Khomusi 1995). For example, histrionic personality disorder (characterized by 'a pervasive pattern of excessive emotionality and attention seeking' [APA 2000:714]) is more often attributed to female patients, while antisocial personality disorder (characterized by indifference to the rights of others, repeated physical fights or assaults, deceitfulness, and unlawful behaviour) is more frequently assigned to

Table 5
Diagnoses Selected by Psychiatrists, Cross-Classified by the Gender and Race of the
Psychiatrist and the Described Patient

		Psychiatrist			
		WM	BM	WF	BF
	WM	schizo	reactive	schizo	depress
	BM	paranoid	schizo	paranoid	paranoid
Patient	WF	depress	depress	reactive	reactive
	BF	depress	depress	schizo	schizo
	NI	schizo	schizo	schizo	schizo

Note: WM = white male, BM = black male, WF = white female, BF = black female,
NI = no information about gender or race of the patient was provided.
Schizo = Undifferentiated schizophrenia, the correct diagnosis
Paranoid = Paranoid schizophrenia, the most severe diagnosis
Depress = Depressive disorder, a moderately severe diagnosis
Reactive = Brief reactive psychosis, the least severe diagnosis
Adapted from Loring and Powell (1988)

male patients with the same symptoms (Garb 1997), patterns consistent
with gender stereotypes.

Perhaps the most compelling example of systematic errors in clinicians' judgments can be found in a now-classic study by Loring and
Powell (1988). They drew a random sample of psychiatrists from the
members of the American Psychiatric Association, sent them actual case
studies of patients who were displaying DSM-III symptoms of undifferentiated schizophrenia, and asked the psychiatrists to identify the
proper diagnosis for each case from a list of possible diagnoses. The
case descriptions differed in only one respect across respondents:
the patients in the case studies were randomly described as a white
male, a white female, a black male, a black female, or no information
about the race and sex of the patient was provided. Table 5 (above) summarizes the results from the Loring and Powell study. The cells of the
table list the diagnosis that was chosen by the majority of psychiatrists
who read each case.

When no information was given about the sex or race of the patient
(the row labelled 'NI'), the majority of psychiatrists correctly identified the patient as suffering from undifferentiated schizophrenia. However, when psychiatrists misclassified patients, they did so in directions

biased by gender and race. Focusing first on diagnoses of depressive disorder, female patients (regardless of race) were more often misclassified as suffering from depression by male psychiatrists (again regardless of race). Looking next at diagnoses of paranoid schizophrenia, which was the most severe diagnosis among the available choices, black male patients were misclassified more frequently by white psychiatrists (both male and female) and by black female psychiatrists. Finally, examining diagnoses of brief reactive psychosis, the least severe and most short-term disorder among the possible choices offered, white patients (both male and female) were categorized with this disturbance by black psychiatrists (both male and female) and by white female psychiatrists. Clearly, psychiatrists' judgments were affected by the gender and race of the patient as well as by their own statuses.

These patterns of error suggest that clinicians' gender and racial stereotypes (i.e., cultural beliefs about group traits) filtered their interpretations of presenting symptoms. An alternative possibility, though, is that clinicians' *knowledge* shaped their diagnostic decisions. Histrionic personality disorder and affective disorders in fact are more common in women, and antisocial personality disorder and substance use disorders are more frequent among men (e.g., Kessler et al. 1994, 2005). Blacks have higher rates of paranoid schizophrenia than whites, perhaps due to the experience of racial discrimination (Whaley 1997). It is reasonable to assume that clinicians are aware of such epidemiological patterns from their professional training, reading the psychiatric literature, or perusing descriptive text in the DSM manuals. However, this alternative theoretical possibility remains consistent with my argument because clinical knowledge itself is ideological. Clinical ideology places a value on scientific methods of discovery and bases beliefs about what is empirically true on those methods. In short, cultural stereotypes *or* biases produced by scientific knowledge of epidemiological patterns may distort clinicians' interpretations of the symptoms that are exhibited by patients who differ from one another only in sex or race but not in symptoms.

Studies of clinical judgments do not usually include assessments of practitioners' beliefs, so the influences of stereotypes or professional knowledge remain unobserved and must be inferred from patterns of diagnostic errors. Future research will need to test the hypothesis that assessments of deviance depend on practitioners' belief systems. Given that laypersons' perceptions of emotional deviance vary systematically with their ideology (Thoits 2009), it would be reasonable to suspect that similar findings would be found among clinicians and that ideological differences among practitioners would account, at least in part, for diagnostic disagreements among them.

Conclusions

I have argued and attempted to show that dramatic, persistent, or repeated deviations from social norms that govern the appropriate range, intensity, duration, and targets of emotions indicate the presence of mental illness to clinicians, community mental health researchers, and laypersons. Emotional deviance is an essential defining feature of 30 per cent of all mental disorders outlined in DSM-IV-TR, and these emotional disorders (mood and anxiety disorders) are by far the most prevalent psychological disturbances in the general adult population. Community researchers identify non-specific mental health problems in the general population by measuring prolonged and frequent symptoms of anxiety and depression. Members of the American public, too, distinguish between mentally ill and normally troubled vignette characters by the extent of the characters' emotional deviations. Using traditional and nontraditional gender-role ideologies as an example, I have also shown that assessments of emotional deviance can differ by individuals' ideology. Emotions that are normative within one ideological frame may be viewed as deviant from a different belief system. Although ideological variations among clinicians have not been explored to my knowledge, such differences might help to explain systematic errors in practitioners' assignment of diagnoses. Understanding sources of diagnostic error is crucial, of course, because diagnoses determine patients' prognoses, treatment options, and long-term life chances.

Assuming additional work will further confirm that ideology determines the emotion norms to which individuals adhere and that violations of emotion norms spark attributions of psychological disturbance, there are additional avenues of research that should be pursued next. First, the content of feeling and expression norms need further study because relatively little is known about the norms people hold or the degree of consensus about them. There are notable exceptions to this statement with respect to anger, jealousy, romantic love, parental love, and sympathy (Stearns and Stearns 1984; Stearns 1990; Clark 1987; Cancian 1987; Shields and Koster 1989), and there are numerous

studies of emotion norms held by workers in various professional, service, and manual occupations (e.g., Cahill 1999; Copp 1998; Haas 1977;
Hochschild 1983; Lively 2000; Pierce 1995; Smith and Kleinman 1989;
Stenross and Kleinman 1989; Tolich 1993). But little attention has been
paid to normative beliefs regarding fear/anxiety, sadness, envy, shame,
loneliness, happiness, pride, and a myriad of other emotional states
nor how these emotion norms vary by gender, age, race, ethnicity, and
social class. When investigators do attend to differences in norms by
socio-demographic characteristics, they frequently focus on variations
by gender, neglecting other social statuses.

Attention should also be directed to the underlying ideologies that
define which particular emotions are appropriate or inappropriate
to feel and express. For example, in cultures or subcultures in which
independence is valued and taught, feelings and displays of pride in
personal success may be normative; in cultures that value and promote interdependence, pride in personal success may be deviant, while
pride in sacrificing oneself to help others succeed may be appropriate
(Markus and Kitayama 1991; see also Rosenfield, Lennon, and White
2005). How emotion norms are framed by broad cultural orientations as
well as individuals' social, religious, and even political ideologies will
need careful examination.

Studies of these 'emotion cultures' (Gordon 1989) may also have
practical applications. For example, self-labelling theory (Thoits 1985,
1990) suggests that when people violate important emotion norms,
they experience heightened psychological distress and engage in more
coping efforts to try to contain or transform their deviant feelings. If
these efforts are repeatedly or persistently unsuccessful, individuals
define themselves as having mental health problems and are motivated
to seek counselling or therapy. If they do seek treatment, they encounter mental health practitioners who typically assign diagnoses. I have
suggested that clinicians draw on their own emotional standards when
making diagnostic decisions. In order to be of therapeutic assistance,
however, practitioners must also be attuned to their patients' underlying ideological beliefs, because those beliefs determine the emotion
norms to which patients are attempting and failing to conform, causing
them distress. In short, defining and understanding clients' psychological problems will depend not only on clinicians' own emotional standards, but on their grasp of the ideology and norms that clients have
used to assess themselves as in need of professional intervention.

NOTES

1 Williams (2000) has argued that mental health should be conceptualized as *emotional* health.
2 I will use the terms *mental disorder, psychological/psychiatric disorder, psychological/psychiatric disturbance, psychopathology, and mental illness* interchangeably in this chapter for variability in the text.
3 One could also argue that there are norms that govern what is acceptable to think and the ways in which it is appropriate to reason – i.e., there are cognitive norms. The basic argument I make in this chapter about emotional deviance should apply to cognitive deviance as well.
4 I am grateful to Ashley Thompson for coding and research assistance on the DSM-IV analysis described in this section.
5 Axis I is the set of clinical or functional disorders; Axis II is the set of personality disorders.
6 The author will provide a list upon request.

12 Polyamory or Polyagony? Jealousy in Open Relationships

JILLIAN DERI

Introduction

When discussing polyamory, the two most common responses I receive are, 'I could never do that; I would get too jealous' and 'Where do you find the time?' While I cannot address the time question, I find the issue of jealousy absolutely fascinating. The assumptions implied in this remark sparked my research into how polyamorists are affected by jealousy. Popular rhetoric insinuates that non-monogamy is impossible; if one's lover has sexual encounters outside the relationship, jealousy will be the inevitable and intolerable outcome. At the same time, jealousy is viewed as a sign of love, and is thus the expected and noble reaction to a partner's sexual and/or romantic activities outside of the relationship. By this logic polyamory would cause jealousy – and monogamy would be the cure. By engaging in multiple relationships, polyamorists seek to do exactly what popular culture deems unsavory. And monogamous people do indeed experience jealousy. Jealousy does occur in polyamorous relationships, but its circumstances are different, and, consequently, the experience and embodiment of jealousy is also different from dominant portrayals of jealousy. This chapter explores the following question: How and why do polyamorists manage jealousy?

Non-monogamous relationships have existed throughout recorded history; however it is only recently that polyamory has emerged as a 'burgeoning sexual story' (Barker 2005), with a particular discourse and cultural practice. Polyamory is commonly defined as a form of non-monogamy where people simultaneously maintain multiple sexual and emotional relationships and where all parties are aware and consenting (Sheff 2005; Haritaworn, Lin, and Kleese 2006). Polyamory (often called poly by its practitioners) differs from swinging in its emphasis on emotional intimacy and longer-term commitments. Polyamory differs from polygamy (wherein a husband can have several wives) in its emphasis on gender equality. In polyamory both men and women are free to have multiple partners. Polyamory also differs from adultery in its focus on honesty, consent, and full disclosure by all parties involved (Sheff 2005). The word polyamory (coined from within the community) is used to describe a sexual identity, sexual preference, practice, and/or philosophy. Unlike many sexual minorities who were named by scientific 'experts,' polyamorists continually work to have polyamory recognized as a sexual category and to educate psychological institutions about care for the community (Weitzman 1999, 2006).

Polyamorists resist the intersecting regulation of emotion and sexuality and create alternatives that better meet their needs. First, polyamorists critique the institution of monogamy and its accompanying norms of emotions, sexism, and heterosexism. Second, polyamorists re-craft their understanding of love, relationships, sexuality, and emotions in ways that minimize instances of jealousy. They strive to replace jealousy with *compersion*, a term used by polyamorous people to describe feelings of pleasure in response to a lover's romantic and/or sexual encounters outside the relationship. Polyamorists question how the dominance of monogamy shapes our emotion world (i.e., the encompassing way in which a culture's words and concepts shape people's emotional responses (see Plummer 2001)). This includes the idea that sexual exclusivity is the epitome of love and commitment and that any diversion from this path should be met with distrust and jealousy. In response, polyamory offers alternate values and ideas about emotions. Jealousy is not inevitable or intolerable and the parameters of relationships are flexible. Polyamorists re-imagine and re-craft their preferred guidelines of sexuality by creating norms and strategies that steer their practice as a culture. These rules include ways to initiate communication, negotiate boundaries, and structure disclosure. By doing so, polyamorists create a lifestyle where compersion is not only possible, but actually common. While not always successful in practice, these ideas inform the culture of polyamory and shape polyamorists' embodied experience of jealousy.

For this chapter, I begin with an overview of the sociological research on jealousy and polyamory. Then I discuss how polyamorists have re-imagined jealousy and have developed tools, strategies, and norms that facilitate compersion. To understand polyamorous norms, I examine the common themes of polyamorous practice that emerged through my interviews. I address several tensions and contradictions with which the polyamorous community grapples and document an illustrative moment of this rapidly blossoming culture. Like most social norms, the rules of polyamory are always in flux and are not always followed. The strategies in place to mitigate jealousy do not work for all polyamorists and circumstances. For this reason, I particularly examine the intersection of what polyamorists do and what they wish they were doing.

For my research, I used qualitative, semi-structured, open-ended interviews with 22 self-identified queer, lesbian, and/or bisexual polyamorous women in Vancouver, British Columbia. Interviews focused on how and why they practise polyamory and how they experience and manage jealousy within open relationships. Some questions I sought to understand were: What stories of jealousy emerge from the culture and experiences of queer polyamorous women in Vancouver? How does a re-imagining of love and jealousy shift embodied affect? What contradictions and tensions exist within polyamorous culture? Is the experience of polyamory enough to overcome polyagony? *Polyagony* is a tongue-in-cheek polyamorous term to remind us that jealousy can sometimes be excruciatingly painful. My interest in this 'ugly feeling' (Ngai 2005) stems in part from the soft taboo surrounding jealousy. While jealousy is repeatedly expected in dominant culture, people are also shamed for feeling it. As a result, people often downplay their jealousy and recast actions displayed in a jealous episode as a matter of honour, pride, or anger (Clanton 1996). Jealousy occurs at the intersection of contradictory feelings: love and hate, romance and heartbreak, excitement and fear. This cultural feeling and experience has been linked to such social concerns as difficult feelings (Baumgart 1990; Clanton and Smith 1977), damaged relationships (White and Mullen 1989; Salovey 1991), and male violence (Pines 1998; Kleese 2006). As Ngai (2005) makes clear, an analysis of ugly feelings, so named for their unpleasantness, reveals a great deal about the structures and institutions in which they emerged, since these feelings operate at the intersection of internal feelings, social inequalities, and critical resistance. Polyamorists are forging creative understandings of jealousy, which might answer that initial reaction: 'But I would get jealous.'

Jealousy Research and Polyamorous Culture

The use of the term *jealousy* varies both in academia and lay discourse. People differ in their description of how it feels, the events that 'cause' it, and the behaviours associated with it. Guerrero (Guerrero, Trost, and Yoshimura 2005) defines romantic jealousy as 'a multi-faceted set of affective, behavioural, and cognitive responses that occur when the existence and/or quality of a person's primary relationship is threatened by a third party' (233). While this definition is based on primary relationships, I argue that any relationship can be subject to jealousy. Also, Guerrero's definition does not make the distinction between real or imagined threats. My study looks at how people manage jealousy in relationships where the inclusion of a 'third party' is openly negotiated and thus the absence of other lovers is not the preferred strategy to mitigate jealousy. Jealousy is a complex emotional experience that combines many primary emotions, including fear, anger, sadness, betrayal, and hurt (Turner and Stets 2005; Stearns 1989), and it is for this reason that some theorists are reluctant to call it an emotion on its own (Hupka 1984). Hence for many theorists, jealousy refers to the emotion, feeling, character trait, and/or 'emotional episode' of a situation, a multitude of feelings related to the situation, actions, and often a resolution (Parrott 1991:4). Polyamorists recognize jealousy as part of a spectrum of emotions, ranging from polyagony to tolerance or indifference.

It is useful to distinguish between two types of jealousy: *suspicious* and *fait accompli* jealousy (Parrott 1991) that follows the division between real and imagined threats. Suspicious jealousy is the feeling of distrust or doubt in relation to a partner's unfaithfulness and/or commitment to the relationship. Fait accompli jealousy is where the threat or 'rival' is known and/or the relationship is in real jeopardy, such as when a lover has left one person for another. Envy can also be subdivided into two groups: malicious versus non-malicious envy (Parrott 1991). Non-malicious envy is the feeling of wanting something that someone else has (such as a relationship with a certain person). Malicious envy is the feeling of wanting someone not to have the object/subject that you desire and wanting bad things to occur to this person in relation to the desired object/subject. Malicious envy is reminiscent of the German term *schadenfreude*, which is the feeling of taking pleasure in another's misfortune. To want an object is simply desire, but malicious envy is the adverse feeling in relation to this desire. Fait accompli jealousy frequently accompanies malicious envy when a person wishes had fortune upon their romantic rival, which might explain why some people's jealous anger is directed towards the rival rather than towards the lover (Yates 2007).

Georg Simmel (1955) notes that jealousy and envy require a feeling of entitlement regarding the possession of an object/subject. Similarly, Candida Yates (2007) argues that sometimes envy is about possession for 'possession's sake' as opposed to actually wanting the object/subject. This urge towards possession may reveal one's own 'narcissistic fragility, something that provokes envy of the other's apparent completeness' (25). Simmel (1955) also notes a third distinction within the family of envy and jealousy – begrudging, which he defines as 'the envious desire of an object, not because it is especially desirable but because the other has it [and it is] accompanied by the utter unbearability of the thought that the other possesses it' (51).

Jealousy is manifested on/in the body with physical and psychological symptoms. Culture plays a role in how jealousy is experienced, how one appraises the situation in which it arises, and how jealousy is expressed. Jealousy is a social emotion in that it is experienced in relation to another person (real or imagined) (Parkinson 2005). Consequently, I ground my theory in work that links sociological, cultural, and biological processes in the formation, experience, and expression of emotion (William and Bendelow 1996). Ahmed (2004) argues that 'rather than seeing emotions as psychological dispositions, we need to consider how they work, in concrete and particular ways, to mediate the relationship between the psychic and the social, and between the individual and collective' (27). Additionally, Harding and Pribram (2004) argue that even though emotions tend to be understood as individual and private affairs, 'emotions are formed and function as part of the historical, cultural, and political contexts in which they are practiced to reproduce, and potentially resist, hegemonic relations' (865). I investigate how polyamorists' cultural beliefs (not solely individual beliefs) translate into embodied feelings, for instance both enabling and preventing the experiences of jealousy and compersion. Ahmed suggests that collective sensations are transformed into 'an act of reading and recognition' (2004:29), so that internalized cultural practices and embodied ideas reveal themselves narratively. Through this academic and narrative research, the emotion of jealousy is revealed to be at once a function of social ideas about love, monogamy, and polyamory, and is experienced as bodily sensations that are interpreted by conscious understandings of those feelings.

Research on jealousy often assumes a monogamous relationship, and, hence, also assumes that a third party is never welcome and always a threat. This research often identifies a partner's cheating and/or the suspicion of cheating as a 'crisis event' from which to discuss jealousy (see Bryson 1991:202). For polyamorists, having other lovers is consensual and pre-negotiated, and therefore the presence of another lover is not enough reason to feel jealous. It is therefore under different circumstances that polyamorists experience jealousy. The participants in my study reported feeling jealous when their partner started to date someone new, when a relationship shifted into love, when the other person was too similar to themselves, when there were overlapping roles, when they felt less secure within a relationship, and/or for no identifiable reason. For polyamorists, cheating or lying is more likely the breaking of an agreed-upon rule rather than an outside sexual affair (Wosick-Correa 2008).

Current literature presents a highly gendered portrayal of the experience and expression of jealousy. For example, Buss (2000) argues that men respond with jealousy to a partner's (feared or real) sexual interactions with another, while women tend to become jealous due to a partner's emotional attachment to another person. Buss (2000) also argues that lesbians respond like heterosexual men, while gay men respond like heterosexual women. Clanton (1996) argues that men are more likely to deny jealousy, call it anger, and fight to avoid humiliation, whereas women are more likely to admit jealousy, internalize the blame, and work on the relationship. Popular media representations of jealousy reinforce this dichotomy, in that women express jealousy with cattiness, gossip, or manipulative behaviour, while men express jealousy with anger or violence. Such generalizations, however, may reveal more about cultural ideology and socialization than intrinsic truths about gender or jealousy. When research begins with an assumption that men and women are two discrete entities, one will often find results to suit this assumption (Fausto-Sterling 2000). Such an assumption leads the inquirer to emphasize differences between genders rather than differences within a gender or similarities between genders, let alone questions about the construction of the dichotomy (Peterson 2004).

The expression of jealousy is socially acceptable only within culture- and gender-specific parameters. In certain cultural frameworks, it is only acceptable to verbalize jealousy when there are identifiable reasons for its cause, and instead of acting jealous, one must calmly use psychological vocabulary (Zembylas and Fendler 2007). When emotions are expressed this way, it is assumed that people are speaking their truth and are taking care of themselves (Zembylas and Fendler 2007). Most other expressions of jealousy are seen as 'emotional' or 'excessive.' An understanding of that which is labelled emotional requires an analysis of gender, race, class, and ability, since women, people of colour, the working class, and people with disabilities are disproportionally thought to be over-reacting or 'over the top' (Harding and Pribram 2002, 2004; Parkinson 2005). Kleese (2006) argues that 'jealousy is constructed in a way that justifies the control of women's bodies and sexuality and has the potential to legitimize all kinds of male violence and atrocities' (647). Relatively, there is more room for women to express their emotions, as a man who is emotive is more likely to have his masculinity called into question (Jackson 1993). However, women who act on, rather than verbalize their jealousy-inspired emotions that do not fit conventional gender roles, such as anger, are seen as inappropriate. Crying may be seen as a feminine expression of an emotion, but too much crying is deemed hysterical. 'Normal' jealousy can be expressed in flirtatious jest, but excessive jealousy is seen as a sign of character weakness, low self-esteem, or even insanity (Clanton 2001). Jealousy is further complicated by the way some people take pleasure in knowing that someone is jealous of them, and might even try to elicit this response in others.

Prior to 1970, jealousy was usually described as a 'proof of love,' coinciding with that period's emphasis on commitment in relationships. Since the Sexual Revolution, with its emphasis on personal freedom, jealousy has been understood as a defective characteristic of a person who is unable to trust, 'unduly possessive, insecure, and suffering from low self-esteem' (Clanton 2001: 160). Clanton (1996) evinces that 'jealousy is a socially-constructed emotion that changes to reflect changes in marriage rules, the adultery taboo, and gender roles' (173). I argue that polyamorous discourse has the potential to further shift our understanding of jealousy. If polyamorous discourse increases in cultural representation, compersion may become more common. Not all polyamorous people are good at alleviating jealousy, and at times they reinforce or repeat conventional manifestations of jealousy. The discourse on polyamory challenges hegemonic structures of emotion by exposing the cultural ideologies of jealousy while concurrently developing its own set of norms about jealousy. Polyamorous people are not the only ones who experience compersion; they are, however, actively disseminating this concept.

A popular view within polyamorous (poly) culture is that jealousy is an emotion over which people have a great deal of control. Easton and Liszt (1997) argue that jealousy is not something that is caused by one's partner and therefore cannot be blamed on her/him. Instead, jealousy originates within oneself and thus is one's own responsibility. By this argument, the feeling of jealousy or behaving jealously will not change a partner's actions. The one who suffers most is the one feeling jealous. Easton and Liszt (1997) describe jealousy as an emotion that cannot be experienced in isolation, but rather is representative of other feelings, such as low self-esteem, insecurity, or dissatisfaction with the relationship. They argue that because jealousy is related to these unfavourable emotions, it is also linked to a feeling of shame, which can prevent acknowledgment and mitigation of jealousy. Similarly, in his popular online essay, Veaux (2009) argues that within open relationships, jealousy needs to be addressed by looking at underlying emotional issues rather than changing the actions that are the surface triggers of jealousy, otherwise patterns will repeat themselves. Taormino (2008) argues that it is important to let yourself feel any remaining jealousy and validate whatever feelings you have, instead of 'criticiz(ing) yourself or pil(ing) shame and judgment on top of it – that will just make you feel worse' (162). Additionally, Taormino argues that one must believe that loving multiple people is possible in order to be successful in open relationships. She contends, 'If you don't, you will always see other people and other relationships as infringing on and threatening to yours' (158).

Easton notes that the dominant model for dealing with negative emotions is to deny and avoid them. She argues instead for a socio-political analysis of personal experiences of jealousy that encourages full expression of all emotions (Easton, in Kleese 2006:646). In her popular online essay, Labriola suggests that polyamorous people need to rewrite popular myths about love and relationships.[1] For example, there is a core myth that 'if a partner really loved me, (s)he wouldn't have any desire for a sexual relationship with anyone else.' She re-writes this myth into, 'My partner loves me so much that (s)he trusts our relationship to expand and be enriched by experiencing even more love from others.' My research looks at how these polyamorous ideas are actualized in a way that makes embodied experiences of compersion possible.

From Polyagony to Compersion

Polyamorists are critical of the dominance of monogamy, compulsory monogamy, or mono-normativity (Ritchie and Barker 2006) and how this shapes emotional experiences of jealousy, love, and sexuality. It should be noted that there is a difference between the practice of monogamy and the institution of monogamy. If one accounts for the prevalence of cheating, swinging, and polygamy (and desiring such sexual encounters), the practice of true monogamy is rather rare – both in Western culture and elsewhere (Kipnis 2003; Mead 1977). However, as monogamy is held up as the standard of true love, any breach of this practice is frowned upon. In other words, if true love is necessarily monogamous, breaching monogamy joins love to its adverse counterpart – jealousy. Polyamorists work to remove the connection between love and sexual exclusivity, thereby disrupting the connection between jealousy and non-monogamy.

While popular culture and the emotion world of monogamy do influence the experience of jealousy, emotions cannot simply be liberated from these dominant forces, much like sexuality cannot be liberated from repression (as demonstrated well by Foucault (1976/1978)). Instead, following Weeks's (2008) example, we must look at the 'historically shaped series of possibilities, actions, behaviours, desires, risks, identities, norms, and values that can be reconfigured and recombined, but cannot be simply unleashed' (29). Weeks notes that while the cultural regulation contributes to subjectivity, emotions, and sexuality, agency also matters. Such agency emerges through grassroots organization and 'the democratization of sexuality and intimate life' (32). Polyamorists manifest these kinds of alternatives to jealousy by developing a different set of expectations than those implicit in dominant culture. The culture in which we live, in part, shapes our identities, and our understanding of this identity is somewhat limited by the language available (Weeks 2003). Whereas a monogamous cultural discourse has no word for the opposite of jealousy, polyamorists identified language to express occasions of pleasure ensuing from their non-monogamous practice: compersion.

According to Heaphy, Donovan, and Weeks (2004), the particular practice of consensual non-monogamy in same-sex relationships (such as those I research) reflects Foucault's idea that resistance produces creative outcomes. An unintended benefit of historic homosexual exclusion from institutionalized marriage is that gays and lesbians have ample opportunity to question the institution of marriage. Through their reflexive critique, they creatively produce relationship alternatives to mainstream options that often better reflect their chosen expressions of pleasure. These creative practices include open relationships, the emotional dimension of polyamory, and cultivating the experience of compersion.

Polyamorists actively develop poly philosophy that contributes to the experience of emotions associated with relationships, jealousy, and love – in both positive and negative ways. There is an interesting contradiction within the polyamorous community. On the one hand, jealousy is seen as something to which polyamorists need to give particular attention – they need to be proactive and upfront in managing jealousy and therefore good at its mitigation. On the other hand, several polyamorists in my study reported a certain pressure to be 'over it already,' and this pressure actually stood in the way of mitigating jealousy since it drove it underground. One participant, Coraline,[2] called this 'the posturing of poly cool.' Some participants would tell me how 'jealousy is socially constructed by the monogamy-centric mainstream culture' and thus should not be part of their poly experience. They felt that if they chose polyamory, they could not complain about how hard it could be. Heloise made the analogy, 'If you move to the rainforest of Vancouver, you've got no right to complain about the rain.' When polyamorists feel pressure to not be jealous, they don't talk about their challenges, and this gives the false impression that everything is easy.

Polyamorists are aware of the misconceptions and prejudice around non-monogamy, such as that polyamorists are commitment-phobic, promiscuous, or idealistic. When talking to monogamous people about their relationships, polyamorists sometimes downplay the challenges of being polyamorous in an attempt to avoid adding the stigma of jealousy to the stigma of being poly. Polyamorists work hard to dispel these negative stereotypes, and therefore may gloss over the challenges of being polyamorous that could leave them open to criticism (Kleese 2007). Additionally, some polyamorous people downplay the sexual component of their relationships, emphasizing instead the importance of the emotional connection in an (somewhat successful) attempt to gain mainstream credibility (Peppermint 2007).

The culture of polyamory challenges several ideals of monogamy and romantic love. It rejects the romantic ideal of 'total devotion,' wherein true love must have only one object, and that true love lasts forever (Goussinsky 2008). Polyamorists are critical of ideas of possession, ownership, or entitlement regarding a lover (Robinson 1999), which are central tenets of envy as described above by Simmel. Polyamorists see multiple loves as a more realistic portrayal of love, rather than idealistic. They claim that jealousy is a 'natural' part of a relationship, yet also say it need not be there at all in relation to a lover's other sexual encounters. Polyamorists differentiate and disconnect the source of jealousy from the event. They understand the source of jealousy as one's own insecurities or monogamous socialization. When jealousy does arise, they address the emotion rather than the event that 'caused' jealousy. Polyamorists support their lovers to mitigate adverse emotions, though the individual is ultimately responsible for their own emotional experience. For example, polyamorists will support their partners by offering reassurance or 'being extra sweet,' but will still go on a date with their other lover.

According to Buss (2000), an evolutionary psychologist, jealousy in monogamy developed as a tool to identify a partner's cheating, to show devoted love, and therefore to prevent the partner from straying. Because polyamorists encourage encounters outside the relationship, jealousy functions as a barrier, instead of a tool, to the full actualization of polyamorous love. Polyamorists want to trust their partners to play outside of the relationship, want their partner to have a good time doing so, want them to return afterwards, and they want to feel compersion throughout this process. Because cheating and loss is still possible in polyamorous situations, however, Buss's description of the role of jealousy is still partially applicable. One participant spoke of the 'ultimate poly betrayal' – a partner having unsafe sex with another lover. She noted that her jealous intuition that he was doing so was 'crazy-making,' particularly since her partner always responded to her suspicion as if she was just being insecure. In this case, the polyamorous ideal of addressing the emotion instead of the event would not serve her well. The distinction between suspicious and fait accompli jealousy is relevant here. Clearly, freedom to have multiple sexual relations does not necessarily translate to trustworthy or ethical behaviour.

Polyamorists enable compersion through developing and negotiating rules within their relationships. They nurture a feeling of 'specialness' in each relationship by creating or identifying an aspect that is unique to the couple (Jamieson 2004; Wosick-Correa 2008). While monogamous people often depend on sexual exclusivity to maintain a feeling of specialness, polyamorists find other ways to achieve this. In poly couples where there is a primary/ secondary hierarchy, they may negotiate reserving certain features for their primary relationship, such as acts (often sex acts), certain locations (their bed, for example), or create certain time restrictions ('Be home by 2 a.m.,' 'Only one date a week,' etc). One participant's only rule was 'Don't do anything you'd be ashamed of.' Another site for negotiation is around rules of disclosure. Some variations of these are: 'Tell me only the necessary details,' 'Tell me before you do anything,' 'Tell me within 24 hours after an act,' and 'Tell me all the juicy details.' One participant had a three-question agreement, where her partner could ask her three questions about a date, thus putting the control of information sharing into her partner's hands. Her partner could opt to hear more banal information (such as 'What did you have for dinner?') or choose more intimate questions. After the three questions, she could decide whether or not she wanted to hear more. Among my interview subjects, honesty was highly valued, but notably, full disclosure was rarely practised and rarely idealized. Over-sharing was often seen as disrespectful since it led to 'dumping' onto people information that they may not have wanted to know.

Within polyamorous culture, as one participant stated: 'It's not sleazy to hit on someone's partner.' Poly etiquette suggests that it is okay to flirt with or pursue a person who has a known partner. When one does so, they are not seen as trying to 'steal' one's date, as long as they follow proper etiquette. Such etiquette involves demonstrating respect, clarity, and open communication towards the person with whom one is flirting and their partner(s). Etiquette also suggests that a person devote their full attention to the person (or people) with whom they are on the date. Flirting with other people is usually not done at this time. When polyamorists neglect these subtle social graces, however, others feel disrespected and compersion is difficult. It is important to note that flirting means different things in different cultural contexts. Within polyamory, flirting does not necessarily represent desire to replace, but might represent playfulness, appreciation, friendship, or romantic interest (the subtleties of which are significant, yet not always apparent). Polyamorists are most likely to experience compersion when they feel as though they are being taken care of by their partners and feel secure within these relationships. Notably, like most etiquette, actual practices do not always reflect the unspoken cultural rules.

Given the small size of many poly communities, overlaps of friends and lovers are quite common. Overlapping social networks could be a catalyst for jealousy, but polyamorous people have established etiquette where difficult emotions are minimized through upfront discussion.

In this instance, polyamorous etiquette calls for people to communicate with all the people who might be adversely affected by a relationship, including friends and ex-lovers. Etiquette calls for them to ask for permission or act in a way so as to minimize jealous tensions. Most participants relied on other polyamorous people for relationship support and were particularly caring and accountable to each other. For these reasons, polyamorous people widen the boundaries of their poly family to include lovers, ex-lovers, close friends, and intimate non-sexual friends, treating them all with consideration as one might a relationship. Also significantly, close friendships or deep respect often form between people who are both lovers to one person (also called cohearts).

Celia was a participant who identifies with and practises both monogamy and polyamory, stating that her preference shifts over time depending on the dynamic with her lover(s). She noted that in her poly relationships, it has been common for her partner to check in with her about whether or not it is okay to flirt with a certain person. This act of reaching consent included her in the decision, which mitigated the potential for jealousy. Her monogamous partners, however, did not think to check in about flirting since it is not supposed to exist with in their dynamic and such boundaries are assumed rather than discussed. According to Celia, it was this exclusion from the decision-making process that triggered her jealousy. She also noted that in a polyamorous dynamic, a partner's crush could potentially become a new relationship, whereas in a monogamous dynamic, the fear is that they may leave her entirely for another person. Tianna argued that if a crush remains unexplored because it is taboo, it will likely blossom. If a partner is permitted to explore a crush, they are likely to 'get it out of their system' and find a better balance. In both of these cases, practising polyamory works to decrease instances of jealousy.

There is a joke about polyamory that sums up one apprehension about the lifestyle: How many polyamorists does it take to screw in a light bulb? None; they are too busy processing to screw. In other words, polyamory is a lot of work. Celia noted, 'Polyamory may be many great and wonderful things, but simple is not one of them.' The idea that relationships take work is so pervasive that it often goes unquestioned (Kipnis 2003). Add more relationships into the mix and there will be more work (Taormino 2008). For polyamorists much of this work is done through communication and negotiation, often geared towards reducing jealousy. Non-violent communication was expected and there was an understanding that jealousy should never be dealt with in a violent or aggressive fashion. Polyamorous culture encourages clarity and upfront communication, in particular about attraction to other people, intentions within a relationship, and sexual practices. Although not unique to polyamory, an unintended benefit of such communication is a great depth of intimacy, feeling of freedom, and a sense of interdependence within a relationship.

All of my study participants agreed that communication was the central tool for mitigating jealousy and enabling compersion. Communication involves negotiating boundaries (which are never a given), learning and expressing one's own triggers for jealousy, and building trust. Some participants felt that the vulnerability that comes from discussing one's jealousy was emotionally risky. Through practising polyamory, however, jealousy was normalized and thus minimized. For instance, one participant noted that as soon as she vocalized her feeling of jealousy and had it heard, the feeling dissipated. Grace said, 'One of my yoga instructors said whenever she felt jealous she would tell whoever she was jealous of that she was jealous at the first opportunity that she could, and she found that the other person usually took it as a compliment and that diffused the situation a little bit. It was easier for her to feel this bad feeling when it was actually making someone else feel good, but at the same time there was no power because the other person couldn't use the jealousy over her because it was out there in the open.' Similarly, Janelle argued that polyamorous culture encourages people to experience jealousy rather than deny it, 'So just allowing yourself to even just be jealous is so much more freeing and you end up not being as jealous. And also being able to talk to your partner and say, 'You know what? This threatens me,' or 'I need some reassurance, can you give that to me?' And it kind of just dissipates. Okay, I'm not so jealous anymore.'

The issue of trust arose frequently among polyamorous participants in relation to jealousy and security within a relationship. It was particularly important to trust their partner to have responsible sex outside the relationship, both physically and emotionally. While they may know and trust their partners, they also want to be able to trust their partner's date, which they may or may not know well. Uslaner (2001) argues that there are two kinds of trusters, a distinction that coincides with my participants' approach to polyamorous practice. Moralistic trusters have an optimistic view of people, assume people are generally good, and thus are more likely to trust someone they do not know. They felt that a partner's choice to stay or leave is irrespective of being actively polyamorous, and thus they easily trusted their partner's out-side sexual and emotional actions. Strategic trusters, on the other hand, depend on accumulated information. They approached polyamory with skepticism and hoped to overcome distrustfulness once people proved themselves. While their core reasons for practising polyamory were strong (i.e., philosophically based or towards a more realistic portrayal of their love), they had to work hard to trust the intentions of their partners and cohearts. Moralistic trusters had an easier time with compersion. Some participants straddled both sides of the fence, such as Coraline, who stated, 'You trust what you know,' and thus she approached her relationships not with a lack of trust but with an optimistic lack of expectations.

The above polyamorous narratives lead one to ask why polyamorists continue to practise polyamory through such difficult emotions. My research indicates that the answer is manifold. First, while jealousy within polyamory can be hard, there is jealousy in monogamous practice as well. Second, once tools are in place to manage difficult emotions like jealousy, it is experienced less negatively. Most polyamorists stated that jealousy was more common in their early experiences of polyamory and became increasingly rare. Third, the tools in place to mitigate jealousy in polyamorists' relationships could be applied to other difficult emotions. Fourth, my participants described polyamory as a much more realistic and freeing expression of their love than monogamy would be, and thus welcomed the full package. They see polyamory as no less normal than monogamy, just less common. Fifth, the benefits of polyamory outweigh the difficult feelings, and the pleasure found in compersion was particularly satisfying. Sixth, the challenge of polyamory and its ensuing opportunity for growth was highly gratifying. And lastly, the sexual enjoyment was a significant benefit to polyamorous practice.

Studies have shown that open relationships correlate to increased self-esteem and self-knowledge (Wolfe 2003), personal empowerment (Sheff 2005; Weitzman 1999), and 'boosts in sexual self-confidence . . . and [the] dissolution of jealousy' (De Visser and McDonald 2007:69). My study reveals similar results. One participant, Cheyenne, talked about polyamory as empowering, and felt a great deal of pride and satisfaction in bringing her jealousy to a place of solid compersion: 'You know those moments when you feel really proud of yourself about the way you live and what you do. Like, "Look at us!" And I do, I feel so attached to that word [compersion], really excited that I do receive so much pleasure from my partner being off with someone else and having a great night. I want to hear about it the next day in whatever degree of detail they want to give me. And that's fun.' Another participant, Nora, responded: 'It is all worthwhile for me to do it. It's a beautiful thing. It's like getting your cake and eating it too. Even if it means the making of the cake is six times longer, it's worth it. It's the most difficult cake in the universe to make.'

While most polyamorists maintain 'It's not all about the sex,'[3] the sexual benefits of polyamory were frequently mentioned in the interviews. Several polyamorists talked about eroticizing what may have otherwise triggered jealousy (such as a partner having sex with someone else), thus converting a potentially painful event into one of pleasure. Research on swinging has also demonstrated that certain situations that are ripe for jealousy had an erotically stimulating effect on swingers (De Visser and McDonald 2007; Gould 2000). Similarly, Stearns (1989:15) notes that a certain amount of jealousy can 'provide some enjoyable spice.' Many polyamorists report that having outside sexual experiences increases their overall libido and that this increase transfers to their other partners. One participant expressed a strong sense of sexual compersion: 'If my lover has a lover who I am friends with or who I like, and this is about 98 per cent of the time, watching them hug, kiss, snuggle, love, have sex with that person is so hot I could almost die from it. It's not even a vague pleasure. It's like Oh my God, right. It's the hottest thing ever. Ever. And the better I like the person that my lover is having sex with, the hotter it is.' Heloise described another aspect of compersion: 'It's funny because if you look at the "How do you know if your spouse is cheating" [article in a magazine] and some of the big signs are, he's suddenly bringing you gifts, they're telling you they love you more, and you are having more sex. And I'm like "Right, what's wrong with that?" Okay, so find out who they are cheating with so they stop doing all those wonderful things for you. I mean the concept is that they are doing it out of guilt, but it could be that they are feeling more sexual and more loving and more gregarious.'

Even though it is often neglected in sociological research, love is central to Western culture (Jackson 1993). Love, of course, is also a central organizing principle within polyamory. Love's shadow is jealousy – and jealousy plays a significant role in the polyamorous experience, either by its presence or its absence. The more people open their hearts to truly open relationships, the more vulnerable they are to the experience of jealousy, or, alternatively, the more they can conquer love's shadow. Through their extensive critique and re-imagining of jealousy, polyamorists seek to shift personal and cultural understandings of jealousy. Compersion is a creative act of resistance that places the body, pleasure, and love at centre stage. Polyamorists' practice of compersion challenges emotionally normative constructions of jealousy.

Conclusion

From the interviews I conducted, I found that my participants definitely experienced more polyamory than polyagony. It could be that those who struggled greatly are no longer polyamorous and therefore did not make it into my sample. Although their class backgrounds varied significantly, my sample represents people who have enough privilege and education to be able to persevere with polyamory, which then must also influence their approach to processing jealousy. I would argue, however, that jealousy is manageable in most polyamorous relationships, so long as all practitioners are willing to do the work. The existence of polyamory contradicts conventional beliefs about the naturalness and inevitability of jealousy and the supposed gendered ways that jealousy is embodied. While polyamorists do not necessarily have different emotional experiences than monogamous people, they follow a different model of love that in turn affects their emotional experience. Through the creation of a cultural ideology of poly, polyamorists have enabled the emotional experience of compersion. Polyamory exemplifies a culture where sexual non-exclusivity is not necessarily associated with jealousy, and offers an alternative narrative of the embodiment and expression of jealousy. As to the question, 'Where do you find the time?,' I offer a response provided by one participant, Priscilla, 'There is always room for Jell-O and always time for Facebook – and one more lover.' In other words, we make time for that which we love.

NOTES

1 http://www.cat-and-dragon.com/stef/Poly/Labriola/jealousy.html.
2 All names are pseudonyms.
3 A polyamorous slogan made popular by CunningMinx's podcast Polyamory Weekly.

13 Feeling Cosmopolitan: Experiential Brands and Urban Cosmopolitan Sensibilities

SONIA BOOKMAN

Introduction

Contemporary consumer culture is considered a 'key arena in which the emotional dynamics of our lives are played out' (Williams 2001:3). In this arena, the 'brand' has emerged as a potent platform on which such emotional dynamics unfold. Increasingly patterned through an 'emotionalized approach to brand design,' a strategy referred to as 'emotional branding,' the brand has become a key mechanism for the management, mobilization, and valorization of emotion in the consumer market (Zyman 2001:vi; Gobé 2001; see also O'Shaughnessy and O'Shaughnessy 2003). The emotionality of the brand is the focus of this chapter. Taking the case of specialty coffee brands Starbucks and Second Cup, it explores the ways in which the brands are configured to engage consumers sensually and emotionally, using emotionally driven marketing techniques and devices. Aiming to cultivate emotional connections with consumers and build brand value in what has been termed an 'experience economy' (Pine and Gilmore 1999), I argue that brands are co-shaping passions, feelings, and emotional experiences in a dynamic interplay with consumers.

To make this argument, I draw on data extracted from an extensive empirical study spanning the production and consumption of the brands, conducted mainly in Toronto, and also in Vancouver, over a period of three years.[1] The project employed three main qualitative research strategies including participant observation of both Starbucks and Second Cup branded cafés, semi-structured interviews with over 60 producers and consumers of the brands, as well as a visual analysis of various brand materials such as brochures, coffee labels, and advertisements.

The chapter begins by outlining the different perspectives on emotion that inform my analysis, followed by a discussion of emotional branding. Drawing on recent branding theory and a view of the brand as an interface (Lury 2004; Arvidsson 2006), I then introduce the experiential brands Starbucks and Second Cup. I consider the ways in which the brands are designed to frame and mediate certain affective responses and emotional experiences through the organization of a themed socio-spatial 'servicescape,' focusing in particular on the cosmopolitan possibilities they proffer. 'Cosmopolitan' can be defined both in terms of its popular, everyday usage as an attitude and stance of openness and ability to negotiate and comprehend cultural diversity, and in its more political and philosophical bent as a form of global citizenship, underpinned by an understanding of global interconnectedness and awareness of a global realm of responsibility (see Binnie et al. 2006; Hannerz 1996; Beck 2002; Urry 1995, 2000). Both of these conceptualizations inform the cosmopolitan experience that is structured by the brands.

I focus on cosmopolitanism because many Starbucks and Second Cup consumers identified it as part of the brand experience. For example, Jeff, a regular consumer at Starbucks, was discussing the process of ordering coffee, which involves the use of 'foreign' languages and choosing from a 'global' selection of coffees, when he remarked that Starbucks was 'branding themselves as this more sophisticated, cosmopolitan, exotic experience . . .' When asked to elaborate on this, he suggested that Starbucks expressed a kind of 'cosmopolitan cool' that he described as a modern, urban style. Another regular Starbucks consumer, Sharon, indicated that 'the overall culture of Starbucks, or feeling of Starbucks, is cosmopolitan'; the same 'feeling' she associates with being 'downtown' in the city of Toronto. The final part of the chapter expatiates this urban cosmopolitan sensibility. Encompassing affective and aesthetic elements, it will be argued that such cosmopolitanism comprises a 'structure of feeling' (Williams 1977) that underpins the formation of new urban cosmopolitan lifestyles, and is given cultural expression by the brands.

Approaching Emotion

In exploring the emotional dimension of brands, I draw on recent work in the area of emotional geographies that considers emotion 'in terms of its socio-spatial mediation and articulation rather than as entirely interiorized subjective mental states,' and that takes a 'non-objectifying view of emotions as relational flows, fluxes or currents, in-between people and places rather than "things" or "objects" to be studied or measured' (Davidson, Bondi, and Smith 2005:3). This perspective is useful for considering how certain sentiments, mediated by the brand interface, are constituted in the interplay between brands and consumers in everyday urban life.

Writing in this vein, Thrift (2009) focuses on affect in relation to emotion. He suggests that emotion is an expression of the (incomplete) capture of affect, which is not amenable to representation. Precognitive, and pre-discursive in nature, affect is generally a 'semiconscious phenomenon' that involves bodily states, processes, and knowledges (Thrift 2009:239). It is a form of embodied thinking, 'often indirect and nonreflective,' and a particular 'kind of intelligence' that also shapes how we move, (re)act and 'relate to the world' (175). Bound up with embodied encounters, affect also moves through and between bodies (broadly understood), which are 'not primarily centred repositories of knowledge – originators – but rather receivers and transmitters, ceaselessly moving messages of various kinds on' (236). Of concern for Thrift is the ever more 'explicit engineering of affect' through, for example, the use of 'sensory design' in the production of commodities, or devices such as the brand, and the way this is influencing disposition (235, 245).

The approach to emotion that informs this chapter is also influenced by sociological and cultural analyses that take a fluid view of emotions, in a manner similar to emotional geography perspectives. Burkitt (2002), for example, indicates that emotions are not objects contained in bodies, but rather are 'patterns of relationship' that have 'sense and meaning in the context of relations to other bodies, both human and non-human' (151). This suggests, following Ahmed (2004:4), that emotions involve particular 'orientations towards others' that are shaped through practices in everyday life, and are formed over time with reference to the past.

Using the term *feeling* instead of *affect*, Burkitt conceptualizes emotions as complexes involving bodily states, or feelings, as well as discourse, or the attempt to articulate feeling using emotional vocabularies. While recognizing their intimate connection, Burkitt (2002) distinguishes between feeling and emotion, indicating that 'feeling is part of practical consciousness and involves the way we can act within our social world through a sense of what has to be done. Emotion, however, belongs to discursive consciousness and involves the way we articulate

these feelings . . .' (154). At the same time, feelings are never fully exhausted through the 'emotional vocabularies' used to identify and express them. Delineated in this way, Burkitt's notion of feeling is akin
to Thrift's view of affect, both of which are closely associated with, yet
exceed emotion, involve embodied, practical consciousness, shape dispositions, and give rise to action. However, I prefer Thrift's somewhat
more mobile view of affect as a set of flows that moves through bodies,
which constantly receive, transmit, and interpret affects or feelings. In
this chapter I use both terms at different times to discuss processes related to emotional branding.

To elaborate on feeling in the context of social relations, Burkitt refers
to Williams's (1977) idea of 'structures of feeling.' Williams is attempting to understand the processual, emergent dimension of cultural and
social forms – how they are lived and experienced in the present as
unarticulated, unfixed, and in the process of becoming. He is interested
in general changes with social life, and defines such change in terms of
'style,' referring to a 'particular quality of social experience and relationship' (131). Williams uses the notion of structures of feeling to indicate how such changes in social meanings and values 'are actively lived
and felt' in terms of a 'practical consciousness of a present kind, in a
living and interrelating continuity' (132). Williams suggests that structures of feeling enable us to understand 'our present cultural process,'
and can be especially discerned in forms of art – 'social formations of
a specific kind' – where social content tends to be 'of this present and
affective kind' (133).

This notion is used by Nava (2002) in her work on the emergence
of a popular cosmopolitan consciousness in the commercial culture of
early twentieth-century England. In her study, she traces how women
in particular, through the consumption of global fashion and décor, expressed and contributed to the formation of a cosmopolitan 'structure
of feeling' in which 'cultural difference and the foreign constituted a
source of interest, pleasure and counter-identification that existed in
tension with more conservative outlooks' in that particular time and
place (86). Drawing attention to the affective dimension of cosmopolitanism, which is largely understood as an intellectual and aesthetic
stance, Nava's work provides a useful way of thinking about cosmopolitanism as a particular way of feeling; an emotional disposition
(Nava 2002, 2007). She also indicates that it is mediated through interactions with consumerist objects, and is generated in specific practices
and performances.

This framework for understanding emotion is used in this chapter to think about the emotionality of brands. Suggesting that brands are implicated in processes of affective engineering, it allows a consideration of the ways in which they intentionally 'work on' and cultivate certain feelings and emotions. It provides a way of thinking about the involvement of brands in the socio-spatial mediation of emotions, which are constituted in the interfacing between brands and consumers. This framework also informs my analysis of the ways in which brands, through the structuring of feelings and the mediation of emotion, give rise to certain structures of feeling through which we feel our way. Nava's work will be useful for exploring the specifically cosmopolitan sensibilities constructed on the platform of the coffee brands I am concerned with.

Emotional Branding

Within contemporary consumer culture, the brand has emerged as a powerful, ubiquitous market cultural form. Its increasing salience in economic and cultural life is attributed to a complex set of developments in marketing, production, and design from the 1970s onwards (Klein 1999; Arvidsson 2006; Moor 2008; Lury 2004). Following the theoretical principles of Lury (1999, 2000, 2004), the brand can be understood as a complex media object that articulates and mediates processes of production and consumption, operating as an interface of communication and medium of exchange. It is a frame that organizes the (asymmetrical) two-way exchange of information, operating as a communicative meeting point between consumers and producers. The exchange is not only a matter of 'qualitative calculation, but also of affect, intensivity and the re-introduction of qualities' (Lury 2004:7). The interface and its communicative possibilities are formatted through a process of design – the branding process – that involves the integration and coordination of information in a patterning of activity; the organization and ordering of relations between products and services in time and space. Constituted as performative, the functioning of the interface facilitates the establishment of brand unity or objectivity, and contributes to the emergence of brand image – 'the associations that a brand holds for consumers' – which is central to creating brand value (80).

In recent years, an emotionalized approach to design has been developed to capitalize on the brand's capacity to be 'affective' in processes of exchange, through the communication of information and introduction of qualities that are specifically devised to engage the senses, generate passions, and evoke emotions. This approach, termed *emotional branding*, is described by Gobé (2001) as providing the 'means and methodology for connecting products to the consumer in an emotionally profound way' (xv). In his use of the term *emotional*, Gobé is referring to the ways in which 'a brand engages consumers on the level of the sense and emotions; how a brand comes to life for people and forges a deeper, lasting connection' (xiv). To achieve this, to be culturally and emotionally relevant to consumers, Gobé indicates that brands must develop respectful, dialogic, and intimate relationships with consumers. They need to understand and facilitate the holistic, emotional experiences consumers desire through an imaginative approach to, and emphasis on, sensorial design and emotional appeal. This involves the establishment of brand personality and presence, as well as a brand vision that enables continual reinvention in order to ensure emotional resonance.

While the emotional dimension of the brand is not necessarily new, it has recently risen to the fore in brand design and management, and is increasingly perceived as the key to brand value and success, wherein, 'building a brand empire 'is about staking out emotional turf in our consciousness'' (Wolf, in Arvidsson 2006:82). According to marketing analyst Ying Fan (2005), 'brands are now gunning for a share of consumers' inner lives, their values, their beliefs, their politics; yes, their souls' (342; see also O'Shaughnessy and O'Shaughnessy 2003). The cultivation of an emotional connection with consumers has become a primary aim of brands. To accomplish this, various 'affective techniques' and emotionally oriented marketing strategies have evolved with the intent to mobilize affects and produce compelling experiences that become associated with the brand (Thrift 2009:243). One such strategy consists of the increasingly widespread trend of 'brandscaping.' This is a marketing strategy based on sensorial design that involves the orchestration of space, using lighting, interior décor, architecture, and atmosphere to create a particular ambiance in which consumers are immersed (Lury 2004). This allows the brand to richly engage all the senses and suggest ways of feeling, with the aim of constructing intensive aesthetic and emotional experiences that will produce added value for the brand. Other strategies include brand sponsorship of celebrities or causes that consumers are already emotionally involved with, the facilitation of brand communities through the organization of branded social events, and viral marketing whereby the brand is inserted into already existing patterns of relations and everyday life, the idea of which is to 'tie commodities into the affective landscape of consumers' (Thrift 2009:247; see also Arvisson 2006).

These brand strategies however, require consumers' embodied participation in the performance and production of brand-based emotional experiences, such as the 'experience of family bonding at McDonald's' or the 'experience of empowerment with Nike' (Arvidsson 2006:82). Through the organization and ordering of retail environments, events, and sponsorships, brand management is able to establish particular ambiances that frame and partially anticipate consumers' engagement with the brand, enabling emotional experiences to unfold in particular directions. The aim is to 'guide the investments of affect on the part of consumers,' with the goal of 'creating an affective intensity, and experience of unity between the brand and the subject' (93). This process is carefully co-ordinated and pre-structured in order to ensure that the meanings and experiences generated on the platform of the brand fall within the parameters of brand image, thus adding to (rather than detracting from) brand value (Arvidsson 2006). Drawing on consumers' emotional capacities and affective labour, consumers are thus implicated in the *co-creation* of brand experiences, and ultimately, brand value.

Experiential Brands: Starbucks and Second Cup

> Now the advertising is not what's important, it's more about the experience. The building of the brand is really about your experience, the way you build a brand is one experience at a time, fulfilling the expectations of each consumer every time.
>
> – Greg, VP Operations, Second Cup

Starbucks and Second Cup have been at the vanguard of the trend towards emotional branding. Starting out in the form of a retail store selling high-quality coffee beans to a small target market of discerning middle-class consumers in the 1970s, both brands quickly evolved in the 1980s to their current predominant form as a streetfront café. Expanding tremendously throughout the 1990s and into the next decade, these branded cafés are a prominent feature of Canadian cityscapes, and the café culture they promote is now an integral aspect of everyday life for many middle-class urbanites.

Premised on the provision of customized, gourmet coffee in a stylized, social, café setting, both Starbucks and Second Cup can be defined as *experiential brands*, a term used to designate those brands which, 'in conjunction with their corporate-sponsored symbols and products, offer consumers distinctively themed servicescapes, designed to facilitate certain kinds of hedonic/aesthetic experiences and social interactions' (Thompson and Arsel 2004:632). A particular form of brandscaping, servicescaping is a marketing strategy that involves the 'experientializing' of service industries through their spatialization and use of sensorial design (Moor 2003). It allows a more 'proximal relationship between consumer bodies and brands' through which emotional connections and experiences can emerge (Moor 2003:45). These experiences are shaped through the use of 'theming' – a technique that provides a framework for the organization of environments in such a way as to establish a unifying image or experience (Lukas 2007:1). The marketing literature suggests that theming is key to creating experiences that are engaging, rich, and memorable (Pine and Gilmore 1999). It works through the identification of a particular theme, as well as a set of feelings and emotional cues that will convey that theme, using this inventory to guide the process of design (Pine and Gilmore 1991). Theming operates as a mechanism through which 'affective response can be designed into spaces' (Thrift 2009:187).

In the case of Starbucks and Second Cup, the organization of the themed servicescape involves the coordination of spatial, material, and relational elements, namely coffee, baristas, and the café space, to convey information and introduce certain qualities that will generate carefully calculated effects. Smells, images, sounds, gestures, and textures are configured as cues to prompt affective responses and cultivate feelings that point to the theme. Consumers are called on to interact with and qualify (Callon, Méadel, and Rabeharisoa 2002) the various cues they encounter as they enter the café, order beverages and potentially linger in the café space. In this process of bodily and tactile engagement, consumers are deeply implicated in production and circulation of the affects, feelings, and emotions that are associated with the themed experience they co-perform. The ongoing everyday co-production of this experience is central to what Second Cup's marketing director terms *living the brand*. This is vital to brand value, which is attained in part by the way a brand 'comes to life' for consumers and is entwined in their everyday lives through the establishment of affective and emotional connections. Consumers pay for the experience they co-create, and which forms the basis of exchange.

Delineated by brand engineers as the 'Starbucks Experience,' or the 'Ultimate Coffee Experience' in the case of Second Cup, the brand experience, in the case of both brands, is structured through two main themes, including a 'third place' coffeehouse theme and the romance of coffee drinking. As summarized by Howard Schultz, chairman and chief global strategist of Starbucks: 'People connect with Starbucks because they relate to what we stand for. It's more than great coffee. It's the romance of the coffee experience, the feeling of warmth and community people get in the Starbucks stores' (Schultz and Yang 1997:5).

The Third Place

The widely recognized third place coffeehouse theme draws on Oldenburg's (1989) notion of the 'third place,' which he describes as an informal gathering place outside of home and work, characterized by social interaction ranging from an exchange of glances to conversation, and marked by a sense of playfulness, community, and camaraderie. Reflecting this formulation, a marketing director for Starbucks Canada remarked:

> 'I like to think of the cafés as the third place, so customers have their home and their work, and Starbucks is, and for a lot of people, the third place that they go to. So when you go in you'll see warm colours making you relax, the music is generally jazzy, which is also relaxing, it's not invasive, it's just there . . . um, we always put in every store we possibly can a space for couches, chairs, in some stores we have a fireplace . . . the ambiance and atmosphere is all about creating a very comfortable space where you can come, have your cup of coffee, read a paper if you want, or visit with a friend.'

A third place ambience is thus framed through configurations of café space, including the use of architecture and interior design. It also involves the 'performatting' (Adkins 2005) of baristas, who are trained to convey third place qualities such as friendliness, hospitality, and recognition through emotional labour intended to foster feelings of belonging and circulate a sense of community among patrons. Consumers are invited to 'hang out' in these spaces, configured as a comfortable and familiar 'home-away-from-home,' and actively co-construct a third place experience, which is constituted as much from consumers' emotional engagement and social activity as it is from the features of café design (Arvidsson 2006).

The Romance of Coffee

Of particular interest for this chapter, and thus elaborated in more depth, is the romance of coffee drinking, which is linked to a 'cosmopolitan connoisseur' experience. Coffee drinking is romanced by the brands, in part through the configuration of specialty coffees, which are introduced to consumers in 'the way wine stewards bring forward fine wines,' with an emphasis on origins as a distinguishing factor in discriminating coffee quality and 'taste' (Schultz and Yang 1997:246). Designed to both 'educate' consumers and encourage emotional involvement, information about specialty coffees and their diverse origins is conveyed aesthetically for the most part through the use of colour, textures, images, and sounds assembled in the form of brochures, wall murals, or even background music.

For example, consumers encounter displays of coffees that are designed to express a variety of coffee styles through colourful, illustrated packaging and stamp-like coffee labels. Second Cup offers take-away cups patterned to tell the 'story of coffee' through artistic images of coffee plants, producers, and global coffee expeditions. Meanwhile, Starbucks provides brochures that act like tour guides to a 'world of coffee' (Starbucks 2002a). Decorated with vintage maps, travel notes, and postage stamps, these brochures introduce consumers to fine coffee such as Ethiopia Sidamo, described as a magical brew with a fleeting, floral aroma, a bright yet soft finish, and an exotic lemon-pepper taste (Starbucks 2002a). Provided with brand-based 'coffee passports' to collect coffee 'stamps' and record their travels, consumers are invited to sensually and imaginatively discover the 'world of coffee' and 'taste' the differences (in origin) configured culturally as an 'authentic' tradition to encounter, an 'exotic' destination to venture to, or a 'mysterious' flavour to imbibe (Second Cup 2008; Starbucks 2002a).

Information designed to convey coffee origins are intended to suggest feelings and circulate certain emotions that will convey the romance of coffee. Discussing a newly created Huehuetenango single origin coffee label, Second Cup's marketing director explained the significance of aesthetic presentation in terms of emotional appeal: '. . . yeah I mean there is a sense of adventure, it's a bit of an escape that allows you to go off to an exotic destination, and uh, you know, I think that adds a little bit to the mystique of the coffee; another way that we continue to try and support and build value for the product that we're developing . . . and also there's an education piece plus creating a sense of intrigue and involvement, which I think gets people more involved in the overall experience.' Designed to stir a host of potential emotions, such as the 'excitement' of adventure, a sense of 'intrigue,' and 'delight' in discovering new tastes, origins, and cultures, consumers are encouraged to get 'caught up' in the romance and to develop a shared 'passion' for coffee through the cultivation of connoisseurship (of the playful or serious sort) with the brand.

The romance of coffee is further invoked through an emphasis onethical consumption, wherein the 'love' of coffee (diversity) is extended to a 'care' for coffee origins. This involves the formatting of corporate social responsibility to frame and mediate altruistic, affective relations between the brands, their consumers, and coffee origin communities. To this end, both Starbucks and Second Cup have developed elaborate programs focused on improving coffee production practices, establishing environmental initiatives as well as pioneering socially responsible coffees such as Second Cup's 'Rwandan Cup of Hope.' Starbucks's 'Commitment to Origins' initiative, for example, involved the development and promotion of a series of ethical coffees (Starbucks 2002b). The aim was to express and communicate, as a marketing director put it, 'our passion about our coffee,' which encompasses 'everything in terms of where we buy, how we buy, how we help origin countries, the kind of blends we make, the kinds of products that we sell' (interview). Displayed in 'authentic' burlap sacs, these coffees were presented to consumers through packaging aesthetics that employed 'natural' materials, and fair trade testimonials to evoke ethical sentiments and mobilize emotions such as empathy for others and hope for change.

Gobé (2001) has flagged this kind of 'cause marketing' as an important trend that is 'perfectly in sync with the premise of Emotional Branding; it has everything to do with getting to know who your consumers really are, what really matters to them, and showing them you feel the same way' (298). Pointing to Starbucks' programs as exemplary of this approach, he suggests that the 'effort to give something back to the often Third-World countries where their product is harvested shows a recognition of the need for respect for human conditions at the product's source and a perspective of global diversity' (300). Going a step further than simply demonstrating their concern to consumers, Starbucks and Second Cup invite consumers to become involved in such efforts. A paragraph from Starbucks 'Commitment to Origins' brochure declares: 'We try to make a difference to the people and places that produce coffee, to the countries we visit and the families we touch. Every time you purchase Starbucks coffees, you're also making a difference, helping to improve people's lives, and encouraging conservation where our coffee is grown' (Starbucks 2002b).

Constituting an ethical 'frame of action' the brands pattern possibilities for consumers to act out feelings of 'care' and 'empathy,' and demonstrate a 'perspective of global diversity' by becoming responsible consumers. Such programmed, altruistic practices allow consumers to 'feel good' about consuming specialty coffees and 'doing good' in the global coffee community, facilitating the circulation of emotions such as pleasure in the consuming encounter.

Romancing Coffee, Invoking Cosmopolitanism

Bound up with the complex set of emotions inspired by the romance of coffee – such as the 'excitement' of adventure to distant places, 'delight' in diversity, and 'empathy' for coffee growing others – the brands construct a cosmopolitan experience. By 'working on emotions,' consumers are potentially aligned with the brands as cultural connoisseurs and concerned global citizens; they are encouraged to feel and be cosmopolitan with the brand (Ahmed 2004). This is a cosmopolitanism premised on an interest in, passion for, and openness to cultural diversity as constituted via the medium of coffee, as well as an awareness of global community and its interrelatedness through altruistic engagement with coffee growing 'others.' Following Nava (2002), it is an emotional as well as aesthetic disposition.

In order to enact this alignment, however, the brands establish a cosmopolitan context for action that attributes coffee origins and coffee producing 'others' as the source of 'our feeling' – of the cosmopolitan orientation afforded by the brands (Ahmed 2004). Aestheticized and culturally framed as 'exotic,' 'authentic,' and 'underdeveloped,' coffee producers and origins are differentially positioned in relation to an audience of primarily (though not exclusively) urban middle-class Western coffee consumers as the source of cosmopolitan 'interest' and 'altruism.' As Ahmed (2000) notes, 'emotions may involve 'being moved' for some precisely by fixing others as 'having' certain characteristics' (11). Here, the 'fixing' of coffee producers and origins in terms of a 'third world difference,' is precisely what enables the unfixing and becoming of the brands and their consumers as cosmopolitan.

Feeling Cosmopolitan: Consumers and the Co-creation of an Urban Cosmopolitan Sensibility

While Starbucks and Second Cup orchestrate distinctive brand experiences – encompassing a range of feelings and emotional performances – they nonetheless require consumers' active participation in order for these to be realized. As Arvidsson (2006) suggests, 'brands do not so much provide ready made experiences, as much as they enable the production, or co-creation, of an experience . . .' (35). Although this dynamic process is tightly managed by the brands, it is not fully determined. It is not assumed that consumers are straightforwardly seduced by the romance of coffee, that they conduct emotional performances as suggested, and co-produce a narrow cosmopolitan experience as engineered. Implicated as 'interactants' in the café servicescape, consumers engage with the brands in embodied, proximal processes of qualification, negotiating emotional appeals and affective pulls, co-generating brand experiences in a way that 'tends to exceed the programming efforts of marketing' (35). Turning to this interplay, in what follows I trace the co-creation and contours of a specifically urban cosmopolitan sensibility and structure of feeling constituted in the interfacing between consumers and the brands.

An Urban Cosmopolitan 'Feel'

Many of the consumers I interviewed in Starbucks and Second Cup cafés indicated that the presence of coffees from around the world, the 'rich and earthy' colours used in café decor, the sounds of 'world' music, and images of coffee growers elicited a cosmopolitan 'feel.' For example, Chris, a creative producer and regular Starbucks consumer, pointed to a connection between Starbucks' global array of coffees and a cosmopolitan sentiment in the following excerpt:

> CHRIS: Just being exposed to the fact that there's lots of different varieties from all over the world; I didn't think about that too much before Starbucks culture came about . . . I guess that's where the gourmet, that's where it comes in, when people start becoming attuned to the various tastes of the various countries and regions, it's almost become like a wine, to some degree. Um, but the environment itself tends to lend to that as well, right, they have that sort of, now I can't say that this one has that, but um, yeah at various points throughout their décor, throughout the year, they tend to sort of have that travel theme happening

> I think. Almost like, I don't know if this is accurate, but it's almost that travel-stamps-on-the-side-of-a-suitcase type of feel.
>
> INTERVIEWER: Where do you get that from?
>
> CHRIS: From the décor. Not this particular décor, but in general that's a common theme in Starbucks.
>
> INTERVIEWER: So, do you get a sense of travel and adventure, being here?
>
> CHRIS: Hmmm, I don't know if it's travel and adventure, or if it's more of a sort of cosmopolitan feel. That's more accurate.

Aestheticized elements designed to invoke the romance of coffee, such as coffee labels, packaging, and murals, are perceived by Chris in terms of a travel theme, constituting an ambiance described as a 'travel-stamps-on-the-side-of-a-suitcase type of feel.' This affective backdrop is fundamental to the emergence of the cosmopolitan sensibility he identifies. When asked what he meant by cosmopolitanism later in the same interview, Chris replied, 'Urban cosmopolitan. So you're in the city, and it's part of the variety of city life, you know, different people come together to experience that whole thing, I don't know' (interview). While not fully or clearly articulated in terms of specific emotions, Chris described the cosmopolitan 'feel' he connects with Starbucks as an 'urban' cosmopolitan orientation, premised on engagement with cultural diversity and difference, experienced as part of everyday urban life.

Qualified in this way, Chris's response reflected a common trend among consumers, who often referred to the cosmopolitan 'feel' they identified as urban, metropolitan, or downtown, bound up with experiences of daily city life and associated with urban lifestyles. This was the case for business owner and Starbucks consumer Jeff, who associated Starbucks with a particular urban style, which he termed 'North American cosmopolitan cool.' When asked to explain what he meant by this, he responded:

> Um, okay, North American cosmopolitan cool is jazz, Miles Davis, American Indie movies, more like modern. I tend to associate North Americans who adhere or latch onto European things as, I guess there's people that seem to consume things that have greater legitimacy as a result of their classical old status, or ballet, opera, Shakespeare . . . These guys give greater legitimacy to things that are older. So in contrast to that, North American urban cool would be much more avant-garde in the sense that it's looking at things that are very recent . . . European cool would be like the Stratford Festival or Shaw Festival, whereas North American cosmopolitan cool would be like the newest plays.

Differentiated from the 'European feel' he attributed to traditional Italian cafes, Jeff described Starbucks' 'cosmopolitan cool' as modern, urban, and innovative. Such cosmopolitanism involves an 'interest' in cultural variety, but 'delights' in popular culture especially, and 'avant-garde' cultural innovation. Indeed, both Starbucks and Second Cup are configured as culturally open and progressive, not only through café design, but also through strategic brand sponsorship of 'cutting edge' cultural events including film, jazz, and fringe festivals.

Jeff's account of 'cosmopolitan cool' reflects the 'popular usage' of 'cosmopolitan' to express 'a modern style of urbanity characterized by cultural liveliness and a certain sophistication' (Haylett 2006:187). It is particularly identified with 'chic cafés, arts festivals, international fashion and food, and vibrant streetlife' (187). This particular urban 'style' underpins what analysts have identified as the emergence of new urban 'cosmopolitan lifestyles' evident among certain factions of the new middle- and gentrifying classes (Binnie et al. 2006; Brown 2006; Young, Diep, and Drabble 2006). Especially constituted through consumption practices, it is also manifest in the rise of ever more 'cosmopolitan spaces of consumption' designed to cater to and support the articulation of such lifestyle formations (Binnie et al. 2006; also see Shields (1992) for a discussion of lifestyle consumption). Configuring a 'cosmopolitan space of consumption,' Starbucks gives cultural expression to this cosmopolitan form, or, following Williams (1977), structure of feeling.

Situated Cosmopolitan Sentiments

The urbanness of the cosmopolitan style and sentiment produced on the platform of the brands is an outcome of a dynamic interplay between consumers and brands (both of which are in open-ended relations with external environments) in particular urban settings. As Moor (2003) has indicated in her study of the brand Witnness' spatialized event-oriented marketing strategies, 'the "effects" of affect must always be actualized or made sense of "locally" ' (52; see also Massumi 1996). This points to the significance of the broader environments in which brand encounters occur, in conditioning affective responses and mediating emotions in the interfacing between brands and consumers.

Prominent features of the urban 'consumptionscape,' the Second Cup and Starbucks cafés where I conducted my research were located in urban shopping and leisure areas, financial districts, and up-and-coming

or gentrified neighbourhoods in the cities of Toronto and Vancouver.
Their location is tactically coordinated as part of brand strategy, which is
designed to incorporate urban environments into the third place brand
image, and connect with target audiences of primarily affluent urbanites
as they go about their daily urban routines and engage in mundane consumption practices. Consumers' affective and emotional involvement
with the brands is influenced by these broader contexts in which such
relations unfold.

This is particularly apparent in the following excerpt from an interview with Starbucks consumer Sharon, a professional working in the
financial district of Toronto: Compared to Tim Hortons – Tim Hortons
is you know, rural, small town, and there's a warm and fuzzy feeling,
and we all grew up with Tim Hortons; now Starbucks is new, and it's
very lively, the colours are very bright and bold, and it's part of my
downtown, it's part of my everyday, and if I, you know, if I'm going
on vacation I will likely go to another city; that's what appeals to me, is
sensory overload. There's a little bit of stimulation at Starbucks which
I associate with life around me, cosmopolitan; it's downtown.[2] Con-
trasted with Tim Hortons, which is perceived as 'small town' and parochial, Starbucks is considered by Sharon to be urban and cosmopolitan.
Characterized by a certain cultural liveliness, it enables her to 'feel very
cosmopolitan,' as she put it, expressed as openness to new cultural experiences, a search for contrasts rather than the comfortable familiarity
she associates with Tim Hortons. Forming the basis for an 'affective
intensity,' Sharon articulates an experience of unity between the way
she feels cosmopolitan and the feeling of cosmopolitanism that is attributed to the brand. The cosmopolitan feeling Sharon associates with
Starbucks is bound up with her impressions of city life. She qualifies affective cues and information designed to convey the romance of coffee
through an urban lens, interpreting 'bright and bold' colours as the vi-
brancy of urban life. The urban cosmopolitan 'feel' that emerges in this
process reflects a complex interplay between the brand and Sharon's
urban disposition (including her emotional 'orientations') and context
of consumption.

As Crossley indicates, emotions are situated and context-specific:
they 'form part of our point of view on the world; we do not just have
them, we exist in and by way of them' (in Williams 2001:59). A specific
way of feeling and emotional orientation, an urban cosmopolitan 'feel'
is shaped through the intersection of brands with consumers and their
everyday urban rhythms and routines of going to work 'downtown,'

hanging out with friends in a 'hip' neighbourhood, or simply reading the weekend newspaper. This cosmopolitan sensibility is clearly *situated*, rooted in the particularity of urban locations, environments, spatial practices, and embodied performances (Cheah and Robbins 1998; Savage, Bagnall, and Longhurst. 2005). It produces a particular kind of cosmopolitan experience associated with the brands, which diverges from the generic cosmopolitan experience they frame. Interestingly, some of the more difficult aspects of the intended experience, such as recognition of global responsibility through the performance of altruistic actions do not figure as part of the popular cosmopolitan sensibility constituted in the interplay with consumers. While exceeding the engineering efforts of brand management, a specifically urban cosmopolitanism nonetheless falls within the parameters of brand image, still constituting a cosmopolitan experience as part of the overall brand image, with a slight variation in kind.

Brand-Based Diversity and Local Cosmopolitan Openness

Engagement with cultural diversity is a central component of the cosmopolitan experience that consumers associate with the brands. It enables the circulation of feelings and emotions such as 'intrigue' with cultural variety, as well as a 'delight' in this diversity, which are bound up with expressions of cosmopolitan openness. As mentioned earlier, Starbucks and Second Cup assemble a global diversity of coffee origins, styles, and cultures in the themed servicescape. Designed to invoke a 'passion' for (coffee) variety as part of a 'cosmpolitan connoisseur' experience, consumers are presented with aesthetic information designating distinct coffee sources and destinations. For consumers, this conveys the idea that the brands are bringing together a 'world of coffee' and cultures, constituting a kind of global diversity that they notice within the café. Nonetheless, several consumers also pointed out the limits to such diversity; as Starbucks consumer and graduate student Jennifer declared, 'they have an Italian CD, they have a Brazilian CD, so in that way, they sort of . . . it's diversity, but it's rigidity-conformed diversity in terms of music, and in terms of atmosphere.' Interacting with the brands in localized practices and embodied performances as they go about their everyday urban lives, consumers qualify and reconfigure such diversity as urban multicultural difference, or the 'variety of city life,' as Chris put it. Illustrated in the quotes above, consumers tend to relate information, such as the 'bright and bold colours' used to convey 'exotic' origins, or murals containing images of 'distant' destinations, to their urban environments, characterised by an array of cultural flows and 'in situ' cultural difference (Latham 2006:95). The experience of brand-based diversity is bound up with routine engagement with variety in the multicultural cities of Toronto and Vancouver. In this interchange, global cosmopolitan awareness and cultural interest is reworked as local openness via the brand; an instance of the 'global grounded in the local' (Binnie et al. 2006:15). This is illustrated in the following commentary by Second Cup consumer Sean, who works and studies part-time in Toronto:

> I think it [Second Cup] is trying to project that image [as being cosmopolitan], and the people who are going there are also trying to project that image. Um, here on this street corner it is relatively multicultural, but a Second Cup in North York is going to be all white, and yet the people in there are somehow in some sense thinking of themselves as taking part in the world culture or something like that . . . I know there's tons of Starbucks in suburbs and in smallish towns, and that's one of the things that's attractive about them, is that you can be in a strip mall in an utterly homogeneous area and you can think of yourself as taking part in; it's projecting itself as being urban and as being worldwide, so you get to think of yourselves as a big city person who knows about the world.

Appealing to emotional imaginations, the brands enable consumers to feel and be cosmopolitan, to imagine themselves as 'a big city person who knows about the world.' As Ahmed (2004) suggests, there is a 'pleasure' associated with sitting in a café and 'feeling' cosmopolitan, which involves a certain way of thinking about and seeing oneself as a 'good or tolerant subject.' However, as Sean also intimates, the openness that is structured in this interplay is limited, involving relatively easy and superficial encounters with difference. Patterned as part of the servicescape, consumers can experience a multiplicity of highly staged and selective cultures from the safety of their window seats, without ever leaving the café environment. Performed in this way, consumers co-create a narrow, urban cosmopolitan experience on the platform of the brand.

Through the structuring of feelings and framing of emotional experiences, the brands give rise to a contemporary cosmopolitan structure of feeling that is linked to the experience of the multicultural Canadian city, and involves an orientation of (limited) openness to diversity and delight in popular culture. It reflects a particular quality of urban experience marked by the banality of cultural diversity, which has become a 'routinized part of cultural practice and social interaction' in everyday urban life (Nava 2002:94). Particularly available to middle-class consumers, it is a style and sentiment that reflects cosmopolitanism in its popular mode, and underpins the construction of cosmopolitan lifestyles.

Conclusion

The growing emphasis on emotional branding and rise to prominence of experiential brands speaks to Ahmed's (2004) concern with the intensification of emotionality in contemporary society (see also Hunt, chap. 8), suggesting that brands and consumer culture are important sites in which this process is occurring and can be fruitfully explored. This chapter has focused on the experiential brands Starbucks and Second Cup, considering the ways in which they frame a range of affective responses and emotional performances through the design of a sensorial café servicescape and the use of theming to program distinctive brand experiences. Arguing that consumers are implicated in the co-generation of emotions and experiences on the platform of the brand, I traced the emergence of an urban cosmopolitan sensibility constituted in the dynamic interplay between urban Canadian consumers and these specialties coffee brands. This situated cosmopolitan aesthetic and structure of feeling forms part of the brand experience. Giving cultural expression to this structure of feeling, the brands enable certain consumers to feel and be 'cosmopolitan' with the brand, and to assemble urban cosmopolitan lifestyles through participation in such cosmopolitan spaces of consumption.

This analysis points to the ways in which brands have become an 'affective force' in consumer culture; they are spun into, and shape our everyday emotional lives, structuring possibilities for feeling, influencing dispositions, and patterning emotional performances. It draws attention to the ways in which corporations are increasingly 'working on' our emotions through the use of 'affective techniques' and knowledges. It also suggest that emotions as cultural practices are shifting through consumer culture, with significant social and cultural implications that are as yet unfolding. As Thrift (2009:73) cautions: 'Through history, of course, landscapes have been constructed and experiences have been put up for sale but I think the new developments which, by engaging all the senses, produce new realms of experience to exchange should give us pause.'

NOTES

1 The research was conducted as part of my doctoral research project,
   'Framing Consumption, Configuring Production, Generating Culture: An
   Enquiry into the Branding Processes of Starbucks and Second Cup.' In total,
   80 participant observations were conducted at 22 cafés in Toronto (11 each
   of Starbucks and Second Cup cafés), and 10 participant observations
   were conducted in Vancouver. Forty-one interviews were conducted with
   Starbucks and Second Cup consumers (20 of whom were Second Cup
   consumers and 21 Starbucks consumers). A further 22 interviews were
   conducted with production-oriented participants, including baristas,
   managers, franchise owners, marketing directors, and creative designers in
   both companies.

   The author wishes to thank Susan Frohlick and Liz Millward for reading
   earlier versions of this chapter, the editors and reviewers for their helpful
   comments, as well as the research participants and cafés that hosted me
   during the research.
2 Founded in 1964 in Hamilton, Ontario, Tim Hortons is the dominant
   mainstream coffee and donut chain in Canada. Having established over 2000
   sites by 2005, it has become a well-known Canadian institution and icon
   (Tim Hortons 2008).

14 Autistic Autobiographies and More-than-Human Emotional Geographies

JOYCE DAVIDSON AND MICK SMITH[1]

> Autism made social life hard, but it made animals easy.
> – Dr Temple Grandin, *Animals in Translation*

Introduction

Qualitative analysis of recent autobiographies by individuals with autism spectrum disorders (ASDs) (Davidson 2007, 2008) reveals that authors' relations with nonhuman others comprise a significant emergent theme. Such autobiographical writings suggest that autistic interactions with animals – and sometimes-inanimate aspects of the 'natural' environment – have profoundly emotional qualities of a kind more usually associated with social settings. This suggestion is conspicuously at odds with widespread popular views, largely supported by clinical accounts, that autistic individuals[2] are exceptionally asocial and almost entirely unconcerned with the beings and doings of others (Frith 1996; Tidmarsh and Volkmar 2003). The name given to the disorder does, after all, derive from the Greek *autos* (meaning 'self'), and is fully intended to connote the aloneness and separation of those frequently described as living as if 'in a world of their own' (Szatmari 2004; see Davidson 2007).

This chapter sets out to provide a hermeneutic context for the self-reported experiences of ASD authors' relations to the more-than-human phenomenal world, paying special attention to emotional geographies. Emotions are, as Heidegger (1988) argues, vital modes of appropriating and connecting to the phenomenologically experienced world, modes of understanding and relating that are, moreover, often pre-interpretative and/or resistant to being fully communicated. The clinical and externalist focus on the relative absence of ASD connections to the social world necessarily undervalues these, often intense, kinds of emotional engagements. What is more, ASD authors' insider accounts are themselves attempts to render these emotional experiences into a socially communicable (linguistic) form.

ASD authors recount narratives that present radical challenges to the 'self-centred' stereotypes of autism. As Biklen (2005) states: 'Far from confirming the deficit model, where the person labeled autistic is presumed isolated and uninterested, recent autobiographical accounts reveal people in search of connections with the world' (49). These *connections* are, for a significant number of ASD authors, often experienced most readily and most intensely with(in) a 'natural' world that apparently offers some respite from the disruptive, intrusive, and communicatively overburdened social world. These personal geographies are characterized by rich, rewarding, and meaningful relationships with more-than-human entities such as animals or trees, which, in this broader sense, offer a form of agreeable sociality, a kind of being-with-others imbued with many varied phenomenal and emotional resonances.

Such a claim might be perceived as uncritically accepting precisely the kind of distinction between 'natural' and 'social' worlds that has been deemed problematic in recent geographical and philosophical literature (Braun and Castree 2001; Latour 2004). The idea that our understandings of nature are socio-historically variable and that our experiences and evaluations of 'natural' entities necessarily differ according to prevailing interpretations is widely accepted. But this should not be taken to mean that all there is to the world is human interpretations, that 'nature' is *just* a social construct (Smith 1999). The phenomenal reality of the more-than-human world is not dependent upon the degree to which that world is socially pre-interpreted – our chemical knowledge of the molecular structure of water, for example, will not stop us drowning or slaking our thirst.

Indeed, the case of autism seems to offer a wide spectrum of possibilities where such social pre-interpretations are minimized or even entirely absent precisely because of a lack of access to socially mediated and communicated understandings – whether through 'choice' (i.e., a concern by those with ASD to avoid and shield themselves from social situations) or 'necessity' (i.e., the difficulty or even impossibility of understanding socially articulated meanings). Ironically, in such circumstances, experiences of the 'natural' world might actually appear more *immediate*, more 'real,' engaging, and evocative precisely because the mediating and disturbing effects and affects of human sociality are, *relatively speaking*, absent. The entity on which concern is focused is not being constantly over-written, taken-up by, or involved in those socially contrived and socially meaningful activities that seem to confuse and confound those with ASDs. The point here, then, is not to posit an absolute distinction between nature and culture or between nature and artifice, but, by beginning with 'insider' accounts of autistic experiences, to explain how, and to some extent why, emotional involvements with elements of a world that is always both more-than and irreducible to human (social) interpretations becomes an important focus for a different form of sociality: an emotionally experienced being-with-others who are more-than-human.

Researching Autistic Worlds: Context and Method

Perhaps surprisingly, given the wide range of disorders, disabilities, and differences that have featured in geographical and social science research, and despite its increasing prevalence and extensive presence in the popular and cultural imagination (e.g., Haddon 2004), first-hand experience of autism had, until very recently, attracted relatively little attention (see Bagatell 2007; Biklen 2005; and Jones, Zahl and Huws 2001; Jones, Quigney and Huws 2003, reviewed in Silverman 2008). Of the various core features of autism discussed in clinical literature and the increasing number of published first-hand accounts, it is the affective, relational differences that are of particular interest for this chapter. The professionals' view of the presence, or rather absence, of such socio-emotional qualities is best summarized by Baron-Cohen's (2004) statement that 'autism is an empathy disorder: those with autism have major difficulties in "mindreading" or putting themselves into someone else's shoes, imagining the world through someone else's eyes and responding appropriately to someone else's feelings' (137). The question though is whether this inability to 'mind-read' is necessarily linked to an *emotional deficit* or is tied in more complex ways to problems associated with experiencing and understanding social interactions that consequently finds such encounters particularly (emotionally) disturbing.

Autistic people are often described as preferring the 'company' of objects, maps, timetables, and mechanical 'systems' to people (Baron-Cohen

2000:490). Attraction to technical/cultural systems does indeed feature heavily in ASD writings, but so also, and arguably just as significantly, do *natural* systems: things and others, with whom apparently comfortable and comforting lasting relations are formed. The point is not to argue that 'nature' is more important than 'culture' in ASD worlds and writings, but rather to question why such natural relations are so often overlooked by external clinical accounts.

The increasing publication of ASD autobiographies mirrors the dramatic increase in the reported incidence of autism. The methodological implications of drawing on autobiographical materials are discussed at length in several recent texts, for example Smith and Watson (1996, 2001), Avrahami (2007), and Davidson (2008a, b). Such implications include issues concerning the reliability of memories and their recursive interpretation (especially when inserted into a totalizing and linear life-narrative), the pressure to conform to a particular (post-Enlightenment) textual form and model of the self, and the potential influence of previous works. The fact that ASD autobiographies are sometimes 'facilitated' by others (see Smith 1996) adds a further level of interpretative difficulty.

There are also problems in trying to generalize from ASD autobiographical accounts to the experience of autism in general. First, many of those with ASDs lack the skills or resources, whether cognitive, social, or financial, to present their accounts in a publishable form. Second, in light of the fact that the ratio of males to females diagnosed with autism is 10:1 (Baron-Cohen 2004), there appears to be a disproportionate number of ASD accounts written by women. Indeed, in the present study, only 40 per cent of texts identified and analysed prior to the point at which data saturation was judged to have occurred were male-authored.

Without underestimating the methodological limitations of this approach, however, we argue that autobiographical writings constitute uniquely suitable 'data' for qualitative research on autism (Davidson 2007, 2008; Smith 1996), a view that is explicitly supported by many of the ASD authors whose work informs this chapter. Not only do such texts present insider accounts, but the very communicative and social challenges that typify autism also mean that those with ASDs often prefer to interact with others via the written rather than the spoken word (see Davidson 2008a; Miller 2003; Prince-Hughes 2002). As Dawn Prince-Hughes (2002) explains in arguing for the importance of insider accounts of autism, 'there is simply no way for nonautistic people to gather this kind of information through questionnaires or interviews, or through reading what nonautistic people have said about us' (xiv).

The present study draws on 45 ASD autobiographies and edited collections of autobiographical accounts identified through academic search engines, by snowballing from academic research papers and first-hand accounts, and via non-academic literature searches (e.g., Amazon.com and the *New York* and *London Review of Books*). These autobiographical writings were subjected to a sequential process of detailed annotation, coding for emergent themes and critical discourse analysis (Fairclough 1995). However, the emphasis in this chapter is very much on the interpretative potential of phenomenological and hermeneutic approaches. The challenge in interpreting these texts is to allow the descriptive immediacy underlying ASD authors' experiential accounts to emerge in ways that challenge the reader to attend to the far-from-usual meanings they acquire. The focus is on what life looks like, feels like, and *means* for these authors. This requires that we trust insiders' accounts – despite sometimes surprising departures from typical experience, expectations, or what is widely considered common sense – about how, for example, we cannot have emotional or social relations with piles of sand or patches of grass, or that we cannot really be 'friends' with worms or rocks (Gaita 2002).

Phenomenological and Hermeneutic Dimensions of More-than-Human Emotional Geographies

While *phenomenology* is not the only qualitative approach where evidence is 'derived from first-person reports of life experiences' (Moustakas 1994:84), it does offer an approach that is unusually sensitive to accounts of experiential differences, since its starting point, as the term suggests, is the phenomenon (the immediate experience) itself as it is presented to thought. In other words, and especially as it developed out of the original work of Edmund Husserl (Welton 1999), phenomenology has been concerned with 'bracketing' the naturalistic presuppositions we usually hold about *how* our experiences accord with the world's underlying reality and our subsequently greater concern for uncovering the cause of these experiences rather than thinking about the experiences themselves. The naturalistic or 'common sense' attitude is, as Moran (2000) notes, 'deeply embedded in our everyday behaviour towards objects and also at work in our most sophisticated natural science' (147). By contrast, bracketing, referred to by Husserl as the *epoché*, requires that we are required to take others' experiences at face value rather than trying to squeeze them into our own preconceived ideas of how the world actually is, of what is possible or meaningful to experience.

Those seeking to apply Husserl's approach tend to emphasize how this process of bracketing seeks to attain a kind of a-situational purity insofar as it attempts to approach phenomena in a way that is entirely free of suppositions. Thus Moustakas (1994) claims '[i]n the *Epoche*, we set aside our prejudgements, biases and preconceived ideas' (85). This 'setting aside' is an aim to be worked towards as a 'preparation for new knowledge' (85).

Aspects of bracketing, however, seem at variance with hermeneutic approaches such as Gadamer's (1998), which claims that all interpretation must inevitably start from 'historically effected consciousness' (*Wirkungsgeshichtliches Bewusstsein*) – that is, from within our already 'socially' pre-given horizon of understanding. Moustakas's decontextualized, almost unworldly notion of phenomenological abstraction is partly a result of not recognising the problems inherent in simply trying to extrapolate Husserl's *introspective* methodology to cover the experiences of *other* people. Our encounters with others' experiences, and perhaps especially others' textual or otherwise reported accounts of experiences, necessarily have a hermeneutic aspect.

That said, the important methodological point is precisely the manner in which both phenomenology and hermeneutics foster openness towards different experiences as an ongoing task. In the case of phenomenology, this is a recognition of the importance of (others' potentially different) experiences as such, while, as Gadamer (1998) argues, the act of interpretation is itself dependent upon maintaining an openness towards what the other expresses to us (about those experiences). In this sense, they supplement each other in the ways they foster openness to other experiences as a methodological virtue.

Indeed, the tension between a pure (Husserlian) phenomenology and a socio-historically emplaced hermeneutics might be understood as mirroring the tension between the actual (more or less pre-interpretative) experiences of the autistic insider and the need to communicate these experiences to themselves and others within a given social horizon. And to this degree, the hermeneutic phenomenology of Gadamer might prove especially informative precisely because it draws 'outside' researchers' attention to the limits of their own interpretative presuppositions.

Hermeneutically, the researcher necessarily works within the recognized and unrecognized 'prejudices' that are associated with, amongst other things, particular academic traditions. That is to say, within the 'effective historical consciousness' of his/her own situation. In our case, these effects might include the discourses, practices, vocabularies, ideologies, and so on, which have influenced and contributed to the development of human geography. So when Gadamer emphasizes the interpretative importance of these *prejudices*, he does not intend this term to be understood pejoratively because such effects are, to some degree, both inevitable and invaluable. His point, too, is that we have to start all our interpretations from some*where*, from a given interpretative situation. This also means that if we are not open to different possibilities, this 'horizon' of understanding can limit what we regard as important and constrain our ability to reach an understanding with others who do not share our presuppositions. This helps explain why many approaches to those with ASDs, including clinical interpretations, have tended to focus on their deficiencies in emotional and communicative relations to other humans. Modern Western forms of knowledge, influenced by traditions of academic humanism and dominant human-centred ideologies, regard relations to other humans as key to, and definitional of, human sociality.

Phenomenologically, the claims of ASD authors remain problematic so long as we stay within these socially and academically dominant horizons. Claims to experience emotional relationships with non-humans seem to run up against the problem of transposing a person's position into that of, for example, the animals those with ASDs claim to understand so well. For example, although Heidegger's (1995) phenomenology allows that the human 'already finds himself [*sic*] transposed into the animal in a certain manner' (211), he also claims that the animal is that which it is most difficult to think that there is, in effect, an unbridgeable gulf between us. We cannot, he suggests, think what it is like to be an animal precisely because its world, its phenomenal experiences, are so very different to those of human beings and in particular because so much of our understanding revolves around the importance of a linguistic capacity that the animal lacks.

The phenomenological/hermeneutic question raised in trying to understand ASD authors' claims is whether non-ASD people can begin to know what it is like to be a person who claims to *feel more like* an animal, or even a place, than they feel like other people. What would that even mean, and what are the implications of asking such questions?

Autistic and Ab/normal Emotion

As suggested above, first hand autistic accounts challenge the idea that those with ASDs have an impoverished emotional capacity (Davidson 2007; Jones, Zahl, and Huws 2001), emphasizing instead differences in experiencing and difficulties in communicating or understanding emotions. Many ASD authors describe feeling terrible pressure in the presence of others to perform in particular ways, to act – in order to pass as – 'normal': 'A person with autism has been described as being a distant and cold-hearted type of person [. . .] I feel a lot inside only I cannot express my feelings as openly as a normal person can' (Cowhey 2005:71). Passing entails determining and learning rules of behaviour that seem to come 'naturally' to non-autistic others, such as when and where it is appropriate to smile, exactly how to do so, and even for how long. Thus, 'every autistic person is a sociologist. We have to be' (Dave, in Osborne 2002:68). Those with ASDs seem to face a hermeneutic challenge if and when they attempt to understand, or be understood by, non-ASD humans. What they 'lack' is not, on their own accounts, an emotional capacity as such (although it may appear to others to be so), but certain capabilities concerning interpretative intuitions that are more usually assumed as 'second nature,' and hence assumed to constitute a shared ground for the interpretative community. This makes any 'fusion of horizons' of understanding, in Gadamer's terms, much more difficult since those with ASDs have, instead, to make these implicitly assumed commonalities explicit through 'socio-logical' experimentation.

This interpretative difficulty is further complicated by phenomenological differences – that is to say, their emotional *experience* as well as expression (a distinction broadly accepted although conceptualized differently by various theorists of emotion [see Solomon 2003]) tends to be far from typical, too. ASD authors describe feelings around others that are unusually and often intolerably vivid and complex (Tidmarsh and Volkmar 2003:518). Relating her own experience of sensory distortion, Prince-Hughes (2004) writes: 'I lived in a kaleidoscope [. . . looking] at broken colored fragments of people,' whose faces appeared as 'blurry objects exploding with invasive stimuli' (67, 169). Her account is fairly typical, and such sensory confusion can involve blurring of other kinds of boundaries. As Kamran Nazeer (2006) explains in his autobiographical account: 'There is a high incidence of synesthesia too, that is, minds that correlate certain sounds, tastes or textures with colors' (69). Given that such melting of 'common sense' distinctions can render people an overwhelming mess of noisy eyes, arms, and legs, it is unsurprising that emotions commonly associated with their presence are strongly negative, tending to involve fear and anxiety that leads to avoidance in a manner reminiscent of agoraphobic social avoidance (Davidson 2003).

Phenomenal and hermeneutic challenges compound each other since language, with all its layers of expressive, communicative, and bodily complexity, is experienced as being extraordinarily difficult and demanding for ASD individuals: 'you need to comprehend tone and gestures as well as context and the words used in order to get the meaning' (Nazeer 2006:11). In a light-hearted illustration of his point, Nazeer claims that '[s]triking up conversation with strangers is an autistic person's version of extreme sports' (31).

Attending to ASD authors' accounts allows us to see that antisocial tendencies need not necessarily mean that the autistic person is unfeeling. In fact, the opposite may be the case, as the very intensity of autistic feeling can mean other people are simply (felt) *too much*: One contributor to Miller's (2003) collection, 'MM,' illustrates common misunderstandings when she claims, 'people think that because I need more quiet that I am a selfish bitch [. . . but] I need the quiet not because I have a cold heart but because I can hear every plea from every being in whatever space I stand or sit or lie down in' (MM, in Miller 2003:30). Like many ASD authors, she is *too* sensitive to, and over stimulated by, others' actions and affects. Being with human others can be exhausting, as MM continues to explain, while at the same time highlighting that her preferred alternative is not solitude: 'I can only afford a certain amount of time among humans, and if I don't get to moving my senses will overload, and the rest of the day Iwill have to put myself in the quiet of my room, and miss out on the trees and rocks and streams that talk to me so much more gently than any human (30).

Williams (1994) feels similarly about social avoidance of a kind that seeks out different kinds of connection, rather than aloneness per se. She writes that: 'The rewards for friendship seemed a sick joke: closeness, attachment, belonging. Closeness made earthquakes go off inside of me and compelled me to run. Attachment reminded me painfully of my own vulnerability and inadequacy and was a threat to security. Belonging was with things and nature, not with people' (113). Thus, we begin to see that while ASD authors cherish protected time and territory, the space they require to sense safety isn't necessarily the 'empty' space (or 'fortress') of aloneness.[1] It may be unpopulated by people, but the environment they desire can still be alive with nonhuman otherness, in whose company a rich and rewarding range of positive emotions can be experienced. In other words, they develop unusual or atypical emotional geographies. Most ASD authors are aware of this atypicality. Grandin (1996) writes, 'I am told by my nonautistic friends that relationships with other people are what most people live for, whereas I get very attached to my projects and to certain places' (140), and again 'my strong emotional bonds are tied up with places more than people' (92). Even, and perhaps especially in the face of extreme perceptual distortion, natural objects and places can be profoundly, delightfully interesting, so long as there are no demands from others or pressures to 'make sense.' ASD authors recount experiences of taking pleasurable sanctuary in hypnotically beautiful aspects of the nonhuman world. The senses of sand falling between her fingers – its shifting appearance and texture – could occupy Grandin (1996) for many happy hours: 'Each grain was different [. . .] as I scrutinized their shapes and contours, I went into a trance which cut me off from the sights and sounds around me' (44).

While this 'interaction' seems clearly one-sided, others' relations appear more 'social' in nature, at least in the sense that they involve unusual openness to other beings and posit some kind of reciprocal connection. Prince-Hughes (2004), for example, states, 'I could feel the personalities of the rocks, the trees, the grass, the hills' (50), and in her own striking terms, Williams (2003) writes: 'I was a social kid: social with the dirt, the trees, the grass [. . .] I felt the world deeply and passionately. I was cheerful in my own world and I had a fascination with anything that was not directly confrontational and which would allow me to simply be (16).

It seems that many and varied non-human others often match these criteria, allowing ASD authors to simply be and feel themselves, comfortably and even pleasurably, however divergent from the norm their feelings are taken to be by clinicians.

Autistic Friendships and Feeling Different

Wendy Lawson's (2005) autobiography describes the supposedly atypical emotional relations with nonhuman others she began to form in
childhood: 'Although I was unable to relate to other children (or even
most other people, whatever their age), with animals it was different'
(28). She writes in detail about one particular companion animal, a gin-
ger mongrel from whom she became inseparable: 'During my teenage
years, my dog Rusty was my most loyal companion and we explored
life together as only trusted friends know how [. . .] she never changed.
We understood one another, even without words. She demanded nothing from me except my acceptance and availability' (52).

The understanding Lawson (2005) experienced, to the exclusion and
bafflement of even 'close' family members, was felt to be *shared* with
her friend: 'To bark like a dog seemed perfectly normal to me' (44). This
communicative connection with companion animals is not unusual in
accounts of autism, as Jean Kearns Miller (2003) illustrates: 'I was raised
by our Siamese cat. I could understand her language better than the
human language, and so I spoke Siamese way before I spoke English,
and I thought the cat was my real mother because I could understand
her more than I could understand humans' (54).

This latter quotation is drawn from an anthology of writings by
women with autism that began on an Internet listserv. In one thread reproduced in the book, participants discuss the question of whether they
'have ongoing relationships with animals and/or with inanimate aspects of the world that are just as strong/important as (or more so than)
your relationships with humans?' (Miller 2003:54). Several do, and one
respondent, Wendy, writes, 'I talk to cats like they are people, because
I have this feeling that they can understand me. And if I treat them as
friends, they become friends' (in Miller 2003:45). Another, Diane, states:
'I fixated on cats. But isn't it sad that, so often, our parents and others have tried to take away these very fixations that have made our
hearts open? When growing up (and even still now) I was frequently
criticized by my family about liking cats so much' (in Miller 2003:45).
Parents, understandably, typically prefer that their child act and have
friends like other children, and ASD authors often write about the extent to which family have tried to force them into moulds of normality that simply don't fit. Often, however, they are also sensitive to the
fact that there may be good and caring reasons for doing so. Gunilla
Gerland's (2003) book contains the following revelation: 'Earthworms

were one of my great delights [. . .] I fondled them and kissed them. I dug them up in my garden and cautiously patted them. My mother did not approve of my love of worms and wanted me to be less intimate with them' (36). Gerland's (2003) mother tried to persuade her not to kiss the worms, but she didn't respond: 'Then my mother made a good decision – the family should buy a cat. It worked. I loved our cat [. . .] Love in the cat way, a love with one's integrity maintained, suited me very well' (36). Her mother is understandably pleased when Gerland's infant affections take a more conventional turn – 'it was more acceptable to fondle a cat' (37) – and indeed it is common for childhood relations to be formed with furry feline friends. For ASD authors, however, relationships are often established with less typical animals, not traditionally viewed as suitable 'companion' material.

Temple Grandin describes her particularly empathetic relations with cows in several publications that combine autobiographical and scholarly approaches to both (e.g., Grandin 1996, 2005).[5] She claims that these 'animals saved me' (2005:4), and takes pains to explain that she feels closer to cows than to people. At times she suggests that she feels more *like* these animals – not simply that she likes or feels more *for* them – than people. She refers to a strong connection:

> between autistic people and animals: autistic people have mostly simple emotions, too. That's why normal people describe us as innocent. An autistic person's feelings are direct and open, just like animal feelings. We don't hide our feelings, and we aren't ambivalent. (Grandin 2005:89)

> Autistic people can think the way animals think. Of course, we also think the way people think – we aren't *that* different from normal humans. Autism is a kind of way station on the road from animals to humans, which puts autistic people like me in a perfect position to translate 'animal talk' into English. (6–7)

Grandin (2005) acknowledges that '[s]ome people will probably think this is an insulting thing to say about autistic people' (89), and she certainly does go further than the majority of ASD authors in stressing her sense of feeling different from humans in such potentially divisive, animalistic terms. Again, 'my feelings are simpler and more overt, and like cattle' (Grandin and Scariano 1996:92). But, bracketing 'common sense,' humanist presuppositions about the potentially insulting nature of such comparisons in terms of the way that Grandin's remarks might be taken to render those with ASD 'less than fully human,' her account, like those of other ASD authors, actually offers an interpretative opening on autistic emotional geographies that would otherwise be unavailable.

Grandin explicitly situates autism as a 'way station' between abilities to understand animals and (non-ASD) humans, and explains this position as one of 'translation.' Miller, too, claims to speak cat before English, to have an ability to understand animals that non-ASD people tend to lack themselves and thus fail to understand in others. Lawson writes of understanding her dog despite (or because of) a lack of words between them. The feelings of closeness these authors express between themselves and other animals – the 'love,' 'intimacy,' and 'delight' felt in touching the worm; the relations of 'trust' and 'friendship' with the dog; the maternal relation posited with the cat – are all directly correlated with degrees of hermeneutic intimacy; that is, in terms of the ASD authors' self-described experience of *understanding* animals, of an ability to translate between the animal's world and their own. This claimed fusion of horizons of understanding reflects the emotional geography of their lives, their daily practices and behaviour; it provides and delimits a comfort zone.

This (hermeneutic) situation, this ability to translate, is presented as both an explanation *of* (i.e., a phenomenal account) and an explanation *for* (i.e., the cause underlying) the different feelings and relations experienced by those with ASDs. In other words, their hermeneutic situation is inseparable from the phenomenological experience of an empathic association that supposedly goes beyond the hermeneutic limits of human language. In most cases (although again Grandin tends to be more explicit than usual about this) the translation taking place with those who lack (human) words is described in terms of a shared *feeling*, an understanding of how the animals, whether cow, cat, worm, or dog, themselves are supposed to feel. Dominant humanist approaches would undoubtedly find such a claim implausible, regarding it as just an example of misunderstanding the interpretative indeterminacy of nature, of self-projection and/or wishful thinking. However, the phenomenological point is not whether such understandings are actually possible – whether Grandin, for example, does understand cows better than any non-ASD person – but that such experiences, and such a self-understanding, define the contours of her world. Once we bracket out the question of how such experiences relate to 'reality,' we can concentrate on their 'reality effects' in terms of how they *affect* the emotional geographies of those with ASDs because it is precisely these feelings that allow them the space to compose and understand their worldly relations to other animals, places, and, when possible, people. How they live their daily lives – and in Grandin's specific case of how animals end theirs – since she is responsible for the design of half of all North American slaughterhouses (Grandin 2005:7) – is not something scholars should ignore. Interestingly, and despite the fact that this might seem a strange mode of employment for someone claiming to empathically understand how cattle 'feel,' Grandin's employment in this capacity is certainly based on her having convinced at least some non-ASD people that her hermeneutic, as well as her phenomenological claims, are valid.

Animal Magic and Animistic Affect

The nature of ASD encounters with animals/places also reflects ASD understandings of self-identity and often constitutes a key aspect of developing the kinds of social self-reflexivity that non-ASD people take for granted. In a very important way, self-constitutive relations with animals often come first, and the phenomenology of feelings experienced concerning non-humans is only later taken up by autistic individuals as an educative illustration of the possibilities of human-to-human relations. The phenomenology of non-human relations described by ASD authors belies any accusation of unjustifiable anthropomorphism. Understandings of social relations (in the usual, narrowly human sense) are interpreted through the lens of prior non-human encounters. For example, ASD author Prince-Hughes (2004), who, like Grandin, is also an academic, has written at length about her close relations and subsequent ethological studies with gorillas. Even as a child, her non-human companions were not entirely typical, and she describes time spent not with a pet pony, but rather, with a 'herd of old Morgan horses that had been let go to roam wild in the hundred acres across the road from the trailer. My relationship with them andthe emotional sustenance it gave me was a foreshadowing of the closeness I later had with the gorillas. I watched them, learned their habits, and knew where to find them at all times of the day' (49).

The emotional sustenance and intense pleasure Prince-Hughes and others describe is often derived from a sense that 'natural others' leave ASD authors *space to be themselves.* Animals make minimal demands and rarely pass judgment: after all, '[n]o animal can be a snob' (Kojève, in Agamben 2004:11). The animal gaze can be felt to affirm rather than weaken a sense of self and self-worth. Their gentle recognition and (almost unconditional) acceptance seems to extend to natural environments and 'objects,' experienced by some ASD authors as 'genuine others' in relation to themselves. Williams (2003), for example, states: 'I felt in company with trees. I couldn't distinguish between the sense of company in being friends with a tree versus a person except the company with a tree was easier. I didn't just climb a tree, I was in company with it like two friends sharing beingness together [. . .] My experience with trees is social' (40).

This is actually very close to the kind of experience that many environmentalists trying to defend old-growth forests from clear-cut logging or road developments identify (Merrick 1996). Williams (2003) goes on to elaborate this sense of *being* at ease in a style that is, in places, strikingly reminiscent of Heidegger's phenomenological writings: 'I used to cry and stroke our old palm tree in my front yard, telling it in silence all my feelings of despair and rage, but also sitting at its elephant-like trunk-feet and jointly appreciating the day and good feelings too. The tree, unlike people, lived a self-in-relation-to-self world. Unlike the self-in-relation-to-other world of people, the tree was by nature indirectly confrontational and good "simply being"' (40).

This similarity in style of expression with certain phenomenological writings may be accidental, but the attention to phenomenal detail and the sense of connective rather than separative 'sociality' does speak to an experiential *openness* to the world, a kind of be-holding, that is often lost in the hustle and bustle of social life, in what Heidegger (1988) refers to as a 'lostness in the everydayness of the they-self' (307), an involved attitude of reciprocation that allows us to feel part of the world rather than standing apart from it. In taking up such a stance, we cease to be spectators, and become open to affective (emotional) contagion. Moreover, and in terms that resonate with ASD narratives, 'nothing is more contagious than genuine tranquility' (Jacoby, in Behnke 1999:109). Many ASD accounts illustrate something of this sense of openness to contagion, to otherness: 'All around me I could feel the personalities of the rocks, the trees, the grass, the hills' (Prince-Hughes 2004:50); 'I seem to be able to feel the trees, the rocks, the water and voices from the past of a land' (MM, in Miller 2003:49).

This animistic presence and sense of agency, and even personality in nature, is not only strongly felt, but also highly valued and somehow humbling. In a continuation of the thread from which MM's statement is drawn, Ava writes: 'Many of us here clearly feel a connection with rocks, plants and animals. For me, this is not just an intellectual thing, it is something passionate and living that I experience deeply in mind, emotions and body all at once (e.g., my response to a familiar tree). Bound with that is a sense of love, respect and responsibility for life, that is most simply and purely experienced in the world of nature, but which also extends to the complexities of human life and the wonders of the wider universe' (Ava, in Miller 2003:49).

Again, this seems very reminiscent of the accounts of deep ecologists and radical environmentalists (Smith 2001). For Ava, the non-human world is truly awesome and she describes her sense of connection with it as the basis of her religious experience. These relational bonds with the natural world do however 'extend to' humanity, and this sense of learning about culture from nature is present in others' accounts as well. Miller (2003) comments on this in the following way: 'A perhaps startling suggestion is that we may even have learnt empathy and other moral attributes, through our early relationships with the nonhuman world, despite a common NT [neurotypical] assumption that fascination with the nonhuman risks making us more robotic' (54).

ASD authors learn to relate to and appreciate humanity in and through relations with nature that *feel* genuinely reciprocal. If, as accounts suggest, this feeling of the 'personality' of the non-human world comes first, if we take these accounts at face value, then they cannot be indicative of what humanism might regard as a wrong-headed extension of understandings of human personality beyond their acceptable (human or near-human) limits. It is quite the contrary. And this coming to self-awareness through felt reciprocation with, and being sheltered by, natural beings extends to coming to social awareness of other humans and their expectations. Prince-Hughes (2004) writes at length about being taught sociality by animals who create an atmosphere of sufficient calm for her to learn, a 'place' apart from the negative emotions long associated with human contact: 'I am blessed to have found a place to escape that chronic anxiety. The gorillas had an enormously calming effect on me . . . their social subtleties and calm demeanor allowed me to relax and really watch what they were doing. I saw social *cause* and *effect* for the first time. When I realized their behaviour was so much like human behaviour I knew I would learn everything I needed to know from them. I began to cautiously apply the things I'd learned from the gorillas . . . and I began to have some success. I actually made some friends' (117).

The notion that nonhuman others have the capacity to teach us about emotion is not exclusive to the writings of those with autism. However, theorists of emotion who press beyond the anthropocentrically drawn bounds of typical life-worlds are few and far between. Phenomenologist Alphonso Lingis (1999) is among those who do, and his questions illuminate much that is often considered beneath us, in more ways than one: 'Is it not animal emotions that make our feelings intelligible? [. . .] Is not the force of our emotions that of the other animals?' (44). Illustrating our early affective interconnections, Lingis writes of human infants: '[their] first heavy toddling shifts into tripping vivacity with the robins hopping across the lawn. They come to feel buoyancy in the midst of the park pigeons shifting so effortlessly from ground to layers of sun-drenched air. They come to feel sullenness from the arthritic old dog the retired cop was walking in the park and that they try to pet. They contract righteousness and indignation from the mother hen suddenly ruffled up, her beak stabbing when they try to remove a chick. They pick up feelings of smoldering wrath from the snarling chained dog in the neighbor's yard, and try out those feelings by snarling when they are put under restraints or confined' (44–5).

The dominant modern Western worldview fails to see the emotional power and potential of our relations with non-human others. Drawing lessons from ASD and other boundary-breaking perspectives, we might begin to question the extent to which *typical* lives are, therefore, restricted, emotionally impoverished, and 'alienated' in oddly unrecognized ways, just as we might reconsider the view that people with autism live as if 'in a world of their own.' ASD authors themselves explicitly challenge this view, drawing on their personal experience with the non-human world to argue that, in fact, it is non-autistic life-worlds that are narrowly drawn, self- (or at least human-) centred, and thus closed to interactions with others. Turning once more to Grandin (2005) for illustration: 'I always find it kind of funny that normal people are always saying autistic children "live in their own little world." When you work with animals for a while you start to realize you can say the same thing about normal people. There's a great big, beautiful world out there that a lot of normal folks are just barely taking in. It's like dogs hearing a whole register of sound we can't. Autistic people and animals are *seeing* a whole register of the visual world normal people can't, or don't' (24).

Perhaps, then, paying attention to the writings of ASD authors also offers non-ASD people ways of re-thinking their own worldly relations and emotional geographies, re-cognizing the potential to be open to sensations of awe and exhilaration in the face of a sensorially marvellous non-human world. Rather than regarding encounters with nature as a distraction from everyday human activities, we might also 'catch' something, however little, of its emotionally contagious possibilities. This is especially so of a culture inoculated by its humanist presuppositions, its lack of phenomenal or hermeneutic openness to non-human otherness: 'Most of humanity is ignorant for not hearing and seeing what is around them. I hear the rocks and the trees' (MM, in Miller 2003:54). Perhaps on this level at least it is also possible to understand why ASDs could, at least in some instances, be thought of by those who experience them in terms of different ability rather than disability – even in terms that lead some ASD authors to refer to the 'everyday heaven' (Williams 2004), or the 'wonderful world of autism' (Cowhey 2005:125): 'People thought that my standing in the heat for one and a half hours to watch an insect was a crazy thing to do. I think it is they who are crazy. By choosing not to stand and watch, they missed out on sharing an experience that was so beautiful and exhilarating' (Lawson 2005:115). This is precisely how many, more neurotypical individuals – for example, those that enjoy hill-walking – describe their experiences with a 'natural' world that, if never entirely unaffected by society, is relatively free from and resistant to the presence of constant social intrusions.

Conclusion

Approaching the autobiographical writings of those with ASDs in terms of phenomenological and hermeneutic openness suggests a possibility of understanding the wider implications of the remarkable insights into different kinds of emotional experience these texts offer. Such authors challenge the view prevalent in clinical and lay writings that autism involves impoverished or even absent emotionality. Further, it draws attention to the extent to which non-human others feature in the surprisingly 'social' emotional geographies of at least some ASD authors. Approximately half of these personal narratives reveal that while perceptual differences often render other people offensive to the highly acute senses of those with ASDs, non-human beings can, to some extent, be experienced as profoundly pleasurable companions who shelter the development of ASD personalities and even open edu-cative insights into human culture that later come to facilitate social (human) contact (even if such contact remains difficult and never be-comes 'second nature'). Since this chapter focuses on those texts that emphasize this most heavily, and given the necessarily selective nature of the texts studied, it is clearly impossible to use this material to gen-eralize about the nature of ASD experiences as a whole. Nonetheless, it does provide important insights into many ASD lives, and the depth and breadth of feelings associated with these non-human environments is truly extraordinary. Recognising this also offers those without ASDs a possibility of bringing to mind what is often lacking in 'our' own taken-for-granted everyday encounters, a chance to recognize the lim-its of the effective (and affective) history of modern Western societies.

NOTES

1 This chapter is adapted from a longer version originally published in *Environment and Planning D: Society and Space* (2009), and the authors are grateful to the publishers for permission to reproduce the text in its current form. Thanks to all authors whose work inspired and informed this chapter and to the Social Sciences and Humanities Research Council of Canada for providing financial support. Thanks also to Sara Ahmed, Stuart Elden, Victoria Henderson, Dale Spencer, and Kevin Walby for helpful comments.
2 'Person-first' language is avoided in this chapter to reflect the preference of the majority of authors whose work contributes to this study. As Elesia Ashkenazy (2009) explains, 'Though it is common for both the medical and cure-focused communities to refer to an autistic person as a person *with* autism, such references are not the lingo of the greater whole of the autistic community. In a nutshell, saying a person *has* autism may imply that the person is defective or that there is an inherent problem or sickness within the person. It also implies that autism can somehow be separated from the person' (original emphasis; see also Jim Sinclair's (2009) influential 'Why I dislike "person first" language').
3 Difficulties in interpreting the more-than-human world also, somewhat ironically, expose the limits of Gadamer's own focus on *human language* which tends to overlook affective (emotional) embodied aspects of our interpretative relations to social *and natural* circumstances. This is why Smith (2005) suggests that Gadamer's notion of an 'effective human historicity' needs to be supplemented with an 'affective natural historicity' when we want to understand human relations to, and especially their feelings about, the wider non-human world.

4 *The Empty Fortress* was the title given to Bettelheim's (1967) controversial account of what he described as the protective autistic shell.
5 While Canadian composer Glenn Gould's candidacy for an ASD diagnosis is a matter of some dispute, his behaviour has certainly led commentators to reflect on this possibility. Interestingly, one biographer recounts his penchant for spending time with and singing to cows (Ostwald 1997:93).

References

Aboraya, A., E. Rankin, C. France, A. El-Missiry, and C. John. 2006. 'The reliability of psychiatric diagnosis revisited: The clinician's guide to improve the reliability of psychiatric diagnosis.' *Psychiatry (Edgemont)* 3:41–50.

Adkins, L. 2005. 'The new economy, property and personhood.' *Theory, Culture and Society* 22(1):111–30.

Agamben, G. 2004. *The open: Man and animal.* Palo Alto, CA: Stanford University Press.

Ahmed, S. 2000. *Strange encounters: Embodied others in post-coloniality.* London: Routledge.

– 2004. *The cultural politics of emotion.* New York: Routledge.

– 2004a. 'Affective economies.' *Social Text* 22(2):117–39.

– 2004b. 'Collective feelings: Or, the impression left by others.' *Theory, Culture and Society* 21(2):25–42.

– 2006. *Queer phenomenology: Orientations, objects, others.* Durham, NC: Duke University Press.

– 2008. 'Introduction: The happiness turn.' *New Formations* 63:7–14.

Aldrich, R. 2004. 'Homosexuality and the city: An historical overview.' *Urban Studies* 41(9):1719–37.

Alvesson, M., and Y. Billing. 1992. 'Gender and organization: Towards a differentiated understanding.' *Organization Studies* 13(12):73–102.

Amerine, R., and J. Bilmes. 1990. 'Following instructions.' In *Representation in scientific practice.* Ed. M. Lynch and S. Woolgar. Cambridge, MA: MIT Press.

American Psychiatric Association. 1952. *Diagnostic and statistical manual: Mental disorders.* Washington, DC: American Psychiatric Association, Mental Hospital Service.

– 1968. *Diagnostic and statistical manual of mental disorders.* 2d ed. Washington, DC: American Psychiatric Association.

– 1980. *Diagnostic and statistical manual of mental disorders.* 3d ed. (DSM-III). Washington, DC: American Psychiatric Association

– 1987. *Diagnostic and statistical manual of mental disorders.* 3d ed. Rev. (DSM-III-R). Washington, DC: American Psychiatric Association

– 1994. *Diagnostic and statistical manual of mental disorders.* 4th ed. (DSM-IV). Washington, DC: American Psychiatric Association.

– 2000. *Diagnostic and statistical manual of mental disorders.* 4th ed. Text rev. (DSM-IV-TR). Washington, DC: American Psychiatric Association.

Aminzade, J., and D. McAdam. 2001. 'Emotions and contentious politics.' In *Silence and voice in the study of contentious politics.* Ed. R. Aminzade, J. A. Goldstone, D. McAdam, E.J. Perry, W.H. Sewell, and C. Tilly. Cambridge: Cambridge University Press.

Ansell-Pearson, K., and J. Mullarkey, eds. 2002. *Bergson: Key writings.* London: Continuum.

Appleby, G.A. 2001a. 'Ethnographic study of gay and bisexual working-class men in the United States.' *Journal of Gay and Lesbian Social Services* 12(3–4):51–62.

– 2001b. 'Ethnographic study of twenty-six gay and bisexual working-class men in Australia and New Zealand.' *Journal of Gay and Lesbian Social Services* 12(3–4):119–32.

Archer, M. 2000. *Being human: The problem of agency.* Cambridge: Cambridge University Press.

Ariès, P. 1975. *Western attitudes towards death: From the middle ages to the present.* Baltimore: Johns Hopkins University Press.

Aristotle. 1998. *Nicomachean ethics.* Ed. W. Kaufman. New York: Dover.

Arvidsson, A. 2006. *Brands: Meaning and value in media culture.* London: Routledge.

Ashford, B., and R. Humphrey. 1995. 'Emotion in the workplace: A reappraisal.' *Human Relations* 48(2):97–125.

Ashkenazy, E. 2009. 'Understand autism-first language.' *Change.org.* 15 January 2009. Retrieved from http://autism.change.org/actions/view/understand_autism-first_language.

Attwood, T., and T. Grandin 2006. *Aspergers and girls.* Arlington, TX: Future Horizons.

Austrin, T., and J. Farnsworth. 2005. 'Hybrid genres: Fieldwork, detection and the method of Bruno Latour.' *Qualitative Research* 5(2):147–65.

Avrahami, E. 2007. *The invading body: Reading illness autobiographies.* Charlottesville: University of Virginia Press.

Badhwar, N.K. 1993. 'Altruism versus self-interest: Sometimes a false dichotomy.' *Social Philosophy and Policy* 10(1):90–117.

Bagatell, N. 2007. 'Orchestrating voices: Autism, identity, and the power of voices.' *Disability and Society* 22:413–26.

Baird, G., E. Simonoff, A. Pickles, S. Chandler, T. Loucas, D. Meldrum, and T. Charman. 2006. 'Prevalence of disorders of the autism spectrum in a population cohort of children in South Thames: The special needs and autism project (SNAP).' *The Lancet* 368(9531):210–15.

Baker, D.L. 2006. 'Neurodiversity, neurological disability and the public sector: Notes on the autism spectrum.' *Disability and Society* 21(1):15–29.

Barbalet, J. 1998. *Emotion, social theory and social structure: A macrosociological approach*. Cambridge: Cambridge University Press.

– 2002. 'Introduction: Why emotions are crucial.' In *Emotions and Sociology*. Ed. J.M. Barbalet. Oxford: Blackwell.

– 2002a. 'Science and Emotions.' In *Emotions and Sociology*. Ed. J.M. Barbalet. Oxford: Blackwell.

– 2002b 'Moral indignation, class inequality and justice: An exploration and revision of Ranulf.' *Theoretical Criminology* 6(3):279–97.

Barker, M. 2005. 'This is my partner, and this is my . . . partner's partner: Constructing a polyamorous identity in a monogamous world.' *Journal of Constructivist Psychology* 18(1):75–88.

Barnett, M. 2005. 'Humanitarianism transformed.' *Perspectives on Politics* 3(4):723–40.

Baron-Cohen, S. 2003. *The essential difference: Male and female brains and the truth about autism*. New York: Basic Books.

Barrow, R. 1980. *Happiness*. Oxford: Martin Robertson.

Barthes, R. 1980. 'Deliberation.' Trans. Richard Howard. *Partisan Review* 4:532–43.

Baumgart, H. 1990. *Jealousy: Experiences and solutions*. Chicago: University of Chicago Press.

Beard, G.M. 1869. 'Neurasthenia, or nervous exhaustion.' *Boston Medical and Surgical Journal* 3:217–22.

– [1881] 1972. *American nervousness, its causes and consequences: A supplement to nervous exhaustion (neurasthenia)*. New York: Arno Press.

Beck, A.T., M. Ward, M. Mendelsohn, J. Mock, and J. Erbaugh. 1961. 'An inventory for measuring depression.' *Archives of General Psychiatry* 4:561–71.

Beck, U. 2002. 'The cosmopolitan society and its enemies.' *Theory, Culture and Society* 19(1–2):17–44.

Becker, H. 1968. *Through values to social interpretation: Essays on social contexts, actions, types, and prospects.* New York: Greenwood Press.

– 1963. *Outsiders: Studies in the sociology of deviance.* New York: Free Press.

Behnke, E.A. 1999. 'From Merleau-Ponty's concept of nature to an interspecies practice of peace.' In *Animal others: On ethics, ontology and animal life.* Ed. H.P Steeves. New York: SUNY Press.

Belenky, M., B. Mcvicker-Clinchy, N. Rule-Goldberger, and J. Mattuck-Tarule. 1986. *Women's ways of knowing: The development of self, voice, and mind.* New York: Basic Books.

Bendelow, G., and S. Williams. 1995a. 'Pain and the mind-body dualism: A sociological approach.' *Body and Society* 1(2):83–103.

– 1995b. 'Transcending the dualisms: Towards a sociology of pain.' *Sociology of Health and Illness* 17(2):139–65.

Bennett, K. 2009. 'Challenging emotions.' *Area* 11:2–10.

Berger, P. 1963. *An invitation to sociology: A humanistic perspective.* New York: Anchor Books.

Bergson, H. [1889] 2001. *Time and free will: An essay on the data of immediate consciousness.* Mineola, NY: Dover.

– [1902] 1998. *Creative evolution.* Mineola, NY: Dover.

– [1932] 1977. *The two sources of morality and religion.* Notre Dame: Notre Dame University Press.

– [1938] 1974. *The creative mind: An introduction to metaphysics.* New York: Citadel.

Berlant, L. 2000. 'The subject of true feeling: Pain, privacy and politics.' In *Transformations: Thinking through feminism.* Ed. Ahmed, J. Kilby, C. Lury, M. McNeil, and B. Skeggs. London: Routledge

– 2004. *Compassion.* New York: Routledge.

Biklen, D., ed. 2005. *Autism and the myth of the person alone.* New York: New York University Press.

Binnie, J., S. Holloway, S. Millington, and C. Young. 2006. 'Introduction: Grounding cosmopolitan urbanism: Approaches, practices and policies.' In *Cosmopolitan urbanism.* Ed. J. Binnie, J. Holloway, S. Millington, and C. Young. London: Routledge.

Bhugra, D. 1997. 'Coming out by South Asian gay men in the United Kingdom.' *Archives of Sexual Behaviour* 26(5):547–57.

Blackman, L. 2008. 'Is happiness contagious?' *New Formations* 63:15–32.

Blumer, H. 1969. *Symbolic interactionism.* Englewood Cliffs, NJ: Prentice-Hall.

Bogue, R. 2006. 'Fabulation, narration and the people to come.' In *Deleuze and Philosophy.* Ed. C. Boundas. Edinburgh: Edinburgh University Press.

Bohan, J.S. 1996. 'Diversity and lesbian/gay/bisexual identities: Intersecting identities, multiple oppressions.' In *Psychology and sexual orientation: Coming to terms.* Ed. J.S. Bohan. New York: Routledge.

Bolton, S. 2009. 'Getting to the heart of the emotional labour process: A reply to Brook.' *Work, Employment and Society* 23(3):549–60.

Bondi, L. 2005. 'Making connections and thinking through emotions: Between geography and psychotherapy.' *Transactions of the Institute of British Geographers* 30:433–48.

– 2005. 'The place of emotions research: From partitioning emotion and reason to the emotional dynamics of research relationships.' In *Emotional Geographies.* Ed. L. Bondi, L.J. Davidson, and M. Smith. Aldershot: Ashgate.

Bourdieu, P. 1979/1984. *Distinction: A social critique of the judgement of taste.* London: Routledge

– 1986. 'From rules to strategies.' *Cultural Anthropology* 1(1):110–20.

– 1987. 'The biographical illusion.' In *Working papers and proceedings of the centre for psychosocial studies.* Vol. 14. Chicago Centre for Psychosocial Studies.

– 1999. *The weight of the world: Social suffering in contemporary society.* Stanford: Stanford University Press.

– 2003. 'Participant objectivation.' *Journal of the Royal Anthropologica Institute* 9:281–94.

– 2008. *Sketch for a self-analysis.* Chicago: University of Chicago Press.

Bourdieu, P., and L. Wacquant. 1992. *An invitation to a reflexive sociology.* Chicago: University of Chicago Press.

Bourke, J. 2005. *Fear: A cultural history.* London: Virago.

Brandt, A. 2007. *The cigarette century: The rise, fall, and deadly persistence of the product that defined America.* New York: Basic Books.

Braun, B., and N. Castree. 2001. *Social nature: Theory, practice and politics.* Oxford: Blackwell.

Brennan, T. 2004. *The transmission of affect.* Ithaca: Cornell University Press.

Brewis, J. 2005. 'Signing my life away? Researching sex and organization.' *Organization* 12(4):493–510.

Brook, P. 2009. 'In critical defense of 'emotional labour': Refuting Bolton's critique of Hochschild's concept.' *Work, Employment and Society* 23(3):531–48.

Brown, B.S. 1978. 'Social and psychological correlates of help-seeking behaviour among urban adults.' *American Journal of Community Psychology* 6:425–39.

Brown, G. 2006. 'Cosmopolitan camouflage: (Post-)gay space in Spitalfields, East London.' In *Cosmopolitan urbanism.* Ed. J. Binnie, J. Holloway, S. Millington, and C. Young. London: Routledge.

Brown, L.M. 1994. *Raising their voices: The Politics of girls' anger*. Cambridge, MA: Harvard University Press.

– 1998. 'Standing in the crossfire: A response to Tavris, Gremmen, Lykes, Davis and Contratto.' *Feminism and Psychology* 4:382–98.

Brown, L.M., and C. Gilligan. 1992. *Meeting at the crossroads: Women's psychology and girls' development*. Cambridge, MA: Harvard University Press.

Bruni, A. 2005. 'Shadowing software and clinical records: On the ethnography of non-humans and heterogeneous contexts.' *Organization* 12(3):357–78.

Bryson, J. 1991. 'Modes of responses to jealousy-evoking situations.' In *The psychology of jealousy and envy*. Ed. P. Salovey. New York: The Guilford Press.

Burkitt, I. 1997. 'Social relationships and emotions.' *Sociology* 31:37–55.

– 2002. 'Complex emotions: Relations, feelings and images in emotional experience.' In *Emotions and sociology*. Ed. J. Barbalet. Oxford: Blackwell.

Buss, D. 2000. *The dangerous passion: Why jealousy is as necessary as love or sex*. London: Bloomsbury Publishing.

Butt, L. 2002. 'The suffering stranger: Medical anthropology and international morality.' *Medical Anthropology* 21:1–24.

Cahill, S.E. 1999. 'Emotional capital and professional socialization: The case of mortuary science students (and me).' *Social Psychology Quarterly* 62:101–16.

Callon, M. 1986. 'The sociology of an actor network.' In *Mapping the dynamics of science and technology*. Ed. M. Callon, J. Law, and S. Rip. London: Macmillan.

Callon, M., C. Méadel, and V. Rabeharisoa. 2002. 'The economy of qualities.' *Economy and Society* 31(2):194–217.

Cancian, F.M. 1987. *Love in America: Gender and self-development*. New York: Cambridge University Press.

Cancian, F.M., and S.L. Gordon. 1988. 'Changing emotion norms in marriage: Love and anger in U.S. women's magazines since 1900.' *Gender and Society* 2(3):303–42.

Cariou, M. 1976. *Bergson et le fait mystique*. Paris: Aubier Montaigne.

Cass, V. 1984a. 'Homosexual identity: A concept in need of definition.' *Journal of Homosexuality* 7(2–3):105–26.

– 1984b. 'Homosexual identity formation: Testing a theoretical model.' *Journal of Sex Research* 20:143–67.

Cavell, S. 1979/1999. *The claim of reason: Wittgenstein, skepticism, morality, and tragedy*. Oxford: Oxford University Press.

Caygill, H. 1995. *A Kant dictionary*. Oxford: Blackwell

– 2006. 'Kant and the relegation of the passions.' In *Politics and the passions, 1500–1850*. Ed. V. Kahn, N. Saccamano, and D. Coli. Princeton: Princeton University Press.

Charmaz, K. 2000. 'Experiencing chronic illness.' In *The handbook of social studies in health and medicine*, 277–92. Ed. G. Albrecht, R. Fitzpatrick, and S. Scrimshaw. London: Sage.

Cheah, P., and B. Robbins, eds. 1998. *Cosmopolitics: Thinking and feeling beyond the nation*. Minneapolis: University of Minnesota Press.

Chirrey, D.A. 2003. '"I hereby come out": What sort of speech act is coming out?' *Journal of Sociolinguistics* 7(1):24–37.

Chong, Kelly H. 2008. 'Coping with conflict, confronting resistance: Fieldwork emotions and identity management in a South Korean evangelical community.' *Qualitative Sociology* 31(4):369–90.

Chouliaraki, L. 2010. 'Post-humanitarianism: Humanitarian communication beyond a politics of pity.' *International Journal of Cultural Studies* 13:107–26.

Clanton, G. 1996. 'A sociology of jealousy.' *International Journal of Sociology and Social Policy* 16(9–10):171–89.

Clanton, G., and D. Kosins. 1991. 'Developmental correlates of jealousy.' In *The psychology of jealousy and envy*. Ed. P. Salovey. New York: The Guilford Press.

Clanton, G., and L. Smith. 1977. *Jealousy*. Englewood Cliffs, NJ: Prentice Hall.

Clark, C. 1987. 'Sympathy biography and sympathy margin.' *American.Journal of Sociology* 93(2):290–321.

– 1990. 'Emotions and micropolitics in everyday life: Some patterns and paradoxes of "place."' In *Research agendas in the sociology of emotions*. Ed. T. Kemper. Albany, NY: SUNY Press.

Clarke, J.N. 2004. *Health, illness and medicine in Canada*. Don Mills, ON: Oxford.

Clay-Warner, J., and D. Robinson, eds. 2008. *Social structure and emotions*. San Diego, CA: Elsevier.

Cloward, R.A., and L.E. Ohlin. 1960. *Delinquency and opportunity: A theory of delinquent gangs*. New York: Free Press.

Code, L. 1991. *What can she know? Feminist theory and the construction of knowledge*. Ithaca, NY: Cornell University Press.

Coffey, A. 1999. *The ethnographic self: Fieldwork and the representation of identity*. London: Sage.

Cohen, A. 1955. *Delinquent boys: The culture of the gang*. New York: Free Press.

Cohen, S., and L. Taylor. 1992. *Escape attempts: The theory and practice of resistance in everyday life*. London: Routledge.

Cohler, B.J. 2004. 'The experience of ambivalence within the family: Young adults "coming out" gay or lesbian and their parents.' *Contemporary Perspectives in Family Research* 4:255–84.

Collins, M. 2003. *Modern love: An intimate history of men and women in twentieth-century Britain*. London: Atlantic Books.

Collins, R. 1975. *Conflict sociology: Towards an explanatory science*. New York: Academic Press.

– 1981. 'On the micro-foundations of macro-sociology.' *American Journal of Sociology* 86:984–1014.

– 2004. *Interaction ritual chains*. Princeton, NJ: Princeton University Press.

Connolly, W.E. 2008. *Capitalism and Christianity, American style*. Durham, NC: Duke University Press.

Copp, M. 1998. 'When emotion work is doomed to fail: Ideological and structural constraints on emotion management.' *Symbolic Interaction* 21:299–328.

Corrigan, P. 2004. 'How stigma interferes with mental health care.' *American Psychologist* 59:614–25.

Cotterill, P. 1992. 'Interviewing women: Issues of friendship, vulnerability and power.' *Women's Studies International Forum* 15:593–606.

Coupland, C., A.D. Brown, K. Daniels, and M. Humphreys. 2008. 'Saying it with feeling: Analyzing speakable emotions.' *Human Relations* 61(3):327–53.

Cowhey, S.P. 2005. *Going through the motions: Coping with autism*. Baltimore, MD: Publish America.

Cox, S., and C. Gallois. 1996. 'Gay and lesbian identity development: A social identity perspective.' *Journal of Homosexuality* 30(4):1–30.

Crawford, J., S. Kippax, J. Onyx, U. Gault, and P. Benton. 1992. *Emotion and gender*. London: Sage.

Crossley, N. 1998. 'Emotions and communicative action.' In *Emotions in social life: Critical themes and contemporary issues*. Ed. G. Bendelow and S.J. Williams. London: Routledge.

Csordas, T. 1994. 'Introduction: The body as representation and being-in-the-world.' In *Embodiment and experience*. Ed. T. Csordas. Cambridge: Cambridge University Press.

Curtis, S., W. Gesler, G. Smith, and S. Washburn. 2000. 'Approaches to sampling and case selection in qualitative research: Examples in the geography of health.' *Social Science and Medicine* 50:1001–14.

Czarniawska, B. 2004. *Narratives in social science research*. London: Sage.

– 2006. 'Doing gender unto the other: Fiction as a mode of studying gender discrimination in organizations.' *Gender, Work and Organization* 13(3):234–53.

Damasio, A. 1995. *Descartes' error: Emotion, reason, and the human brain*. New York: Quill, Harper Collins.

– 2000. *The feeling of what happens: Body, emotion and the making of consciousness*. London: Vintage.

Darwin, C. 187? *The expression of the emotions in man and animal*. London. Oxford University Press.

Davidson, A. 1993. 'Religion and the distortions of human reason: On Kant's *Religion within the limits of reason alone.*' In *Pursuits of reason: Essays in honor of Stanley Cavell*. Ed. T. Cohen, P. Guyer, and H. Putnam. Lubbock: Texas Tech University Press.

Davidson, J. 2003. *Phobic geographies: The phenomenology and spatiality of identity*. Aldershot: Ashgate.

– 2007. 'In a world of her own . . .': Re-presentations of alienation in the livesand writings of women with autism.' *Gender, Place and Culture* 14(6):659–77.

– 2008a. 'Autistic cultures online: Virtual communication and cultural expression on the spectrum.' *Social and Cultural Geography* 9(7):791–806.

– 2008b. 'More labels than a jam jar . . .': The gendered dynamics of diagnosis for girls and women with autism.' In *Power and illness*. Ed. P. Moss and K. Teghtsoonian. Toronto: University of Toronto Press.

Davidson, J., L. Bondi, and M. Smith. 2005. 'Introduction: Geography's "emotional turn."' In *Emotional geographies*. Ed. J. Davidson, L. Bondi, and M. Smith. Aldershot: Ashgate.

Davidson J., and M. Smith. 2009. 'Autistic autobiographies and more-than-human emotional geographies.' *Environment and Planning D: Society and Space* 27(5):898–916.

De Beauvoir, S. 1997. *The second sex*. Trans. H.M. Parshley. London: Vintage Books.

De Visser, R., and McDonald, D. 2007. 'Swings and roundabouts: Management of jealousy in heterosexual "Swinging" Couples.' *British Journal of Social Psychology* 46:459–76.

Deleuze, G. 1966/1988. *Bergsonism*. New York: Zone.

– 1969/1990. *The Logic of Sense*. New York: Columbia University Press.

–1983/1986. *Cinema 1: The movement-image*. Minneapolis: University of Minnesota Press.

– 1985/1989. *Cinema 2: the Time-Image*. Minneapolis: University of Minnesota Press.

– 2004. 'Cours sur le chapitre III de *L'évolution créatrice* de Bergson.' In *Annalesbergsoniennes II: Bergson, Deleuze, la phénoménology*. Ed. F. Worms. Paris: PUF.

Denzin, N.K. 1983. 'A note on emotionality, self and interaction.' *American Journal of Sociology* 89:402–9.

– 1984. *On understanding emotion*. San Francisco: Jossey-Bass.

– 1985. 'Emotion as lived experience.' *Symbolic Interaction* 8(2):223–40

– 1990. 'On understanding emotion: The interpretive-cultural agenda.' In *Research agendas in the sociology of emotions.* Ed. T. Kemper. New York: SUNY Press.

Dhaouadi, M. 1990. 'Ibn Khaldun: The founding father of eastern sociology.' *International Sociology* 5(3):319–35.

Dixon, J., C. Gordon, and T. Khomusi. 1995. 'Sexual symmetry in psychiatric diagnosis.' *Social Problems* 42:429–48.

Dixon, T. 2003. *From passions to emotions: The creation of a secular psychological category.* Cambridge: Cambridge University Press.

Doka, K. 1989. *Disenfranchised grief: Recognizing hidden sorrow.* Lexington, MA: Lexington books.

– 2002. *Disenfranchised grief: New directions, challenges and strategies for practice.* Champaign, IL: Research Press.

Doucet, A. 2006. *Do men mother? Fathering and domestic responsibilities.* Toronto: University of Toronto Press.

– 2008. ' "On the other side of gossamer walls": Reflexive and relational knowing.' *Qualitative Sociology* 31(1):73–87.

Doucet, A., and N.S. Mauthner. 2002. 'Knowing responsibly: Ethics, feminist epistemologies and methodologies.' In *Ethics in qualitative research.* Ed. M. Mauthner, M. Birch, J. Jessop, and T. Miller. London: Sage.

– 2006. 'Feminist methodologies and epistemologies.' In *Handbook of 21st century sociology.* Ed. C.D. Bryant and D. Pleck. Thousand Oaks, CA: Sage.

– 2008. 'What can be known and how? Narrated subjects and the Listening Guide.' *Qualitative Research* 8(3):399–409.

Dunner, J. 1964. *Dictionary of political science.* London: Vision Press.

Durkheim, E. [1912]1961. *The elementary forms of religious life.* New York: Collier Books.

Easton, D., and C. Liszt. 1997. *The ethical slut: A guide to infinite sexual possibilities.* Eugene, OR: Greenery Press.

Ekman, P. 1973. *Darwin and facial expression.* New York: Academic Press.

– 1984. 'Expression and the nature of emotion.' In *Approaches to emotion.* Ed. K. Scherer and P. Ekman. Hillsdale, NJ: Lawrence Erlbaum Associates

– 1992. 'An argument for basic emotions.' *Cognition and Emotion* 6:169–200.

Ekman, P., ed. 1982. *Emotions in the human face.* Cambridge: Cambridge University Press.

Elias, N. 1978. *The civilizing process. Vol. 1: The history of manners.* New York: Urizen Books.

– 1982. *The civilizing process. Vol. 2: State formation and civilization.* New York: Pantheon Books.

– 1994. *The civilizing process. Vol 1: The History of manners*. 2d ed. Oxford: Blackwell.

– 1996. *The Germans: Power struggles and the development of habitus in the nineteenth and twentieth centuries*. Trans. E. Dunning and S. Mennell. Cambridge: Polity Press.

– 1998. 'Informalization and the civilizing process.' In *The Norbert Elias reader: A biographical selection*. Ed. J. Goudsblom and S. Mennell. Oxford: Blackwell.

Elias N., and Eric Dunning. 1986. *The quest for excitement: Sport and leisure in the civilizing process*. Oxford: Basil Blackwell.

Eliason, M.J. 1996. 'Identity formation for lesbian, bisexual, and gay persons: Beyond a "minoritizing" view.' *Journal of Homosexuality* 30(3):31–58.

Ellis, D., and J. Cromby 2009. 'Inhibition and reappraisal within emotional disclosure: The embodying of narration.' *Counselling Psychology Quarterly* 22(3):319–31.

Ellison, J. 1999. *Cato's tears and the making of Anglo-American emotion*. Chicago: University of Chicago Press.

Emerson, R., R. Fretz, and L. Shaw. 1995. *Writing ethnographic fieldnotes*. Chicago and London: University of Chicago Press.

Emerson, R.W. [1841] 2000. 'Self reliance.' In *Essential writings*. Ed. M. Oliver. New York: Random House.

Erickson, B., P. Abanese, and S. Drakulic. 2000. 'Gender on a jagged edge: The security industry, its clients and the reproduction and revision of gender.' *Work and Occupations* 27(3):294–318.

Erickson, R. 2009. 'The emotional demands of nursing.' In *Nursing policy research: Turning evidenced-based research into health policy*. Ed. G. Dickinson and L. Flynn. New York: Springer.

Erikson, K.T. 1966. *Wayward puritans: A study in the sociology of deviance*. New York: Macmillan.

Esterberg, K.G. 1997. *Lesbian and bisexual identities: Constructing communities, constructing selves*. Philadelphia: Temple University Press.

Evans, K. 2002. *Negotiating the self: Identity, sexuality, and emotion in learning to teach*. New York: Routledge.

Eyerman, R., and B.S. Turner. 1998. 'Outline of a theory of generations.' *European Journal of Social Theory* 1(1):91–106.

Fairclough, N. 1995. *Critical discourse analysis: The critical study of language*. London: Longman.

Fan, Y. 2005. 'Ethical branding and corporate reputation.' *Corporate Communications: An International Journal* 10(4):341–50.

Fausto-Sterling, A. 2000. *Sexing the body: Gender politics and the construction of sexuality*. New York: Basic Books.

Field, F. 2003. *Neighbours from hell: The politics of behaviour*. London: Politico's.

Figert, A.E. 1995. 'The three faces of PMS: The professional, gendered, and scientific structuring of a psychiatric disorder.' *Social Problems* 42:56–73.

Fineman, S. 1993. 'Organizations as emotional arenas.' In *Emotion in organizations*. Ed. S. Fineman. London: Sage.

– 2004. 'Getting the measure of emotion – and the cautionary tale of emotional intelligence.' *Human Relations* 57(6):719–40.

Fineman, S., and A. Sturdy. 1999. 'The emotions of control.' *Human Relations* 52(5):631–63.

Finch, J. 1984. ' "It's great to have someone to talk to": The ethics and politics of interviewing women.' In *Social researching: Politics, problems, practice*. Ed. C. Bell and H. Roberts. London: Routledge and Kegan Paul.

Flam, H. 2005. ' "Emotions" map: A research agenda.' In *Emotions and social movements*. Ed. H. Flam and D. King. London: Routledge.

Floyd, F.J., and T.S. Stein. 2002. 'Sexual orientation identity formation among gay, lesbian, and bisexual youths: Multiple patterns of milestone experiences.' *Journal of Research on Adolescence* 12(2):167–91.

Flyvbjerg, B. 2006. 'Five misunderstandings about case-study research.' *Qualitative Inquiry* 12(2):219–45.

Foucault, M. 1965. *Madness and civilization: A history of insanity in the age of reason*. New York: Vintage Books.

– 1976/1978. *The history of sexuality. Vol. I: An introduction*. New York: Pantheon Books.

Francis, L.E. 1997. 'Ideology and Interpersonal Emotion Management: Redefining Identity in Two Support Groups.' *Social Psychology Quarterly* 60:153–71.

Freund, P. 1998. 'Social performances and their discontents: The biopsychosocial aspects of dramaturgical stress.' In *Emotions in Social Life*. Ed. G. Bendelow and S.J. Williams. London and New York: Routledge.

Frey, B.S., and A. Stutzer. 2002. *Happiness and economics: How the economy and institutions affect human well-being*. Princeton, NJ: Princeton University Press.

Friedman, L.M. 1999. *The horizontals society*. New Haven: Yale University Press.

Friedman, M. 1993. *What are friends for? Feminist perspectives on personal relationships and moral theory*. Ithaca, NY: Cornell University Press.

Frith, U. 1996. 'Asperger and his syndrome.' In *Autism and asperger syndrome*. Ed. U. Frith. Cambridge: Cambridge University Press.

Furedi, F. 2004. *Therapy culture: Cultivating vulnerability in an uncertain age*. London: Routledge.

Gadamer, H-G. 1998. *Truth and method*. New York: Continuum.

Gailus, A. 2006. *Passions of the sign: Revolution and language in Kant, Goethe, and Kleist*. Baltimore: Johns Hopkins University Press.

Gaita, R. 2002. *The philosopher's dog: Friendships with animals*. New York: Random House.

Game, A. 1997 'Sociology's emotions.' *Canadian Review of Sociology and Anthropology* 34(4):385–99.

Garb, H.N. 1997. 'Race bias, social class bias, and gender bias in clinical judgment.' *Clinical Psychology: Science and Practice* 4:99–120.

Geertz, C. 1973. 'Thick description: Towards an interpretive theory of culture.' In *The interpretation of cultures: Selected essays*. Ed. C. Geertz. New York: Basic Books.

– 1988. 'Being there: Anthropology and the scene of writing.' In *Works and lives: The anthropologist as author*. Ed. C. Geertz. Palo Alto, CA: Stanford University Press.

George, M. 1994. 'Riding the donkey backwards: Men as the unacceptable victims of marital violence.' *Journal of Men's Studies* 3(2):137–59.

Gerland, G. 2003. *A Real person: Life on the outside*. London: Souvenir Press.

Gesler, W. 2003. *Healing places*. Lanham, MD: Rowman and Littlefield.

Gevers, I. 2000. 'Subversive tactics of neurologically diverse cultures.' *Journal of Cognitive Liberties* 2(1):43–60.

Gherardi, S., D. Nicolini, and A. Strati. 2007. 'The passion for knowing.' *Organization* 14(3):315–29.

Gibbs, A. 2001. 'Contagious feelings: Pauline Hanson and the epidemology of affect.' *Australian Humanities Review*. December 2001. Retrieved from http: www.lib.latrobe.edu.au/AHR/archive/Issue-December-2001/gibbs.html.

Gibbs, J.P. 1965. 'Norms: The problem of definition and classification.' *American Journal of Sociology* 70:586–94.

Giddens, A. 1992. *The transformation of intimacy: Love, sexuality and eroticism in modern societies*. Cambridge: Polity Press.

Gijswijt-Hofstra, M., and R. Porter, eds. 2001. *Cultures of neurasthenia: From Beard to the First World War*. New York: Rodopi.

Gilligan, C. 1982. *In a different voice: Psychological theory and women's development*. Cambridge, MA: Harvard University Press.

– 1988. 'Remapping the moral domain: New images of the self in relationship.' In *Mapping the moral domain: A contribution of women's thinking to psychological theory and education*. Ed. C. Gilligan, J.V. Ward, and J.M. Taylor, with B. Bardige. Cambridge, MA: Harvard University Press.

Gilligan, C., N.P. Lyons, and T.J. Hanmer. 1990. *Making connections: The relational worlds of adolescent girls at Emma Willard School*. Cambridge: Harvard University Press.

Gilligan, C., R. Spencer, K.M. Weinberg, and T. Bertsch. 2006. 'On the Listening Guide: A voice-centred relational method.' In *Emergent methods insocial research*. Ed. S.N. Hesse-Biber and P. Leavy. Thousand Oaks, CA: Sage.

Glendon, M.A. 1991. *Rights talk: The impoverishment of political discourse*. New York: The Free Press.

Gobé, M. 2001. *Emotional branding: The new paradigms for connecting brands to people*. New York: Allworth Press.

Goffman, E. 1961. *Encounters: Two studies in the sociology of interaction*. New York: Bobbs-Merrill.

– 1963. *Stigma*. Englewood Cliffs, NJ: Prentice Hall.

Gordan, A. 1996. *Ghostly matters: Haunting and the sociological imagination*. Minneapolis: University of Minnesota.

Gordon, S.L. 1989. 'The socialization of children's emotions: Emotional culture, exposure, and competence.' In *Children's understanding of emotions*. Ed. C. Saarni and P. Harris. New York: Cambridge University Press.

Gordon, T., J. Holland, and E. Lahelma. 2000. *Making spaces: Citizenship and difference in schools*. Basingstoke: Macmillan.

Gould, D.B. 2002. 'Life during wartime: Emotions and the development of ACT UP.' *Mobilization* 7(2):177–200.

Gould, T. 2000. *The lifestyle: A look at the erotic rites of swingers*. Toronto and New York:Vintage.

Goussinsky, A. 2008. *In the name of love: Romantic ideology and its victims*. Oxford: Oxford University Press.

Gove, W.R. 2005. 'The career of the mentally ill: An integration of psychiatric, labeling/social construction, and lay perspectives.' *Journal of Health and Social Behaviour* 45:357–75.

Grandin, T. 1996. *Thinking in pictures: And other reports from my life with autism*. New York: Vintage Books.

– 2005. *Animals in translation: Using the mysteries of autism to decode animal behaviour*. Orlando: Harcourt.

Grandin, T., and M.M. Scariano. 1996. *Emergence labelled autistic*. New York: Warner Books.

Green, L., and Grant, V. 2008. 'Gagged grief and beleaguered bereavements?': An analysis of multidisciplinary theory and research relating to same sex partnership bereavement. *Sexualities* 11(3):275–300.

Grosz. E. 1994. *Volatile bodies: Towards a corporeal feminism*. Bloomington: Indiana University Press.

Guerrero, L., M. Trost, and S. Yoshimura. 2005. 'Romantic jealousy: Emotions and communicative responses.' *Personal Relationships* 12:233–52.

Gusfield, J. 1963. *Symbolic crusade: Status politics and the American temperance movement.* Urbana: University of Illinois Press.

Haas, J. 1977. 'Learning real feelings: A study of high steel ironworkers' reactions to fear and danger.' *Sociology of Work and Occupations* 4:147–69.

Haddon, M. 2004. *The curious incident of the dog in the night-time.* Toronto: Anchor Canada.

Hadot, P. 2001/2009. *The present alone is our happiness: Conversations withJeannie Carter and Arnold I. Davidson.* Stanford: Stanford University Press.

Halford, S., and P. Leonard. 2006. *Negotiating gendered identities at work: Place, space and time.* New York: Palgrave Macmillan.

Halbertal, T.H. 2002. *Appropriately subversive: Modern mothers in traditional religions.* Cambridge, MA: Harvard University Press.

Hall, S. 1986. 'Gramsci's relevance for the study of race and ethnicity.' *Journal of Communication Inquiry* 10:5–27.

Hannerz, U. 1996. *Transnational connections.* London: Routledge.

Harding, J., and E.D. Pribram. 2002. 'The power of feeling: Locating emotions in culture.' *European Journal of Cultural Studies* 5(4):407–26.

– 2004. 'Losing our cool; Following Williams and Grossberg on emotions.' *Cultural Studies* 18(6):863–83.

Haritaworn, J., C. Lin, and C. Kleese. 2006. 'Poly/logue: A critical introduction to polyamory.' *Sexualities* 9(5):515–29.

Hart, D., and M.K. Matsuba. 2007. 'The development of pride and moral life.' In *The self-conscious emotions.* Ed. J. Tracy, R. Robbins, and J.P. Tagney. New York: The Guilford Press.

Haug, F. 1987. *Female sexualisation: A collective work of memory.* Trans. E. Carter. London: Verso.

Haylett, C. 2006. 'Working-class subjects in the cosmopolitan city.' In *Cosmopolitan Urbanism.* Ed. J. Binnie, J. Holloway, S. Millington, and C. Young. London: Routledge.

Heaphy, B., C. Donovan, and J. Weeks. 2004. 'A different affair? Openness and nonmonogamy in same sex relationships.' In *The state of affairs: Explorations in infidelity and commitment.* Ed. J. Ducombe, K. Harrison, G. Allan, and D. Marsden. Hillsdale, NJ: Lawrence Erlbaum Associates.

Heidegger, M. [1926]1962. *Being and time.* San Francisco: Harper Collins.

– 1988. *Being and time.* Oxford: Blackwell.

– 2001. *The fundamental concepts of metaphysics: World, finitude, solitude.* Bloomington: Indiana University Press.

Heinz, B., L. Gu, A. Inuzuka, and R. Zender. 2002. 'Under the rainbow flag: Webbing global gay identities.' *International Journal of Sexuality and Gender Studies* 7(2–3):107–24.

Held, V. 1999. 'Liberalism and the ethics of care.' In *On feminist ethics and politics*. Ed. C. Card. Lawrence: University Press of Kansas.

Hendrickson, David C. 1999. The ethics of collective security. In *Ethics and international affairs: A reader*, 221–41. 2d ed. Ed. Joel H. Rosenthal. Washington, DC: Georgetown University Press.

Herdt, G., and B. Koff. 2000. *Something to tell you: The road families travel when a child is gay*. New York: Columbia University Press.

Hesse-Biber, S.N., and Patricia L. Leavy. 2006. *Emergent methods in social research*. Thousand Oaks, CA: Sage.

Hill, C. 1972. *The world turned upside down: Radical ideas during the English Revolution*. New York: Viking Press.

Hobsbawm, E.J. 1959. *Primitive rebels: Studies in archaic forms of social movement in the nineteenth and twentieth centuries*. Manchester: Manchester University Press.

Hochschild, A. 1975. 'The sociology of feeling and emotion: Selected possibilities.' In *Another Voice*. Ed. M. Millman and R. Kanter. Garden City, NY: Anchor.

– 1979. 'Emotion work, feeling rules, and social structure.' *American Journal of Sociology* 85:51–75.

– 1983. *The managed heart: Commercialization of human feeling*. Berkeley: University of California Press.

– 1989. *The second shift: Working parents and the revolution at home*. Berkeley: University of California Press.

– 1990. 'Ideology and emotion management: A perspective and path for future research.' In *Research agendas in the sociology of emotions*. Ed. T. Kemper. Albany, NY: SUNY Press.

– 2007. 'Exploring the managed heart.' In *The emotions: A cultural reader*. Ed. H. Wulff. New York: Berg.

Holland, J. 2007. 'Emotions and research.' *International Journal of Social Research Methodology* 10:195–209.

Hollway, W. 2008a. 'Turning psychosocial? Towards a UK network.' *Psychoanalysis, Culture and Society* 13(2):199–204.

– 2008b. 'The importance of relational thinking in the practice of psycho-social research: Ontology, epistemology, methodology and ethics.' In *Object relations and social relations*. Ed. S. Clarke, P. Hoggett, and H. Hahn. London: Karnac.

Hollway, W., and T. Jefferson. 2000. *Doing qualitative research differently: Free association, narrative and the interview method.* London: Sage.

Holstein, J.A., and G. Miller. 1990. 'Rethinking victimization: An interactional approach to victimology.' *Symbolic Interaction* 13(1):103–22.

Holt, M., and C. Griffin. 2003. 'Being gay, being straight and being yourself: Local and global reflections on identity, authenticity and the lesbian and gay scene.' *European Journal of Cultural Studies* 6(3):404–25.

hooks, b. (2000) *Feminist theory: From margin to centre.* London: Pluto Press.

Hubbard, Gill, Kathryn Backett-Milburn, and Debbie Kemmer. 2001. 'Working with emotion: Issues for the researcher in fieldwork and teamwork.' *International Journal of Social Research Methodology* 4:119–37.

Hume, D. 1949. *Treatise of human nature.* Oxford: Clarendon Press.

– 1975. *Enquiries concerning human understanding and concerning the principles of morals.* Oxford: Clarendon Press.

Hupka, R. 1984. 'Jealousy: Compound emotion or label for a particular situation?' *Motivation and Emotion* 8:141–55.

Illouz, E. 1997. *Consuming the romantic utopia: Love and the cultural contradictions of capitalism.* Berkeley: University of California Press.

– 2007. *Cold intimacies.* Cambridge: Polity Press.

– 2008. *Saving the modern soul: Therapy, emotions and the culture of self-help.* Berkeley: University of California Press.

Izzard, C. 1977. *Human emotions.* New York: Plenum.

– 1984. 'Emotion-cognition relationships and human development.' In *Emotions, cognition and behaviour.* Ed. C. Izzard, J. Kagman, and R. Zajonc. Cambridge: Cambridge University Press.

Jackson, K., and L.B. Brown. 1996. 'Lesbians of African heritage: Coming out in the straight community.' *Journal of Gay and Lesbian Social Services* 5(4):53–67.

Jackson, S. 1993. 'Even sociologists fall in love: An exploration in the sociology of emotions.' *Sociology* 27(2):201–20.

Jaffe, A. 2000. *Scenes of sympathy: Identity and representation in Victorian fiction.* Ithaca, NY: Cornell University Press.

Jaggar, A., and S. Bordo, eds. 1992. *Gender/body/knowledge: Feminist reconstructions of being and knowing.* New Brunswick, NJ: Rutgers University Press.

Jamieson, L. 2004. 'Intimacy, negotiated nonmonogamy, and the limits of the couple.' In *The state of affairs; Explorations in infidelity and commitment.* Ed. J. Ducombe, K. Harrision, G. Allan, and D. Marsden. Hillsdale, NJ: Lawrence Erlbaum Associates.

Jeffery, R. 1979. 'Rubbish: Deviant patients in casualty departments.' *Sociology of Health and Illness* 1(1):90–107.

Johns, D.J., and T.M. Probst. 2004. 'Sexual minority identity formation in an adult population.' *Journal of Homosexuality* 47(2):81–90.

Johnson, J.G., M.B. First, S. Block, L.C. Vanderwerker, K. Zwin, B. Zhang, andH.G. Prigerson. 2009. 'Stigmatization and receptivity to mental healthservices among recently bereaved adults.' *Death Studies* 33(8): 691–711.

Jones, R.S.P., C. Quigney, and J.C. Huws. 2003. 'First-hand accounts of sensory perceptual experiences in autism: A qualitative analysis.' *Journal of Intellectual and Developmental Disability* 28(2):112–21.

Jones, R.S.P., A. Zahl, and J.C. Huws. 2001. 'First-hand accounts of emotional experiences in autism: A qualitative analysis.' *Disability and Society* 16(3):393–401.

Jones, S.J., and Beck, E. 2007. 'Disenfranchised grief and monfinite loss as experienced by the families of death row inmates.' *OMEGA* 54(4):281–99.

Jones, T.C., and N.M. Nystrom. 2002. 'Looking back . . . looking forward: Addressing the lives of lesbians 55 and older.' *Journal of Women and Aging* 14(3–4):59–76.

Jutel, A. 2009. 'Sociology of diagnosis: A preliminary review.' *Sociology of Health and Illness* 31:278–99.

Kain, P.J. 1988. *Marx and ethics.* Oxford: Clarendon Press.

Kant, I. [1787] 1996a. *Critique of pure reason.* New York: Hackett.

– [1798] 1996b. *The conflict of the faculties.* Cambridge: Cambridge University Press.

– [1788] 2002. *Critique of practical reason.* New York: Hackett.

– [1790] 1987. *Critique of judgment.* New York: Hackett.

– [1793] 2009. *Religion within the bounds of bare reason.* New York: Hackett.

– 1967. *Philosophical correspondence, 1759–99.* Ed. and Trans. A. Zweig. Chicago: University of Chicago Press.

– 2004. *Critique of practical reason.* Trans, T.K. Abbott. New York: Dover.

– 2005. *Groundwork for the metaphysics of morals.* Ed. L. Denis. Trans. T.K. Abbott. Toronto: Broadview Editions.

Katz, J. 1988. *Seductions of crime.* New York: Basic Books.

Katz, S.J., R.C. Kessler, R.G. Frank, P. Leaf, E. Lin, and M. Edlund. 1997. 'The use of outpatient mental health services in the United States and Ontario: The impact of mental morbidity and perceived need for care.' *American Journal of Public Health* 87:1136–43.

Kellow, M.M.R. 2009. 'Hard struggles of doubt: Abolitionists and the problem of slave redemption.' In *Humanitarianism and suffering: The mobilization of empathy*. Ed. R.A. Wilson and R.D. Brown. New York: Cambridge University Press.

Kemper, T. 1978. *A social interactional theory of emotions*. New York: Wiley.

– 1987. 'How many emotions are there? Wedding the social and the autonomic components.' *American Journal of Sociology* 93(2):263–89.

– 2004. 'The differential impact of emotions of rational schemes of social organization: Reading Weber and Coleman.' *Advances in Group Processes* 21(3):223–44.

Kemper, T., and R. Collins. 1990. 'Dimensions of microinteraction.' *American Journal of Sociology* 96(1):32–68.

Kendon, A. 1990. *Conducting interaction*. New York: Cambridge University Press.

– 2004. *Gesture: Visible action as utterance*. Cambridge and New York: Cambridge University Press.

Kennedy, D. 2004. *The dark side of virtue: Reassessing international humanitarianism*. Princeton, NJ: Princeton University Press.

Kenney, J.S. 1999. *Coping with grief: Survivors of murder victims*. Unpublished doctoral thesis. Hamilton, ON: McMaster University.

– 2002a. 'Metaphors of loss: Murder, bereavement, gender, and presentation of the victimized "self."' *International Review of Victimology* 9:219–51.

– 2002b. 'Victims of crime and labeling theory: A parallel process?' *Deviant Behaviour* 23:235–65.

– 2004. Human agency revisited: The paradoxical experiences of victims of crime. *International Review of Victimology* 11:225–57.

Kenney, J.S., and D. Clairmont. 2009. 'Using the victim role as both sword and shield: The interactional dynamics of restorative justice sessions.' *Journal of Contemporary Ethnography* 38(3):279–307.

Kerfoot, D., and D. Knights. 1998. 'Managing masculinity in contemporary organizational life: A "man"agerial project.' *Organization* 5(1):7–26.

Kessler, R.C., K.A. McGonagh, S. Zhao, C.B. Nelson, M. Hughes, S. Eshleman, U. Wittchen, and K.S. Kendler. 1994. 'Lifetime and 12-month prevalence of DSM-III-R psychiatric disorders in the United States: Results from the National Comorbidity Survey.' *Archives of General Psychiatry* 51:8–19.

– 2003. 'Screening for serious mental illness in the general population.' *Archives of General Psychiatry* 60:184–9.

– 2005. 'Prevalence, severity, and comorbidity of 12-month DSM-IV disorders in the National Comorbidity Survey Replication.' *Archives of General Psychiatry* 62:617–27.

Khaldun, I. 1989. *The Muqaddimah: An introduction to history*. Trans. F. Rosenthal. Princeton, NJ: Princeton University Press.

Kipnis, L. 2003. *Against love: A Polemic*. New York: Vintage Books.

Kirk, S.A., and H. Kutchins. 1992. *The selling of DSM: The rhetoric of science in psychiatry*. New York: Aldine de Gruyter.

Kirsch, G.E. 2005. ' Friendship, friendliness, and feminist fieldwork.' *Signs: Journal of Women in Culture and Society* 30:2163–72.

Kitsuse, J.I. 1980. 'Coming out all over: Deviants and the politics of social problems.' *Social Problems* 28(1):1–12.

Kitzinger, C., and S. Wilkinson. 1995. 'Transitions from heterosexuality to lesbianism: The discursive production of lesbian identities.' *Developmental Psychology* 31:95–104.

Kleese, C. 2006. 'Polyamory and its "others": Contesting the terms of non-monogamy.' *Sexualities* 9(5):515–29.

– 2007. *The spectre of promiscuity: Gay male and bisexual non-monogamies and polyamories*. Aldershot: Ashgate.

Klein, N. 1999. *No Logo*. Toronto: Knopf Canada.

Kleinman, S., and M.A. Copp. 1993. *Emotions and fieldwork*. Sage.

Kleinman, A., and B. Good, eds. 1985. *Culture and depression: Studies in the anthropology and cross-cultural psychiatry of affect and disorder*. Berkeley: University of California Press.

Kleinman, A., and J. Kleinman. 1985. 'Somatization: The interconnections in Chinese society among culture, depressive experiences, and the meanings of pain.' In *Culture and depression: Studies in the anthropology and cross-cultural psychiatry of affect and disorder*. Ed. A. Kleinman and B. Good. Berkeley: University of California Press.

Knights, D., and E. Surman. 2008. 'Editorial: Addressing the gender gap in studies of emotion.' *Gender, Work and Organization* 15(1):1–8.

Knorr-Cetina, K. 1997. 'Sociality with objects: Social relations in postsocial knowledge societies.' *Theory, Culture and Society* 14(4):1–30.

– 1999. *Epistemic cultures: How the sciences make knowledge*. Cambridge, MA: Harvard University Press.

Knowles, C. 2006. 'Handling your baggage in the field: Reflections on research relationships.' *International Journal of Social Research Methodology* 9:393–404.

Kozol, W. 2008. 'Visual witnessing and women's human rights.' *Peace Review: A Journal of Social Justice* 20:67–75.

Kring, A. 2000. 'Gender and anger.' In *Gender and emotion: Social psychological perspectives*. Ed. A.H. Fischer. Cambridge: Cambridge University Press.

Kuhn, A. 2002. *Family secrets: Acts of memory and imagination*. London: Verso.

– 2007. 'Photography and cultural memory: A methodological exploration.' *Visual Studies* 22:283–92.

Labriola, K. 2009. 'Unmasking the green-eyed monster: Managing jealousy in open relationships.' *Cat and Dragon.* Retrieved from www.polycat.org/node/46, 1 June 2009.

De Laet, M., and A. Mol. 2000. 'The Zimbabwe bush pump: Mechanics of a fluid technology.' *Social Studies of Science* 30(2):225–63.

Landri, P. 2007. 'The pragmatics of passion: A sociology of attachment to mathematics.' *Organization* 14(3):413–35.

Lapoujade, D. 2005. 'The normal and the pathological in Bergson.' *MLN* 120(5):1146–55.

Laqueur, T. 1989. 'Bodies, details, and the humanitarian narrative.' In *The new cultural history.* Ed. L. Hunt. Berkeley: University of California Press.

– 2009. 'Mourning, pity and the work of narrative in the making of "humanity."' In *Humanitarianism and suffering: The mobilization of empathy.* Ed. R.A. Wilson and R.D. Brown. New York: Cambridge University Press.

Latouche, S. 1996. *The Westernization of the world.* Trans. R. Morris. Cambridge, UK: Polity Press.

Lash, S. 2002. *Critique of information.* London: Sage.

Latham, A. 2006. 'Sociality and the cosmopolitan imagination: National, cosmopolitan and local imaginaries in Auckland, New Zealand.' In *Cosmopolitan urbanism.* Ed. J. Binnie, J. Holloway, S. Millington, and C. Young. London: Routledge.

Latour, B. 1987. *Science in action.* Milton Keynes: Open University Press.

– 1996. *Aramis or the love of technology.* Cambridge, MA: Harvard University Press.

– 2004. *Politics of nature: How to bring the sciences into democracy.* Cambridge, MA: Harvard University Press.

Law, J. 2002. 'Objects and spaces.' *Theory, Culture and Society* 19 (5–6): 91–105.

– 2004. *After method: Mess in social science research.* London: Routledge.

Law, J., and V. Singleton. 2005. 'Object lessons.' *Organization* 12(3):331–55.

Lawlor, L. 2003. *The challenge of Bergsonism.* London: Continuum.

Lawson, W. 2005. *Life behind glass: A personal account of autism spectrum disorder.* London and Philadelphia: Jessica Kingsley Publishers.

Layard, R. 2005. *Happiness: Lessons from a new science.* London: Allen Lane.

LeDoux, J. 1998. *The emotional brain.* New York: Phoenix Paperbacks.

Lefebvre, A. 2008. *The image of Law: Deleuze, Bergson, Spinoza.* Palo Alto, CA: Stanford University Press.

– 2011. 'Human rights in Deleuze and Bergson's later philosophy.' *Theory & Event* (14):3.

– 2012. 'Bergson and human rights.' In *Bergson, politics, religion.* Ed. A. Lefebvre and M. White. Durham, NC: Duke University Press.

– forthcoming. 'Human rights in Deleuze and Bergson's later philosophy.' In *Deleuze and jurisprudence*. Ed. L. de Sutter and K. McGee. Edinburgh: Edinburgh University Press.

Lemert, E. 1951. *Social pathology*. New York: McGraw-Hill.

Leventhal, H., and L. Patrick-Miller. 2000. 'Emotions and physical illness: Causes and indicators of vulnerability.' In *Handbook of emotions*. Ed. M. Lewis and J.M. Haviland-Jones. New York: Guilford Press.

Levine, H. 1997. 'A further exploration of the lesbian identity development process and its measurement.' *Journal of Homosexuality* 34(2):67–78.

Lewis, M. 2007. 'Self-conscious emotional development.' In *The self-conscious emotions*. Ed. J. Tracy, R. Robbins, and J.P. Tagney. New York: The Guilford Press.

Li, L., and M. Orleans. 2001. 'Coming out discourses of Asian American lesbians.' *Sexuality and Culture* 5(2):57–78.

Lidchi, H. 1999. 'Finding the right image: British development NGOs and the regulation of imagery.' In *Culture and global change*. Ed. T. Skelron and T. Allen. London: Routledge.

Lindsey, B.B., and W. Evans. 1927. *Companionate marriage*. New York: Boni and Liveright.

Lingis, A. 1999. 'Bestiality.' In *Animal others: On ethics, ontology and animal life*. Ed. H.P. Steeves. New York: SUNY Press.

Link, B.G., and J.C. Phelan. 2010. 'Labeling and Stigma.' In *A handbook for the study of mental health: Social contexts, theories, and systems*, 571–87. 2d ed. Ed. T.L. Scheid and T.N. Brown. New York: Cambridge University Press.

Link, B.G., J.C. Phelan, M. Bresnahan, A. Stueve, and B.A. Pescosolido. 1999. 'Public conceptions of mental illness: Labels, causes, dangerousness, and social distance.' *American Journal of Public Health* 89:1328–33.

Linstead, S. 2001. 'Comment: Gender blindness or gender suppression? A comment on Fiona Wilson's research note.' *Organization Studies* 21(1): 297–303.

Little, J. 2003. ' "Riding the rural love train": Heterosexuality and the rural community.' *Sociologia Ruralis* 43(4):401–15.

Lively, K.J. 2000. 'Reciprocal emotion management: Working together to maintain stratification in private law firms.' *Work and Occupations* 27:32–63.

Locke, J. 1997. *An essay concerning human understanding*. London: Penguin Books.

Lorde, A. 1982. *Zami: A new spelling of my name*. London: Sheba Feminist Publishers.

– 1984. *Sister outsider: Essays and speeches*. Trumansburg, NY: The Crossing Press.

– 1997. *The cancer journals.* San Francisco: Aunt Lute Books.

Loring, M., and B. Powell. 1988. 'Gender, race, and DSM-III: A study of the objectivity of psychiatric diagnostic behaviour.' *Journal of Health and Social Behaviour* 29:1–22.

Loseke, D. 1993. 'Constructing conditions, people, morality and emotion: Expanding the agenda of constructionism.' In *Constructionist controversies: Issues in social problems theory.* Ed. G. Miller and J.A. Holstein. New York: Aldine.

Lucey, H., J. Melody, and V. Walkerdine. 2003. 'Project 4:21 transitions to womanhood: Developing a psychosocial perspective in one longitudinal study.' *International Journal of Social Research Methodology* 6:279–84.

Lukas, Scott. 2007. 'The themed space: Locating culture, nation, and self.' In *The themed space: Locating culture, nation, and self.* Ed. S. Lukas. Lanham, MD: Lexington Books.

Lupton, D. 1998. *The emotional self: A sociocultural exploration.* London: Sage.

Lury, C. 1999. 'Marking time with Nike: The illusion of the durable.' *Public Culture* 11:499–526.

– 2000. 'The united colors of diversity.' In *Global nature, global culture.* Ed. S. Franklin, C. Lury, and J. Stacey. London: Sage.

– 2004. *Brands: The logos of the global economy.* London: Routledge.

Luther, M. [1525]1969. *On the bondage of the will.* In *Luther and Erasmus: Free will and salvation.* Ed. G. Rupp and P.S. Watson. Philadelphia: Westminster Press.

Lynch, J.M. 2004. 'The identity transformation of biological parents in lesbian/ gay stepfamilies.' *Journal of Homosexuality* 47(2):91–107.

Lynch, J.M., and K. Murray. 2000. 'For the love of the children: The coming out process for lesbian and gay parents and step-parents.' *Journal of Homosexuality* 39(1):1–24.

Lynch, M., and S. Woolgar, eds. 1988. *Representation in scientific practice.* Cambridge, MA: MIT Press.

Lyotard, J.F. 1986/2009. *Enthusiasm: The Kantian critique of history.* Palo Alto, CA: Stanford University Press.

Maffesoli, M. 1996. *The time of the tribes: The decline of individualism in mass society.* London: Sage.

Mallon, G.P. 2001. 'Oh, Canada: The experience of working-class gay men in Toronto.' *Journal of Gay and Lesbian Social Services* 12(3–4):103–17.

Marrati, P. 2006. 'Mysticism and the foundation of the open society: Bergsonian politics.' In *Political theologies: Public religions in a post-secular world.* Ed. H. de Vries and L. Sullivan. New York: Fordham University Press.

Marion, J.L. 2003/2007. *The erotic phenomenon.* Chicago: Chicago University Press.

Markus, H.R., and S. Kitayama. 1991. 'Culture and the self: Implications for cognition, emotion, and motivation.' *Psychological Review* 98:224–53.

Marshall, T.H. 1963. 'Citizenship and social class.' In *Sociology at the crossroads and other essays*. Ed. T.H. Marshall. London: Heinemann.

Maruna, S. 2001. *Making good: How ex-convicts reform and rebuild their lives*. Washington, DC: American Psychological Association.

Massumi, B. 1996. 'The autonomy of affect.' In *Deleuze: A critical reader*. Ed. P. Patton. Oxford: Blackwell.

Mauthner, N.S., and A. Doucet. 1998. 'Reflections on a voice centred relational method of data analysis: Analysing maternal and domestic voices.' In *Feminist dilemmas in qualitative research: Private lives and public texts*. Ed. J. Ribbens and R. Edwards. London: Sage.

– 2003. 'Reflexive accounts and accounts of reflexivity in qualitative data analysis.' *Sociology* 37(3):413–31.

Mauthner, N.S., and A. Doucet. Forthcoming. *A guide through qualitative analysis: Listening, seeing and reading qualitative data*. London: Sage.

Mayes, R., and A.V. Horwitz. 2005. 'DSM-III and the revolution in the classification of mental illness.' *Journal of the History of the Behavioural Sciences* 41:249–67.

McCormack, C. 2004. 'Storying stories: A narrative approach to in-depth interview conversations.' *International Journal of Social Research Methodology* 7:219–36.

McDonald, G.J. 1982. 'Individual differences in the coming out process for gaymen: Implications for theoretical models.' *Journal of Homosexuality* 8(1):47–60.

McDonald, S. 2005. 'Studying actions in context: A qualitative shadowing method for organizational research.' *Qualitative Research* 5(4):455–73.

McKenna, K.Y., and J.A. Bargh. 1998. 'Coming out in the age of the Internet: Identity "demarginalization" through virtual group participation.' *Journal of Personality and Social Psychology* 75(3):681–94.

McMahon, D.M. 2006. *Happiness: A history*. New York: Atlantic Monthly Press.

McMahon, M. 1996. 'Significant absences.' *Qualitative Inquiry* 2:320–36.

McNeil, D. 1992. *Hand and mind: What gestures reveal about thought*. Chicago: University of Chicago Press.

– 2005. *Gesture and thought*. Chicago: University of Chicago Press.

Mead, M. 1977. 'Jealousy: Primitive and civilized.' In *Jealousy*. Ed. G. Clanton and L. Smith. Englewood Cliffs, NJ: Prentice Hall.

Mee, J. 2000. 'William Blake, songs of innocence and experience.' In *A companion to literature from Milton to Blake*. Ed. D. Womersley. Oxford: Blackwell.

Meisiek, S., and X. Yao. 2005. 'Nonsense makes sense: Humor in social sharing of emotion at the workplace.' In *Emotions and organizational behaviour*. Ed. C. Hartel, W. Zerbe, and N. Ashkanasy. Hillsdale, NJ: Lawrence Erlbaum Associates.

Meltzer, B.N., and G.R. Musolf. 2002. 'Resentment and *ressentiment*.' *Sociological Inquiry* 72(2):240–55.

Merleau-Ponty, M. 1960. *Eloge de la philosophie, et autres essais*. Paris: Gallimard.

Merrick. 1996. *Battle for the trees*. Leeds: Godhaven.

Meštrovicÿaa, S.G. 1997. *Postemotional society*. London: Sage.

Miller, J.B. 1976/1986. *Towards a new psychology of women*. London: Penguin Books.

Miller, J.K. 2003. *Women from another planet: Our lives in the universe of autism*. Bloomington, IN: Dancing Minds.

Miller, K., J. Considine, and J. Garner. 2007. '"Let me tell you about my job": Exploring the terrain of emotion in the workplace.' *Management Communication Quarterly* 20(3):231–60.

Miller, W.I. 1997. *The anatomy of disgust*. Cambridge, MA: Harvard University Press.

Millett, K. 1970. *Sexual politics*. Garden City, NY: Doubleday.

Mint, P. 2004. 'The power dynamics of cheating: Effects on polyamory and bisexuality.' *Journal of Bisexuality* 4(3–4):55–76.

– 2007. 'The strange credibility of polyamory.' *Freaksexual*. Retrieved from http://freaksexual.wordpress.com/2007/11/27/the-strange-credibility-of-polyamory/.

Mirowsky, J., and C.E. Ross. 2003. *Social causes of psychological distress*. Hawthorne, NY: Aldine de Gruyter.

Molloy, H., and L. Vasil. 2002. 'The social construction of Asperger's Syndrome: The pathologising of difference?' *Disability and Society* 17(6):659–69.

Moor, L. 2003. 'Branded spaces: The scope of new marketing.' *Journal of Consumer Culture* 3(1):39–60.

– 2008. 'Branding consultants as cultural intermediaries.' *The Sociological Review* 56(3):408–28.

Moran, D. 2000. *Introduction to phenomenology*. London: Routledge.

Morgan, D., and I. Wilkinson. 2001. 'The problem of suffering and the sociological task of the theodicy.' *European Journal of Social Theory* 4(2):199–214.

Morris, J.F. 1997. 'Lesbian coming out as a multidimensional process.' *Journal of Homosexuality* 33(2):1–22.

Moustakas, C. 1994. *Phenomenological research methods*. Thousand Oaks, CA: Sage.

Mullan, J. 1988. *Sentiment and sociability: The language of feeling in the eighteenth century*. Oxford: Oxford University Press.

Munt, S.R., E.H. Bassett, and K. O'Riordan. 2002. 'Virtually belonging: Risk, connectivity, and coming out on-line.' *International Journal of Sexuality and Gender Studies* 7(2–3):125–37.

Myers, G. 1999. *Ad worlds*. London: Arnold.

Nadesan, M. 2005. *Constructing autism: Unravelling the 'truth' and understanding the social*. New York: Routledge.

Nagel, T. 1974. 'What is it like to be a bat?' *The Philosophical Review* 4:435–50.

Nash, J.M. 2002. 'The secrets of autism: The number of children diagnosed with autism and Asperger's in the US is exploding. Why?' *Time Magazine* 159 (18):47–56.

Nava, M. 2002. 'Cosmopolitan modernity: Everyday imaginaries and the register of difference.' *Theory, Culture and Society* 19(1–2):81–100.

– 2007. *Visceral cosmopolitanism: Gender, culture, and the normalisation of difference*. Oxford: Berg.

Nazeer, K. 2006. *Send in the idiots: Or how we grew to understand the world*. London: Bloomsbury.

Ngai, S. 2005. *Ugly feelings*. Cambridge, MA: Harvard University Press.

Nietzsche, F. 1968. *The will to power*. Trans. W. Kaufman and R.J. Hollingdale. New York: Vintage Books.

– [1887] 1989. *On the genealogy of morals*. Trans. W. Kaufmann and R.J. Hollingdale. New York: Vintage Books.

– 2007. *On the genealogy of morality*. Ed. K. Ansell-Pearson. Trans. C. Diethe. Cambridge: Cambridge University Press.

Norum, K. 2000. 'Black (w)holes: A researcher's place in her research.' *Qualitative Sociology* 23:319–40.

Nussbaum, B. 1990. *Love's knowledge: Essays on philosophy and literature*. Oxford: Oxford University Press.

– 2001. *Upheavals of thought: The intelligence of emotions*. Cambridge: Cambridge University Press.

Oakley, A. 1981. 'Interviewing women: A contradiction in terms.' In *Doing feminist research*. Ed. H. Roberts. London: Routledge and Kegan Paul.

Oldenburg, R. 1989. *The great good place*. New York: Marlowe and Company.

O'Malley, P., and S. Mugford. 1994. 'Crime, excitement and modernity.' In *Varieties of criminology*. Ed. G. Barak. New York: Praeger.

O'Neill, J.L. 1999. *Through the eyes of aliens: A book about autistic people*. London: Jessica Kingsley.

Osborne, L. 2002. *American normal: The hidden world of Asperger's Syndrome*. New York: Copernicus Books.

O'Shaughnessy, J., and N. O'Shaughnessy. 2003. *The marketing power of emotion*. Oxford: Oxford University Press.

Ostwald, P.F. 1997. *Glenn Gould: The ecstasy and tragedy of genius*. New York: W.W. Norton.

Oswald, R.F. 2000. 'Family and friendship relationships after young womencome out as bisexual or lesbian.' *Journal of Homosexuality* 38(3): 65–83.

Parkinson, B. 2005. *Emotion in social relations: Cultural, group and interpersonal processes*. New York: Psychology Press.

Parks, C.A., T.L. Hughes, and A.K. Matthews. 2004. 'Race/ethnicity and sexual orientation: Intersecting identities.' *Cultural Diversity and Ethnic Minority Psychology* 10(3):241–54.

Parrott, W. 1991. 'The emotional experiences of envy and jealousy.' In *The psychology of jealousy and envy*. Ed. P. Salovey. New York: The Guilford Press.

Payton, A.R. 2009. 'Mental health, mental illness, and psychological distress: Same continuum or distinct phenomena?' *Journal of Health and Social Behaviour* 50:213–27.

Peterson, A. 2004. *Engendering emotions*. New York: Palgrave Macmillan.

Phelan, S. 1993. '(Be)coming out: Lesbian identity and politics.' *Signs* 18(4):765–90.

Philo, C., and C. Wilbert, eds. 2000. *Animal spaces, beastly places: New geographies of human-animal relations*. London: Routledge.

Pierce, J.L. 1995. *Gender trials: Emotional lives in contemporary law firms*. Berkeley: University of California Press.

Pine, J., and J. Gilmore. 1999. *The experience economy*. Boston: Harvard Business School Press.

Pines, A.M. 1998. *Romantic jealousy: Causes, symptoms, cures*. London: Routledge.

Plummer, K. 2001. *Documents of life 2: An invitation to critical humanism*. London: Sage.

Plutchik, R., and H. Kellerman, eds. 1980. *Emotion: Theory, research and experience. Vol. 1: Theories of emotion*. New York: Academic Press.

Polanyi, K. 1957. *The great transformation*. Boston: Beacon Press.

Power, C. 2003. 'Freedom and sociability for Bergson.' *Culture and Organization* 9(1):59–71.

Prince-Hughes, D. 2002. *Aquamarine blue 5: Personal stories of college students with autism*. Athens, OH: Swallow Press.

– 2004. *Songs of the gorilla nation: My journey through autism*. New York: Harmony Books.

Probyn, E. 2005. *Blush: Faces of shame*. Minneapolis: University of Minnesota Press.

Purvis, T., and A. Hunt. 1993. 'Discourse, ideology, discourse, ideology, discourse, ideology . . .' *British Journal of Sociology* 44:473–99.

Radloff, L.S. 1977. 'The CES-D Scale: A self-report depression scale for research in the general population.' *Applied Psychological Measurement* 1: 385–401.

Radway, J. 1991. *Reading the romance: Women, patriarchy, and popular literature book description*. Chapel Hill: University of North Carolina Press.

Rafaeli, A., and M. Worline. 2001. 'Individual emotion in work organizations.' *Social Science Information* 40(1):95–123.

Raissiguier, C. 1997. 'Negotiating school, identity, and desire: Students speak out from the Midwest.' *Educational Foundations* 11(1):31–54.

Ramsay, K. 1996. 'Emotional labour and qualitative research: How I learned not to laugh or cry in the field.' In *Methodological imaginations*. Ed. E.S. Lyon and J. Busfield. Basingstoke: Macmillan.

Ranulf, S. 1938/1964. *Moral indignation and middle class psychology: Sociological study*. New York: Schocken Books.

Rawls, J. 1989/1999. 'Themes in Kant's moral philosophy.' In *Collected papers*. Ed. S. Freeman. Cambridge, MA: Harvard University Press.

Reinharz, S. 1992. *Feminist methods in social research*. Oxford: Oxford University Press.

Riessman, C. 2008. *Narrative methods for the human sciences*. Thousand Oaks, CA: Sage.

Ritchie, A., and M. Barker. 2006. 'There aren't words for what we do or how we feel so we have to make them up: Constructing polyamorous language in a culture of compulsory monogamy.' *Sexualities* 9(5):515–29.

Robins, L.N., and D.A. Regier, eds. 1991. *Psychiatric disorders in America: The epidemiologic catchment area study*. New York: The Free Press.

Robinson, D., J. Clay-Warner, and T. Everett. 2008. 'Introduction.' In *Social structure and emotions*. Ed. J. Clay-Warner and D. Robinson. San Diego, CA: Elsevier.

Robinson, V. 1999. 'My baby just cares for me: Feminism, heterosexuality and non-monogamy.' *Journal of Gender Studies* 6(2):143–58.

Robnett, B. 2004. 'Emotional resonance, social location, and strategic framing.' *Sociological Focus* 37(3):195–212.

Rousseau, J. 1993. *Émile*. Trans. B. Foxley. London: Everyman.

Rosaldo, M. 1980. *Knowledge and passion: Ilongot notions of self and social life*. Cambridge: Cambridge University Press.

Rose, N. 1989. *Governing the soul: The shaping of the private self*. London: Routledge.

Rosenfield, S., M.C. Lennon, and H.R. White. 2005. 'The self and mental health: Self-salience and the emergence of internalizing and externalizing problems.' *Journal of Health and Social Behaviour* 46:323–40.

Rubin, G.S. 1993. 'Thinking sex: Notes for a radical theory of the politics of sexuality.' In *The lesbian and gays studies reader*. Ed. H. Abelove, M.A. Barale, and D.M. Halperin. New York: Routledge.

Rubington, E., and M. Weinberg. 2005. *Deviance: The interactionist perspective* (9E). Boston: Pearson.

Ruddin, L. 2006. 'You can generalize stupid! Social scientists, Bent Flyvbjerg, and case study methodology.' *Qualitative Inquiry* 12(4):797–812.

Rust, P.C. 1993. ' "Coming out" in the age of social constructionism: Sexual identity formation among lesbian and bisexual women.' *Gender and Society* 7(1):50–77.

Ryan, P. 2003. 'Coming out, fitting in: The personal narratives of some Irish gay men.' *Irish Journal of Sociology* 12(2):68–85.

Sacks, O. 1995. *An anthropologist on Mars*. Picador: London.

Sachs, W., ed. 1992. *The development dictionary*. London: Zed Books.

Salovey, P. 1991. *The psychology of jealousy and envy*. New York: The Guildford Press.

Samuels, E. 2003. 'My body, my closet: Invisible disability and the limits of coming-out discourse.' *GLQ* 9(1–2):233–55.

Sandelands, L., and C. Boudens. 2000. 'Feeling at work.' In *Emotion in organizations*. Ed. S. Fineman. London: Sage.

Sartre, J.P. 1949. *The emotions: Outline of a theory*. New York: Philosophical Library.

Saurette, P. 2005. *The Kantian imperative: Humiliation, common sense, politics*. Toronto: University of Toronto Press.

Sauvagnargues, A. 2004. 'Deleuze avec Bergson: Le cours de 1960 sur *L'évolution créatrice*.' In *Annales bergsoniennes II: Bergson, Deleuze, la phénoménology*. Ed. F. Worms. Paris: PUF.

Savage, M., G. Bagnall, and B. Longhurst. 2005. *Globalization and belonging*. London: Sage.

Savin-Williams, R.C., and L.M. Diamond. 2000. 'Sexual identity trajectories among sexual-minority youths: Gender comparisons.' *Archives of Sexual Behaviour* 29:607–27.

Scarry, E. 1985. *The body in pain: The making and unmaking of the world*. Oxford: Oxford University Press.

Schatzki, T. 2005. 'Peripheral vision: The site of organizations.' *Organization Studies* 26(3):465–84.

– 2006. 'On organizations as they happen.' *Organization Studies* 27(12):1863–73.

Scheff, T. 1966. *Being mentally ill: A sociological theory*. Chicago: Aldine.

– 1984. *Being mentally ill: A sociological theory*. 2d ed. New York: Aldine de Gruyter.

– 1990. 'Socialisation of emotions: Pride and shame as causal gents.' In *Research agendas in the sociology of emotion*. Ed. T. Kemper. Albany: SUNY Press.

– 2000. Shame and the social bond: A sociological theory. *Sociological Theory* 18(1):85–99.

Scheler, M. [1912]1961. *Ressentiment*. Glencoe, IL: Free Press.

– 2008. *The nature of sympathy*. Trans. P. Heath. New Brunswick, NJ: Transaction Publishers.

Schickel, R. 1985. *Intimate strangers: The culture of celebrity*. Garden City, NY: Doubleday.

Schneider, B.E. 1986. 'Coming out at work: Bridging the private/public gap.' *Work and Occupations* 13(4):463–87.

Schrock, D., D. Holden, and L. Reid. 2004. 'Creating emotional resonance: Interpersonal emotion work and motivational framing in a transgender community.' *Social Problems* 51(1):61–81.

Schultz, H., and D.J. Yang. 1997. *Pour your heart into it: How Starbucks built a company one cup at a time*. New York: Hyperion.

Schutz, A. 1962. 'On multiple realities.' In *Collected papers*. Vol. 1. The Hague: M. Nijhoff.

Schwartz, R.D., and J.H. Skolnick. 1962. 'Two studies of legal stigma.' *Social Problems* 10(fall):133–8.

Scott, J.C. 1990. *Domination and the arts of resistance: Hidden transcripts*. New Haven: Yale University Press.

Scott, M.B., and S.M. Lyman. 1968. 'Accounts.' *American Sociological Review* 33:46–62.

Schwartz, R.D., and J.H. Skolnick. 1962. 'Two studies of legal stigma.' *Social Problems* 10 (fall):133–8.

Seale, C. 1999. *The quality of qualitative research*. London: Sage.

The Second Cup Ltd. 2008. 'Second Cup coffee bean passport: Discover the world.' Brochure. Second Cup, Winnipeg, 1 September 2008.

Sedgwick, E. 1990. *Epistemology of the closet*. Berkeley: University of California Press.

– 2003. *Touching feeling: Affect, performativity, pedagogy*. Durham, NC: Duke University Press.

Seed, J., J. Macy, P. Fleming, A. Naess and D. Pugh. 1988. *Thinking like a mountain: Towards a council of all beings.* Philadelphia: New Society Publishers.

Sheff, E. 2005. 'Polyamorous women, sexual subjectivity and power.' *Journal of Contemporary Ethnography* 34(3):251–83.

Sherman, N. 1998. 'Empathy, respect, and humanitarian intervention.' *International Affairs* 12(1):103–19.

Sherry, M. 2004. 'Overlaps and contradictions between queer theory and disability studies.' *Disability and Society* 19(7):769–83.

Shields, R. 1992. 'Spaces for the subject of consumption.' In *Lifestyle shopping.* Ed. R. Shields. London: Routledge.

Shields, S.A., and B.A. Koster. 1989. 'Emotional stereotyping of parents in childrearing manuals, 1915–1980.' *Social Psychology Quarterly* 52:44–55.

Shilling, C. 1997. 'Emotions, embodiment and the sensation of society.' *The Sociological Review* 45(2):195–219.

– 2002. 'The two traditions in the sociology of emotions.' In *Emotions and sociology.* Ed. J. Barbalet. Oxford: Blackwell.

– 2003. *The body and social theory.* London: Sage.

Shore, S. 2003. *Beyond the wall: Personal experiences with autism and Aspergers Syndrome.* Shawnee Mission, KA: Autism Asperger Publishing Company.

Shweder, R.A. 1994. ' "You're not sick, you're just in love": Emotion as an interpretive system.' In *The nature of emotion: Fundamental questions.* Ed. P. Ekman and R.A. Davidson. Oxford: Oxford University Press.

Silverman, C. 2008. 'Critical review, fieldwork on another planet: Social science perspectives on autism.' *BioSocieties* 3:325–41.

Simmel, G. 1955. *Conflict and web of affiliations.* Glencoe, IL: Free Press.

Simon, R.W., and L.E. Nath. 2004. 'Gender and emotion in the United States: Examining emotion culture in the U.S.: Do men and women differ in self-reports of feelings and expressive behaviour?' *American Journal of Sociology* 109:1137–76.

Sims, D. 2005. 'You bastard: A narrative exploration of the experience of indignation within organizations.' *Organization Studies* 26(11): 1625–40.

Sinclair, J. 2009. 'Why I dislike "person first" language.' J. Sinclair personal website. Retrieved 15 January 2009 from http://web.syr.edu/%7Ejisincla/person_first.htm.

Smith, A. [1759] 2006. *The theory of moral sentiments.* New York: Dover.

– 1984. *The theory of moral sentiments.* Indianapolis: Liberty Fund.

– 2000. *The theory of moral sentiments.* New York: Prometheus Books.

Smith, A.C., and S. Kleinman. 1989. 'Managing emotions in medical school: Students' contacts with the living and the dead.' *Social Psychology Quarterly* 52:56–69.

Smith, M. 1999. 'To speak of trees: Social constructivism, environmental values, and the future of deep ecology.' *Environmental Ethics* 21(4):359–76.

– 2001. *The ethics of place: Radical ecology, post-modernity and social theory.* Binghampton, NY: SUNY Press.

– 2005. 'Lost for words? Gadamer and Benjamin on the nature of language and the "language" of nature.' *Environmental Values* 10(1):59–75.

Smith, S. 1996. 'Taking it to a limit one more time: Autobiography and autism.' In *Getting a life: Everyday uses of autobiography*. Ed. S. Smith and J. Watson. Minneapolis: University of Minnesota Press.

Smith, S., and J. Watson, eds. 2001. *Reading autobiography: A guide for interpreting life narratives.* Minneapolis: University of Minnesota Press.

– 2006. *Getting a life: Everyday uses of autobiography.* Minneapolis: University of Minnesota Press.

Solnit, R. 2000. Wanderlust: A history of walking. New York: Viking.

Solomon, R.C. 2003. *What is an emotion?* Oxford: Oxford University Press.

Somers, M.R. 1994. 'The narrative constitution of identity: A relational and network approach.' *Theory and Society* 23:605–50.

Soulez, P. 1989. *Bergson politique.* Paris: PUF.

Spickard, J. 2001. 'Tribes and cities: Towards an Islamic sociology of religion.' *Social Compass* 48(1):103–16.

Spielberger, C.D., and S.J. Sydeman. 1994. 'State-Trait Anxiety Inventory and State-Trait Anger Expression Inventory.' In *The use of psychological testing for treatment planning and outcome assessment*. Ed. M.E. Maruish. Hillsdale, NJ: Lawrence Erlbaum Associates.

Spinoza, B. [1677] 2002. *The ethics.* New York: Hackett.

Spector, M., and J. Kitsuse. 1977. *Constructing social problems.* Menlo Park, CA: Benjamin/Cummings.

Stacey, J. 1991. 'Can there be a feminist ethnography?' In *Women's words*. Ed. S.B. Gluck and D. Patai. New York: Routledge.

Starbucks Coffee Company. 2002a. 'The world of coffee: A guide to Starbucks® whole bean selections.' Brochure. Toronto: Starbucks Coffee Company.

– 2002b. 'Commitment to Origins™: Starbucks involvement in coffee-origin countries.' Brochure. Toronto: Starbucks Coffee Company.

Stearns, C.Z., and P.N. Stearns. 1985. 'Emotionology: Clarifying the history ofemotions and emotional standards.' *American Historical Review* 90:813–36.

– 1986. *Anger: The struggle for emotional control in America's history*. Chicago: University of Chicago Press.

Stearns, P.N. 1989. *Jealousy: The evolution of an emotion in American history*. New York: New York University Press.

– 1990. 'The rise of sibling jealousy in the twentieth-century.' *Symbolic Interaction* 13:83–101.

– 1993. 'History of emotion: The issue of change.' In *Handbook of emotion*. 2d ed. Ed. J. Haviland-Jones and M. Lewis. New York: The Guilford Press.

– 1994. *American cool: Constructing twentieth-century emotional style*. New York: New York University Press.

– 1999. *Battleground of desire: The struggle for self-control in modern America*. New York: New York University Press.

– 2000. 'History of emotions: Issues of change and impact.' In *Handbook of emotions*. 2d ed. Ed. M. Lewis and J. Haviland-Jones. New York: Guilford Press.

Stenross, B., and S. Kleinman. 1989. 'The highs and lows of emotional labor: Detectives' encounters with criminals and victims.' *Journal of Contemporary Ethnography* 17:435–52.

Stolzman, J. 2000. 'Social dimensions of mental illness.' In *Social issues and contradictions in Canadian society*. Ed. B. Singh Bolaria. Toronto: Harcourt-Brace.

Sturdy, A. 2003. 'Knowing the unknowable? A discussion of methodological and theoretical issues in emotion research and organizational studies.' *Organization* 10(1):81–105.

Suchman, L. 2005. 'Affiliative objects.' *Organization* 12(3):379–99.

Susman, W.I. 1984. *Culture as history: The transformation of American society in the twentieth century*. New York: Pantheon.

Swidler, A. 1986. 'Culture in action: Symbols and strategies.' *American Sociological Review* 51:73–86.

Sykes, G., and D. Matza. 1957. 'Techniques of neutralization: A theory of delinquency.' *American Sociological Review* 22:664–70.

Szasz, T.S. 1960. 'The myth of mental illness.' *American Psychologist* 15:113–8.

– 1994. 'Mental illness is still a myth.' *Society* (May/June):34–9.

Szatmari, P. 2004. *A mind apart: Understanding children with autism and Asperger Syndrome*. New York and London: The Guilford Press.

Sznaider, N. 1998. 'A sociology of compassion: A study in the sociology of morals.' *Cultural Values* 2(1):117–39.

Tagney, J.P., J. Stuewig, and D. Mashek. 2007. 'What's moral about self-conscious emotions?' In *The self-conscious emotions*. Ed. J. Tracy, R. Robbins, and J.P. Tagney. New York: The Guilford Press.

Talay-Ongan A., and K. Wood. 2000. 'Unusual sensory sensitivities in autism:
A possible crossroads.' *International Journal of Disability, Development and Education* 47(2):201–12.

Taormino, T. 2008. *Opening up: A guide to creating and sustaining open relationships*. San Francisco: Cleis Press.

Taylor, V. 1995. 'Self-labeling and women's mental health: Postpartum illness and the reconstruction of motherhood.' *Sociological Focus* 1:23–47.

– 2000. 'Emotions and identity in women's self-help movements.' In *Self, identity, and social movements*. Ed. S. Stryker and T.J. Owens. Minneapolis: University of Minnesota Press.

Taylor, V., and N.C. Raeburn. 1995. 'Identity politics as high-risk activism: Career consequences for lesbians, gay, and bisexual sociologists.' *Social Problems* 42(2):252–73.

Tereda, R. 2001. *Feeling in theory: Emotion after the death of the subject*. Cambridge, MA: Harvard University Press.

Tester, K. 2001. *Compassion, morality and the media*. Buckingham, UK: Open University Press.

Thagard, P. 2002. 'The passionate scientist: Emotion in scientific cognition.' In *The cognitive basis of science*. Ed. P. Carruthers, S. Stich, and M. Segal. Cambridge: Cambridge University Press.

Thoits, P.A. 1985. 'Self-labeling processes in mental illness: The role of emotional deviance.' *American Journal of Sociology* 92:221–49.

– 1990. 'Emotional deviance: Research agendas.' In *Research agendas in the sociology of emotions*. Ed. T. Kemper. Albany: SUNY Press.

– 1995. 'Stress, coping and social support processes: Where are we? What next?' *Journal of Health and Social Behaviour* (Extra Issue):53–79.

– 2005. 'Differential labeling of mental illness by social status: A new look at an old problem.' *Journal of Health and Social Behaviour* 46:102–19.

– 2009. 'Gender, emotional deviance, and psychological distress: The role of gender-role ideology.' Unpublished manuscript. Indiana University, Department of Sociology.

Thoits, P.A., and R.J. Evenson. 2008. 'Differential labeling of mental illness by social status revisited: Patterns before and after the rise of managed care.' *Sociological Forum* 23:28–52.

Theodosius, C. 2006. 'Recovering emotion from its management.' *Sociology* 40(5):893–910.

– 2008. *Emotional labour in health care: The unmanaged heart of nursing*. Abingdon, UK: Routledge, Taylor and Francis.

Thien, D. 2005. 'After or beyond feeling? A consideration of affect and emotion in geography.' *Area* 37(4):450–56.

Thompson, C.J., and Z. Arsel. 2004. 'The Starbucks brandscape and consumers' (anticorporate) experiences of glocalization.' *Journal of Consumer Research* 31(3):631–42.

Thomson, R., and J. Holland. 2005. 'Thanks for the memory: Memory books as a methodological resource in biographical research.' *Qualitative Research* 5:201–19.

Thomson, R., and J. McLeod. 2009. *Researching social change: Qualitative approaches*. London: Sage.

Thrift, N. 2009. *Non-representational theory*. London: Routledge.

Tidmarsh, L., and F.R. Volkmar. 2003. 'Diagnosis and epidemiology of Autism Spectrum Disorders.' *The Canadian Journal of Psychiatry* 48(8):517–25.

Tim Hortons. 2008. 'The story of Tim Hortons.' *Tim Hortons*. Retrieved from http://www.timhortons.com 6 January 2008.

Todd, J. 1986. *Sensibility: An introduction*. London: Methuen.

Tolich, M.B. 1993. 'Alienating and liberating emotions at work: Supermarket clerks' performance of customer service.' *Journal of Contemporary Ethnography* 22:361–81.

Tolman, D.L. 2002. *Dilemmas of desire: Teenage girls talk about sexuality*. Cambridge, MA: Harvard University Press.

Tracy, J., and R. Robbins. 2007. 'The self in the self-conscious emotions: A cognitive appraisal approach.' In *The self-conscious emotions*. Ed. J. Tracy, R. Robbins, and J.P. Tagney. New York: The Guilford Press.

Tronto, J.C. 1993. *Moral boundaries: A political argument for an ethic of care*. New York: Routledge.

Turkle, S. 2004. *The second self: Computers and the human spirit*. Cambridge: MIT Press.

Turner, B.S. 2002. 'Cosmopolitan virtue, globalization and patriotism.' *Theory, Culture and Society* 19(1–2):45–63.

Turner, J. 2010. 'The stratification of emotions: Some preliminary generalizations.' *Sociological Inquiry* 80(2):168–99.

Turner, J., and J. Stets. 2005. *The sociology of emotions*. Cambridge: Cambridge University Press.

Urry, J. 1995. *Consuming places*. London: Routledge.

– 2000. *Sociology beyond societies*. London: Routledge.

Uslaner, E. 2001. 'Producing and consuming trust.' *Political Science Quarterly* 115(4):569–90.

Valentine, G., and T. Skelton. 2003. 'Finding oneself, losing oneself: The lesbian and gay "scene" as a paradoxical space.' *International Journal of Urban and Regional Research* 27(4):849–66.

Van Maanen, J. 1988. *Tales of the field: On writing ethnography*. Chicago: University of Chicago Press.

Veaux, F. 2009. 'Jealousy management for love and profit: Or, how to fix a broken refrigerator.' *Xeromag*. Retrieved from http://www.xeromag.com/fvpoly.html, 1 June 2009.

Veroff, J., R.A. Kulka, and E. Douvan. 1981. *Mental health in America: Patterns of help-seeking from 1957 to 1976*. New York: Basic Books.

Viano, E.C. 1989. 'Victimology today: Major issues in research and public policy.' In *Crime and its victims: International research and public policy*. Ed. E.C. Viano. New York: Hemisphere.

De Vries, H. 1999. *Philosophy and the turn to religion*. Baltimore: Johns Hopkins University Press.

– 2002. *Violence and metaphysics: Philosophical perspectives from Kant to Derrida*. Baltimore: Johns Hopkins University Press.

Wacquant, L. 2009a. 'Habitus as a topic and as a tool: Reflections on becoming a prizefighter.' In *Ethnographies revisited: Constructing theory in the field*. Ed. A.J. Puddephatt, W. Shaffir, and S.W. Kleinknecht. London:Routledge.

– 2009b. 'The body, the ghetto and the penal state.' *Qualitative Sociology* 32:101–29.

– 2009c. Personal e-mail communication, 5 March.

Wahl, O.F. 1997. *Media madness: Public images of mental illness*. Piscataway, NJ: Rutgers University Press.

Wainwright, D., and M. Calman. 2002. *Work stress: The making of a modern epidemic*. Buckingham, UK: Open University Press.

Walkerdine, V., H. Lucey, and J. Melody. 2001. *Growing up girl: Psychosocial explorations of gender and class*. Basingstoke: Palgrave.

– 2002. 'Subjectivity and qualitative method.' In *Qualitative research in action*. Ed. T. May. London: Sage.

Waltz, M. 2005. 'Reading case studies of people with autistic spectrum disorders: A cultural studies approach to disability representation.' *Disability and Society* 20(4):421–35.

Ward, J., and D. Winstanley. 2003. 'The absent presence: Negative space within discourse and the construction of minority sexual identity in the workplace.' *Human Relations* 56(10):1255–80.

Watzlawik, M. 2004. 'Experiencing same-sex attraction: A comparison between American and German adolescents.' *Identity: An International Journal of Theory and Research* 4(2):171–86.

Wax, R.H. 1971. *Doing fieldwork: Warnings and advice*. Chicago: University of Chicago Press.

Way, N. 1998. *Everyday courage: The lives and stories of urban teenagers.* New York: New York University Press.
– 2001. 'Using feminist methods to explore boys' relationships.' In *From subjects to subjectivities: A handbook of interpretive and participatory methods.* Ed. D. Tolman and M. Bryden-Miller. New York: New York University Press.
Weeks, J. 2003. *Sexuality.* 2d ed. London: Routledge.
– 2008. 'Traps we set ourselves.' *Sexualities Journal* (11 February):27–33.
Weitzman, G. 1999. 'What psychology professionals should know about polyamory.' *Polyamory.* Retrieved from http://www.polyamory.org/joe/polypaper.htm, 1 June 2009.
– 2006. 'Therapy for clients who are bisexual and polyamorous.' *Journal of Bisexuality* 6(1–2):137–64.
Welton, D., ed. 1999. *The essential Husserl.* Bloomington: Indiana University Press.
Wentworth, W., and D. Yardley. 1994. 'Deep sociality a bioevolutionary perspective on the sociology of emotions.' In *Social perspectives on emotion.* Ed. D. Franks, W. Wentworth, and J. Ryan. Greenwich: JAI Press.
Weston, K. 1995. 'Get thee to a big city: Sexual imaginary and the great gay migration.' *GLQ* 2:253–77.
Whaley, A.L. 1997. 'Ethnicity/race, paranoia, and psychiatric diagnoses: Clinician bias versus sociocultural differences.' *Journal of Psychopathology and Behavioural Assessment* 19:1–20.
White, G., and P. Mullen. 1989. *Jealousy: Theory, research and clinical strategies.* New York: The Guilford Press.
Whitley, E., and M. Darking. 2006. 'Object lessons and invisible technologies.' *Journal of Information Technology* 21(3):176–84.
Willey, L.H. 1999. *Pretending to be normal: Living with Asperger's Syndrome.* London: Jessica Kingsley Publishers.
Williams, A. 1999. *Therapeutic landscapes.* Lanham, MD: University Press of America.
Williams, D. 1992. *Nobody nowhere: The extraordinary autobiography of an autistic.* New York: Random House.
– 1994. *Somebody somewhere: Breaking free from the world of autism.* New York: Random House.
– 1996. *Autism: An inside-out approach.* London: Jessica Kingsley Publishers.
– 2003. *Exposure anxiety, the invisible cage: An exploration of self-protection responses in the Autism Spectrum and beyond.* London: Jessica Kingsley Publishers.
– 2004. *Everyday heaven: Journeys beyond the stereotypes of autism.* London: Jessica Kingsley Publishers.

– 2006. *The jumbled jigsaw: An insider's approach to the treatment of Autistic Spectrum "fruit salads."'* London: Jessica Kingsley Publishers.

Williams, R. 1977. *Marxism and literature*. Oxford: Oxford University Press.

Williams, S. 1998. 'Emotions, cyberspace and the "virtual" body: A critical appraisal.' In *Emotions in social life: Critical themes and contemporary issues*. Ed. G. Bendelow and S. Williams. London: Routledge.

– 2000. 'Emotions and health: Rethinking the inequalities debate.' In *Health, medicine and society: Key theories, future agendas*. Ed. S.J. Williams, J. Gabe, and M. Calnan. London: Routledge.

– 2000. 'Reason, emotion, and embodiment: Is "mental" health a contradiction in terms?' *Sociology of Health and Illness* 22:559–81.

– 2001. *Emotion and social theory: Corporeal reflections on the (ir)rational*. London: Sage.

Williams, S., and G. Bendelow. 1996. 'The "emotional" body.' *Body and Society* 2(3):125–39.

Wilson, R.A., and R.D. Brown. 2009. 'Introduction.' In *Humanitarianism and suffering: The mobilization of empathy*. Ed. R.A. Wilson and R.D. Brown. New York: Cambridge University Press.

Wolf, D. 1996. *Feminist dilemmas in fieldwork*. Boulder, CO: Westview Press.

Wolfe, A. 1998. 'What is altruism?' In *Private action and the public good*. Ed. W.W. Powell and E.S. Clemens. New Haven: Yale University Press.

Wolfe, L. 2003. 'Jealousy and transformation in polyamorous relationships.' *Dr. Leanna Wolfe*. Retrieved from http://drleannawolfe.com/Dissertation. pdf, 24 June 2003.

Wolfe, S.J., and J.P. Stanley. 1980. *The coming out stories*. Watertown, MA: Persephone Press.

Wolfinger, N.H. 2002. 'On writing fieldnotes: Collection strategies and background expectancies.' *Qualitative Inquiry* 2(1):85–95.

Wollstonecraft, M. 1975. *A vindication of the rights of women*. New York: W.W. Norton.

Woodward, K. 2004. 'Calculating compassion.' In *Compassion: The culture and politics of an emotion*. Ed. L. Berlant. New York: Routledge.

Woolf, V. 1953. *Mrs. Dalloway*. New York: Harvest Books.

World Health Organization. 1992. *The ICD-10 classification of mental and behavioural disorders: Clinical descriptions and diagnostic guidelines*. Geneva: World Health Organization.

Wosick-Correa, K. 2008. 'Contemporary fidelities: Sex, love and commitment in romantic relationships.' *Dissertation Abstracts International, Humanities and Social Sciences* 68(09):408 pp.

Wouters, C. 1989. 'The sociology of emotions and flight attendants: Hochschild's managed heart.' *Theory, Culture and Society* 6(1):95–123.

– 1992. 'On status competition and emotion management: The study of emotions as a new field.' *Theory, Culture and Society* 9(1):229–52.

– 2001. 'The integration of classes and sexes in the twentieth century: Etiquette books and emotion management.' In *Norbert Elias and human interdependencies*. Ed. T. Salumets. Montreal: McGill-Queen's University Press.

– 2007. *Informalization: Manners and emotions since 1890*. London: Sage.

Yates, C. 2007. *Masculine jealousy and contemporary cinema*. London: Palgrave Macmillan.

Yin, R. 2003. *Case study research: Design and methods*. London: Sage.

Young, C., M. Diep, and S. Drabble. 2006. 'Living with difference? The "cosmopolitan city" and urban reimagining in Manchester, UK.' *Urban Studies* 43(10):1687–1714.

Young, J. 2007. *The vertigo of late modernity*. London: Sage.

Zeldin, T. 1973. *France 1848–1945. Vol. I: Ambition, love and politics*. Oxford: Clarendon Press.

Zembylas, M., and L. Fendler. 2007. 'Reframing emotion in education through lenses of parrhesia and care of the self.' *Studies in Philosophy and Education* 26(4):319–33.

Zyman, S. 2001. 'Foreword.' In *Emotional branding: The new paradigms for connecting brands to people*. Ed. M. Gobé. New York: Allworth Press.

Index